SECRETARIAL PROCEDURES in the ELECTRONIC OFFICE

An integrated approach to IT-based and traditional secretarial practice

Desmond W Evans

Pitman

PITMAN PUBLISHING
128 Long Acre, London WC2E 9AN

A Division of Longman Group UK Limited
© Desmond W Evans 1989

First published in Great Britain 1989

British Library Cataloguing in Publication Data
Evans, Desmond W.
   Secretarial procedures in the electronic office
   1. Office practices. Clerical procedures
   I. Title
   651.3'7

ISBN 0-273-03002-7

All rights reserved; no part of this publication may be reproduced, stored in a retrieval system, or transmitted in any form or by any means, electronic, mechanical, photocopying, recording, or otherwise without either the prior written permission of the Publishers or a licence permitting restricted copying in the United Kingdom issued by the Copyright Licensing Agency Ltd, 33–34 Alfred Place, London WC1E 7DP. This book may not be lent, resold, hired out or otherwise disposed of by way of trade in any form of binding or cover other than that in which it is published, without the prior consent of the Publishers.

Typeset by Avocet Robinson, Bicester, Oxon
Printed in Great Britain at The Bath Press, Avon

Contents

Foreword v

Acknowledgements vi

Using this book vii

UNIT 1
Organisations: activities and structures 1
Overview 1
1.1 Organisations 3
Defining features of a business organisation; new terms and phrases; types of organisation; key people in organisations; the work of departments in business organisations; centralised support services and functions; information technology in organisations
1.2 Personal relationships in organisations 15
The line relationship; the staff relationship; the functional relationship; the roles of the manager and secretary; the secretary and career development;
Summary of main points 22
Activities 23
Practice questions from past examination papers 25
Glossary of terms and phrases 26

UNIT 2
Information processing in the office 29
Overview 29
2.1 Daily routines 31
The office as information processing centre; information processing in the electronic office; working in an electronic and traditional office environment; sorting and routing overnight messages; dealing with incoming mail; dealing with outgoing mail

2.2 Dairies, appointments and work scheduling 43
Dairies and appointments; key features of the electronic diary; the secretary's diary; self organisation and management of time
2.3 Filing and records management 49
Office records: classifying, filing, storing and retrieving data; major features of popular office filing systems; media for storing electronic data; filing and database software application packages; manual and paper/card-based filing systems; micrographics, microform and microfilm
2.4 Visitors to the office 64
First impressions; receiving visitors; visitors calling into the office; sources of information and support in reception; personal qualities needed for reception; the office environment
Summary of main points 72
Activities 73
Practice questions from past examination papers 78
Glossary of terms and phrases 81

UNIT 3
Information handling: how to use the equipment and systems effectively 85
Overview 85
3.1 Networks 87
Information handling in the electronic office; the arrival of the local area network
3.2 Fax, telex, viewdata and videotex 100
Facsimile transmission; telex; viewdata and videotex
3.3 The telephone – CABX and mobile phones 109
Telephone services in organisations; using a CABX system; mobile phones for mobile people; how directories can help
3.4 Office reprographics 120
B-IT: before information technology; printers; photocopiers; desktop publishing
Summary of main points 131
Activities 132
Practice questions from past examination papers 137
Glossary of terms and phrases 138

UNIT 4
Creating and presenting office documents 141
Overview 141

4.1 Letters 143
Choosing the best medium for a document; major applications of the letter; effective letter presentation; checklist for effective letter creation;
4.2 Memoranda 153
Components; how to handle memoranda effectively;
4.3 Reports and forms 158
Major applications of the written report; reports: referencing, typography and presentation; pre-printed forms and documents; effective document presentation; summary
4.4 Computer graphics 171
Applications of graphics software in the office; driving the software; graphics and the secretary;
Summary of main points 176
Activities 177
Practice questions from past examination papers 179
Glossary of terms and phrases 181

UNIT 5
Meetings, conferences, seminars and presentations 183
Overview 183
5.1 Meetings 185
Types of meeting and degrees of formality; calling meetings; the agenda; the chairman's agenda; minutes; how to take and transcribe effective minutes; terms and phrases used in meetings;
5.2 Conferences, seminars and presentations 202
Organising a conference; the main stages of organising a conference; seminars and presentations
Summary of main points 211
Activities 212
Practice questions from past examination papers 214
Glossary of terms and phrases 217

UNIT 6
Services and the secretary 219
Overview 219
6.1 Personnel services 221
The functions of a personnel department; checklists of major sections of personnel forms and schedules; contents of a contract of employment
6.2 Financial services 231
How PAYE income tax payments are calculated; payroll and pay as you earn; how to operate an imprest petty cash system; checklist of finance and accounting terms
6.3 Banking services 243
Customer accounts; banking services related to the account; bank travel services; checklist of banking terms in general business use; the secretary and plastic money
6.4 Post Office services 251
Mailing letters and parcels; other services
6.5 Travel services 254
Travelling in the UK by rail; travelling in the UK by air; hotel reservations in the UK; foreign travel; the travel itinerary
Summary of main points 261
Activities 262
Practice questions from past examination papers 265
Glossary of terms and phrases 268

Appendix 1
External agencies and bureaux 270

Appendix 2
Major legislation affecting organisations 271

Appendix 3
Checklist of reference information 273

Appendix 4
Reference list of sizes, dimensions and extents 275

Index 278

Foreword

As a member of the Institute of Qualified Private Secretaries it is my privilege to write the foreword to Desmond Evans' *Secretarial Procedures in the Electonic Office*.

In the rapidly changing business world where information technology and the ultimate fully electronic office is fast becoming a reality, secretaries cannot be complacent and rely on their basic office skills/secretarial training. Although skills and disciplines will be necessary, the ability to be conversant with word processors, computers, desktop publishing equipment, computer applications and future innovations will be an essential requirement.

It is in the secretary's own interest to be knowledgeable by reading, learning and first-hand experience, wherever possible. The Institute of Qualified Private Secretaries (IQPS) is a professional organisation which aims to provide members with information on appropriate professional matters, organising workshops to enable members to continue their own education and keep up to date with developments.

As executives become more involved in IT, secretarial tasks will change.

From conglomerates to small offices, one of the functions of a secretary is to input reports for managers to access and amend. Desmond Evans clearly defines throughout his book how information can be gathered from within and outside the company, displayed on VDUs at any appropriate desk and accessed.

Time will be of the essence. Offices will be streamlined to use maximum facilities and human resources. Maybe this will result in secretaries being at their workstations for longer time periods, as information and messages are easily keyed in and accessed.

The secretary's role will still be supportive, but with the added requirements of IT knowledge will encompass data administration and information management, allowing the secretary to analyse complex situations and submit practical recommendations.

Within this new business concept managerial skills will be allowed to develop and opportunities increase for career development.

For those secretaries or executives who travel within the scope of their job, confidential disks can be prepared and, where necessary, transported for accessing, updating and transmitting back to base. Telecommunications and facsimile machines have speeded up vital information-gathering, eliminating many wasted hours.

Desmond Evans has produced a book of benefit to all students and secretaries in setting out the requirements of the future. IT is a challenging, exciting world, in which the skills and expertise of the secretary are being stretched and tested to an extent scarcely imagined only a few years ago! As a secretary in training, make sure you go 'all out' to master IT and in so doing help to ensure a satisfying and enriching secretarial career.

Barbara V Thomas FIQPS

Acknowledgements

The author gratefully acknowledges the help, advice and support – including permission to reproduce copyright material – supplied by the people and organisations listed below. Without their generous interest and assistance, the illustrative concept of this textbook could not have been attained:

Acco Europe
Aldus Europe Limited (Pagemaker)
Barclays Bank plc
British Standards Institute
British Telecom plc
Chichester College Of Technology Governing Body
Chichester District Council
Compsoft plc
C W Cave & Tab Limited
Envopak Group Limited
Epson (UK) Limited
Fellowes Manufacturing (UK) Limited
Ferranti GTE Limited
GEC Plessey Telecommunications Limited
Headway Computer Products
William Heinemann Limited
Her Majesty's Stationery Office (Publications Division)
The Staff of Hogg Robinson (Travel) Limited, Chichester Branch
Hewlett Packard (UK) Limited
Mr John Hopkins, Author
IBM United Kingdom Limited
Miss Alison George and Mr Paul Quin, IBM United Kingdom Limited (Havant Plant)
Informix Software Limited (Multi-user Smart)
The Inland Revenue Service
Mrs Barbara V Thomas, The Institute Of Qualfied Private Secretaries
Kodak (UK) Limited (Business Imaging Systems)
The London Chamber Of Commerce Examinations Board
Longman Group Limited
Mar-Com Systems Limited
Minolta (UK) Limited
Muirhead Office Systems Limited
National Telephone Systems Limited
Pitman Examinations Institute
Pitman Publishing Limited
The Post Office
Prestel
Quantec Systems & Software Limited
The Royal Society Of Arts Examinations Board
Select Office Services, Chichester & Mr C H Longley, (Rinnai UK)
SPSS (UK) Limited
Mr Roger Swaffield, Partner, Evans, Weir Chartered Accountants, Chichester
Torus Systems Limited
Waterlow Business Supplies
West Sussex County Council
Mr Geoffrey Whitehead, Author

The production of a text – from initial idea to distributed printed copy – is dependent upon a publishing team including editors, designers, printers, distribution and administrative staff. The author also gratefully acknowledges their suggestions, support and advice in the creation of this text.

Throughout the book I have referred to a secretary as 'she' and a manager as 'he'. This is simply for fluency and is in no way meant to infer that the roles may not be reversed. Similarly I have adopted the term 'chairman' rather than 'chair' or 'chairperson' but here again the holder may be male or female.

DE

Using this book

This book is designed to provide you – as a secretary in training – with a series of practical insights into the procedures and applications which make up current good and effective secretarial practice.

The theory or body of knowledge you will need is presented in a practical way, with an extensive range of photographs, diagrams, document specimens and models to aid your development and confidence. The book's Units are also flexibly structured so that, with your teacher, you may organise and structure your learning programme in the best sequence suited to your studies.

USING THE ASSIGNMENTS

Each Unit includes an Activities section designed to give you plenty of opportunities to practise what you have learned – by working on your own, or as a member of a group. Activities include:

- Discussion topics
- Quick review quizzes
- Research and report back assignments
- Work simulation and work experience assignments
- Case studies
- Case histories
- Past examination practice questions

The Activities sections enable you to develop the 'good practice', practical competence expected of top secretaries and to promote your initiative, researching and presentation skills.

Provided that you work at them conscientiously and make the most of your contacts with local employers, the assignments will give you a thorough preparation for your secretarial career.

Good luck, and – a first and last tip – the Top Secretary *never* stops learning!

Desmond Evans
May 1989

UNIT 1
Organisations: activities and structures

OVERVIEW

Unit 1 examines the role of the secretary within the organisation. It looks first in detail at the various ways in which organisations are structured in order to achieve particular aims and to operate as effectively as possible.

Both private and public sectors are surveyed, each with its very different goals. Commercial and industrial organisations, on the one hand, sell products and services at a profit, and central and local government agencies, on the other, provide a range of services for businesses and the public, and put government policies into practice.

What each department of a large business organisation undertakes is explained – production, accounts, marketing, personnel, etc – and how employees fit into departmental structures.

In addition, the roles of the manager and the secretary/personal assistant are analysed and the ways in which they need to work closely together to achieve success.

Most people starting out on an office career will work for organisations of at least fifty employees. Some may join organisations employing many thousands in dispersed locations. The secretary/PA, in particular, will interact with colleagues and customers. It is therefore important at the outset to have a sound understanding of what makes organisations work and of people's relationships with one another in carrying out their daily tasks. This helps in giving a clear picture of the secretary's duties.

1.1 Organisations

Defining features of a business organisation; types of organisation; key people in organisations; the work of departments in business organisations; centralised support services and functions.

Starting out as a secretary in a large private or public sector organisation can prove very bewildering – until you think about what organisations are for, how they are structured and how various people in different posts fit into them. Firstly, organisations start small and grow big – usually as a result of success in meeting their basic aims, whether to make a profit in the private sector, or to serve the public well and cost-effectively in the public sector. As you will see in this section, growing larger usually results in specialised departments being set up and in employees occupying tiers or 'hierarchic' layers in the organisation, according to their job responsibilities and levels of authority. Also, as markets and demands change, so do organisations, with the result that they are in constant process of development – they are dynamic rather than static.

DEFINING FEATURES OF A BUSINESS ORGANISATION

1 The profit motive

All business organisations are created and developed in order to attain specific goals such as making and selling goods at a profit, selling a professional service, such as legal advice, at a profit or carrying out equipment maintenance under contract at a profit. Indeed, it is the ability of commerce and industry to make profits that keeps the country's economy going. The organisations make **gross profits**, from which taxes and other deductions are taken, to leave the **net profits**.

2 Clearly defined roles and responsibilities for employees

In order to achieve such goals or objectives, people in organisations are given clearly defined roles and responsibilities for particular activities which go to make up the overall purpose of the organisation. In manufacturing, perhaps the machine operator on the factory floor will concentrate upon only a small part of the process of making a motor-car. In the design office, the senior designer will be pondering over the shape and structure of a new model. At the top level of the organisation, the finance director will be concerned to ensure that *all* models produced are at the right price to cover costs and give a profit.

3 The hierarchy effect: the higher up, the more authority

In larger organisations, jobs vary in their scope and significance. As the jobs of certain people become more important to the organisation, so the people doing them are given more authority to see them properly carried out. This authority typically extends to having responsibility for the work of others, using the organisation's finances to buy and sell, and helping to decide upon the future direction the organisation should take.

4 The organisational pyramid

Most organisations work according to a cascade effect of **delegation**: most power and authority is located at the top of the pyramid and delegated outwards and downwards from directors via department heads and supervisors to office and factory personnel working at junior levels of the organisation.

As a result of this practice of granting more authority to fewer people, many organisations are said to be pyramidic in shape.

Fig 1.1 The organisational pyramid

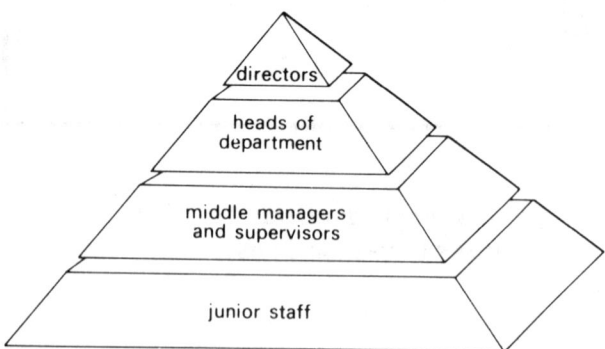

The layer-sandwich structure of the pyramid is termed an **organisational hierarchy**. In this, people work at different levels and receive instructions and action requests from senior staff, either to carry out themselves or to manage through staff reporting to them.

5 The stepped hierarchy or ladder in organisations

This stepped or hierarchical structure is a very common feature of both business and public sector organisations as you can see from the diagrams below of the structure of a typical company and of local government.

DISCUSSION TOPIC

Why do organisations so often take on pyramidic structure, with a few senior staff holding extensive authority?

6 Division of activity into departments, sections and units

A further feature of organisations is the division of activity into specialised units or departments. As the activities of business became more complex, it made sense for groups or units of people within the organisation to concentrate upon an area which had a common theme – the actual making or production, the

Fig 1.2 The stepped hierarchy

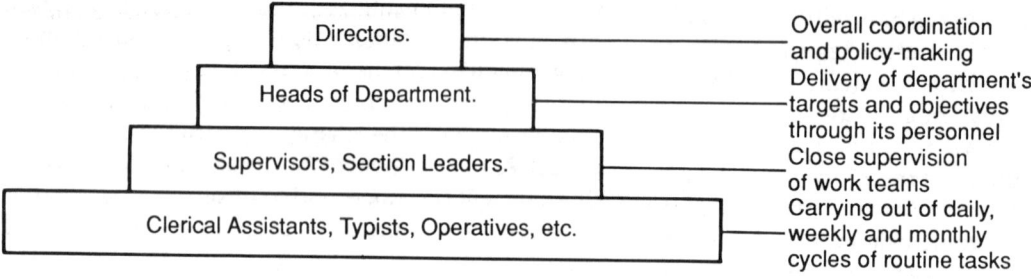

Fig 1.3 Hierarchies in county councils: members and employees

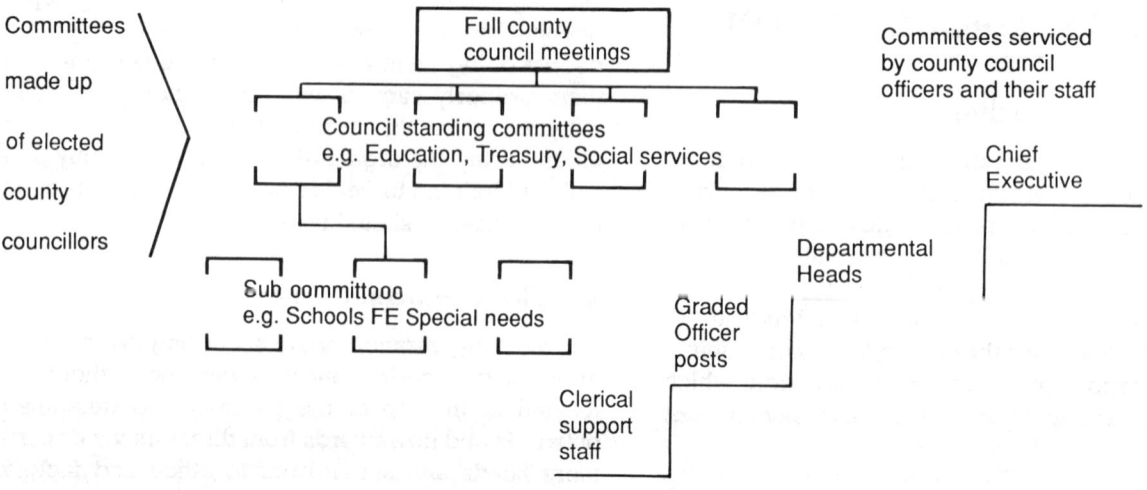

Organisations: activities and structures

financial aspects of the business, the sales side and so on. Each department, section or unit forms part of the structure of the whole organisation.

The organisational chart

Many companies and public service institutions find it helpful to construct organisation charts and diagrams like the one shown in Fig 1.4 in order to illustrate clearly how the various parts of the organisation are related and interconnect to form the whole.

Factors which influence the structure of organisations:

- What they do
- How large they are
- Where they are sited
- Who their customers are
- What kind of tasks employees do daily
- The impact of information technology applications

The impact of information technology has affected all aspects of the organisation – operation, size, siting and customer contact. With rapid telecommunications through electronic mail networks, facsimile transmission (fax) and interconnected databases on computer (see Unit 3), it matters much less where a person works from. An employee can be linked by computer to the organisation's network while working alone at home and customers can order goods without visiting the shops.

> **DISCUSSION TOPICS**
>
> Do you think that the days when groups of people travel to a common office centre are numbered and that people will work from home by means of a computer network? Or can you think of good reasons why people will still need and want to work in purpose-built offices and maintain physical contact with one another?

7 Authority: bestowed on managers by general consent

Another defining feature of most organisations is that authority lies in the post and not in the person. In effect this means that staff will associate with the post of managing director or head of department the power and authority which goes with either job, rather than with the particular individual who happens to hold it. Thus an organisation's personnel can move on or retire and successors can take on the vacant posts confident that they will be accorded due respect at the outset. Of course, the newcomers will have to continue to earn it by dint of personal example and leadership! In this way, organisations work as hierarchies because the people within them agree to abide by the custom of accepting reasonable orders or instructions from those whose posts give them the right to issue them.

Fig 1.4 The organisational chart

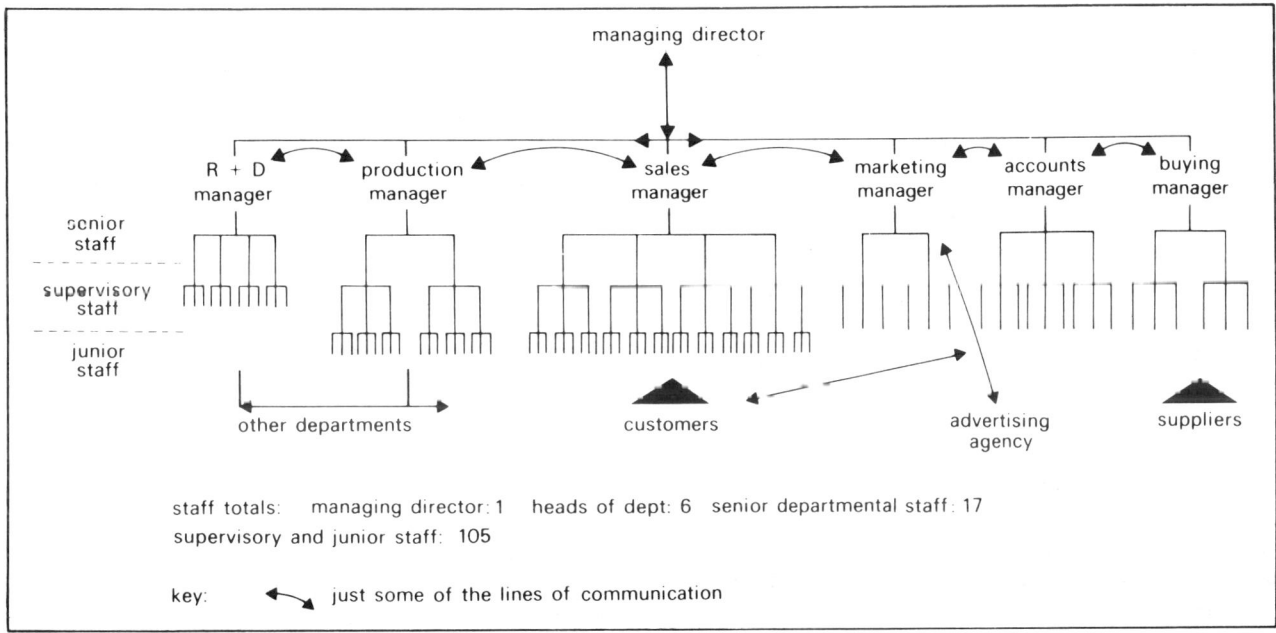

8 Job descriptions: written schedules which communicate responsibilities

In small organisations, the various activities of, say, the shopkeeper and his assistants are pretty straightforward and understood most of the time by all concerned on the basis of the spoken word. Since everyone rubs shoulders all the time, there is very little need for messages to be written down and circulated. However, in large organisations word-of-mouth messages sometimes become garbled as the 'What did he say? Pass it on.' effect comes into play. Moreover, neither managers nor secretaries work very well without some clear notion - understood and communicated to all concerned - of the range and limit of their responsibilities. Thus the written **job description** serves to clarify the duties and responsibilities of all organisational personnel, and in open, sensible organisations, it is made available to those staff affected by the duties it defines and describes. (See Unit 6 for a detailed look at job descriptions.)

9 Organisational change

In order to survive, an organisation must be responsive to changes in, say, consumer buying habits or taxpayers' expectations. For example, as a result of increased requests for details about county councils' activities, public relations departments and information officials were added to county council structures. By the same token, new departments, such as export sales or training and staff development may be grafted on to expanding companies.

DISCUSSION TOPIC

Companies employing thousands of people - sometimes international companies spanning the globe - have grown considerably in the past fifty years. What problems do you think this poses for their managerial and secretarial staff?

NEW TERMS AND PHRASES

Entire dictionaries of business terms and definitions have been compiled to aid students, and this initial checklist will get you started on drawing up your own personal list of terms and phrases. Make a habit of jotting down each new specialist word or phrase you encounter in your studies, since you will recall much better those entries you researched and set down yourself. Indeed, you and your fellow students may well wish to set up a computer database of such terms for constant access through the year.

TYPES OF ORGANISATION

Franchise
Large companies marketing well-known products or processes sometimes license small entrepreneurs to use their name and (for a fee) help them to run successful outlets; franchising, for example, is popular in the fast-food market.

Limited company
Many small businesses are created as limited companies since in law their directors are not personally liable for the debts incurred by the business beyond their shareholdings in it; limited companies may be private, public or limited by guarantee. The Royal Society Of Arts Examinations Board is limited by guarantee and this type of company structure is favoured by charities.

Multinational
A term used to describe a private sector company or group of companies with divisions or wholly owned subsidiary companies in various countries.

Multiple
Retailing firms with numerous High Street stores or branches in a national network are often called multiples.

Nationalised industry
A state-owned industry like the national Coal Board and British Rail; *note*: many former nationalised industries have recently been privatised - turned into public limited companies (see below).

Partnership
A partnership is formed when between two and twenty people draw up a deed of partnership which formally sets down who does what and how profits and liabilities are shared out; accountants, solicitors and doctors often form partnerships, sharing risks, workload and profits.

public corporation
A term used to describe large state-owned organisations like the energy industries, now being privatised.

public limited company (PLC)
These are usually large national or multi-national (international) companies with an issued share value of at least £50,000; shares in such companies are offered for sale each day in stock exchanges and may be purchased by the general public; private limited company shares may not be sold in this way.

Quango
A 'quasi autonomous non-government organisation' to undertake specific tasks; the Equal Opportunities Commission is a good example of a quango.

Sole trader
The formal title given to the 'one-man-band' single owner business (which is how many mutlinationals started); note also the term 'proprietor' is used for the owner of a small business.

Organisations: activities and structures

DISCUSSION TOPIC

Dr E F Schumacher wrote a famous book in 1973 entitled *Small Is Beautiful*. His view was that small organisations were more effective than large ones and that people worked better in them. Do you agree?

External organisations which interact with private sector companies

Registrar of Companies
Factories Inspectorate
Fire Service
Training Agency
Employment Bureau
Job Centre
Careers Office
Office of Fair Trading
Advertising Standards Authority
Equal Opportunities Commission
Race Relations Board
EEC European Commission
Department of Trade & Industry
Department of Social Security
Inland Revenue
Customs & Excise
Patents Office
Industrial Tribunal
Advisory Conciliation and Arbitration Service (ACAS)
Trade Unions
Wage Councils
Clearing banks
Merchant Banks
Insurance Brokers
Chartered Accountant

ASSIGNMENT

Carry out your research into *one* of the above external organisations and produce a factsheet of the essential information you discover. Give a 3–5 minute oral presentation to your group based on your factsheet and ensure that each member receives a photocopy of it as part of their Unit 1 database.

SUMMARY OF FEATURES OF AN ORGANISATION

- An organisation is a group of people working together to achieve goals which they set themselves.

- An organisation tends to become structured so that senior experts at the top plan, direct and monitor the work of others. That is, they *manage* those working for them.

- Organisations need money, buildings and equipment to enable their personnel to achieve the pre-set goals.

- Organisations tend to become broken down into specialised departments or units which interrelate and enable groups of people to specialise in particular tasks

- For organisations to work successfully, employees at each level of activity must agree to work to and abide by the rules of the organisation and the authority given to its managers and supervisors. To this end, each employee is given a contract of employment and, usually, a personal job description.

- Nothing stays the same. Organisations are constantly reacting to outside events and situations which may cause them to expand, contract or modify their activities. In this way they are said to be dynamic.

Fig 1.5 Key people in the private sector organisation

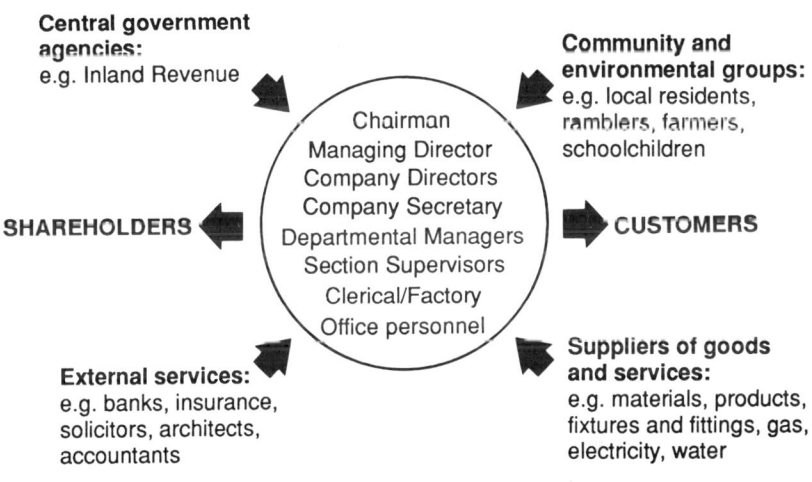

KEY PEOPLE IN ORGANISATIONS

Private sector organisations

The shareholder
- private and public limited companies are financed by money (capital) from people buying shares in the company
- shareholders may be individual members of the public, organisations like trade unions or other companies with cash to invest
- public company shares may be purchased by anyone through a stock exchange, whereas private company shares can only be bought from the shareholder, and are usually held by the company's directors
- shareholders attend annual general meetings and extraordinary general meetings of the company
- they have legal rights of access to information
- they vote to elect the directors
- they may acquire sufficient shares to control or take over the company

The chairman
- at the top of the organisational pyramid
- elected by the board of directors
- chairs meetings of the board of directors
- may have executive status or may leave day-to-day running of the company to the managing director

The directors
- decide on important matters at board meetings
- have legal obligations and responsibilities under the Companies Act 1985
- may exert influence on company activities by having extensive shareholdings in the company
- the board of directors presents its annual report to the shareholders for approval at the end of each trading year

The managing director
- the executive head of most organisations, with authority over all the staff
- is a member of the board of directors

The company secretary
- responsible to the managing director and board to ensure all the company's affairs are conducted according to legal requirements
- services and attends meetings of the board of directors
- attends to all correspondence involving shareholders and the calling of shareholders' meetings
- usually responsible for fire, health and safety regulations, company contracts, trade mark registrations, etc
- acts as legal advisor to the company

The departmental manager
- responsible to the managing director for the work of one department in the organisation
- directs the work carried out by the members of staff in the department
- ensures targets are met, eg projected (budgetted) annual sales turnover is achieved at the desired level of gross profit (profit before tax)
- is provided by the company with the human, equipment and financial resources to reach the pre-set targets

The section supervisor
- responsible to the head of department for the work of a section or unit in the department (eg a large accounts department may have sections for the sales ledger, purchase ledger, nominal ledger, payroll, credit control, etc.)
- reviews work in progress with the head of department to ensure targets are met
- responsible for section staff

The shop steward
- responsible for trade union matters within the section/organisation
- represents the trade union members in negotiations with management
- responsible to area branch secretary and trade unions' officers

Public sector organisations

County councillor/District councillor
- elected by those registered to vote in each local area
- usually a member of a political party
- makes decisions in full council meetings or in committees
- responsible for setting budgets and carrying out legally imposed duties

Local government officer
- full-time official who carries out the policies of the elected members under the direction of a chief executive
- officials are divided into departments and sections covering specific areas of the work

The chairman of a public corporation
- responsible to a central government department for the administration of a public corporation; the central government department will be headed by a Permanent Secretary responsible to a Minister – a senior Government Member of Parliament
- duties resemble those of a company chairman.

Fig 1.6 Key people in the local government public sector organisation

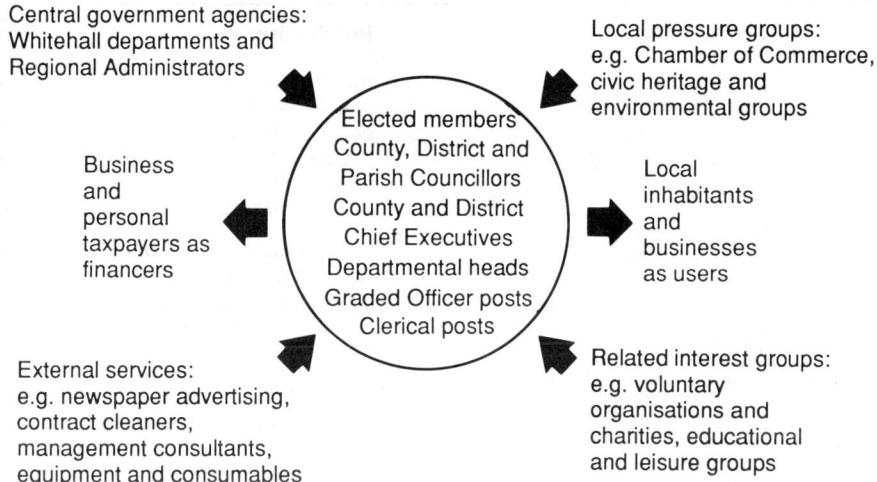

DISCUSSION TOPIC

'Organisations are not bricks and mortar or plant and equipment, or even neat little diagrams on paper. They are people!' Is this an over-simplified view of organisations?

THE WORK OF DEPARTMENTS IN BUSINESS ORGANISATIONS

Although as a secretary you will naturally be preoccupied with the work of your own department, it is important right from the start to appreciate that the success of any business enterprise depends entirely on the cooperation between departments which are interdependent. Furthermore, as a secretary you will undoubtedly be in daily contact with many colleagues in other departments and so it is important for you to gain a thorough knowledge of what they do and what preoccupies them.

Research and development department

- designs and tests new products
- improves and updates existing products
- researches into new areas of interest
- analyses and tests competing products
- works with the production department to develop **prototypes** (initial models) and construct the equipment to manufacture new products
- helps to ensure that new products comply with legal requirements, **British Standards** and safety laws.

Production department

- manufactures the company's range of products
- monitors factors like wastage and costs of bought-in parts so as to maintain profit margins
- designs tools to help make products and buys in the necessary plant and equipment
- writes or buys in computer programs which control much of the set routines of production-line manufacturing – **Note:** 'Computer-Aided Manufacture And Design' (CADCAM) and the term 'robotics'.
- controls and coordinates the rate and quantity of manufacture so as to meet given orders within pre-set deadlines – plans its activities in advance
- monitors trends in production techniques internationally so as to remain competitive

Accounts department

- is responsible for overall financial aspects of the organisation's activities
- records and monitors all areas of financial activity: sales, purchases, running costs (heat, light, payroll, etc), manufacturing costs, **dividends issued**, etc and checks these against annual **budgets**.
- supplies timely information aimed at ensuring that the organisation works at a profit, ie that **sales revenue** is not exceeded by **cost of sales**; provides financial reports for senior management on a regular basis
- produces information for shareholders at regular intervals – in the form of financial reports including **balance sheets** and **profit and loss accounts**

Fig 1.7 The work of company departments

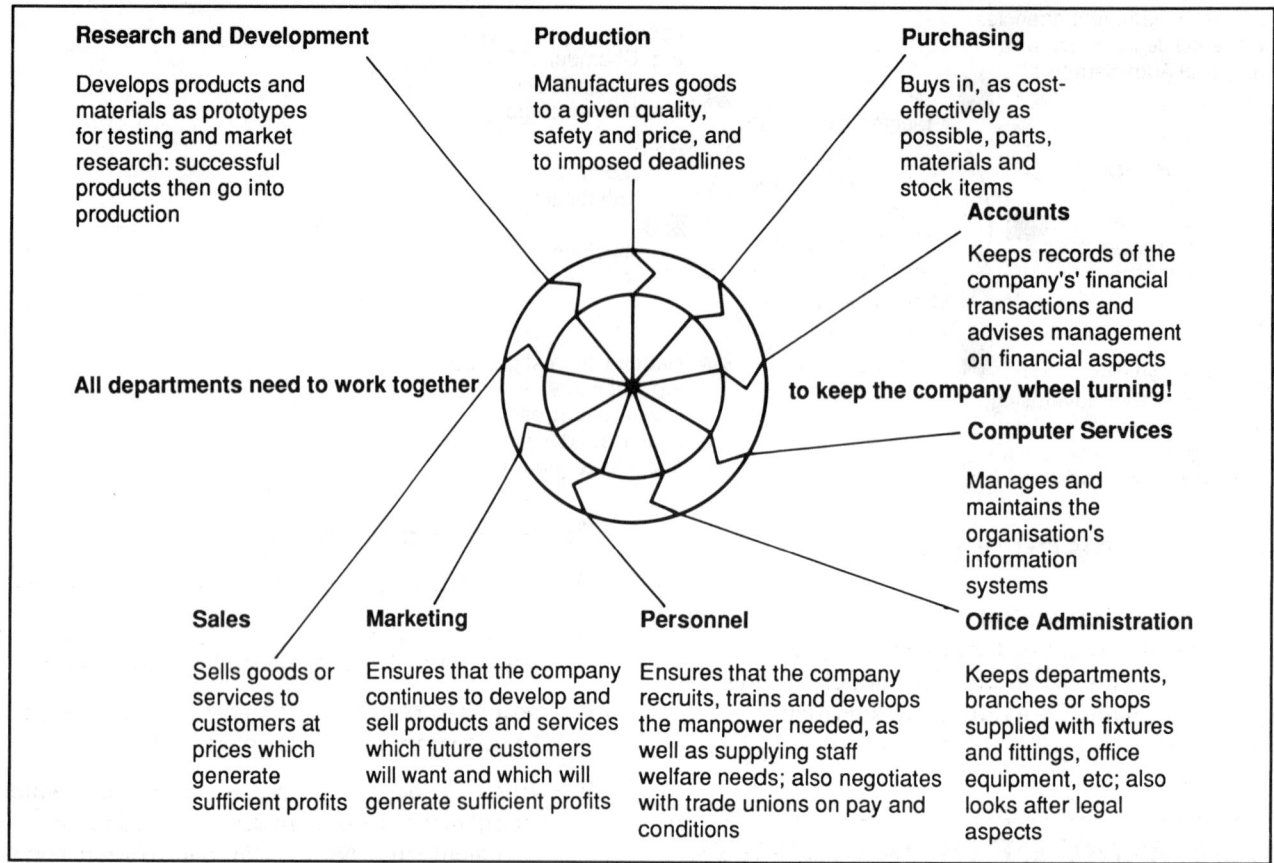

- maintains financial information required by law, such as the details of income upon which tax must be paid

Marketing department

- ensures that the organisation remains competitive by providing information about what products and services the market wants and what sort of prices it will pay
- maintains a **market research** function to explore new markets and new product opportunities; monitors the success/failure of its own products and competing products
- works with R & D and production departments in the design of attractive and 'sellable' new products, as well as the updating and improving of existing ones
- designs and develops advertising materials and campaigns aimed at increasing sales
- monitors local and national trends in consumer demand or industrial marketing needs
- provides advice on the termination of existing products and the introduction of new ones at appropriate intervals; in large companies, maintains computerised models of markets and uses them to predict what will sell.

Sales department

- prepares an **annual sales plan** which breaks down how many of what type of product will be sold at what profit in the year; divides the plan up into regions, districts and branches, or sales representatives' territories
- supplies **point-of-sale** material and advice to customers to help sell products
- monitors discreetly the sales of competing products in customers' outlets
- supplies **market intelligence** to the marketing department on current sales activities; sales representatives provide weekly sales reports to senior sales department personnel
- aims to secure new business with new customers and to increase sales with existing customers on a given target basis

Personnel department

- ensures that the organisation has the human resources needed to achieve its aims
- coordinates employee selection, promotion and termination; supervises appraisal schemes
- provides a staff training and development service

- maintains the organisation's employee records, including pension, sickness benefit and superannuation payments
- supervises industrial negotiations on pay and conditions of work with trade unions and associations
- provides a confidential employee counselling service and runs welfare and social activities in many instances
- monitors personnel activities in competing companies so as to avoid key staff being lured away by increased offers on pay and fringe benefits, etc

Office administration department

- provides a service for other departments in areas such as **centralised purchasing** of stationery and office supplies, and advice on what equipment to purchase for office use
- coordinates the internal or external design and printing of forms and schedules
- oversees a **centralised reprographics service** for bulk photocopying/printing for other departments
- provides **word processing/desktop publishing**/text production services, if required
- maintains the organisation's insurance requirements
- monitors any leasing arrangements
- where an organisation has dispersed branches or retail outlets, supervises their administration with the help of branch inspectors.

Computer services department

- acquires and maintains company computing equipment
- secures or creates computer software needed by all departments: in larger organisations many computer functions are supplied via custom-designed software
- maintains computer records of organisational information and **archived data**: large companies have a single database of information which is constantly extended and updated and accessible according to **security clearance**: back-up duplicate records are essential!
- coordinates and supports national and international computer-based communications on behalf of staff
- maintains a watching brief on new developments in information technology to ensure competitiveness and efficiency
- may run staff training schemes for new staff in various computer/data-processing functions
- installs new/updated versions of **software** as they are released; ensures **hardware** is able to match growth in company's activities and increased use by staff.

Transport department

- coordinates the organisation's transport needs, from directors', managers' and sales representatives' cars to acquisition and maintenance of fleets of lorries and/or vans
- keeps service records and renews insurances, vehicle registrations etc
- designs cost-effective delivery routes via computer for delivery fleets
- negotiates purchases and leasings with car/HGV dealers
- provides training as needed

Note: Some business organisations have separate purchasing departments and training departments, while some amalgamate marketing and sales. They may also have a press or public relations office to promote their company image and publicise the company's products in a general way, perhaps by sponsorship of a sports event. Generally, the larger the organisation, the more specialised departments it is likely to create. Remember that the number of departments and the work they do depends directly upon the nature of the organisation's activities, its size and the degree to which it can afford to employ specialist as opposed to generalist employees and managers.

CENTRALISED SUPPORT SERVICES AND FUNCTIONS

Most organisations reach a point in their development when it makes sense to bring together the fragmented, departmentalised functions or services, such as filing or computing. Such activities, which are made use of throughout a company's departments, are restructured so as to report directly either to a managing director or an office administration manager with an overall servicing brief.

The chart on page 12 illustrates some of the major services which tend to be centralised in larger organisations. Note that some centralised services, like the personnel function may be run from a department which in many respects is structured just like any other department, with a hierarchical system of responsibility. At other times, units may be set up quite outside the departmental structure and this may create its own problems in communication and interpersonal relations.

Fig 1.8 Centralised company support services and functions

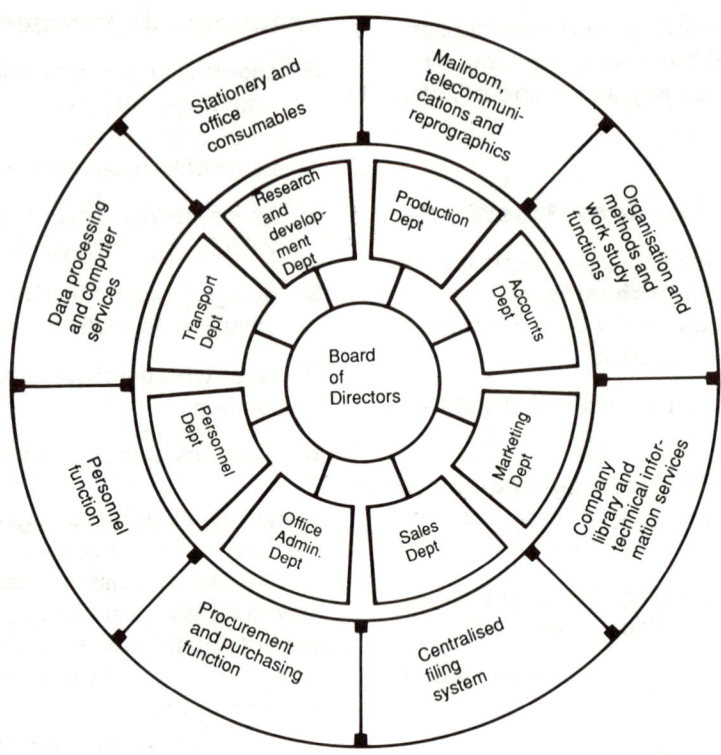

Advantages

- Easier for directors to exert overall control and direction.

- Uniform, company-wide policies quicker and easier to introduce.

- By providing extra support, encourages departments to do their own work faster.

- Security and continuity improved (see DP and filing especially).

- Rationalisation secures lower costs and a higher level of service equally available to *all* departments.

- Gathers into a single group staff who can develop an expert company-wide service.

Disadvantages

- Departments compete for a service which is finite.

- Being external to the departments, the services suffer from 'the distancing effect' and intermittent contact inhibits communication.

- Uniform policies and procedures stifle departmental initiative and innovation.

- 'Things' take longer to happen!

- Face-to-face contact and 'the personal touch' suffer.

- Possible lack of consultation about policy changes.

- Increase in costs of running support services – at expense of, say, production and sales activities.

● **Note:** Some centralised services are set up as departments, e.g. personnel. Centralised services need excellent administrative and communication skills in their staff if they are to work well

Examples of frequently centralised services

1 Office administration
Used frequently in national retail and distribution organisations to administer branches and depots.

2 Personnel Function
Provides a comprehensive service from staff recruitment to pensions fund administration, including training, welfare, industrial relations, and legal advice to management.

3 Organisation and methods/work study
O & M provides a service which monitors office practices and procedures in order to improve efficiency. Work Study in factories vets production processes so as to maximise efficiency and minimise costs and wastage.

4 Data processing and computer services
Provides an around-the-clock, non-stop service, backing up and maintaining an organisation's computing and information processing needs. DP also provides a computer program-writing service for departments needing to administer specific tasks via computers.

5 Mailroom and telecommunications
With the widespread use of information technology in organisations today, the function of the mailroom to administer internal and external mail is being superseded in many instances by telecommunications services located at key access points. Such services include: fax, telex, BT data transmission services (like SATSTREAM), Prestel, teletex and Email (see Unit 3 for a detailed description of these services). Thus, area networking is bringing such services to every computerised desktop!

6 Filing and records
Many organisations run a centralised filing and records system which loans out paper-based files on request and logs respective users. Advantages include better control, security, avoidance of duplication and fewer lost documents – at the cost of accessibility, time taken to obtain documents and slower pace of updating.

The computerisation of information enables the organisation's database to be kept constantly up to date and made available to all terminals from a mainframe or mini-computer (subject to security clearance). This makes centralised paper-based filing and records systems obsolete, save where legal requirements oblige papers to be kept. Also, computer output microfilm (COM), linking microfilm technology with computers, greatly reduces the need for archiving paper documents.

7 Library and technical information services
Many large organisations, like ICI, IBM (UK) and Shell, include scientific/technical libraries in their range of centralised services. Such services offer computerised databases of information from remote locations to all company desktop terminals. Also, optical scanning equipment and computer networks, enable staff to access and to look at paper-originated documents (stored in the form of electronic files on their desktop computer screens.

8 Procurement and purchasing
Both public and private sector organisations make sigificant economies by centralising their purchasing functions and take advantage of bulk purchasing discounts by doing so.

INFORMATION TECHNOLOGY IN ORGANISATIONS

No examination of the activities and structures of organisations would be complete without emphasising the all-embracing impact which information technology – IT – has made upon the ways in which organisations work. Since 1971, the microprocessor or silicon-chip has revolutionised the ways in which all kinds of office equipment function and widely extended their versatility. For example, even modest electronic typewriters now have built-in memories to enable stored text to be edited, and can also be connected to desktop computers to act as computer printers.

Revolution in telecommunications

The greatest impact upon organisational activities prompted by IT has undoubtedly been in the field of electronic telecommunications. Managers and secretaries alike are now able to access both local and wide area networks, fax, telex and Prestel from their personal desktop computers and similarly to use all the facilities of a computerised telephone switchboard (CABX) through a phone and modem connected also to the same PC. (Unit 3 examines such equipment in detail). Thus the organisation's personnel and customers – all over the world – have become almost instantly accessible at the touch of a few buttons or keys!

Records and information management

IT has also made possible a completely new approach to the management of records and information systems. The electronic file – whether stored on a 5.25" or 3.5" disk, or within the hard disk inside the computer – is replacing many paper-based systems of record keeping. Moreover, computer technology allied to various types of microform technology (which photographs paper documents on to miniature photo-frames) enables large organisations like insurance companies or building societies to cope with keeping – and finding quickly – millions of individual records. Similarly, managers and secretaries are increasingly accessing files and records on their desktop computer monitors by 'fetching them out' of mainframe computers in the twinkling of an eye!

Changing jobs and roles in organisations

Whatever else IT has done in organisations, no one will deny that it has quickened the pace of change much more rapidly than could have been imagined in the early 1970s. Some types of office job, such as copy typist, have been entirely replaced by that of word processor operator in many firms. Personal secretaries have seen their jobs and careers enlarged by being transformed into information assistants and then communication managers. Hardly a single office-based occupation has remained unaffected by the onward sweep of IT applications. Accounts clerks now use spreadsheets as often as they used to employ electronic calculators. Secretaries and managers have adapted to computerised diaries, daily faxing and frequent electronic mailing. Meetings are now called in a trice by computer at the first common opportunity available to five busy executives. Teleconferencing links company managers across the EEC. Electronic mail from the UK to Sydney Australia is patched across international telecommunications channels in seconds!

Top Secretary Tip

Developing a successful secretarial career today depends upon the secretary in training acquiring IT-based skills and expertise. Whether in the area of text processing, information management, computerised records or telecommunications. MAKE SURE YOU USE YOUR TRAINING TIME TO BECOME AN 'IT' EXPERT!

QUICK REVIEW QUIZ

1 What does the term 'profit-motive' mean?

2 Why do organisations tend to be structured as hierarchies?

3 List the factors which influence the ways organisations are structured.

4 Note down five different external organisations which have dealings with a private sector company.

5 What are the main responsibilities of a company secretary?

6 In what ways are company directors answerable to their shareholders?

7 Explain briefly the major activities of a marketing department.

RESEARCH AND REPORT BACK ASSIGNMENTS

1 Investigate the major aspects of one of the following. Make your notes and either deliver your findings orally to your group or as a factsheet on one side of A4:

(a) A deed of partnership
(b) The Companies Act 1985
(c) A memorandum and articles of association

2 Shareholders invest their cash in companies hoping it will increase in value. Find out the difference between: (a) a debenture and (b) an ordinary share.

3 Where in your locality may shares be bought and sold? Find out how much it costs, including comission, to buy, say, £300 worth of shares at £5.00 each.

4 Contact the local branch office of one of the trade unions and find out how the union organisation is structured. Which local companies have members of the trade union working for them? What benefits do they provide for their members?

5 In pairs, research into the way in which one of the following is structured and design a suitable organisational chart to display in your base room:

(a) Your college or school
(b) A local bank branch
(c) A large supermarket in your district
(d) A manufacturing company
(e) A large firm of local solicitors
(f) Your nearest district council

DISCUSSION TOPICS

1 How do you think organisations are likely to change in the next ten years in the light of developments in information technology?

2 What do you consider to be the main motivators of people working in organisations?

1.2 Personal relationships in organisations

The line relationship; the manager and secretary; the secretary and career development.

An old but true definition of the art of management is 'The achievement of predetermined goals through the work of others'. In order to enable managers to work effectively, a number of relationships have evolved between people in organisations which directly affect how employees respond and relate to one another. This section explains three types of relationship central to the working of private and public sector organisations.

You will find it essential in your secretarial work to understand how the three relationships – **line, staff** and **functional** – influence the ways in which company personnel interact with those for whom you work – probably a manager (or managers). In the same way, when relaying instructions or requests from your manager to various people within the company, your approach will vary.

THE LINE RELATIONSHIP

A **line relationship** occurs within an organisation when there is a system of 'reports to' requirements. For example, in an accounts office, the clerical assistant will report to a supervisor or senior clerk, who oversees his work; in turn, the supervisor will report to the head of department, who may be responsible for the work of several supervisors – and, through them, for their clerical assistants. The accounts manager will report to his company' managing director and be responsible for the entire work of the accounts department. Thus the clerical assistant, supervisor, head of department and managing director are said to enjoy a 'line relationship' in which instructions and requests for work to be done go *down* the line and responses go *up* it.

The **scalar chain** is sometimes used to describe the line management relationship where each employee reports to a single superior.

It is important to be aware that employees working within such a line relationship tend to resent others who are outside such a line of authority giving them orders or instructions. In fact, effective management depends a very great deal on all employees understanding and respecting the line relationship. A watchword among managers is that it is unfair to give them the responsibility to achieve certain aims without the authority that should go with it. It is this line relationship which transmits authority from the top to the bottom of the organisation.

THE STAFF RELATIONSHIP

However, not all people working in an organisation interrelate in a line relationship. Indeed, secretaries and administrative assistants, who report directly to a manager (or managers) and who are not responsible for the work of junior staff, enjoy what is known as a **staff relationship** with their manager(s) in the organisation.

As the diagram on page 16 illustrates, the manager's personal assistant or secretary does not possess the authority to insist that any of the manager's departmental staff carry out an instruction. They do not report to the secretary, but to the manager. Nevertheless, the secretary very often has to relay orders and instructions to the manager's

Fig 1.9 Example of a line and staff relationship in a department

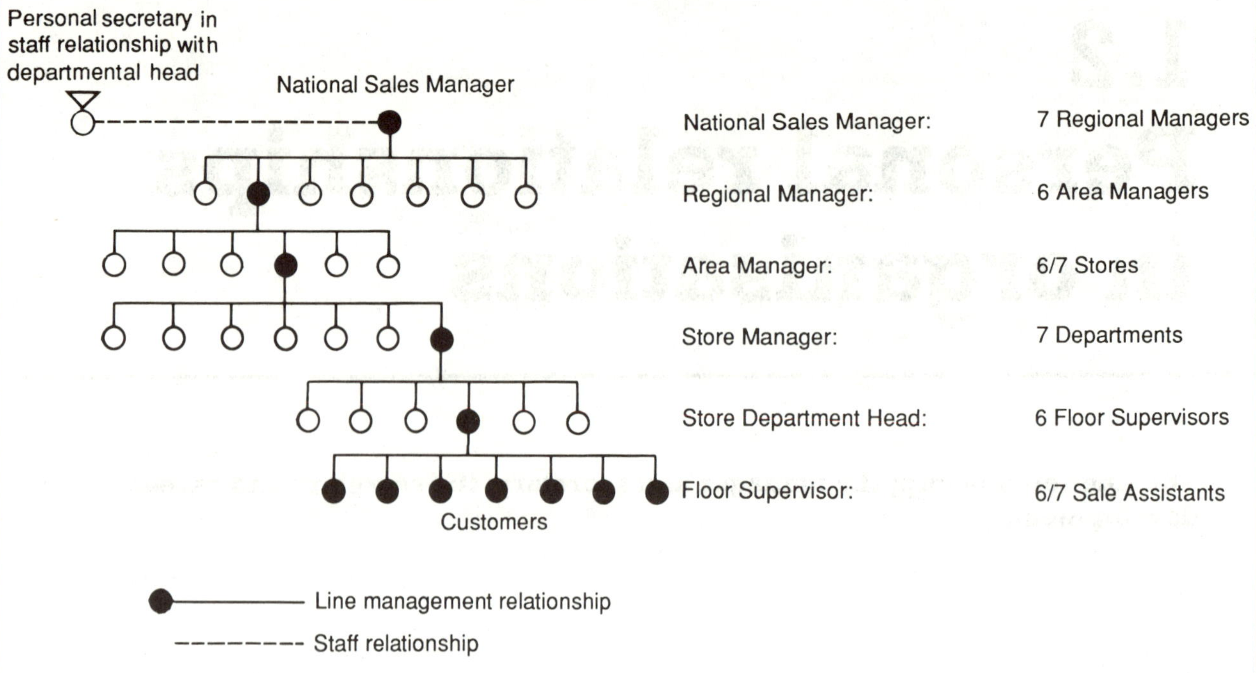

Personal secretary in staff relationship with departmental head

National Sales Manager

Role	Reports to/manages
National Sales Manager:	7 Regional Managers
Regional Manager:	6 Area Managers
Area Manager:	6/7 Stores
Store Manager:	7 Departments
Store Department Head:	6 Floor Supervisors
Floor Supervisor:	6/7 Sale Assistants

Customers

● —— Line management relationship
- - - - - Staff relationship

---

subordinates. In such instances, the instructions are likely to be issued courteously and prefaced with a phrase such as:

'Mr Johnson has asked me ... to remind you that your sales report is overdue ...'

Thus the secretary communicates in a way which is acceptable to someone whose post lies outside the secretary's line of authority by making use of the manager's position and authority.

In larger organisations a number of staff relationships exist between managers and their assistants, and between the managing director and individual advisers and personal aides, such as a financial advisor, a legal assistant or a researcher.

THE FUNCTIONAL RELATIONSHIP

The term **functional relationship** within the context of the organisation usually refers to personnel who have an overall (centralised) organisational responsibility for a particular function or activity. For example, the personnel manager and his department will have an overall responsibility for recruiting the kind of people the organisation needs – not only immediately, but for the organisation's future development. The personnel function will also coordinate training and staff development across the entire organisation. Even so, the line manager running a particular department will have a strong say in who is appointed to work for him and who is most in need of training.

Other kinds of functional activities in organisations include caretaking and maintenance, management services (monitoring the effectiveness of organisational activity) and computer services.

Such functional staff tend to report directly to the managing director or public service chief executive.

THE ROLES OF THE MANAGER AND SECRETARY

Delegating and monitoring

As we have already established, the fundamental role of the manager is to assist in achieving the goals and objectives of the organisation by coordinating and overseeing the activities of those who report to him. Most managers occupy positions in line relationships which span the organisation, from top to bottom. As a consequence they spend much time in receiving information and instructions from their senior colleagues. In turn, the departmental manager sifts and interprets such messages before transmitting them on to his various sections of subordinates as requests or requirements for specific jobs and tasks to be carried out.

It is common for busy managers to have numerous

departmental activities going on simultaneously and so it becomes essential to devise methods which will provide the manager with regular feedback on the progress being made by section teams or individuals. Such a process is termed **delegating**, where particular jobs are assigned to teams or individuals who work to a brief or set of instructions given to them by the manager.

Correspondingly, the manager will organise his working week so as to include a number of feedback or review meetings at which a particular activity, such as the preparations for launching a new snack product nationally, may be reviewed and progress discussed by members of the promotional team. At such meetings the manager's secretary frequently sits in to take notes which will subsequently be circulated as a form of action minutes (see Unit 5), summarising what was agreed and who was identified to carry out what.

While such meetings may have a semi-formal air about them, much of the manager's feedback on work in progress comes as a result of informal chats in his office with various members of staff who may have called in to discuss something quite different but who are gently asked to report back by questions like:

'Oh, before you go, Jack, tell me how the Manchester project is going. I've got to report back myself to the Board next week.'

Since the manager has a complex role to discharge in this aspect of his job, it is important that his secretary also ensures that she holds regular meetings with the manager to ensure that she is kept fully up to date with what is happening in the department, particularly since it is often the secretary who is approached to answer queries or to provide confirmation that certain actions are in order when the manager is away.

Decision-making and problem-solving

Another important part of the role of the manager is his acceptance of responsibility or **accountability** for the work his department has been set up to do. However, part of the 'deal' the manager has with his superiors is that he is likewise given sufficient authority, delegated to him by senior management, so as to provide the 'clout' which will ensure his instructions are carried out promptly and readily. This being the case, the manager has to make many decisions – many of them snap decisions – in the course of the day or week which will affect the success of the operation he is managing. In a similar way, the manager personally will be expected to solve problems and to troubleshoot in matters of conflict or disagreement among his staff as part of his routine activities.

The secretary must also play a part in this central management activity of making the decision-making and problem-solving processes easier by:

- Filtering out calls and callers when the manager needs to concentrate fully on, say, a new product development decision.

- Ensuring that the files and documents, which are a major part of the department's information assets, are kept up to date and instantly accessible when, for instance, the manager requests, say, a copy of last year's sales figures or stock levels.

- Alerting the manager to problems or clashes among departmental staff before a molehill becomes a mountain.

- Using diplomatic and counselling skills to ensure that the manager does not arrive at an ill-advised decision because of momentary stress or irritation. Indeed, many secretaries become highly skilled at discreetly modifying in dictated letters, memoranda or reports, those remarks or observations which are abrasive or inappropriately expressed.

- Acting as a sounding board for ideas and first thinking; indeed, the able secretary or administrative assistant has a crucial role to play in providing the manager with a trustworthy confidante who is in close touch with departmental staff outlooks and views and who can therefore give informed advice about the best way to proceed in reaching a decision or solving a problem.

Communication and the dissemination of information

A great deal of the manager's time is spent in acting as a communicator – explaining, cajoling, interpreting and briefing staff in a host of matters – and also in relaying by various available media all sorts of messages and information.

As a result, the manager and his secretary devote much time to the processing of information, whether in the form of a notice on the departmental noticeboard, a circular letter to customers or a report to the board of directors. **Information technology** developments also enable the manager to communicate by computer via **local area networks** and to participate in **teleconferences** or to make telephone calls while on the move with a **cellular telephone**.

This being so, both the manager and the secretary need to possess highly developed skills in creating, editing, formatting and visually presenting information in a variety of media — **overhead projector** (OHP) transparencies, printed text, desktop computer published newsletters or **electronic mail** (Email) messages. Underpinning such skills are those of skim-reading, proofreading, and expertise in spelling, punctuation, grammar and numeracy.

In addition, the manager and secretary will carry

out much of their communication orally. They will both therefore need to have acquired fluent speaking skills allied to techniques of oral communication which convey assurance, confidence, sympathy, interest, enthusiasm and so on.

Interpersonal skills

Fundamentally, an organisation is people. Organisations both large and small will contain people with very different responsibilities, outlooks and personalities. Since the manager has to maintain an extensive network of relationships – with superiors, subordinates, peers and customers – it is essential that he has first-rate people skills. Such skills include the ability to make someone feel at ease, to be a good listener, to be able to interpret the body language signals people display and to grasp quickly the mood or views of colleagues or clients and modify his own responses accordingly.

By the same token, the secretary will need to acquire just the same such skills, for in many instances the secretary acts as a direct substitute for an absent principal. Also the secretary will develop in his or her own right a network of contacts and associates very similar to those of the manager.

Organising the workload

By now you will have gained a clear – and indeed accurate – impression of the manager and secretary working as a closely knit team of two. Many managers in fact tend to treat their secretaries or personal assistants very much as equals rather than as subordinates and come to rely very much upon them.

Nowhere is such close cooperation more evident than in the organisation of the workload. While the junior manager may be able to cope with a 'secretary' who is more decorative than efficient, the busy manager values immensely the organisational skills of his capable secretary.

Thus it often falls to the secretary to devise and implement the systems through which the office will run. These will include procedures for prioritising the morning's mail, running various memory aid systems for checking on work in progress or awaited responses, making appointments, maintaining the manager's diary and so on.

Similarly, procedures will need to be set up and maintained for early daily meetings between manager and secretary to plan the day's activities according to priorities and to review any backlog of work outstanding.

Reception techniques and the general treatment of callers – both by appointment and unexpected – will need to have been discussed and agreed upon so that the secretary has a clear brief on how to handle them. Similarly, the manager will need to have reached a general understanding with his secretary on the type of situation when a personal initiative may be taken in dealing with a caller or customer. It takes much experience and sensitivity for a secretary to walk the line between acting as a total blocker, barring allcomers from the boss and as an indecisive 'pushover' allowing one and all to take up the boss's time and energy in trivial matters!

The diagram below illustrates the major roles of the manager and secretary and emphasises the importance of their working as an integrated team.

Fig 1.10 The roles of the manager and secretary

THE SECRETARY

- **As an assistant:**
  Loyalty, integrity, tact, cooperation.
- **As an executor of tasks:**
  Initiative, resourcefulness, accuracy, delivery on time.
- **As a supervisor:**
  Delegating, checking, helping development.
- **As a receptionist:**
  Charm, courtesy, alertness, perception, rapport.

THE MANAGER

- **As a leader:**
  Motivating, setting example, fair-mindedness, loyalty.
- **As a decision-maker**
  Analysing, evaluating, comparing, reviewing.
- **As a problem-solver:**
  Listening, balancing views, appreciating, anticipating.
- **As a subordinate:**
  Cooperating, relaying, achieving.

A team offering mutual support and showing mutual respect for each other's skills

THE SECRETARY AND CAREER DEVELOPMENT

The last twenty years have seen radical changes in the ways in which women are regarded at work. Changes in the economic structure of the country have obliged both parties to marriage or long-term relationships to work full-time. Better education and an increased consciousness of women's rights – among men as well as women at work – have resulted in women developing successful careers across a wide range of professional and managerial posts, where ability rather than gender is what counts.

During the coming years, women will play an increasingly important role in commerce and industry, not least because of the downturn in numbers of teenagers following the drop in births in the early 1970s. As a result, employers will be only too anxious to fill their vacancies for office staff, and promotion will go to the best qualified.

Developing your skills

There has never been a time, then, when prospects and opportunities for well qualified secretaries have been better! However, career development and promotion still rely on skills and expertise which are in demand.

The following examples show how foundation secretarial/office skills may be developed and, as a result aid career prospects and promotion. As you will have noticed, skill development through study *after* full-time education has ended is often a must for those who wish to advance their careers, and part-time study does require a good deal of 'stickability' and commitment.

Extending your experience

Having worked hard to attain secretarial expertise and, having developed good relationships with a network of colleagues, it is very tempting for the proficient secretary to stay put. However, if climbing the company career ladder is important to you, then you should be prepared to move posts in order to extend your experience. For example, a secretary who has worked for both sales and accounts department executives is in a much stronger position in applying for the post of buyer than her counterpart who has never moved out of personnel.

Forward planning

It is often said of politicians that they always have their eyes on the next promotion but one! In other words, that they are consciously seeking to gain experience and insight which will help their advancement. The ambitious secretary should also seek to plan a career rather than allowing it to drift. And here, a secretary is often in an advantageous position, working in, say, a regional or head office supporting managers who are handling high-status information. The alert secretary in this situation can learn as much in ten months as a field sales representative may in ten years! However, it is essential to identify a specialist area in which to develop – whether sales, communications, personnel, finance or office administration.

In the publishing field, for example, a frequent entry point is as a junior secretary. As knowledge and skills develop, such post-holders migrate to assistant editor then commissioning editor posts – responsible for finding prospective authors, negotiating contracts and delivering books on time. Further advancement

Examples of secretarial career development

Secretarial skill	Development	Resultant opportunities
Shorthand at note-taking speed	To speeds of 100/130	PA work with senior management and meetings servicing at board level
Information/word processing at basic competence levels	Expert operation of database, spreadsheet and integrated information management packages	Move from secretarial support role to communications/ information management post
Aptitude for working with people, good records management skills, secretarial experience in personnel work	Evening classes in Institute of Personnel Management courses: IPM certification	Progression to supervisory, then management post in personnel department
Facility with one or more European languages and ocasional use in, say, export sales secretarial work	Part-time study for, say, RSA Secretarial-Linguist Certificate or Diploma	Move across into sales representation and management, especially with EEC single market prospects

lies in divisional management, of sectors such as business education, sports, etc.

It therefore pays to keep fully abreast of accepted routes to more senior posts within the organisation and field you have chosen, and to make sure that your personnel department is aware of your aspirations.

Maintaining a personal skills audit

The next practical step to take is to measure your own skills and expertise against those needed in the post you wish to obtain. In other words, to take an audit at regular intervals of your marketable features. These will fall under the following headings:

Knowledge
How much do I know about the way my organisation works, what each department does, how sales are made, records kept, finances monitored, etc?

Skills
As my interest lies in finance, can I yet draw up a trading account or read a balance sheet? How developed are my spreadsheet operating skills? How can I develop them quickly? Is there a local college short course?

Qualifications
What further qualifications do I need to support a future application for a more senior post? A Bilingual Secretarial Certificate? Membership of a professional institution by examination? (like the Institute of Personnel Management, Institute of Marketing, or Institute of Administrative Management).

Experience
What further experience of the organisation (or sector of commerce, etc) do I need to round out my current experience? A move into export sales? A period in marketing? A secondment to data processing?

Appraisal
How do my seniors rate me? What are my current strengths and weaknesses? (If you are not regularly appraised, seek an informal interview with your manager to explore these areas. While such an appraisal may prove uncomfortable, you will end up knowing what weak spots to strengthen!

Such a personal audit, if conducted honestly, will prove invaluable in identifying those areas you need to develop within a clear career plan.

Testing the market

Some people have an inborn tendency to underestimate their own worth and value. Consequently, they tend to shy away from better job opportunities. But it is only by going for a better job that people find, not only that they could do it, but they are, in fact, offered it!

So you should keep a regular eye on the situations vacant columns of office-based publications and, if genuinely interested, send off for the particulars of advertised posts. In this way you will soon discover the precise requirements which are expected of, say, a personal assistant to a company chairman, or the administrative secretary of a county council chief executive. And, if you have been conscientiously developing your career, you may discover you can match them!

QUICK REVIEW QUIZ

1   What is the difference between a line and a staff relationship in an organisation?

2   Explain the difference between a private and public limited company

3   In what ways do the branch of a multiple and a franchised outlet differ?

4   List four different ways in which Information Technology has changed business practices in the past ten years.

RESEARCH AND REPORT BACK ASSIGNMENTS

1   Find out what are the major aspects of *one* of the following, make your notes and either deliver your findings orally to your group or as a factsheet on one side of A4:

   (a)   a deed of partnership
   (b)   the Companies Act 1985
   (c)   a memorandum and articles of association

2   In pairs, make arrangments to interview one of the following:

   (a)   A personal secretary
   (b)   A departmental manager or deputy
   (c)   The owner of a small business

Your aim is to find out: what they regard as the major areas of their job, how they organise themselves, and what sort of equipment they use in the process. Remember to draw up a checklist of the questions you wish to ask beforehand.

Write a short account of what you discover, which can be duplicated for the rest of your group after you have given them a 3-5 minute oral presentation. Use any audio-visual aids you think helpful for your presentation (for example, you may be able to tape-record part of the interview or use an OHP foil and colour pens).

3 In groups of three to four decide how best you can pool your efforts to produce a report on three sides of A4 entitled:

'How information technology applications are being used in business **or** the public sector to process information.'

Copy your report to each class group and decide who has dealt with the project most effectively and why.

4 Make use of your own network of relatives, neighbours, friends and acquaintances and ask one of them who works in a medium-to-large firm how information technology has changed his or her job. Report back orally on your findings to your group and swap notes. Make a group checklist of what emerges as a common theme, etc.

DISCUSSION TOPICS

1 Having just embarked upon a course of secretarial study, what career aims do you have? What sort of challenges and satisfactions are important to you? What do you see at present as the main personal qualities a secretary should possess?

2 Within a short space of time you will be working for one or several managers. What do you see as the skills and personal qualities essential in a good manager? Do these vary from person to person or are there general traits you can identify and agree upon?

UNIT 1
Summary of main points

1 **Definition of an organisation**: A group of people working together to achieve agreed, predetermined goals with the help of human, material and financial resources and capable of changing in the light of circumstances.

2 **Pyramidic hierarchies**: Organisations tend to be structured in the shape of pyramids stepped downwards from senior managers who direct activities to middle and junior employees who carry them out.

3 **Factors affecting the shape and structure of an organisation**: Size, location, nature of activities, type of customer, kind of work procedures and the extent of IT applications in use.

4 **Key people in private sector companies are**: Shareholders, the company chairman, managing director, director, company secretary, departmental manager, section supervisor and clerical/production assistant, and, of course, customer.

5 **Key people in public sector (local government) organisations are**: The elected member, chief executive, departmental head, local government officer, clerical assistant and local taxpayer.

6 **Typical company departments are**: Research and development, production, accounts, marketing, sales, personnel, office administration, computer services, transport and customer services. Note also the purchasing or procurement department and the training functions.

7 **Line, staff and functional relationships**: the line relationship links together tiers of people with a 'reports to' relationship to the immediate superior; employees in a staff relationship with a superior report to him on matters outside the line relationship and usually provide a range of services to line managers and personnel; the functional relationship defines those activities which are provided for the company as a whole e.g. computer services and personnel.

8 **Sole trader, partnerships, private and public limited companies**: These are four different ways of legally organising a private sector trading enterprise; sole traders tend to be shopkeepers, partnerships tend to be associated with professional services, private limited companies with smaller businesses and PLCs with national/multinational companies.

9 **The roles of manager and secretary**: The manager plans, leads, administers, monitors delegated tasks, makes decisions and carries out policies determined by his seniors; the secretary assists her manager by dealing with correspondence, organising his time, maintaining a records system, dealing with visitors and calls, administering delegated tasks and generally aiding his effectiveness.

10 **Information Technology in organisations**: The impact of IT has been to transform the speed of access to people and data and to process information much faster and more efficiently. It has radically changed many office jobs and redefined the ways in which offices operate to process information. As a secretary you must develop and update your skills and plan your career path.

Sources of further information

The Organisation in its Environment
   J Beardshaw and D Palfreyman, Pitman
People, Communication and Organisations,
   Desmond W Evans, Pitman
*The Structure of Business Systems
   and Organisation*, Kilgannon & Warson,
   Edward Arnold
Modern Business Administration, R Appleby,
   Pitman
Background To Business A Leal, Pitman
Working in Organisations, D Davison, Pitman

ACTIVITIES

Time to get organised
A case study

There was no doubt about it – as a sole trader Bob Milton was becoming a successful businessman. Indeed, his business, Milton's School of Motoring in Redbury New Town, had grown rapidly – thanks to Bob's good manner with his customers and his wife's shrewd common sense over business matters. It was Stella Milton who had advised Bob to concentrate on the teenage learner group 'who are mad keen to drive, learn quickly and, round here, have got indulgent parents with cash to spare for driving lessons.'

In the space of two years, Bob had managed to obtain four cars for his School of Motoring, and employed three instructors, Harry Brooks, Jean Carr and Tommy Simpson. Bob's cars were being paid for with a loan from his bank and his monthly payments were high – but, in six weeks' time, two of the four would be paid for and Bob was looking forward to being some £480 a month better off.

The Miltons had two children. Ken, aged 23, was a motor-car salesman for a local main dealership, a keen advanced motorist and rally driver in his spare time. Jane was just 18, and nearing the end of her two-year secretarial course at Redbury College of Technology.

Bob's office – or rather his front sitting room, which had served as his office for the past two years – was becoming increasingly difficult to get into. On the sofa were various piles of documents: sales receipts, invoices and tax payment requests. Bob had the habit of skewering these on to hooks with wooden bases. 'Don't worry about my filing system, I know where everything is!' he would say, with less assurance as each week slipped past. The wood and glass bureau, a relic of the 1930s taste for glass-encased bookshelves, with a pull-down desk which revealed partitions and little drawers, looked rather like the storage bin for a recycled paper mill. It had long since given up the unequal struggle of keeping the Milton School of Motoring's records in anything resembling a system.

In fact, Bob spent as little time as possible in his 'office'. 'Look after your customers, and the paperwork'll look after itself!' was a favourite motto of Bob's, and there was little doubt that Bob's crowning asset was his ability to keep on getting his customers through the driving test at their first, or at least second, attempt. Indeed, money seemed to be no problem, in spite of having taken on Tommy Simpson only two months ago, and buying another car (thanks to a handsome legacy of some £30 000 left to Bob by a spinster aunt.) The Milton School Of Motoring's only problem appeared to be too many new customers, in no small part due to the influx of people to the high-tech computer industries which made up much of Redbury's expanding commercial growth.

And yet ... Stella was becoming increasingly 'up-tight' about customers turning up for driving lessons they had booked over the phone, only to find that there had been a slip-up and all four cars were out on lesson instruction ... 'Well, it's not my fault,' retorted Bob, when Stella confronted him with just such a situation one lunch time, 'I can't do *everything* myself, and you know how much Harry, Jean and Tommy love the admin side of the job,' he added sarcastically and with feeling.

'I'll tell you what, Bob Milton', responded Stella, 'if you don't start getting yourself organised you'll drop dead of a heart attack or something – and I don't even know where to look in that dratted bureau of yours for a will, insurance policies or *anything*!'

That tea-time, a thundery sort of early evening in late June, matters came to a quite unexpected head.

'Here, look at this, Stella! Fancy that, I've had a letter from a firm of solicitors in Fitcham (about 15 miles from Redbury). Seems some old cove's snuffed it and his kids want to meet me to discuss the possibility of my taking over the management of his business – a driving school, believe it or not!'

'Humph!' sniffed Stella, 'you can't even manage the one you've got properly! And before you go gallivanting over to Fitcham, I'm giving you a final ultimatum: either you find yourself some office premises away from this house, or I move out! I've had more than I can take of losing half my home to your office junk and being your unpaid telephone answering system, not to mention car-washer and Teasmaid!'

This time, Bob could tell from the tone of her voice that Stella was in deadly earnest. No one had given him more initial support, and it wasn't as if he couldn't afford it. In fact, Bob mused that perhaps he couldn't afford *not* to expand.

His thoughts were interrupted by Jane swinging happily round the dining-room door. 'That's it! Last exam finished! No more Coll – and what do you think, I reckon I got the 120 words a minute passage OK!'

A heavy clumping noise heralded Ken's homecoming – in fact even heavier than usual. He slumped down into his usual place at the tea-table. 'What on earth's the matter with you?' asked Stella. 'You look blacker than the sky outside!'

'Got a right to, haven't I,' answered Ken, 'Just been made ruddy redundant – firm's been taken over by one of them conglomerates or whatever you call 'em! Blue Shield Blinkin' Motors Limited, some big, set-up in the south London area!'

CASE STUDY ASSIGNMENTS

1 First, on your own, make a checklist of the different types of problem – and opportunity – which face the Milton School of Motoring, according to your interpretation of the case study.

2 Then, in groups of three to four, re-read the case study carefully and:

   (a) Make a checklist of the actions you think Bob and his family should take in the light of the events outlined in the case study. Give your reasons for the actions you list.

(b) Compare your response to the Milton family's situation with those devised by other groups in your class.

3 What do you think would be the best way for Bob and Stella's business to develop, given its rapid initial growth and Bob's strengths and weaknesses as a businessman?

Write your answer in the form of a plan which Bob might carry out over the next twelve months.

4 If you were in Jane's or Ken's position, what would you do? Give your reasons for your views.

5 What kind of organisational structure do you think most likely to prove effective in any new phase of the development of the Milton School of Motoring?

Construct a chart to illustrate your solution and add any comments you think useful.

6 Select one of the following and devise an action plan which you think would prove effective for the Milton School of Motoring in the coming six months:

(a) A scheme to increase sales (ie more customers paying for more lessons)
(b) A system which will more effectively administer the business
(c) An organisational chart to explain the new personnel structure you think would prove most effective

7 What benefits do you think would stem from the Milton School of Motoring becoming either a partnership or a private limited company? Which would you recommend, and why?

8 Do you anticipate any dangers ahead if Bob expands his business and takes on more staff? if so, of what kind, and how would you seek to avoid these?

WORK SIMULATION ASSIGNMENTS

Managers of local companies and public service organisations are increasingly working with colleges and schools to provide work experience for students in full-time study. Many firms go to great lengths to ensure that attached students obtain varied and stimulating experiences. For your part, while attached to a local organisation, you should ensure you learn as much as possible about *real* work practices and procedures – especially about the area of work you are likely to pursue – carried out under the pressures of earning a profit and keeping customers satisfied:

1 Find out what type of work staff carry out:

(a) in the department in which you are working
(b) in the organisation as a whole

Then design two organisational charts aimed at explaining who does what to someone unfamiliar with the organisation. Your charts may include supportive notes.

2 Make arrangements to interview a senior secretary within the organisation and to ask what kind of tasks are carried out:

daily; weekly; monthly; quarterly annually; occasionally.

Draw up a well laid-out checklist of your findings and compare it with those drawn up by others in your group, so as to ascertain what sort of tasks and routines are common to most secretarial work.

3 Find out what use the organisation makes of various external agency services such as printing, employment bureaux, advertising, car rental, travel, and what services it provides for itself from within the organisation. In interviews with two or three managers, seek to establish what factors led to work being given to external agencies – like degree of expertise, cost or time, and what factors led to work being kept within the organisation, like security or cost-saving.

Having carried out your research, compose a briefing for secretaries in general advising on what kind of work is most suited to internal or external delivery.

4 Through a range of interviews with organisational staff, find out what impact and relationship the following may have upon the organisation:

The Registrar of Companies, The Patents Office, The Fire Service, The County Council Planning Department, The Inland Revenue, Customs and Excise Office, The local Job Centre and Careers Offices, The Office of Fair Trading, The Training Agency, The Department of Social Security.

5 Explore the range of work carried out by the department in which you work. Then design and produce a brochure to be part of an induction 'kit' for new arrivals, which aims to explain simply and clearly the work of the department. Your brochure should also explain how the department relates to the rest of the organisation. Your brochure will probably benefit from the inclusion of diagrams, charts and other illustrations.

6 You work as secretary to the Sales Manager of a medium-sized firm making high quality sets of golf clubs. Reporting to Mr Gordon Jenkins, Sales Manager, are the following heads of section:

Jean Jones	Sales order section
Pat Davies	Advertising and sales promotion
Helen Simpson	Sales administration and sales force coordination
Suresh Patel	Customer service

The following items of mail arrived in this morning's

post. Sort them into a priority sequence, starting with what you consider most important. Against each item indicate the person to whom you would pass it – if you consider it does not require Mr Jenkins' attention. If you think any item should be redirected to another department, give your reasons and indicate any arising action you might take:

- An invitation to join the Traveller's Club Gold Card leisure card service.

- A letter from an old-established customer querying the bill for a consignment of clubs ordered at an old price and invoiced at a new one.

- A faxed enquiry for 10 sets of Sam Ball's Masterplay De Luxe clubs from the Glenairey Golf Club Professional, Perth, Scotland – delivery has to be in five days, in time for the British Masters' Tournament being held there.

- A memorandum from the Accounts Manager reminding Mr Jenkins that his sales turnover figures for the second quarter are overdue.

- A letter from Jack Lacey, the General Manager of Southern Sports Shops Limited, complaining about the length of time being taken to deliver a consignment of putters being endorsed by Jane Dexter, a leading ladies' circuit player due to visit Southern's premier store next week.

- A letter confirming the latest fleet leasing rates from Sentinel Car Leasing Limited.

- A schedule of the company's latest salary rates for sales department employees from the personnel manager.

- A letter from the company's advertising agency enclosing draft copy for a national sales campaign due to start in six weeks' time.

PRACTICE QUESTIONS FROM PAST EXAMINATION PAPERS

(a) How does a public corporation differ from a public limited company?
(b) What has happened to some public corporations in recent years? (LCC First Certificate in Office Technology)

2 You have received a number of letters and other items some of which are not intended for your department. Redirect the following items in each case, giving reasons for your decision:

(a) A query from the tax authorities about an employee's PAYE
(b) an order for bulk delivery of sun dresses
(c) an account from the company's advertising agents
(d) a letter from the Trade Marks Owners Association about a possible infringement
(e) a cover note from ECGD about a consignment of dresses to Finland
(f) confirmation of a Telegraphic Transfer for 200 000 Escudos to Portugal
(g) a letter from the Company's lawyers about a proposed Licensing Agreement
(h) a Shipping Note and Airways Bill from a Freight Forwarding Agent
(i) a letter from an irate shareholder of Comlon International plc about the low rate of dividend paid.

LCC PSC, Office Organisation and Secretarial Procedures)

UNIT 1
Glossary of terms and phrases

accountability
A term which indicates that a member of staff carries a personal responsibility for specified tasks and duties.

annual sales plan
The sales budget (see page 27) in national/international companies will be broken down into regions and districts, and also by products going to make up the total sales range; individuals will then be given targets to reach and exceed if possible.

archived data
Some information, like balance sheets or patents, needs to be kept safely for many years, in a system which permits prompt retrieval; such documents are said to be archived.

balance sheets and profit and loss accounts
At frequent intervals (usually monthly), accounts departments analyse in a profit and loss account their trading position – whether they are selling enough and controlling costs sufficiently to make a profit (so as to take corrective action if need be); once a year, the entire financial position of the company is drawn up in a balance sheet which compares what is owned and due with what is owed and what profits (or losses) have been made.

British Standards Institute
This is a national public institution which sets approved standards and qualities for product design and manufacture.

cellular telephones
These are cordless/wireless telephones which operate within a network of cells (covering a locality or district – hence the word 'cellular'. A user's call is picked up as radio waves by telephone exchanges on the boundary of the cell which the user is in, and then relayed over the national telephone network to the recipient of the call.

centralised purchasing
In order to gain the best buying terms and discounts, large organisations channel *all* their purchasing needs through a single specialist department.

centralised reprographics service
For the same reasons, all a firm's copying and duplication needs will be met through a single unit serving all departments.

delegation
Managers cannot undertake everything themselves and so they entrust responsibility for a series of tasks to their various subordinates whom they monitor; however, the manager still 'carries the can' if anything goes wrong with delegated duties.

desktop publishing
Follows a process similar to word processing and also enables the operator to include photographic and graphics (drawn) images, as well as a variety of typefaces and sizes on a screened master which is printed after editing and approval.

dividends issued
Public companies are run on the finance generated by the sale of shares; annually, at the discretion of the directors, shareholders may be issued a share of profits pro rata to their shareholdings, termed a dividend.

electronic mail
An important term which describes the messages which are keyed into a computer workstation that is linked to a LAN (see page 27), and then 'posted' to an intended recipient (also on the LAN); note a single message may be sent simultaneously to groups of 'tagged' (designated) users, thus saving much time and effort in producing and distributing paper memos; the LAN operating system provides each user with an 'IN' and 'OUT' tray for sending and receiving electronic mail.

functional relationship
This term describes those employees generally outside a line management relationship, who provide an 'all-company service' like company librarian or data processing manager (note that line relationships will exist within the library and DP functions).

gross profit
The gross profit is what remains when the cost of sales is deducted from sales turnover. (**Net profit** is what remains after taxes due, dividends issued, etc, are deducted from gross profit.)

hardware
A term grouping together computers and allied equipment used to process information.

information technology
Widely referred to as 'IT', this term stands for the host of systems, equipment and materials, essentially computer-based, which are used to obtain, store, process and distribute information.

job description
This takes the form of a written schedule which details precisely those duties and responsibilities which go to make up an employee's job (see also **personnel specification** in Unit 6).

line relationship or scalar chain
Employees are said to be in a line relationship if they are all connected in a direct 'reports to' line, eg national sales manager – regional sales manager – district sales manager – sales representative.

local area networks
Now usually called LANs, this term describes a series of computer terminals or workstations (together with printers and allied equipment) which is linked by cable so as to enable any user to communicate electronically with all other network users through electronic mail, etc. (Note also the term *wide area network (WAN)* which works in the same way nationally and internationally).

market intelligence
This is data, information or hot news – often gleaned by sales reps in the field, about what competing firms are doing, or what buying habits or trends are evolving – to be digested by marketing personnel.

market research
Larger firms possess marketing departments, part of whose role is to keep a constant check on what people want to buy and what the competition is doing and planning; they also set up research programmes aimed at developing new products and services.

OHP
Short for Overhead Projector/ion – OHP equipment is used in seminars and presentations to enlarge and project drawings, text and diagrams produced on transparent plastic sheets for an audience to see clearly on a large white projection screen over the head of the lecturer; such OHP transparencies are sometimes called viewfoils and are nowadays produced by computer graphics software of DTP systems and printed on a colour printer or plotter (a device which draws computer-designed graphs).

organisational hierarchy
This term similarly describes the tiers or layers of authority in an organisation on a 'reports to, responsible for' basis.

organisational pyramid
A useful short way to describe the structure of organisations, in which the number of people reduce as responsibility and authority increase in stages up to the point (chairman of the board) of the pyramid.

point-of-sale material
Shops and forecourts usually have plenty of placards, posters, window-stickers, etc, which seek to persuade the consumer to buy a product while on the premises – often on impulse.

prototypes
In manufacturing, a first 'trial go' form of a product is produced for testing and examination; if accepted, the prototype (after any modification) will go into full production.

sales revenue and cost of sales
Larger companies set themselves annual targets (**budgets**). One of these is for sales turnover – money brought in from goods sold. Clearly to make a profit, sales turnover must exceed the cost of making the sales, which include sales reps' salaries, expenses, production and distribution costs of products, etc.

security clearance
With so much industrial espionage and theft taking place today, companies set up strict procedures to authorise specific staff to access confidential data; photographs and holograms are used on passes, and secret passwords with computer software.

software
Refers to the **programs** specialists write and market on floppy and hard disks which enable computers to carry out tasks (like word processing, computing the payroll, drawing graphs, etc); the user's work disks are also 'software'.

staff relationship
This term describes an employee – often a personal assistant or secretary – who works directly for a manager outside of the chain of line relationship.

teleconferences
In this system, groups of executives may be interconnected by means of closed circuit television; all groups (spread over a wide area or in different countries) can see each other on TV monitors and hear each other's live comments, etc. BT provides an international teleconferencing service.

word processing
Is replacing typewriting as a means of processing information; text and data is keyed into a computer, edited while displayed on a visual display unit (VDU) and then printed out on a printer driven by the computer.

UNIT 2
Information processing in the office

OVERVIEW

This unit examines the role of the office as an information processing centre, accepting, processing, storing and issuing a wide variety of messages to many different kinds of recipient.

It also highlights the changes which have taken place – and still are – in the ways in which IT equipment and applications are replacing more traditional methods of handling information.

In particular it provides a thorough treatment of the central tasks which, as a secretary, you will undertake on a regular basis – dealing with the mail, maintaining diaries and appointments schedules, administering a records system, prioritising and routing messages, receiving visitors, organising yourself and your time and helping to ensure that your manager's time is also used as cost-effectively as possible.

Unit 2 considers these aspects both in terms of the computer-based software applications and techniques now widely in use and of the paper-based systems which pre-date them. As well, Unit 2 reviews the latest computer-aided microform records and management information systems available.

While working through this unit, you should keep firmly in mind that IT applications and systems are being constantly updated and superseded. You should, therefore, aim to master the principles involved in computerised information processing while remaining receptive to new systems and practices which you can absorb into your secretarial expertise.

2.1 Daily routines

The office as an information processing centre; information processing in the electronic office; working with electronic and traditional office systems; sorting and routing overnight messages; dealing with incoming mail; dealing with outgoing mail.

THE OFFICE AS INFORMATION PROCESSING CENTRE

In today's national and international business world, information is a priceless commodity, whether in the form of the daily fluctuating values of the dollar, yen or pound sterling, the latest costs of motor-car components or the level of stocks held in a chainstore's branches.

Without up-to-the minute, accurate information, most commercial organisations would quickly founder. Indeed, in the UK today there are over 400 000 offices which accommodate some 10 million office workers – about 40% of the country's entire labour force.

Such offices serve as hubs or centres of information which take in, process, store and relay data and messages in a host of situations – financing, selling, building, making, servicing or advising – so as to enable all sorts of people to function in their jobs, ranging from senior managers planning company activities over the next five years to shop assistants querying the current retail price of a hair shampoo.

The diagram shown (Fig. 2.1) illustrates this information processing function of the office according to the systems model which identifies the following stages in the process.

Stages of computerised information processing: 1 INPUT 2 PROCESS/STORAGE 3 OUTPUT 4 FEEDBACK.

Examples of the input phase:

- Incoming electronic mail item
- Incoming fax message
- Selected Prestel page
- Memo being dictated
- Incoming telephone call
- Viewing of video-tape
- Discussion at a meeting
- Incoming letter or invoice

Examples of the process phase:

- Keying an appointment into an electronic diary
- Entering fresh figures on to a spreadsheet
- Producing a staff holiday rota for visual display
- Revising a report via word processing
- Arranging the time, date and location of a meeting for dissemination via electronic mail

(Remember that part of the process phase is the

The essential functions of an office

- To receive incoming information from a variety of sources, both external and internal to the organisation
- To generate information as part of the task of helping to meet the aims and goals of the organisation
- To prioritise and evaluate information before acting upon it
- to communicate information to relevant personnel in appropriate forms via effective communications media
- To maintain an efficient system for storing and retrieving information for future consultation and reference
- To maintain a system for discarding obsolete information and updating information relevant to the organisation's activities

Fig 2.1 Information processing function of the office

Media of incoming information
- Telephone calls
- Letters
- Memos
- Customer orders
- Requisitions
- Reports (including financial) articles, circulars, advertisements, catalogues, brochures
- Callers and visitors
- Briefings from staff
- Teleconferences
- Fax and telex messages
- Viewdata pages
- Telemessages
- Electronic mail (Email)
- Computer printout
- Answerphone messages and notes
- Government directives and circulars

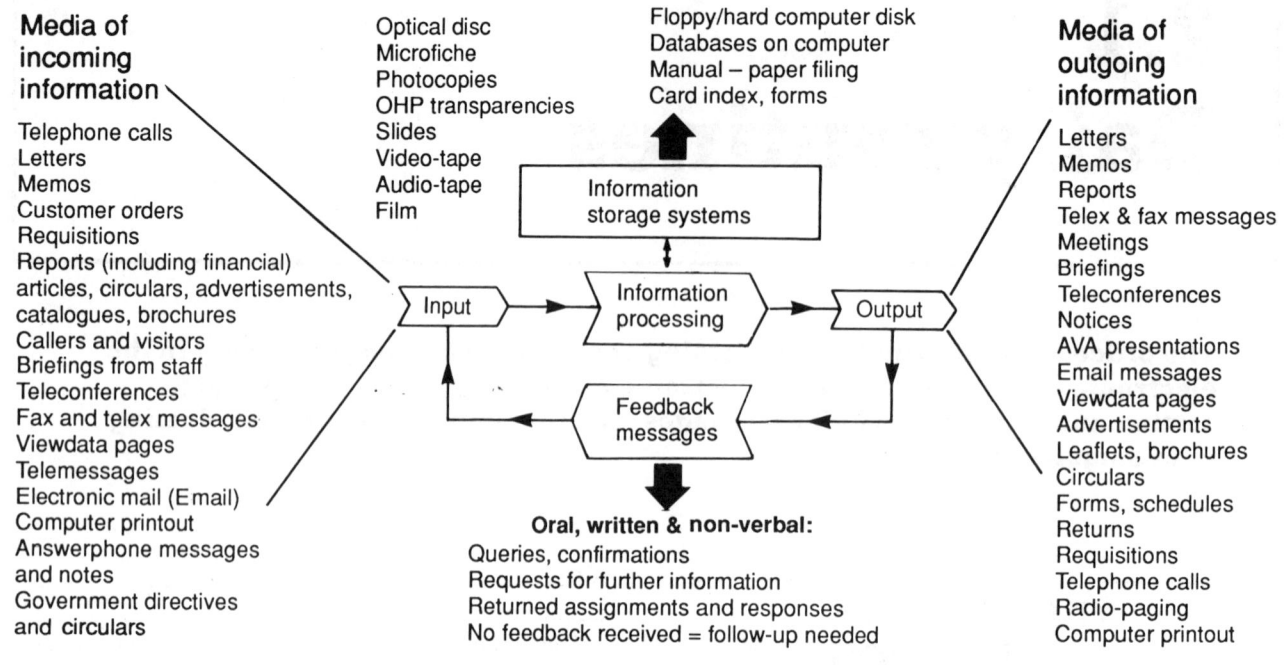

STORAGE MEDIA
- Optical disc
- Microfiche
- Photocopies
- OHP transparencies
- Slides
- Video-tape
- Audio-tape
- Film
- Floppy/hard computer disk
- Databases on computer
- Manual – paper filing
- Card index, forms

Input → Information processing → Output
Information storage systems
Feedback messages

Oral, written & non-verbal:
- Queries, confirmations
- Requests for further information
- Returned assignments and responses
- No feedback received = follow-up needed

Media of outgoing information
- Letters
- Memos
- Reports
- Telex & fax messages
- Meetings
- Briefings
- Teleconferences
- Notices
- AVA presentations
- Email messages
- Viewdata pages
- Advertisements
- Leaflets, brochures
- Circulars
- Forms, schedules
- Returns
- Requisitions
- Telephone calls
- Radio-paging
- Computer printout

All kinds of information is received via various media, dealt with and processed into appropriate forms of message for onward distribution. Copies, records and back-up files are stored in a wide range of paper and media, as archived data or for future reference.

---

storage of processed data in an appropriate medium – on computer disk, on video or audio tape, as a microfiche, or as a paper photocopy etc.)

Examples of the output phase:

- Fax message dispatched to Hong Kong

- Email (electronic mail) message calling meeting sent to staff computer terminals

- Advice note sent with consignment of goods to customer

- Confirmation of an order sent by sales rep to sales office via British Telecom Gold Email Service

- Dictated, typed letter mailed to client via Post Office service

The feedback phase

It is important to remember at all times the need to check whether a message transmitted to one or more recipients has been received, understood and acted upon. For this reason managers and secretaries customarily set deadlines for receiving feedback confirmations:

'Please let me know by 28 January 19-- whether you wish to confirm your provisional booking.'

'So as to deliver your personalised Christmas cards in good time for posting, your order should reach us no later than 15 November 19--.'

Note: A helpful tip for securing feedback is to include a reminder in your '**bring forward**' system before a deadline occurs:

22 March 19— Check JJ has remembered wife's birthday card and present – 25 March.

INFORMATION PROCESSING IN THE ELECTRONIC OFFICE

The 1970s and 1980s saw a very rapid and all-embracing revolution in the technology used in processing information. Central to this revolution has been the **microprocessor** or silicon chip which is used in a wide range of office equipment.

While manual and paper-based systems of information processing are still much in use, in the form of book diaries, letters, invoices and so on, more and more office activities and functions are today being undertaken by electronic and computer-based technology. For example **optical character recognition** equipment (**OCR** scanner) instantly converts incoming letters on paper into electronic files stored on the computer. These files are accessible to any personnel linked by a **wide area network (WAN)** into the computer in other company offices, which may be many hundreds of miles apart, as well as to other personnel in the originating office who are linked up to the computer by a local area network (**LAN**). In addition, radio-wave and telephone-line **telecommunications systems** now enable messages to be transmitted across the world in seconds in typescript, photographic or diagrammatic form, say, by telex and fax. (See Unit 3.)

The technological revolution which has brought about the automated electronic office is far from over – rather, it is gaining increased momentum. Computers are now able to learn from experience; **optical disc storage** can enhance the storage capacity of computers many times; and the voice inputting of information into computers is being developed. Many companies have a **mainframe** computer, which is a large computer to which many small desktop **personal computers** (**PCs**) can be linked to form a network. This enables them to use the information stored on the big mainframe computer and to communicate with each other.

Therefore, this unit will emphasise the automated office approach and show how your secretarial tasks may be made easier and more effective as a direct result of information technology (IT) office applications.

ASSIGNMENT: THE ELECTRONIC OFFICE

Working in groups of three to five, make contact with a local office which is using IT equipment to process information.

Arrange to interview the office manager, together with some of the office staff, and find out how information is processed, and what equipment and systems are used for this purpose.

Before your visit, make out a checklist of questions you wish to ask about the range of information which has to be handled, the advantages and disadvantages of IT equipment and systems and the likely future trends and developments in information processing which the manager anticipates. The offices of banks, building societies, insurance companies and manufacturing companies will have a great deal to show you.

Make notes of your findings and give a 10-minute oral presentation to your class. Discuss what each group learned about IT and the electronic office. Then, write up your findings and photocopy them to each group. If you have access to a personal computer, key your factsheet into this as part of the communal database for your class.

ROUTINE ACTIVITIES IN A SECRETARY'S TYPICAL DAY

Time	*Activity*	*Equipment/system used*
8.45	Arrival: greets colleagues.	
	Checks that there are no security breaches, logs on to office's LAN (Local Area Network) from her desktop computer and reads Email messages sent in overnight.	Personal desktop computer linked to company mainframe computer and LAN/WAN networks
	Similarly, checks fax, telex and answerphone system for incoming messages.	Fax transceiver, telex, and computerised CABX telephone systems
	Takes hard-copy printouts as required – to work on, etc.	Electronic Printer
	Accesses electronic notebook on desktop computer and keys in a note for her manager indicating priority of messages needing his attention; notes those to deal with herself; Emails note to manager's personal computer.	Desktop PC's integrated Information Manager software
9.00–9.10 am	Greets manager on arrival; they check day's appointments and commitments via VDU display of manager's electronic diary and he notes overnight messages to be dealt with.	Electronic diary and notepad software

Time	Activity	Equipment/system used
9.10–9.25 am	Incoming paper mail sorted prioritised and date-stamped; electronic file copies made of appropriate items via OCR scanner for office personnel to access subject to security clearance; paper mail needing manager's attention given to him to read.	OCR scanner linked to computer storage disk and LAN network
9.25–10.00 am	Secretary supervises work of office assistant reporting to her: checks what work left over from previous day, provides instructions on deadlines for word processing work in progress, quantities and circulation list of documents for photocopying etc.	Word processing files Office/company photocopiers
10.00–10.30 am	Secretary takes dictation from manager in shorthand of messages for transcription and transmission via most effective medium; tasks to be completed that day agreed upon – eg booking of hotel accommodation for manager's imminent trip, invitations to clients for a sales seminar, which secretary composes and then passes to assistant for merging with addresses and printing out.	From shorthand notebook to WAN EMAIL message to sales branches Fax or Telex or Email booking to hotel Mailmerged letter to clients done on word processor and laser printer
10.30 am–12.30 pm	Manager attends meeting. Secretary uses time to deal with dictated correspondence and alloted tasks. Uses CABX extension to set up a telephone conference between manager and his seven regional managers for the following day.	CABX (computerised automatic branch exchange) British Telecom audio-conferencing telephone service
	Emails sales management meetings documentation to centralised office services department for archiving on microfilm.	COM (computer output microform) microfilming equipment
	Deals with several visitors to office and sets up appointments with manager as a result.	Electronic diary
12.30–1.00 pm	Checks work in progress of clerical assistants; takes in correspondence to manager for signature and checks if any tasks have arisen from meeting. Leaves outgoing mail in out tray for messenger' late morning collection.	Uses LAN system to scan files created by assistants on software used by all office staff, downloaded via file-server
1.00–2.00 pm	Checks her desk and VDU for security (eg confidential correspondence), transfers incoming calls to her assistant's extension before going to lunch	Logs out of LAN system. Re-routes incoming phone calls
2.00–2.30 pm	Sorts and prioritises second delivery of mail. Deals with incoming fax and Email messages. Checks with assistants the stocks of office consumables and stationery and arranges orders; sends off for a new office equipment brochure.	Fax and LAN/WAN networks Uses Prestel Viewdata service to order brochure

Information processing in the office

Time	Activity	Equipment/system used
2.30–3.30 pm	Works on text and audio visual aids support material for manager's forthcoming annual sales presentation to board of directors. Interrupted by upset clerical assistant who is being asked (she thinks) to meet two conflicting priority deadlines – troubleshoots problem.	Uses integrated information manager software and produces WP text for office desktop publishing system
3.30–3.45 pm	Called into manager's office to take dictation following a lengthy telephone call he has had with important customer. Need to check last year's discount and credit arrangements which have been cited in a dispute about a reduction in buying terms.	Retrieves records from mainframe computer's database software; issues WAN Email memo to sales offices.
4.00–4.15 pm	Resolution of problem generates need to amend records and sales representatives' instructions urgently, and to advise accounts department.	Routes a priority LAN message to Accounts Manager
4.15–4.30 pm	Completed sales presentation drafts and other correspondence given to manager for checking and signature etc. Pencils on top right-hand corner of outward mail envelopes the class of postage required and puts into mail out tray for collection.	Sends letter to customer via Post Office Datapost service overnight
	Work processed by assistants checked for despatch. Filing (paper/manual and electronic carried out)	Filing: either into company mainframe computer files or on to office hard-disk micro-computer or into paper-based systems
4.30–4.45 pm	Discussion with manager on following day's priorities, appointments and commitments and respective electronic diaries compared and updated. Arrangements for telephone conference finalised.	Electronic diary
	Manager agrees text for overnight transmission to European agents.	BT Telex Plus service
4.45–5.30 pm	Secretary reviews her work in progress and reorganises her list of outstanding tasks in order of priority and identifies those for delegation.	Electronic notepad
	Supervises the end-of-day routines of assistants, and checks her desk and office for overnight security and safety. Before leaving, reminds manager of evening appointment with European client and wife at theatre and makes sure he has tickets on him.	Computerised fire and safety systems
	Makes final check that equipment for receiving overnight messages – fax, telex, Email computer terminal, telephone answering machine etc, are correctly set up.	Fax, answerphone, desk-top PC, etc

DISCUSSION TOPICS

1 Refer to the diary of Routine activities in a secretary's typical day (see pages 33–35).
   Consider what traditional communication processes and media could be substituted for the electronic ones identified. Decide what the outcomes could be in terms of:

- Time taken to create and transmit data
- Administrative efficiency and effectiveness cost factors
- Communication effectiveness in a large organisation
- Records management effectiveness

2 What do you think are the factors which are likely to affect the wholesale introduction into a large office of automated electronic office equipment? Make a checklist of your group's suggestions and compare it with those drawn up by other class groups.

3 If you had to supervise the transition in an office from traditional paper/manual systems to their computerised/automated counterparts, where would you start? Draw up a checklist of the steps you would take in order of priority and the reasons for your priorities.

4 What *changes* are likely to occur in large organisations' communication processes as a result of the widespread development of IT systems and equipment?

WORKING IN AN ELECTRONIC AND TRADITIONAL OFFICE ENVIRONMENT

The diary of a secretary's typical day (pp. 33–5) has been designed to illustrate the many ways in which automated electronic office systems and equipment are already making the manager's and secretary's work much more effective – by routing messages much faster, accessing records more immediately and processing text and data far more sophisticatedly and efficiently.

However, since technological developments are not adopted by every organisation at the same rate, today's secretary will inevitably find herself needing to master a dual system of office administration in which the more traditional, paper-based processes are used in conjunction with the newer computer-based systems. The most commonly occurring secretarial routines with reference to both electronic and manual/paper systems and processes are therefore described in this section.

Table of regularly occurring secretarial tasks

Arriving at the office

- Conducting an early morning HASAW check before staff arrive for any equipment or machinery in a potentially dangerous state (see Health and Safety at Work Act 1974, Appendix 2).

- Checking for any possible breaches of office security arising from a break-in, safes or cupboards being left unlocked or documents left in sight of office cleaners etc. Report any suspected or certain breaches to the manager.

- Starting the day right with cheerful greetings to manager, and office staff.

- Attending to overnight incoming messages via fax, telex, telephone answering system, BT Gold Email, internal LAN or company WAN networks, etc.

- Sorting, prioritising and date-stamping incoming mail. Deciding what requires manager's attention and distributing mail to various office executives.

- Meeting early with manager or the executives being serviced to decide upon the day's priorities and commitments; checking for any recent developments to be aware of or needing action since last speaking to the manager.

- Comparing, and updating diaries – including any entries made in pocket diaries while staff were out of the office.

- Setting the tasks for the day for any clerical assistants who report to the secretary.

During the course of the day

- Meeting with manager after incoming mail and messages have been scanned to take dictation and receive briefings on tasks requiring action. Subsequent self-organisation to accomplish such delegated tasks including listing of priorities and identifying what can be delegated.

- Ensuring that incoming messages are relayed promptly and clearly to their intended recipient(s), through a mastery of the equipment and media involved.

- Maintaining an efficient diary system and ensuring the continuous matching of the manager's and secretary's diaries; monitoring manager's diary commitments to ensure that he does not become overloaded with meetings and interviews which adversely affect his ability to achieve his own work deadlines and commitments.

- Operating effective **bring-forward** and reminder systems for work in progress, items pending and deadlines, etc, for the manager and yourself.

- Maintaining effective and secure systems for filing and recording information; carrying out intermittent archiving and shredding of documents which are either out of active use or no longer needed – according to company policy directives.

- Topping up supplies of office stationery and consumables in good time and cost-effectively by means of a reliable stock-control system; maintaining and improving the supply and design of forms regularly used by office personnel; ensuring that obsolete and superseded forms are disposed of.

- Creating and processing information using the most efficient and economical means, having regard to urgency, confidentiality, cost, and acceptance factors by means of systems within the organisation or via external services.

- Compiling and updating various databases of useful information: for example, of contact names, addresses and telephone numbers, customer particulars, product prices and specifications etc.

- Keeping accurate records of any localised financial transactions (usually via an *imprest petty cash system*, see Unit 6) supervising the recording of office staff expenses, and, sometimes, maintaining a small payroll system.

Before leaving the office

- Ensuring that the post for the day's final collection is prepared and signed in good time and the postal service required – registered, recorded delivery, first, second class etc. clearly indicated.

- Checking progress on delegated work and passing completed items to the manager or executives for approval and onward despatch. Storing unfinished work safely, and setting priorities for the following day.

- Ensuring that all filing is up to date and, where computer files are involved, checking to ensure that safety back-up files have been made and secured in remote locations according to company policy.

- Making end-of-day checks for security – equipment switched off or left on as appropriate; no fire-hazard litter left on live equipment; no confidential documentation left on desks or in sight; appropriate cupboards and filing receptacles locked, etc.

- Checking that equipment for receiving overnight messages is left switched on, is in the appropriate mode and is safe.

- Reminding the manager of any evening/early following morning commitments and checking that nothing further needs to be done for that day.

SORTING AND ROUTING OVERNIGHT MESSAGES

Having looked at a summary of the secretary's regular tasks in a typical day, these are now discussed in more detail. One of the first tasks is to sort any overnight messages received on office equipment such as telex or fax.

Thanks to the development of a range of national and global telecommunications systems, today's office is always open and ready to receive incoming messages; indeed with so many businesses operating internationally, it is essential for executives and their assistants to be able to contact agents, suppliers, customers and government departments across the world promptly but without rousing them from their beds during their share of earth's night-time periods!

Therefore, one of the first duties of the secretary on arriving in her office is to sort and route the messages which have arrived overnight. The following checklist identifies the principal systems in use.

Telecommuni-cations system	Storage medium
Facsimile transmitted Message	Stacked in receiving tray of transceiver
Telex message	Printed on teleprinter's paper roll or held in desktop computer for VDU display if PC is connected to Mailbox and Telex Manager telex systems
Electronic mail	Stored on computer's memory waiting for VDU display – note various 'in-tray' VDU display listings to show incoming Email waiting to be read.
Telephone answering systems	Recorded voice-input (audio) messages will have been stored on cassette tape for playback.

Hard copy facility: note that, with the exception of the audio telephoned message, it is possible to secure a paper copy of the message – either as a direct result of the reception media: immediate printing onto stored paper – or by securing a print-out of the computer screened version.

> **Top Secretary tip**
> At present, telex messages are *legally binding* but faxed messages are not. Bear this in mind when dealing with incoming messages or when choosing the best medium for outgoing ones.

Procedure

All facsimile, telex and Email messages will display prominently at the top of the paper or screen the name and sometimes designation of the message's intended recipient. Additionally, fax and telex messages indicate the (local) date and time at which they were transmitted and also a status message such as URGENT or CONFIDENTIAL.

Unless the executive staff of the office have personal desktop PCs, it will be necessary to take paper copies of overnight messages and to distribute them, remembering to prioritise urgent messages and *to maintain confidentiality* through the use of envelopes or re-usable message wallets.

Bear in mind that Email messages can be sent to groups of personnel simultaneously and a circulation list will indicate who has what message awaiting them on their own PC workstation. Also, most electronic mail software provides a visual means of checking who has read a recently despatched mail item.

Since international telecommunications do not come cheap – even at low-cost transmission times – it is always good practice to make mention of the receipt of overnight messages as soon as their recipients arrive at the office. Naturally, paper copies of such messages will be placed at the top of the executive's stack of morning mail, and any responses needed should be dealt with straightaway. Non-urgent outgoing fax and telex messages may be stacked until cheap transmission times eg overnight.

Incoming Email messages for the manager will be stored in his desktop workstation and will normally be dealt with by him personally. However, the secretary should make a point of asking if there is any follow-up she can attend to herself. On the other hand, incoming answerphone messages will be accessible to the secretary who should play them through and note those which she herself can take care of. She should then make a series of typed note summaries of those needing the manager's attention for him to deal with as part of his morning mail.

Finally, it is always important to record the date and time at which a telecommunications message was first dealt with, since this message routing system tends to be used for important transactions and spans the many time-zones operating across the world.

DEALING WITH INCOMING MAIL

One of the most important daily routines the secretary undertakes is to deal with incoming mail. Any message which is transmitted in the form of posted correspondence should be handled with respect for a number of good reasons: the mailed item may take the form of a document needed as a legally acceptable record, it may include an enclosed cheque or money-order, it may be a customer's purchase order, and, if it is a letter written to a specified executive in the organisation, it will have cost some £20 to produce and deliver!

Every secretary should possess an informed appreciation of how a mailroom operates in a large organisation. If she works in a small one, this becomes even more important, because she is likely to have to administer her own, informal counterpart.

The mailroom

In large organisations incoming mail is delivered directly to a specialist unit which runs the mailroom, a room or area which is especially equipped to deal with large volumes of incoming and outgoing mail. Normally, a senior clerical officer or supervisor directs activities and is responsible for ensuring that no pilferage or misappropriation of money or securities occurs during the processes of distributing incoming mail or preparing mail for onward posting.

A well equipped mailroom will contain:

- An electronic letter-opening machine (if justified by the volume of mail handled)
- A rack or series of trays for sorting post into departmental stacks
- Trolleys for messenegers to use in their mail routes to various offices
- Tools for opening packages and parcels, including industrial staple removers
- Manual/automatic date-stamping equipment
- A franking machine for imprinting and recording the postage paid on outgoing mail
- A set of manual/electronic scales for weighing items and calculating postage due

- Materials and equipment for wrapping/securing outgoing parcels.
- Equipment for folding bulk mailshot letters or brochures
- Manual/automatic collators for sequencing multi-paged documents
- Equipment for addressing bulk mail, either by printing addresses on continuous, **tractor-fed** envelopes or via sets of adhesive labels printed by computers.
- Sets of reference books and data, including information on current internal and overseas postage rates, information for the express routing of parcels, various means of insuring packages, etc.
- Sets of stamps of various denominations and a range of stickers for envelopes and parcels such as 'fragile', 'urgent', 'airmail', 'recorded delivery'.
- Forms for completion for Red Star, Datapost, couriers and other delivery services.
- Boxes for sorting outgoing mail and equipment for holding mailbags

Note: In mailrooms servicing larger organisations, systems operate to record the value and destination of enclosed cheques or money orders, to cost postage back to respective departments and to record the costs incurred by the mailroom in, say, sending a letter by registered post or a parcel by overnight datapost. The system for keeping such expenditure records is very much like that used to operate an imprest petty cash system in which an initial allocation of cash is shown and items deducted from it as purchasing transactions occur, until a fresh allocation of cash is needed.

Where incoming mail is sent by recorded delivery, a signature from the mailroom supervisor or other authorised staff member will satisfy the Post Office delivery man, but where an item has been sent by registered mail, it must be accepted and signed for by its named recipient. As a general rule, other than in the situations outlined above, the mailroom will deliver a department's mail opened and ready for sorting into respective section or individual staff member stacks.

The secretary should always take pains to acquire a thorough understanding of the organisation's policies for the initial handling of incoming mail. For example, if enclosed cheques are routed directly to the accounts department, a note of the amount and any further details should be sent with the accompanying correspondence to the named recipient as an item of essential information and to avoid subsequent misunderstandings.

Furthermore, it is essential for the mailroom to respect totally the conventions which apply to mail sent either confidentially or as a personal letter to a specific individual. The current conventions which must be respected are:

Envelopes Marked:

CONFIDENTIAL	Under no circumstances should these be opened by mailroom staff; *only* the addressees or personal secretaries with their manager's delegated authorisation may do so.
PRIVATE	
PRIVATE & CONFIDENTIAL	

Envelopes marked:

PERSONAL	In order to respect the privacy required by the 'personal' status of the mailed item, it must *always* be left unopened for its *named recipient to deal with*.

Some additional tips are worth incorporating into the daily mail-handling routine. As there will not be enough time to scrutinise each document minutely, check the tops of letters for status entries such as 'urgent' or 'for the attention of'; note the dates of each item in case of delay in arrival etc, and take in carefully the topic of each letter's upper case subject-heading. Skim-read opening paragraphs for the purpose of the letter and check the final paragraph's action statement to see if what is requested is urgent. Check who wrote the letter or memo and consider its consequent status. Also, whenever an important or urgent item arrives in the post, make a point of advising its recipient directly – he or she may be off to a meeting or visit as the day's first task, and a response may thus be delayed.

Always remember office or departmental security: you may be authorised to open confidential mail – it may need re-insertion into a re-usable office envelope before being left on an executive's desk, especially in an open-plan office.

In many offices trade journals, periodicals, sales leaflets, circulars and catalogues arrive in abundance daily. While senior managers do not have time to read all such mail, many like to be given the opportunity of a preview skim-read before it is distributed to specific sections and staff. Such items are normally included at the bottom of the manager's mail.

Lastly, bear in mind that this procedure needs to be followed – for a reduced volume of mail – in the early afternoon following second postal deliveries.

Guidelines for secretarial handling of incoming mail

Not all organisations have mailrooms and consequently it may fall to the secretaries reporting to departmental heads to collect and distribute incoming mail. The following guidelines highlight the main features of this routine task.

1 Check all addresses on envelopes of unopened mail in case an item for another department has been inadvertently included and redirect it promptly.

2 Use a paperknife or automatic letter opener to open the mail, taking special care not to leave enclosed items in envelopes or hidden under discarded wrappers etc.

3 To avoid related documents from becoming separated, staple them together; many office secretaries dislike using paper clips as they tend to pick up other papers next to them which instantly become lost.

4 Date stamp each incoming item – where appropriate record the time of initial receipt of urgent documents.

5 Sort items into the various stacks which have been identified in the office – head of department, section heads, specific clerks for routine items such as invoices or copy purchase orders etc.

6 Prioritise the sorted stacks according to these guidelines:

- Items marked 'urgent'
- Items from senior organisational staff and clients or customers
- Items which have been delayed in the external/internal post
- Non-routine items – individually composed letters as opposed to forms, dockets and sales literature
- Items for which an existing deadline is imminent
- Items for which an existing deadline is imminent

7 Present incoming mail to a manager with the most important/urgent item first and the rest in descending order of importance in the stack.

Top secretary tip: incoming mail

As you may well be the first person in the office or department to have seen some (if not all) of the incoming mail, make it a regular practice to tell your manager straightaway of any high-priority, unusual or potentially problem-causing item. Managers always appreciate early warnings and prompts.

DEALING WITH OUTGOING MAIL

Central to dealing with outgoing mail are the factors of urgency, cost and visual presentation.

Urgency

Letters may be despatched, according to urgency in the following ways:

Inland
Motor-cycle courier
One-hour delivery guaranteed in larger towns and cities.

Intelpost
A fax-based Post Office service for fast document routing within UK or overseas; messages may be telephoned to the Post Office or handed in to a post office for onward transmission.

Datapost sameday and overnight
Another Post Office service for goods and documents; delivery is guaranteed within zones and overnight deliveries have a next day 10.00 am deadline across most of the UK.

Royal Mail Special Delivery
Here the Post Office operates a money-back next working day delivery guarantee for first-class letter packets provided they are given in by specific times.

Airway and railway letters
British Airways and some British Rail stations accept post for transmission to designated airports/stations for collection.

Overseas
Datapost International
The Post office runs a service to over 90 countries worldwide – with a 'next-day' delivery to most of Europe and to New York. Items can be collected for despatch. Contact Freephone Datapost.

Information processing in the office 41

Fig 2.2 Post Office forms

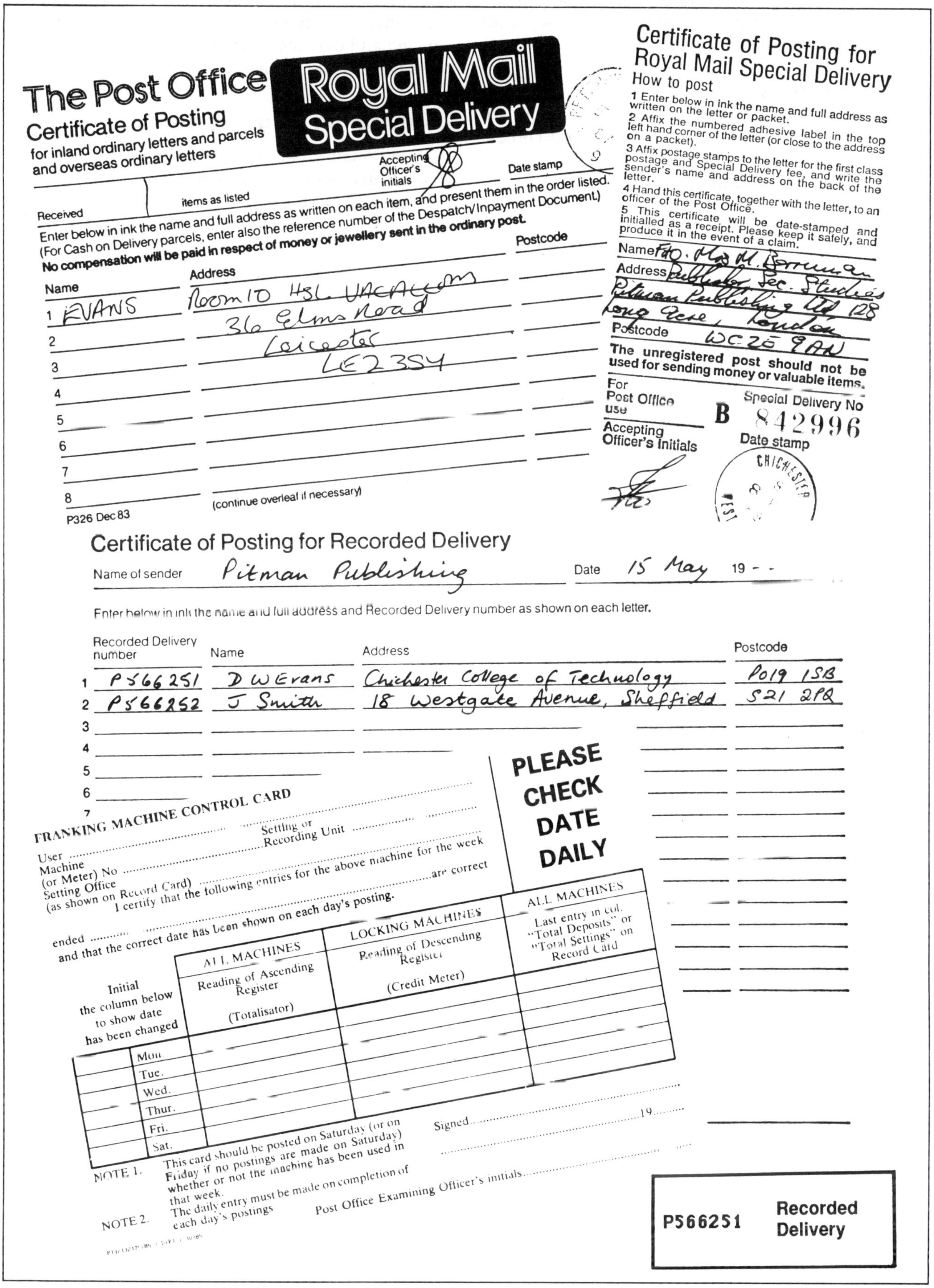

Swiftair
Items may be given in at post offices or separately collected; delivery is scheduled for the day after posting to destination country.

Express delivery
Items travel by normal PO airmail services, but are given express treatment from destination post office.

Normal service inland
First-class Letter Post
The Post Office aims to deliver 90% by the next working day, provided items are posted before locally set deadlines

Second-class post
Used for non-urgent items and the Post Office aim is delivery by the third working day.

Note: Increasingly, private sector distribution firms are offering highly competitive private sector services in the field of high-speed secure delivery. See Unit 6 for details of other postal services.

Costs

Inevitably, in choosing the method of despatch, there is a balance to be struck between urgency and cost. A further factor is the need for a legally accepted record: faxed documents are not legally binding at present, whereas documents sent through the post or by telex are.

Presentation

It is worth noting that a high-quality white or pastel shaded notepaper and envelope allied with a form of express service will impress far more than a duplicated sheet delivered over three to four days in a manilla envelope.

ASSIGNMENT

In groups of three to four, research *one* of the following topics, either for inland or overseas letters:

First carry out your research and then present your findings orally to your group using any AVA (audio-visual aids) facilities available to you:

1 What is the fastest way to get a letter which weighs 60 grams from your local office to Edinburgh OR Alice Springs, Australia? How much will it cost?

2 Draw up a table which lists the various ways of sending a letter packet faster than normal first-class post (inland) or a normal airmail letter (overseas) and a comparison of costs, where the weight does not exceed 1 kilogram.

3 Compose a memorandum for a junior clerical assistant reporting to you which provides guidance on what express postal services are available both inland and overseas and in what typical circumstances they should be used.

Annotating outgoing mail

It is important when using the services of an organisational mailroom to ensure that all outgoing mail is accompanied by a clear instruction as to the type of postal service required. For straightforward mail, a simple '1st' or '2nd' note will suffice where the stamp/franking will go.

Mail intended for express, registered or recorded delivery should be accompanied by a brief, clear note. (See Unit 6 for details of further Post Office services.)

QUICK REVIEW QUIZ

1 Explain what is meant when describing the office as 'an information processing centre'.

2 What action should a secretary take to deal with incoming overnight messages effectively?

3 What do the following stand for: Email, OCR, LAN, WAN?

4 List four advantages which computer-based telecommunications offer over traditional systems.

5 Identify four routine tasks a secretary attends to:
   (a) on arriving at the office
   (b) at the end of the day

6 Explain briefly how messages are stored on:
   (a) a fax transceiver
   (b) a teleprinter
   (c) a computer workstation using electronic mail

7 List the major items of equipment which a large firm's mailroom will contain and what each is used for.

8 How would an envelope be marked which must be left for its recipient to open?

9 To what sort of incoming mail items would you give priority?

10 List three different types of accelerated mail delivery which you could use within the UK and say which would be fastest to a destination 250 miles distant.

2.2 Diaries, appointments and work scheduling

Diaries and appointments; key features of the electronic diary; managing the secretary's diary; self-organisation and management of time.

DIARIES AND APPOINTMENTS

The ability to administer the manager's and secretary's own diaries effectively lies at the very heart of office organisation. The most precious commodity a hard-pressed manager has is his or her time and the use made of it. An able secretary can save her manager – and herself – hours each week by shrewd diary and appointments management. Clearly, each manager and each office will have evolved practices and procedures which have been shown to work effectively and the secretary must always be prepared to adapt to, and adopt, methods which both suit the manager's personality and overall work pattern of the office.

Nevertheless, there are a number of strategies which may be incorporated into any diary and appointments situation, and which work well in both electronic and paper/manual environments.

1 Establishing and maintaining regular routines with the manager to compare respective diaries and to update them. A brief meeting at the day's start ensures a smoother running day, without unexpected visitors arriving whose appointments are known only to the manager, or, worse, visitors with appointments arriving when the manager is out or tied up, because the appointment has been written only into the secretary's diary after a phone call! Similarly, a day-end meeting to review the next day's commitments is very helpful.
Note: Some managers and secretaries make a firm decision that there will be only *one* electronic diary and that only *one* of them shall run it!

2 Maintaining sufficient 'blocked-out' time each day and week to enable the manager – and the secretary – to get on with work uninterruptedly. Some managers, are their own worst enemies in this regard and their 'ever open door' policy can prevent them from meeting deadlines imposed by their own superiors. As a result, the secretary must learn to judge which enquiries or requests to meet with the manager can be satisfactorily dealt with either by another office member or herself, and which need his attention. As a guideline, requests from people external to the organisation and from senior personnel within it should always be brought to the manager's attention.

3 Time spent by visitors with the manager should be carefully allocated and rationed. For instance, a good sales rep can sell a lot in 15 minutes, and a VIP customer can be given the red carpet treatment and every attention in 45–60 minutes. Many managers and secretaries operate a discreet system of terminating interviews or visits by means of a polite head round the door reminder about 'that meeting with the MD' or by other similar pre-arranged signals. Note that informing the caller that 'Mr Brown has set aside 11.00 to 11.30 for you.' helps to prevent meetings from overrunning.

4 It pays to have a mutually understood set of codes and symbols – capital letters, underscoring, use of highlighting pens for priority events and reminders – which both manager and secretary stick to Also, entries like: '4.00 pm Mr Smith with Miss Grainger can be both tiresome and dangerous if they are referred to some four weeks after the appointment was made and the reason for the visit has become hazy or forgotten! Generally, diary entries should include the visitor's *name*, *job title*, *organisation* and *reason for the meeting* in a

Fig 2.3 Effective diary management

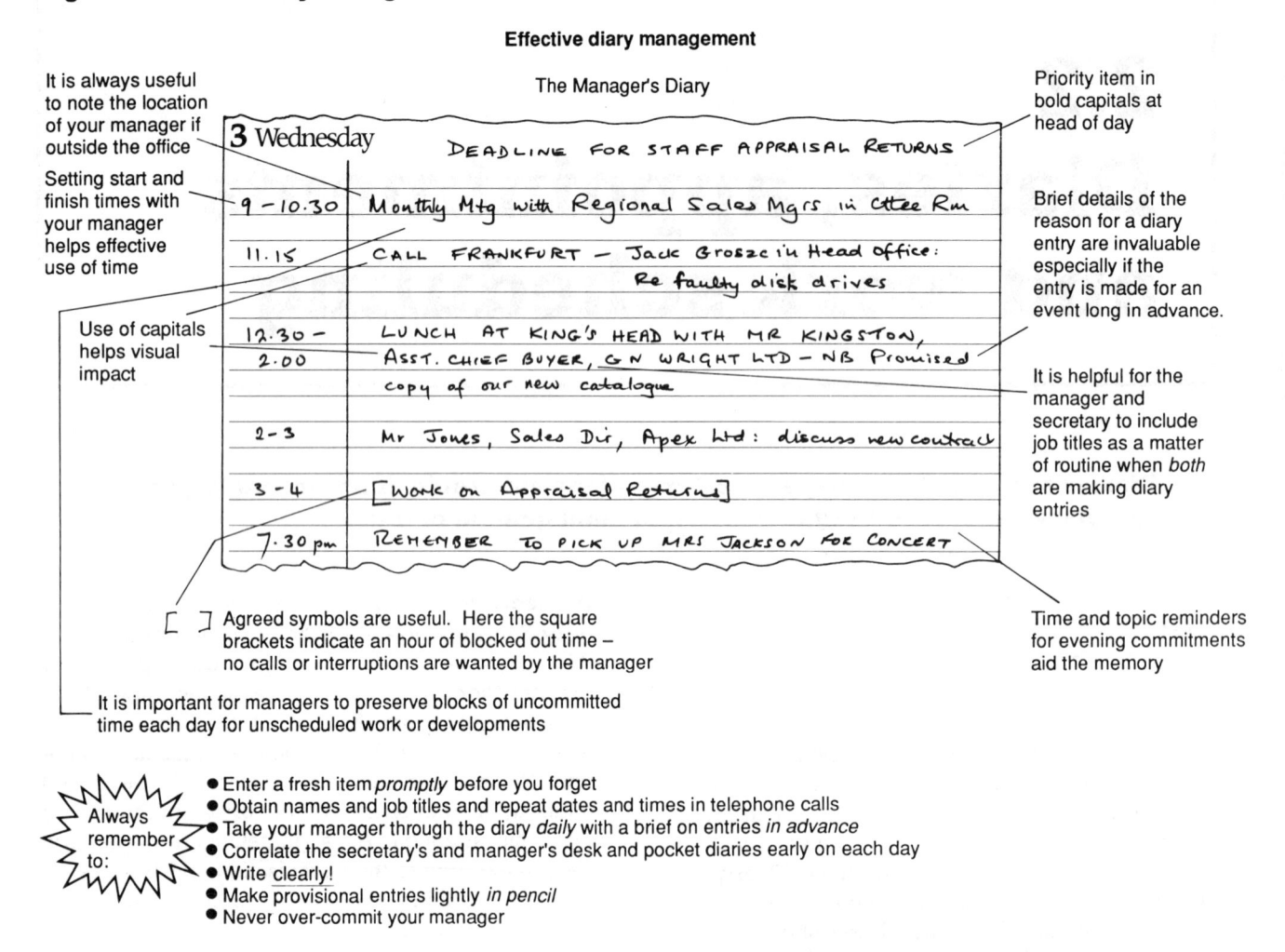

Effective diary management

The Manager's Diary

It is always useful to note the location of your manager if outside the office

Setting start and finish times with your manager helps effective use of time

Use of capitals helps visual impact

Priority item in bold capitals at head of day

Brief details of the reason for a diary entry are invaluable especially if the entry is made for an event long in advance.

It is helpful for the manager and secretary to include job titles as a matter of routine when *both* are making diary entries

Time and topic reminders for evening commitments aid the memory

3 Wednesday — DEADLINE FOR STAFF APPRAISAL RETURNS

9 – 10.30	Monthly Mtg with Regional Sales Mgrs in Cttee Rm
11.15	CALL FRANKFURT – Jack Grosze in Head Office: Re faulty disk drives
12.30 – 2.00	LUNCH AT KING'S HEAD WITH MR KINGSTON, ASST. CHIEF BUYER, G N WRIGHT LTD – NB Promised copy of our new catalogue
2 – 3	Mr Jones, Sales Dir, Apex Ltd: discuss new contract
3 – 4	[Work on Appraisal Returns]
7.30 pm	REMEMBER TO PICK UP MRS JACKSON FOR CONCERT

[ ] Agreed symbols are useful. Here the square brackets indicate an hour of blocked out time – no calls or interruptions are wanted by the manager

It is important for managers to preserve blocks of uncommitted time each day for unscheduled work or developments

Always remember to:
- Enter a fresh item *promptly* before you forget
- Obtain names and job titles and repeat dates and times in telephone calls
- Take your manager through the diary *daily* with a brief on entries *in advance*
- Correlate the secretary's and manager's desk and pocket diaries early on each day
- Write clearly!
- Make provisional entries lightly *in pencil*
- Never over-commit your manager

---

brief but intelligible entry format. (See Fig. 2.3)

Both electronic and paper diaries vary in the formats they offer to aid the manager and secretary and it pays to shop around for good software and book-form diaries. Some managers, for example, prefer 'see the week at a glance' formats while others like large page-a-day layouts. With electronic diaries, some software leaves very little space in which to key in entries, while others are cumbersome to **scroll** for a week's overview. Some others are much more user-friendly and ally the **electronic notepad facility** to each diary entry so that fuller back-up notes can be easily entered and later referred to as reminders and memory-joggers.

Top secretary tip: your manager's diary plan

Always remember that your chief's diary is a confidential item, personal to him and entrusted to you!

KEY FEATURES OF THE ELECTRONIC DIARY

The development of various kinds of integrated software packages for information management (see Unit 3) has revolutionised the ways in which diaries and appointments are managed and as such software offers so many advantages and supportive features, every secretary should be fully aware of these, so as to lobby for access to them! The integrated package links and interconnects these features:

☐ **Diary and appointments** ☐ **Electronic notepad**
☐ **Word processing** ☐ **Spreadsheet** ☐ **Graphics**
☐ **Communications via modem – fax, BT Gold Email, etc**
☐ **Calculator, five-year calendar reference tables, etc** (see 'Multi-user Smart' software contents list on page 96)

Major features of the diary and appointments facilities are:

■ **Calendar five-year display** and **five-year rolling diary**

Information processing in the office

- **Scanning of diary pages**: by morning, afternoon or evening; by week, month or year; via fast or slow scroll
- **Entry of commitments, reminders appointments** at any time for any duration; facility to block out time periods for uninterrupted work
- **Insertion of reminders, priority jobs, memory joggers**; some software highlights PRIORITY ACTION FOR DAY types of entry at any future date; additionally some packages connect electronic notepad entries to such reminders so that detailed supportive entries may be accessed directly to refresh the operator's memory.
- **Facility to search via LAN/WAN networks the diaries of associates/colleagues**: this can be used (via the correct security password) to arrange and make the diary entries for a meeting at the first time/date when all are available, and to order AVA equipment and accommodation from a central resource.
- **By means of windows display feature the facility to consult other integrated package components**, such as a database, spreadsheet or calculator while processing a diary or appointment entry.

THE SECRETARY'S DIARY

Used imaginatively, the secretary's diary is a most helpful self-organisation aid and often a life-saver when office work becomes madly hectic and fraught! The following guidelines illustrate some of the principal aids which it offers:

Fig 2.4 Specimen electronic diary - a week on display

```
                     Appointment Schedule
                          A. George
                     04/04/    - 08/04/

       March                   April                      May
  S  M  T  W  T  F  S     S  M  T  W  T  F  S      S  M  T  W  T  F  S
           1  2  3  4  5                     1  2      1  2  3  4  5  6  7
   6  7  8  9 10 11 12     3  4  5  6  7  8  9      8  9 10 11 12 13 14
  13 14 15 16 17 18 19    10 11 12 13 14 15 16     15 16 17 18 19 20 21
  20 21 22 23 24 25 26    17 18 19 20 21 22 23     22 23 24 25 26 27 28
  27 28 29 30 31          24 25 26 27 28 29 30     29 30 31


  Monday        04/04/
   08:00   18:30      V  ALISON - 1 DAY VACATION
   NOTES:             V  JAN JONES - VACATION 4TH - 8TH INCL.
  Tuesday       05/04/
   00:00   00:01      i  NEW STUDENT STARTS TODAY
   09:00   10:30      m  MONDAY REVIEW - PQ AG
   14:00   16:00      m  MANAGEMENT SUPPORT MEETING - CONF ROOM 2
   NOTES:             V  JAN JONES - VACATION 4TH - 8TH INCL.
  Wednesday     06/04/
   10:00   11:00      M  NEW STUDENT- EMMA JONES - INDUCTION
   11:00   12:00      M  DEPARTMENT REVIEW - CONF ROOM 4
   14:00   16:00      I  MEETING PREPARATION TIME
   16:00   17:30      M  COMMUNICATIONS STATUS - AG OFFICE
   NOTES:             V  JAN JONES - VACATION 4TH - 8TH INCL.
  Thursday      07/04/
   09:00   09:05      i  REMINDER - AG TO TELEPHONE BOROUGH COUNCIL
   10:00   12:30      i  PRESENTATION PREPARATION FOR 16TH
   14:00   14:30      M  ARTICLE REVIEW - D EVANS CHICHESTER COLLEGE / AG
   NOTES:             V  JAN JONES - VACATION 4TH - 8TH INCL.
  Friday        08/04/
   08:00   17:00      i  KEEP FREE - POSSIBLE VISIT- time to be confirmed
   NOTES:             V  JAN JONES - VACATION 4TH - 8TH INCL.
```

Weeks and months may be scanned at will

Key:
I = information
M = meeting
V = vacation

Notes may be keyed in as required

*Professional Office System: IBM's Information Management System

(IBM's PROFS office system. *Reproduced by kind permission of IBM (UK) Ltd*)

Bring Forward Routines. Often copy letters, memos or reminder notes are interleaved into the diary (sometimes a separate diary) with a note to draw them to the manager's attention at a given future date – usually as a memory jogger or to prompt the checking of a set deadline. Electronic diaries handle this job very well and some software packages include the facility of flagging up prominently a reminder on a given electronic diary page for as many as five years ahead!

Reminders to self. Many managers issue requests for future reminders or small jobs to be done with the rapidity of a machine-gun in action during dictation periods! Make it a rule to enter such requests – *sometimes a day or two before the due date* – in your diary as your own memory jogger. Such a practice will help you remind your manager of important business and social events like a customer opening a new branch, or the MD's birthday or silver wedding.

Regular Activities. There are always a number of routine jobs which need to be attended to regularly in the life of the effective secretary, such as checking stocks of stationery, re-issuing forms in use, purchasing office consumables like typewriter ribbons or photocopying toner. Some activities occur in quarterly or annual cycles – like issuing bonuses, creating a summer holiday rota or preparing for the department's annual report, stock-taking or salary reviews. Here the secretary's diary acts as a helpful planning aid used in conjunction, say, with a visual year planner chart – either located in the desktop PC or hung on the wall.

Advance Preparations The battle is half won on the secretarial front when tasks and jobs are well anticipated. Again the electronic or paper diary prove to be a boon to the hard-pressed secretary if entries like this are made suitably in advance of the relevant deadline:

June

12 Monday

Personnel Managers' Meeting Weds 14 June in Conference Room 1100–1230

Check spare copies of minutes available and J.J. has Chairman's Agenda with him; duplicated paper to be tabled on Bournemouth Conference. See members' name plaques on committee tables with notepaper

SELF ORGANISATION AND MANAGEMENT OF TIME

No survey of the secretary's range of routine activities would be complete without considering an aspect which underpins all of this Unit's sections – how the secretary may organise herself to make best use of the time, equipment and resources available to her. The acquisition of self-organisation and time management skills marks the difference between the secretary who is always in charge of herself and her job, always composed, calm and capable, and her disorganised counterpart, always stressed by imminent deadlines, always behindhand with her workload and mostly driven by a series of lurches from one potential crisis to another!

Guidelines on self-organisation and time management

DOs

- Acquire the habit of anticipating events and needs well ahead of their arrival: scan your own and your manager's diaries regularly and make time to plan what is needed for a coming interview, conference, overseas visit, etc.

- Develop a daily and weekly routine in which you tailor your tasks around your manager's needs and intermittent absences. For example, save filing and routine, non-urgent typing for the two hours during which the manager is attending a meeting. Plan larger personal projects to coincide with the manager's 'away days'.

- Keep an electronic or paper notebook of the various 'work in progress' jobs which are delegated to you and reorder their priority (every morning and afternoon or daily), according to the speed of approaching deadlines or the manager's ever-changing sense of what is urgent.

- Encourage your manager to work as far as possible according to a series of routines (such as set times for dictation and reviewing work schedules, signing the outward post, etc), which avoid last-minute rushes and provide you with enough time to complete allocated work each day or week.

- Make a habit of scanning office and business systems magazines for labour- and time-saving devices and resources and develop as helpful a set of equipment and material as possible; avoid the trap of sticking to time-worn routines just because they *are* routines!

- Keep your own bring-forward or memory-jogging diary of items for attention which occur on an infrequent or irregular cycle, such as reordering electronic typewriter ribbons or supplies of departmental letterheaded stationery. Many secretaries become highly esteemed simply because they can manage 'stitch in time' routines!

- Ensure you take the time and trouble to *master* the office equipment and systems available, and always be prepared to absorb a new technique.

DON'Ts

- Waste time in idle gossip; if you're worth your salt you should be earning a good salary, with the emphasis on *earn*!

- Become an informational 'black hole' and gatekeeper denying access to all from your manager. Ensure you act as a responsible communicator with everyone in your network and you will find that an invaluable two-way process develops based on mutual trust between you and your colleagues.

- Waste your time on routine jobs you could easily delegate and monitor.

- Adopt a *reactive* approach to your job. Always adopt a *proactive* approach in which you anticipate jobs, problems and eventualities and plan and control events rather than letting them control you.

- Forget that your main role is to act as an assistant and facilitator for one or more managers. Avoid the temptation to assume responsibility for matters which are more properly in your manager's job description. Whenever in doubt as to the limits of your responsibilities, always confer with your manager and secure prior approval for actions.

- Betray your manager's confidences – even to close friends. Most managers work under much stress and have virtually no one in whom to confide other than the secretary with whom a close professional relationship may develop. Many secretaries have shared their manager's promotional good fortune because they have proved entirely trustworthy.

- Be shy of telling the manager – diplomatically – if you think he or she is wrong. If, for example, the memorandum he dictated in a fit of anger or frustration is dangerously terse or a matter is best left to fade away. Good secretaries develop a much appreciated knack of sometimes saving managers from themselves and of proffering the benefit of another perspective upon a given problem. But neither be too upset if such advice is ignored!

Top secretary tip
When asked what qualities they most desire in their personal secretaries or PAs, many top-echelon managers select a phrase which one way or another may be summed up as *nous*. Deriving from the Greek, the word 'nous' is a synonym for common sense and gumption, but means much more:

NOUS IS:
knowing when to do the job yourself and when to check with JJ;
knowing how to save JJ from time-wasters without appearing bossy or rude;
knowing when to intervene and when to keep quiet;
selecting the best moment to proffer suggestions or advice;
anticipating what JJ will need to do next;
accepting that most managers have poor memories and devising a system to counteract this sad fact!
and, lastly, nous includes an acceptance – however reluctant – that only a very few managers fully acknowledge the credit owed to a top secretary.

TOP SECRETARIES HAVE A DEVELOPED SENSE OF NOUS!

QUICK REVIEW QUIZ

1 Identify four major useful features you would expect to find in an electronic diary applications package.

2 What factors should a secretary take into account when making an appointment for her manager in an appointments diary?

3 How does a 'bring forward' system work?

4 What do you consider to be the essential details to enter in the appointments diary about a visitor to see the manager?

5 What major advantages are offered to the secretary using an electronic as opposed to a book diary?

6 Why is it important for the secretary and manager to 'synchronise' and compare their diaries regularly?

RESEARCH AND REPORT BACK ASSIGNMENTS

1 In pairs, find out what application software is on the market which includes an electronic diary. Make a list of the principal features each possesses. You should be able to obtain these from sales brochures. Then find out whether a local office uses a system you have researched and make arrangements through your teacher to see it demonstrated.

Together, compose a newcomer's guide to electronic diary applications and include guidelines on their effective use. Copy your guide and install it in your class's information database. Note: you may be able to secure non-confidential printouts as useful illustrations.

2 Conduct a survey of the various types of book diary suited to a manager's needs available locally. Decide which you think most useful and, in an oral presentation to your group, explain why.

2.3 Filing and records management

Classifying, filing, storing and retrieving data; major features of office filing systems; media for storing electronic data; filing and database software application packages; manual and paper/card-based filing systems; micrographics, microform and microfilm

OFFICE RECORDS: CLASSIFYING, FILING, STORING AND RETRIEVING DATA

Initially in this unit the office was examined as an information processing centre, able to take in, process, store and disseminate large volumes of information and data. Indeed, some large offices process more than 20 000 items of information each day thanks to **automated office records systems and equipment**.

In some offices the filing and storage of data, whether in the form of paper letters, invoices or memos or as computerised electronic files, is regarded sometimes as a chore or necessary evil. And, not surprisingly, it is in just these same offices that tempers become frayed and staff frustrated and irritable when vital documents cannot be found before, say, a meeting which the MD is attending! Indeed, a recent survey found that one in every ten documents or files stored become immediately lost for ever, thanks to inadequate and careless filing techniques and practices.

Accomplished records management skills and techniques form a most important part of a secretary's repertoire today, particularly since developments in electronic office automation are transforming the speed at which data may be stored and accessed and extending massively the amount of data which organisations wish to retain and refer to at intervals.

Systems for classifying Data

Dewey decimal system

For many years now, librarians, lexicographers, data processing managers and scientists have devised various logical methods for organising and classifying information. For example, compilers of dictionaries in the 17th century used, not unnaturally, the alphabetical sequence from A to Z to list words and their definitions. Dr Peter Roget in the mid 19th century devised six major categories in which to organise his *Thesaurus of English Words and Phrases*, ranging from abstract relations to emotion, religion and morality. Melvil Dewey, father of modern library classification techniques developed his 'Dewey Decimal System' in Albany, USA, in 1876, by dividing all areas of human knowledge into eleven expandable sectors. For instance, the area between 600 and 699 was given over to technology; within it 651 was allocated to the area of business English and, by introducing sub-divisions behind a decimal point, Dewey was able to add any new entry or item to his system indefinitely:

651.74: English for business students
651.77: committees
651.78: report writing

Hierarchical system

More recently, data processing specialists have devised systems for organising information which include the **decision-tree system** which provides the user with a single starting point and then arranges data according to a series of dividing branches taking him into ever-increasing detail, eg:

Fig 2.5 Hierarchical or branching database

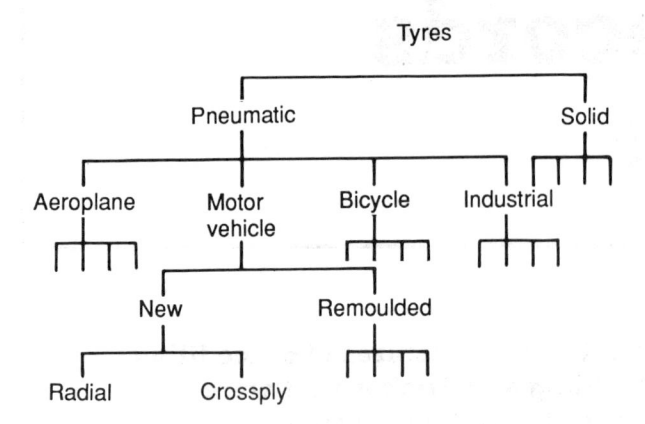

```
                        Tyres
                ┌─────────┴─────────┐
            Pneumatic              Solid
       ┌────┬────┬────┐         ┌──┬──┬──┐
   Aeroplane Motor Bicycle Industrial
            vehicle
            ┌──┴──┐      ┌──┬──┬──┐
           New  Remoulded
         ┌──┴──┐         ┌──┬──┬──┐
      Radial Crossply
```

Decimal point reference system

Another system for organising information frequently used in the composition of long reports is to number each consecutive major section as follows:

1.0   2.0   3.0   4.0   5.0

Sub-divisions within each major section are then divided thus:

1.1, 1.2, 1.3 etc.   3.1, 3.2, 3.3 etc.

Within each sub-division further sub-sections may be created by the addition of another decimal point and number:

1.1.1, 1.1.2, 1.1.3,   4.1.1, 4.1.2, 4.1.3 etc.

Such a system provides a very quick method for referring to a detailed topic within the body of such reports:

... in the case of lost of misfiled documents (para 3.6.4 refers) ...

As you can see, a varied range of systems exists for ordering and classifying the knowledge which we need to access, and it is held in all sorts of storage media — books, filing cabinets, card-indexes, **microfiche film**, computer files on floppy or hard disk, film slides, audio tapes, video cassettes and so on.

The following section concentrates on examining those record storage systems and techniques which are most frequently found in today's offices. However, you should take the trouble to extend and deepen your own appreciation of current systems for storing information since the ability to obtain and present data quickly and skilfully from a wide variety of sources is extremely valuable and much esteemed by perceptive managers.

Factors influencing the design of record management systems

The following factors affect the ways in which records are kept and the methods and media employed:

1   The length of time for which a record must be kept. For some items this may be as long as 30 years!

2   The extent or volume of records for storage and the rate at which this volume is expected to grow.

3   The speed at which access to a given record is demanded or expected, together with the estimated number of people needing to be given access and the frequency of requests for the item.

4   The duration of the short-term, active life of a document or record and the long-term period of its passive existence as an archive.

5   The nature or form of the original record – paper letter, computer file, photograph etc.

6   The cost of storage: paper files occupy much more floorspace than their microform counterparts.

7   The extent of legal requirements: certain documents may be vital originals like deeds, contracts or share certificates which must be kept in fire-proof safes.

As the above checklist illustrates, records management is by no means a dull or boring chore. On the contrary, secure and efficient records administration requires constant imaginative planning and anticipation as well as a logical and consistent approach.

Guide to current archive retention practice

Agreements	12 years
Balance sheets	30 years
Bank statements	6 years
Cheque counterfoils	1 year
Correspondence files	6 years
Credit Notes	6 years
Customs & Excise VAT records	6 years
Delivery notes	1 year
Directors' reports	30 years
Expenses claims	1 year
Insurance claims forms	6 years
Expired leases	12 years
Licences for patents	30 years
Medical certificates	1 year
Expired patents	12 years
Power of Attorney	30 years
Prospectuses	30 years
Paying-in books	1 year
Purchase orders	6 years
Quotations, out	6 years
Royalty ledger	30 years
Sales invoices	6 years
Product specifications	6 years
Tax records	6 years
Share applications	12 years

This guide is reproduced by kind permission of Fellowes Manufacturing UK Ltd and Business Equipment Digest magazine

ASSIGNMENT

By arrangement, visit the offices of, for example, a local district or county council department, an estate agent, an insurance office, an architect or your school/college and obtain a briefing on the kinds of filing systems used and their various advantages and disadvantages. In particular, find out how computerised record systems are improving records management. Make notes of your findings and report back to your group to exchange information by means of an oral/AVA presentation.

To help you to draw up a useful checklist of questions beforehand, refer to the checklist on page 51, 'Factors influencing the design of record management systems.

MAJOR FEATURES OF POPULAR OFFICE FILING SYSTEMS

At the heart of all commonly occurring office filing systems lies the need for them to be simple enough so that a range of staff can use them competently, to be totally logical in the way in which files are classified and sequenced and to be capable of locating and presenting required information quickly and accurately.

The type of filing system an office will employ naturally varies according to the nature and characteristics of source documents or materials – large maps need to be handled very differently from extensive batches of customer invoices or from sets of colour slides. The following checklist includes the principal systems currently in use in office filing systems:

Files may be arranged in:

1 Numerical order

Files may be numbered from 1 to 1000 and major sections may occur at regular intervals (100, 200, 300 etc.) as in the Dewey decimal system. Sub-sections within a file may be introduced by the addition of a decimal point: 100.1, 234.35 etc.

Advantages: Such a system is capable of infinite expansion and can cope with a very large number of sub-sections, sub-divisions and diverging branches of data.

Disadvantages: In order for the numbers to convey readily what they mean, it is necessary for an index to be created, eg;

600 Technology
 650 Business Practices
 658 Management etc.

This system is therefore more time-consuming to use than one in which each file is given an instantly identifiable name.

2 Alphabetical Order

Here files are arranged in a sequence which follows that of the A–Z order of letters. A number of protocols or rules for filing alphabetically must be committed to memory:

- 2.1 The alphabetical sequence must be strictly adhered to: abbess comes before abbot and Richards before Richardson.

- 2.2 Files or entries are sequenced letter by letter:

   Dun
   Dunn
   Dunstable

- 2.3 Indefinite and definite articles (a, the) are ignored in entry titles

- 2.4 Abbreviations are filed as written: Messrs Smith and Williams

- 2.5 Abbreviated names like BBC, ITV, TUC, etc,

are filed according to their abbreviated letter sequence

- 2.6 St is filed as Saint and foreign versions like San or Sainte are filed as spelled. Some filing systems treat Mc, Mac or M' as quite different versions of 'mac' and file them according to their individual letter sequence; others treat them all as 'Mac'.

- 2.7 As a rule entries which are shorter come first:

Elizabeth
Elizabeth I
Elizabeth I, Queen of England

- 2.8 Personal names are normally filed surname first:

Richards, Jack
Richards, Dr John
Richards, Sir Gordon

Titles like Mr, Mrs, Dr, Prof, Sir etc, are ignored, save for forming part of the entry after the initial surname shown.

- 2.9 Where the same word occurs as a name, then the convention is to enter forename followed by surname, followed by corporate name, followed by name as subject:

Heather
Heather, Arnold
Heather Products Limited
Heather, British species

Advantages: Alphabetical filing enables files to be read and accessed quickly; the system is also readily expandable.

Disadvantages: Items within a named file require some additional system of classification – letters to an account client may need to be numbered or filed chronologically, making cross-referencing laborious.

Note: items 2.1–2.9 have been adapted from the British Standard on filing and indexing: BS 1749 specimen filing sequence.

3 Chronological order

Sometimes it is necessary to file items according to the day/date received – such as applications for permits or licences or the dates when vehicles in a company fleet were serviced:

May 19--
   1   F195 BXP   30,000 service
   2   E256 DFX   48,000 service etc.

Advantages: particularly useful when actions need to be taken on a cyclical basis – like relicensing sales reps' cars annually; good for cross-referencing – file on vehicle and relicensing date records quickly matched. Ideally suited to computerised database – all vehicles due for re-taxing on say 31 August 19-- may be located and displayed on the VDU in a trice!

Disadvantages: Need for index and explanatory back-up system. Time-consuming to access data held in manual filing system.

4 Geographical order

Many organisations file data according to geographic region, area or locality, such as sales turnover by region or international sales division; public service departments hold many records in regional, county, district and parish council sections and sub-sections.

Advantages: Such a system enables statistics to be held in manageable and comparable units and also permits a large or 'macro' figure or total to be evaluated in terms of its 'micro' or component parts.

5 Decision – tree branching

As records are being stored increasingly on computer files, new methods of accessing data are being more widely introduced. Popular among these is the decision-tree system for moving from root or basic entry points into a system of off-shoots or branches of information which has been classified according to a logical form of progression or division of data. Some such systems operate on the basis of providing alternative routes according to whether a question is answered by a 'yes' or a 'no':

Must the paint used be waterproof?

YES: (VDU displays menu on marine/outdoor paints)

Top secretary tip: filing

It is good practice in maintaining a filing system to make a habit of:

- **Cross indexing**: making a reference in one file of related or helpful/additional data held in another file.

- **Noting files in use**: a file borrowed without a record of who has it, when it was removed from the filing system, etc, is a file lost! Make sure you have a 'file in use' set of slips to be filled out showing: user, date out, date due back, etc.

- **Maintaining security**: some files will certainly contain highly confidential data; make sure you control who may access what and keep a secure system for sensitive files.

MEDIA FOR STORING ELECTRONIC DATA

Computer files

Today billions of files in offices around the world are stored electronically on computer files. Such files may lie in the heart of mainframe computers within their hard disks as inert electronic pulses waiting to be activated by the appropriate instruction from the user – perhaps operating from a desktop keyboard hundreds of miles distant.

Floppy disk technology

The same technology enables files to be stored on floppy disks either 8, 5.25 or 3.5 inches in diameter, the latter two sizes being the most common forms of disk in use on personal computers.

Early computers used to store files on magnetic cards made of material similar to that of audio tape; each card could only store one or two A4-type pages of memory and a cumbersome process was needed to install and retrieve such cards frequently. The same time-consuming technology was also a major drawback in the small computers of the 1970s which stored files on cassettes. Fortunately, the introduction of the floppy disk enabled much larger and more numerous files to be stored on circular tracks upon both sides of the disk. This floppy disk technology allowed files to be 'written' electronically on concentric tracks and to be 'read' or retrieved for display and interaction very rapidly by means of a head (rather like a record-player's head) which moved over (but not on) the rapidly rotating disks. As a result, it became possible to store up to the equivalent of 2000 A4 typescript pages of information on the largest type of floppy disk. Commonly a 5.25 inch floppy disk will hold the equivalent of between 50–100 of such pages.

Hard disk technology

The process of storing files on hard disks follows a very similar pattern, except that the magnetic disk material is permanently encased in a dust-proof cover. In today's desktop micro-computers such disks are referred to as Winchester disks and are capable of storing some 50 million characters or bytes of information. As a result, the computer's speed in reading and writing files became very much faster and, indeed, such hard disk desktop computers are used as file-servers or master memory storage units in local area networks linking, say, 8–10 dual disk drive PCs.

Computer software and filing techniques

Computerised files exist mainly in two forms. First, there are those which are permanently installed in the electronic microprocessor cards which form part of the computer' structure. Files built into the computer in this way offer **ROM** or Read Only Memory features – the user can access them but, in normal use, cannot change them. Such files store data which the computer needs in order to function.

The files which the user can create and manipulate are made up of **RAM** or Random Access Memory, which means, in effect, that the user can instruct the computer to locate and display data which has been stored on various tracks of the floppy or hard disk which were free at the time. To formulate RAM files, the computer needs to have been booted up (have

Examples of computerised records storage media

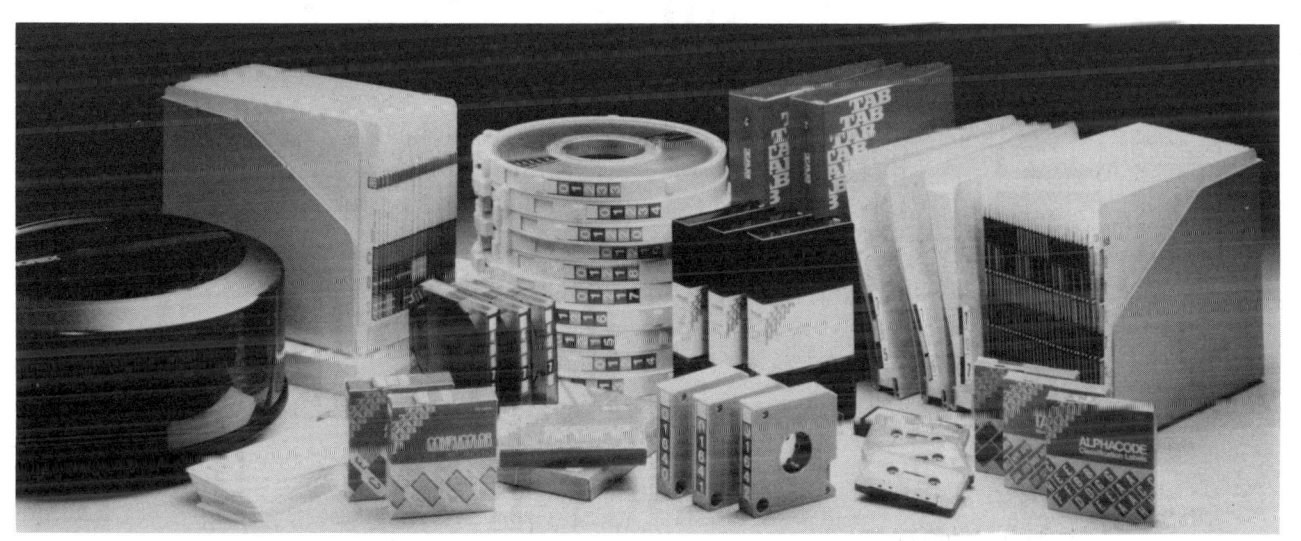

Fig 2.6 Winchester disk, microfiches, computer magnetic tapes, cartridges and hard copy data – today's information comes in all shapes and sizes.

(*Reproduced by kind permission of Cave Tab Ltd*)

Fig 2.7 Information management system using optical disk, desktop scanner and laser printer: the system integrates document capture, indexing and computer-assisted storage and retrieval (*Reproduced by kind permission of Kodak*)

Fig. 2.8 Diagram of Kodak's Information Management System, KIMS 5000

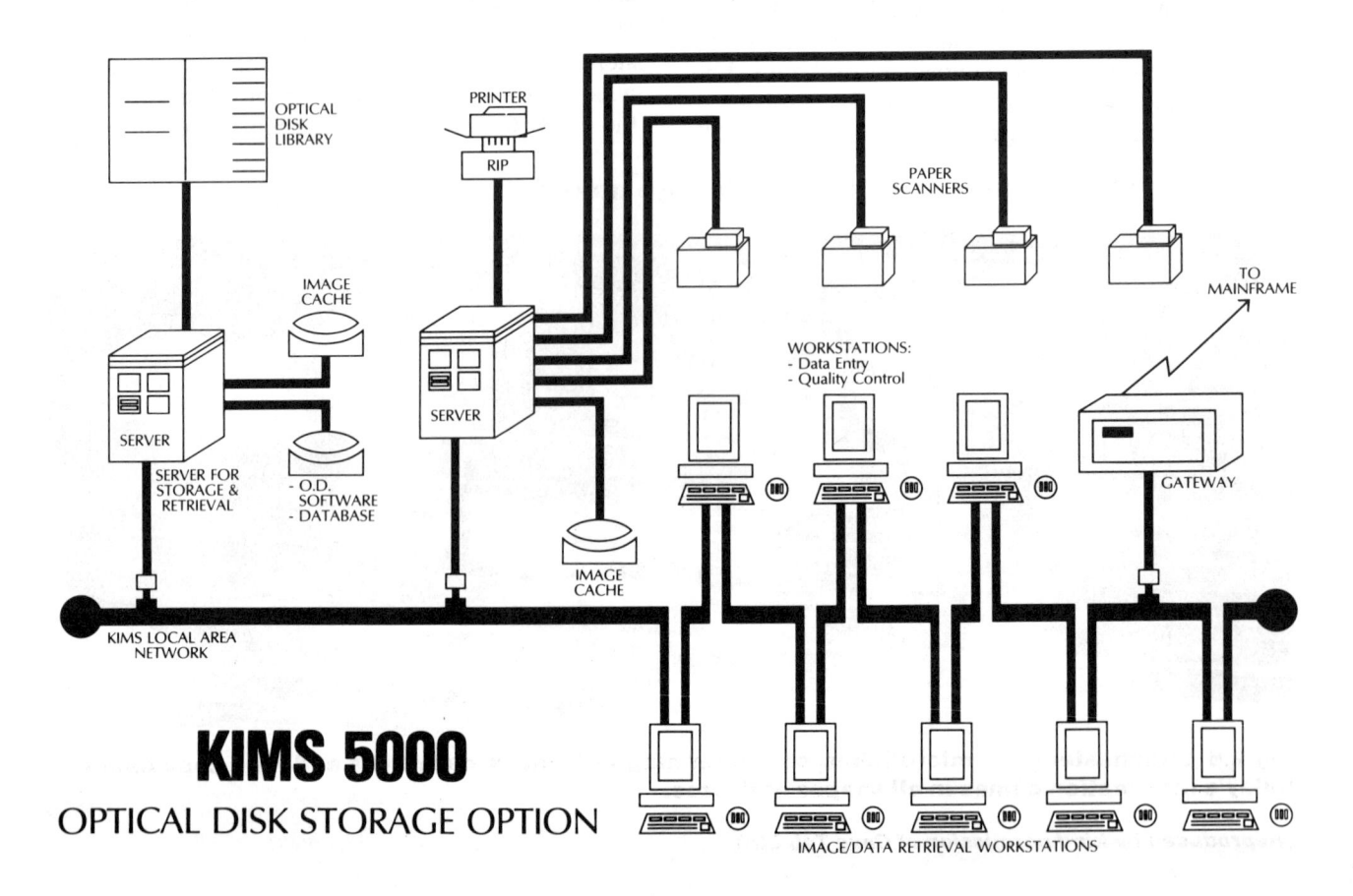

KIMS 5000
OPTICAL DISK STORAGE OPTION

had the preliminary start-up procedure done) and have its DOS (Disk Operating System) installed and the **software applications package** – word processing, database, spread sheet or management information system – inserted into the computer's temporary memory (which lasts until the terminal is switched off), or activated from its permanent residence within the computer's hard disk.

File creation

Each software application package will embody its own particular instruction for creating a file. Wordstar, for example, uses the key 'd' to instruct the computer to create a file, while Delta 4, a database package employs the key 'B' to enable the user to set up or define a data file from scratch. By the same token, similar quick-action instructions via keyboard or function keys permit the user to manipulate and store inserted data in whatever ways the software package can cope with, whether as text, graphics, columns of numbers or pictorial images. Today all software houses proudly advertise the user-friendliness of their packages and various help menus or accessible windows of extra information are readily to hand to enable the user to construct the file.

File interrogation

Undoubtedly the great attraction of computer-based records management for office personnel is the speed, versatility and flexibility with which created files may be summoned, interrogated or accessed for specific data they contain. For example, a database software package enables its user to set up an information file or card on each of, say, 100 university lecturers; essential data may be included on each – full name, age, address etc, and any useful category or, to use its technical name, field of information may be included, such as foreign languages spoken or detailed subject knowledge. Thus, if a visiting delegation of Latin American nuclear physicists is expected, the database may be interrogated to see which lecturers may speak Spanish or Portuguese and also possess a knowledge of applied nuclear physics. Moreover, such information is found and displayed on the VDU in a split second! A further, extremely helpful feature of electronic file interrogation is the search by key word facility which enables a sought-after file to be found and displayed by means of the computer looking for and finding a key word or phrase like 'file interrogation' which is included *somewhere* in the file created – without the user even needing to refer to a file name or index!

File saving and security

Crucial to the process of **electronic file creation and construction** is the capacity to save data which is being produced by means of save instructions – either to save VDU screens of keyed-in data until the file is completed, or to produce two permanent files on the hard or floppy disk, one to work from and refer to and the other as a back-up security copy in case the first is lost or destroyed in error. Naturally, the effective secretary takes pains to master the security systems which relate both to her independently performing desktop PC and the system which obtains when accessing data via an organisational mainframe. Here it is worth noting that the data processing (DP) departments in large organisations spend much time and effort in maintaining safe back-up security systems which may involve 'streamer tape' machines taking high-speed copies of hard disks for storage in locations remote from office buildings for prompt substitution in case of fire or electricity supply failure. One national UK computer company maintains an entire dual system of computer files and records for this reason at opposite ends of Great Britain.

Note that the Data Protection Act 1984 obliged employers to register the type of records they maintain and gave employees, customers and members of the public the right of access to see files about themselves.

Guide to major application software packages

Type of software application	Typical files
Word processing	Letters, memoranda, reports, articles, meetings documents, manuals, etc,
Database	Product key features and specifications, personnel records, stock control data, pupil/student records, patients' case histories, etc.
Spreadsheet	Regional sales turnover, monthly and rolling totals, sales representatives' expense records, payroll data, cash flow projections, etc.
Information management system (integrated package)	Limited versions of all of the above, plus: Electronic diary and appointments schedule, electronic notepad, graphics generator, electronic mail transmission and reception – file storage facility, etc.

Major advantages of computer filing systems

- Instant access to massive banks, files and databases of information.
- Data is constantly updated in large organisational unified databases.
- Remotely located terminals can access mainframe or minicomputer files in seconds.
- Data can be scrutinised either on screen or as a print-out.
- Data created on one file can be instantly transferred and incorporated on to another (eg spreadsheet table to WP report).
- Security is very good, allowing for graded levels of access to specific files and records.

Guidelines on electronic file management

Using a floppy disk system

- Always ensure you purchase top-quality floppy disks: avoid the false economy of buying cheap disks which corrupt and cause the loss of invaluable time and data.
- Take care to follow the maker's instructions for floppy disk storage, avoiding heat, humidity, direct sunlight and proximity to magnetic field sources etc.
- Make sure you are fully proficient in the procedures needed to format and copy disks on the PC you operate; always keep a supply of formatted blank disks to hand for immediate use and employ self-adhesive labels to label such disks using *only* a soft marker pen.
- *Never* use original software floppy disks as working disks: *always* make at least two copy sets – one for daily use and the other for emergencies and store your originals safely in case further copies are needed.
- Remember to make a careful note of any personal identity number you may be given by an application package in the course of its installation – you may need to quote it if you need to obtain further copies over and above those that the manufacturer ordinarily permits.
- Be sure to attach a small self-adhesive tag around the write-protect notch of the floppy disk if it holds files or application software you do not wish to have inadvertently over-written.
- Make it a regular habit to treat your floppy disks respectfully; they are essentially delicate and should be stored upright in paper wallets within dust-proof, lockable desktop boxes or cabinets when not in use.
- *Always* be security conscious in your handling of floppy disks – if left unattended, they are very easily and quickly copied.
- Keep all your user manuals and supportive cards of commands and function key features, etc, on a nearby shelf where they are safe and readily available for consultation.

Using a mainframe, mini or hard disk LAN system

- Make sure you are fully acquainted with the procedures in use for logging on and off the system.
- Keep any personal password code or name carefully secure; the loss or forgetting of passwords can cause a very great deal of inconvenience to DP managers on most mainframe/LAN systems so be warned!
- Remember to change your password periodically in order to maintain good security and avoid your confidential files being accessed improperly
- *Always* log off or 'lock up' your PC if you have to leave your desk, in order to avoid leaving WP text, etc visible on your VDU screen to be read at will by anyone wandering into your office!
- Make it a constant practice to record the names you give to files in a secure and readily accessible manner: this may be effected by creating a **file directory** as an electronic file either on a floppy or hard disk for VDU call-up, or as a manual file in a ring-binder:

FILDIR.89: DIRECTORY OF ELECTRONIC FILES 1989

AJBAX.24   A J Baxter & Sons Ltd Letter 24: Quotation for the supply of shop fittings 24/6/89 JJ/ABC

SALREPX.42   Sales Representatives Expenses: Month 42: June 1989

Note 1: Some secretaries now record the electronic file number as part of the customary reference given on documents, so that they can call up an electronic file copy at will:

Our ref: JJ/ABC/AJBAX.24

and similarly reference all print-out documents

Note 2: If a scanner is being employed to convert incoming paper documents such as letters into electronic files, a similar system of awarding each document an electronic file reference must be similarly introduced.

File saving and storage

- As a regular routine, save any work you are keying in at regular and *short* intervals by using the 'save and resume edit command' – almost every computer user has at least once lost valuable time and text by erasing a long entry which had not been saved.

- *Always* ensure that every file you create has been backed up by the computer – check this by referring to your A, B or C, etc Drive directory on completing a particular job.

- Diskcopy your working disks at regular intervals (if using a floppy disk system) so as to ensure you *always* have a fall-back copy of, say, that long, vital report wanted in two days' time!

- Remember to carry out regular file 'housekeeping', especially if using a hard disk or mini/mainframe terminal; delete files which are of first draft or obsolete data and archive those off the main memory which need to be kept. Avoid 'hogging' computer memory with unwanted files.

FILING AND DATABASE SOFTWARE APPLICATION PACKAGES

As a result of the extensive use of database software application packages in office administration it is important for today's secretary to have a thorough understanding of the principles of database software operations and an appreciation of the uses to which database software may be put.

Database terminology

There are a number of basic concepts which support the operation of a database application package.

Files of data

In the context of database terminology, the term 'file' stands for a series of related items of data. It helps to think of the 'file' as all those items which could be stored, in, say, the total number of suspended wallets of a drawer in a filing cabinet, provided that they all refer to the same root classification, such as, full-time staff, products' specifications or goods for sale held in stock etc.

Records within a file

Each file (in the database sense) will comprise a number of records. In the case of the above examples, this could be the information held on an *individual* full-time staff member, the specification of a motor-car's carburettor or the stock-card details relating to silver-wedding anniversary cards.

Fields within a record

Each individual record will be made up of a number of fields. A field is the term used to describe a particular sector of information into which the record is divided. The following example of a record within a stock file illustrates five chosen fields into which the record has been sub-divided:

Thus the display upon the VDU of the record shown below indicates that it relates to stock item number 123 (for identification purposes), that the item stocked is writing desks, that the desks are located in Warehouse A and that the current number in stock is 23. As the minimum stock level as indicated should be 50, then a reordering process should be set into motion directly.

Fig 2.9 Delta 4 database application package

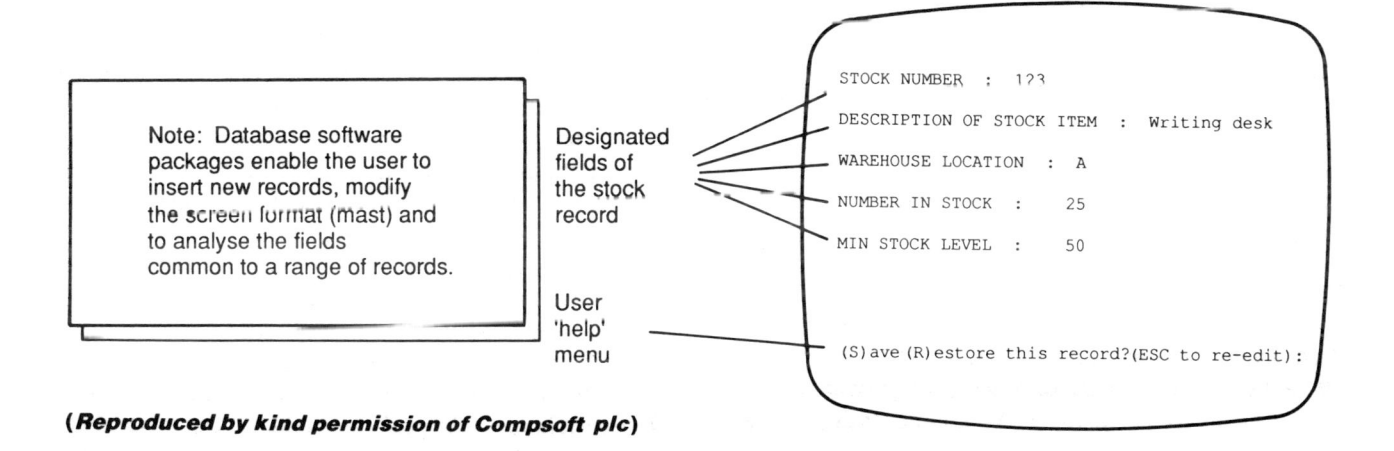

Note: Database software packages enable the user to insert new records, modify the screen format (mast) and to analyse the fields common to a range of records.

Designated fields of the stock record

User 'help' menu

```
STOCK NUMBER         :  123
DESCRIPTION OF STOCK ITEM  :  Writing desk
WAREHOUSE LOCATION   :  A
NUMBER IN STOCK      :  25
MIN STOCK LEVEL      :  50


(S)ave (R)estore this record?(ESC to re-edit):
```

(*Reproduced by kind permission of Compsoft plc*)

Interrogating a computer database

From a filing and records management viewpoint, one of the most attractive features of database software lies in its ability to permit its various fields to be scanned or interrogated and for selected data to be extracted and displayed in a trice on the VDU. For example, it would be possible on a database about stocks to include a field showing the purchase value of individual items, to display a current total for each record and therefore to be able to see at a glance by interrogation techniques built into the software:

1   The current value of a particular number of stock items, eg writing desks.

2   The sum of the value of a sector of stock records, eg office furniture,

3   The total value of all stock items held.

Alternatively, such data could be made to refer to warehouse contents' values or goods held in departmental chainstore branches. The records of a computer database may be compared in their flexibility to a blank page upon which the user draws or designs the required type of format and the nature and number of desired fields into which to locate data. As filing tools, databases are remarkably flexible and extremely time-saving and are nowadays employed in organisations ranging from the sole trader to the mammoth multinational.

MANUAL AND PAPER/CARD-BASED FILING SYSTEMS

Alongside the rapidly growing computerised records management systems are still their traditional, paper-based counterparts in which the secretary also needs to be fully expert.

Such systems use the various numerical, alphabetical, geographic and chronological classification methods outlined above, and the approach is inherently the same. Nevertheless, a number of important features remain to be examined, and these are set out below.

Vertical and lateral filing systems

In considering paper-based records systems, a practical starting point is to remember that, essentially, the vast majority of items to be stored will take the form of either individual paper documents of A4 or A5 size or sets of A4 sheets collated into minutes, reports, brochures etc. As a result, the techniques of filing associated with them all derive from the design of folders, wallets, receptacles and enclosing boxes or cabinets which permit such documents to be stored safely, accessibly and with a minimum of office space occupation.

The vertical filing system

As its name suggests, the vertical filing system describes a means of document or file storage which uses V-shaped wallets suspended from a set of parallel rails constructed within a drawer or compartment of a cabinet which may comprise 2–4 drawers.

Each V-shaped wallet acts as a receptacle for the papers to be filed under the title or name given to it and is identified by means of a flag or tab.

Within the file, letters, memoranda and other documents are likely to be stored chronologically. For example, a file may be set up to hold all the documentation which a sales department creates or receives in its business with, say, Alpha Products Limited. All received and transmitted correspondence held in the file is likely to be stored by date with the most recent letters lying at the top of the storage folder. Also, a system may be employed in which all letters sent out to Alpha Products limited are numbered consecutively, where Our ref: JJ/PD APL 128 refers to the one hundred and twenty-eighth letter composed since the file's creation.

Where a correspondence, say about an insurance claim, is protracted, the outgoing series of letters and replies received may be clipped together as a temporary working file.

The alphabetical system is frequently used in vertical filing and where a numerical system is employed, a key index is commonly kept at the front of the filing drawer for ease of reference.

Note: Some manufacturers of vertical filing cabinets market a means of joining wallets together in a kind of concertina shape at the top to avoid papers falling to the bottom of the drawer and thus becoming lost: always be on the guard against this type of mishap.

The lateral file

Again, the term lateral is descriptive, since in this system, files are stored side by side and their flags or tabs stick out for the user to consult from one side. A series of wallets hang from tracks which are suspended at heights within the filing cabinet which correspond to the depths needed to accommodate files lying on their sides (see Fig. 2.10).

As a rule, filing cabinets are some 2 metres high and 1.5 metres wide, with a capacity of five to six tiers of files. They are thus useful for offices which operate a significant number of active files, and security is achieved by means of lockable cabinet doors. However, lateral filing cabinets take up a good deal of

Fig 2.10 Lateral filing with colour coding, showing 'out' markers

(Reproduced by kind permission of Cave Tab Ltd)

office floorspace and are a luxury in expensive city locations. Similarly accessing top and bottom-most tiers is cumbersome, and tags in such tiers may be hard to read.

Automated/mobile lateral systems

Centralised filing units, – such as a company's technical library – often install automated filing systems in which racks of lateral files are constructed so as to move around upper and lower cogs, rather like an endless loop of trays. Thus the operator can summon up a required tier at will. A further source of assistance in such systems lies in the use of colour coding on files and tags or spines for prompt recognition and identification of a correct file location – a single blue strip in a block of red quickly identifies a misfiled wallet!

Visual filing systems

In addition to vertical and lateral filing designs, a range of visual systems exist, aimed at optimising ease of use and prompt location of data. Indeed the terms 'visual' or 'visible' are used to describe such systems, which include the following:

Rotary filing systems

Here files are inserted into free-standing, circular shelves constructed in columns which users can walk around. Visibility is good but they absorb a great deal of space.

Year planners and project charts

A variety of card or wipe-over charts are available either to pin or hinge to the office wall which display information like staff holiday rotas, key dates, branch visits, plant maintenance records, etc.

T-card slot Indexes

This system takes the form of a large metal framework of slots – like rows of breast pockets – into which coloured cards shaped like the letter T are slotted: main titles or labels are written across the lateral bar of the T and more detailed data down its vertical bar which rests inside the pocket. Such T-cards may be moved around the frame and this system is popular in offices controlling projects or the work of personnel who move from job to job.

Strip indexes

Strip indexes often take the form of metal-edged frames

with removable transparent inserts, beneath which a series of strips of card have been aligned in a particular sequence, each of which displays a piece of relevant information. For example, the displayed data may take the form of the names, addresses and telephone numbers of frequently used suppliers in a garage workshop to which mechanics may refer without greasing up a telephone directory.
Note: Sometimes such strip indexes are fixed around a central plinth as a rotary index.

Wipe-over whiteboards
Many office managers like to jot down memory-joggers and important information on wall-mounted whiteboards using coloured marker pens: while not particularly sophisticated this system is most effective in highlighting key information.

Desktop card indexes
Managers and secretaries alike often insert frequently used information on card-indexes stored in small boxes or pop-up A–Z files encased in spring-loaded metal containers.

Top secretary tip: filing
Computerised, electronic filing systems and their paper-based, manual counterparts are only as effective and reliable as the accurate and up-to-date information they contain. Therefore, no matter how busy you are, *always* make time to update or amend an entry upon receiving a change of address, job-title or telephone number, etc. This routine will pay handsome dividends when an office crisis occurs!

MICROGRAPHICS, MICROFORM AND MICROFILM

An important method of records management takes the form of the miniaturisation of original documents on to frames of film/photographic media. In the USA, this process is called micrographics. For years in the UK it has been known as microfilming, but perhaps it ought to be called 'microform' since this term reflects the various photographic forms that the miniaturisation can take.

Essentially, microform records are produced by the reverse of the process which enables us to have enlargements made of photographs which start out as contact prints. In microforming, special cameras take photographs of, say, A4 documents and reduce them by up to 105 times. In many popular processes, the reduction ranges between 24 and 48 times. As a result, an entire textbook could be transferred on to a set of microfiche cards or 100 foot roll of microfilm!

Furthermore, at higher ratios of reduction it is possible to store the Bible on a strip of microform known as Ultrastrip, no more than 20 cm long!

It is little wonder, then, that microform has been a popular source of record storage and archiving since its invention over 100 years ago. During the past decade, microform technology has taken a new lease of life by combining with computer-based data creation and retrieval techniques to produce Computer Output Microform (COM), Computer Input Microform (CIM) and Computer Aided Retrieval (CAR) – see below.

Types of microform

Roll film
As its name suggests, this type of microform comprises a continuous strip or roll of film made up of juxtaposed frames. Roll films occur primarily in 100- or 200-foot spooled lengths of 16 mm, 35 mm or 105 mm widths. A roll film may contain 2000–4000 individual frames, each one capable of holding the text and/or images of an A4 document on 16 mm film) or set of plans or designs on 105 mm film. While such a medium is ideal for archiving high-volume documents like sales invoices or purchase orders, it is a cumbersome way of storing data which needs to be referred to often, since the operator has to spool through the roll of juxtaposed frames in a linear sequence to arrive at the desired one. However, motorised scanning equipment has improved this situation – but at a price.

Micro jackets and fiches
Two popular media of microform are micro jackets and microfiches, which resemble one another. Both usually are constructed as a kind of card some 15 cm x 10 cm. The microjacket takes the form of a transparent sleeve into which strips of microfilm (say 12 frames long) or individual frames may be arranged in any desired sequence. A typical jacket might hold 30–40 frames. The microfiche embodies a similar structure but is made up of a single piece of microform divided into as many as 400 frames, depending upon the photographic reduction ratio employed.

Micro jackets and microfiches are read by means of a reader which magnifies each frame roughly back to the same size as the original document. (In fact many readers have screens A4 in size.) Some readers possess built-in printers to take a hard copy of the re-enlarged document and are called reader-printers. In this way, a copy invoice can be promptly resurrected from an archive, say, five years old. Micro jackets and fiches are very commonly found in libraries, bookshops, spare-parts departments of garages and stockrooms of manufacturers – in fact anywhere in which a large number of individual items needs to be catalogued, stored and located quickly. Where large numbers of microfiches are used regularly, it is

Information processing in the office

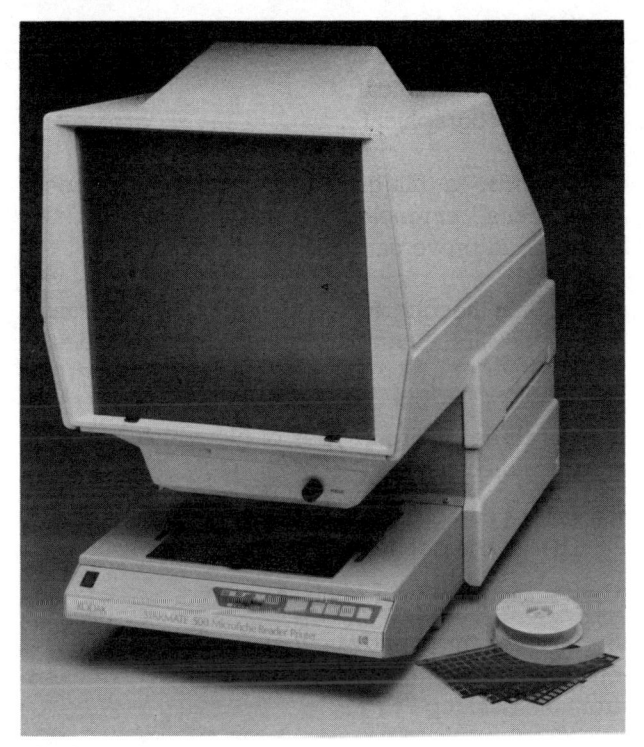

Fig 2.11 Microfiche reader with microfiches and microfilm roll

(Reproduced by kind permission of Kodak)

common practice to index each frame with a number and to catalogue each fiche with a title, etc, and some readers have a facility to take the operator directly to a predetermined frame.

Aperture cards

An aperture card usually holds a single piece of 35 mm film on to which has been recorded a single image – which may be the draughtboard-sized drawing of a single layer of a microprocessor's complex circuitry. The card (about 17.5 cm x 8 cm) also includes a space to hold explanatory notes, etc, and may be filed in a card index or punched hole storage medium for fast location.

Microform and the computer

The widespread expansion of computer-based records management in the 1970s and 80s caused microform equipment manufacturers to work hard to develop an integrated technology which would preserve their investment – and that already made by many large organisations. As a result, three major areas of joint technology were introduced:

Computer output microform (COM)

COM is a system which enables computer-created data to be transferred during its creation *direct* on to microfilm at speeds which emulate those of a laserprinter. The use of such equipment is perhaps best described by means of an example. A large manufacturing company may run its sales invoices for national accounts customers in batches at intervals throughout the month and in so doing potentially create vast piles of copy invoices for its own records. COM enables such company records to be produced directly on to microfilm and thus to save as much as 95% of the storage space needed and, as the process is simultaneous with the production of the paper-invoice for onward despatch, at no extra cost in time.

Computer input microform (CIM)

CIM is a process which enables a computer to read the data held on microform and to transfer it into a computerised electronic file for distribution and examination, etc. In this way it provides a facility very much like that of an OCR scanner.

Computer aided retrieval (CAR)

It is not uncommon nowadays for international companies to hold millions (if not billions) of microform records of past activities in research, production, accounts, sales, and purchases, etc. While the vast majority may remain dormant for years, occasionally – say in the unhappy event of an airline disaster – it may prove necessary to locate quickly the records of parts, specifications, sources of supply and personnel involved in manufacturing an aero engine or wing part which go back 5-10 years. In such cases CAR is invaluable, since it links the memory and classification power of the computer with the vast records storage capacity of the microform media.

Frequently computer and microfilm frame are linked by 'blip' squares – tiny boxes to record serial numbers, etc, which are printed on to each frame. As documents are microfilmed, a unique number is imprinted on to each frame which is also built into an indexing system on computer file. Thus the calling up of a given serial number enables the computer to find the file-roll or fiche in question and to display desired frame in a matter of seconds!

Records management and optical disks

While great strides have been made in integrating computers and microform systems – even to the extent of including a microform reading and printing facility on LAN/WAN networks – the development of the optical disk offers even more economical records and archive management systems. For example, a single 35 cm (14-inch) optical storage disk (rather like an LP record in appearance) is capable of holding the equivalent of 250 copies of *The Complete Works Of William Shakespeare*! While at present it is possible only to read the data on an optical disk and not to amend it (WORM technology = Write Once Read Many Times), the convenience of holding vast quantities of data in such a small space, and within a medium which is considered very safe from accidental damage or corruption is already proving very attractive to personnel managers, lawyers, librarians and scientists, despite the comparatively high cost of optical disks and associated equipment.

Summary

Mircoform technology has rightly earned a central place in the records management systems available to managers of all kinds of data Its plus factors include:

- Enormous savings in the space (and hence cost) needed to store paper documents.

- Data security and completeness: with microform storage, inividual files and records do not go astray and are not easily destroyed by accident.

- Costs: once the capital costs of installing equipment are recovered, the actual cost per frame of microforming can be measured in fractions of a penny.

- Information in microform is cheap and easy to send to widely distributed branches, offices or sites.

- Linked to a computerised management information system (MIS) microform can handle millions of records safely and swiftly.

As with any modern technology, a period of rapid technological change inevitably means that minus factors occur:

- To acquire a fully versatile microform facility is expensive in terms of cameras, lenses, reader-printers, and computer-linked equipment.

- A high standard of indexing and cataloguing skills is needed to manage a large system.

- Some processes, such as obtaining printouts and film copies, are time-consuming.

QUICK REVIEW QUIZ

1 What do you understand by the term 'branching database' in connection with filing data?

2 Explain how the decimal point referencing system works.

3 Can you say how long it is recommended to keep the following records?

    (a) balance sheets
    (b) tax records
    (c) cheque counterfoils
    (d) credit notes

4 Explain briefly how each of the following filing systems works:

    (a) numerical
    (b) alphabetical
    (c) chronological
    (d) geographical

5 Describe a filing need for which numerical, alphabetical, chronological and geographical systems would prove particularly appropriate.

6 Explain the difference between a hard disk and a floppy disk and where you would expect to find each in use.

7 List three different types of file which would be ideally stored on:

    (a) a computer database
    (b) a spreadsheet

Give reasons for your choices.

8 List five major advantages to the secretary of employing computerised filing systems accessed from the desktop PC.

9 Explain the difference between a 'file', a 'record' and a 'field' in database terminology.

10 For what purpose would a lateral filing system prove most appropriate?

11 Explain how the following work and in what situations they would be particularly useful:

    (a) a T-card slot index
    (b) a strip index

12 List three different types of microform and say for what applications they are most suited.

13 In what circumstances are microform record systems most useful?

14 What advantages stem from centralised support services in organisations?

ASSIGNMENTS

1 First, in a group of three to four students, organise your respective areas of investigation, choosing one of the following topics. Having carefully researched this topic, deliver a 5-10 minute oral presentation of your findings to your group:

    (a) The services a mailroom can provide for the departmental secretary.
    (b) Services currently available to despatch valuable articles to inland/overseas destinations, the type of insurance available and the costs involved.

Information processing in the office

- (c) The range of services offered by the Post Office's Datapost both in the UK and internationally.
- (d) The range of courier and delivery services available in your locality from private operators, and how prices compare with those of the Post Office for similar services.

2 Find out what kind of uses local firms are making of *either* a database software package *or* a spreadsheet package within an office context. Having carried out your investigations, produce a factsheet on one side of A4 which details the sort of use a secretary could make of the software you researched. Copy your factsheet to your class members and discuss your suggestions.

2.4 Visitors to the office

First impressions; receiving vistors; visitors calling into the office; sources of information and support in reception; personal qualities need for reception; the office environment.

The act of receiving visitors or organisational staff into the manager's office suite is extremely important for a number of reasons. The ability of a secretary to perform the often very demanding role of effective receptionist quite rightly ranks high among her accomplishments and as a component of the secretary's make-up deserves careful study.

FIRST IMPRESSIONS

As customers, clients or callers, our sensibilities are at their keenest when we first visit a department, suite of offices or business complex. We are quick to notice tired noticeboards with yellowing, dog-eared bulletins pinned on top of each other and also to spot yellowing potted plants, drooping from neglect and cigarette stubs. Likewise, we tend to be particularly impatient if our arrival goes unnoticed, or if noticed, unheeded, as a careless receptionist continues a gossiping conversation with a colleague. In short, the appearance of a reception area and the attitude of staff towards receiving visitors says a very great deal about the overall efficiency and caring attitude of an entire organisation. For this very reason, most organisations go to great lengths in designing and fitting out reception areas and in training staff to become effective ambassadors of the organisation as well as receptionists.

The reception area

It is customary for secretaries to be given the responsibility for ensuring that the reception area of the office suite in which they work is properly cared for and maintained. The following paragraphs highlight those aspects which require regular attention if visitors are to enjoy what may be their first, all-important experience of the organisation:

Furniture

At least one armchair or easy chair and one upright chair should be installed in the reception area (the latter for visitors who may find it difficult to use a chair with a low squab); in addition a coffee-table is needed for visitors to set down coffee cups or tea cups and refreshments comfortably; a magazine rack is useful and prevents newspapers and magazines becoming a messy pile on the table. Essential is a full-length cupboard or coat rack for use in wet and winter weather, with a drip-pan incorporated into its umbrella rack.

Magazines and reading matter

Some organisations use the reception area cleverly as a means of creating good public relations – the latest copies of a company newsletter or quarterly journal are always included in the available reading matter; publishing houses also usually set their latest publications on display for clients to browse through, while manufacturers often display colour brochures and photographs of their most recent components or products.

It also pays to subscribe to at least one quality daily newspaper and weekly news or business magazine – all organisations like to show that they are alert and aware of what is going in the world. By the same token, many firms display trade journals and magazines relevant to their line of business.

Indoor plants and flower arrangements

Increasingly, visitors and office staff are becoming aware of the importance of creating and maintaining an office environment which is visually and aesthetically pleasing; living plants and flowers add precious

Fig 2.12 Reception area at the TSB

(Reproduced by kind permission of Plessey)

colour and flowing form to the inert, angular lines of office furniture and fittings. Well-tended plants and flowers demonstrate a caring and thoughtful environment and help to set a visitor at ease.

Lighting and decor

Interior lighting is a very important feature of a reception area and should provide sufficient reading light (60 100 watts) in the seating area, while creating a warm and pleasant atmosphere elsewhere, perhaps by means of concealed lighting or opaque lampshades.

The design and texture of wall and window coverings are also very important in the reception areas. Traditionally green and blue hues provide a calm atmosphere, while reds and yellows tend to convey impressions of harshness, if not aggressiveness. By the same token, carefully chosen pictures and frames posters can communicate a sense of either reliability and tradition, or a self-confident, avant-garde image.

Refreshments

Almost every office reception area today has access either to a nearby beverage vending machine or coffee/tea-making equipment. Indeed, the ability to offer a visitor a hot drink goes a long way towards coping with an unexpected delay.

Access to an outside telephone line

The provision of a telephone extension in the seating area is especially useful if a visitor wishes to make use of an enforced delay but, clearly, an organisation needs to decide as a matter of policy how far it is prepared to go to subsidise visitors' telephone-calls.

RECEIVING VISITORS

Many organisation's have evolved strict rules about receiving visitors. For example, in the organisation's general reception foyer, each and every visitor (especially in firms where product design or work in progress must be kept totally confidential) is asked to 'log in' by filling out an entry line of a Visitors' Book or Reception Register. An example is shown on page 66.

Having signed in, the visitor may then be given an identification lapel badge or pass, and some compan-

Fig 2.13 Reception register

DATE	ARRIVAL	NAME	ORGANISATION	TO SEE	LEAVING TIME	
22/6/89	11.00	Jack Brown	Apex Office Systems	Jean Watts	11.45	Sometimes completed by receptionist

ies with a developed security sense may even take a photograph of the visitor and laminate it to the badge. At all events, the prevalence of industrial espionage and the cool nerve of its perpetrators have ensured that in very few instances will a visitor get past general reception unescorted by a company employee and without having produced his credentials to prove his identity and reason for calling. For reasons of security, secretaries are often telephoned from general reception to collect a visitor and escort him to the manager's office, provided that he has an appointment.

In order to ensure that expected visitors are accorded a courteous and appropriate treatment, many organisations operate a daily appointments schedule which is compiled at least a day in advance by the general receptionist from information supplied by an organisation's departmental secretaries. (See Fig. 2.14 below)

Such information enables the visitor to be smoothly and efficiently greeted and for security and escorting aspects to be handled without embarrassment:

'Miss King, I'm ringing to say that Mrs Williams — Mr Cartwright's visitor – has arrived in reception, if you'd be kind enough to come down to meet her.'

VISITORS CALLING INTO THE OFFICE

Not all organisations possess general reception areas to regulate visitors' arrivals and so the secretary working in an internal office suite must always be ready to assume the role of courteous but effective receptionist. The following guidelines set out the major aspects of good reception practice which all managers appreciate:

Unknown visitors

When someone arrives whose identity is unknown, it is essential that his or her identity, organisation and reason for calling are courteously but carefully established at the outset. For this reason many business and government executives or officials carry business cards to help establish their credentials.

At this point it is prudent to avoid conveying whether the manager is 'in' or 'out', since visitors without appointments can take up precious time in a day dedicated to, say, the completion of an urgent report. Indeed some companies have a policy whereby visitors may only be seen by appointment (particularly the benighted sales representative). Again, some managers and secretaries evolve tactics which enable the secretary either 'to see if he's in', or to move out of the reception area and to ask the manager, personally, whether he is prepared to see the visitor without an appointment. If the answer is 'no', then the secretary must have a ready repertoire of excuses with which to terminate the visitor's call. While it is customary for secretaries to adopt the gatekeeper role in such matters, it is always worth remembering that over-protectiveness can prove counter-productive, as in the sales cartoon in which a besieged baron is busily supervising the hurling of oil and rocks on to his enemies while behind him a sales rep is waiting his moment to deliver his sales pitch about the machine-gun his firm of medieval armour-

Fig 2.14 Appointments schedule

Date Day Time (From To)	Wednesday 12 September 11.30 – 12.00 pm		
Name Organisation	To See:	Dept.	Floor 16
Alice Hurst Yellow Pages	John Wright, Advertising Manager	Room No. 209	

ers has just invented; the caption is:

Baron: 'Don't waste my time – can't you see I've got a fight on my hands?'

In such matters, the effective secretary uses her judgement!

Operating the appointments diary

The unexpected visitor's departure may be eased if he at least secures a definite appointment for a later date. Appointment requests may also result from a telephone call. It is therefore important for the secretary as receptionist to develop thoughtful appointment-making skills. Here a discussion with the manager at the outset of one's secretarial appointment is essential to establish preferred approaches. Some managers deliberately restrict the number of hours or half-hours each day which they are prepared to devote to visitors. For others, like company buyers, however, interviews with visiting suppliers' salesmen may be the bread of life! At all events, these tips provide a balanced approach:

Tips on making appointments

1 Choose days and times carefully and *always* check the other events of the day or week surrounding the proposed appointment, to judge whether the time can be given to the appointment.

2 Keep appointment times down to what you judge to be an acceptable minimum of time – then if they run over they will not have proved unduly time-consuming.

3 Avoid appointments immediately prior to lunchtimes and in the late afternoons.

4 Never over-commit the manager to appointments on a single day – remember his other priorities and commitments.

5 Always make a note in your diary to fetch out the appropriate customer's file or relevant documents for an appointment in good time for the manager to peruse *beforehand*.

6 Take the trouble to remind the manager of imminent appointments and find a plausible excuse to rescue him from appointments which are clearly overrunning – he will always make it clear if he wants the appointment to carry on.

7 Always be aware of hospitality expectations and ask if coffee or tea is wanted.

8 When making the entry for an appointment in the diary, be sure to note clearly the name, designation and organisation of the visitor and a clear detail of the reason for the appointment – 'Mr Smith 4.00 pm' is pretty feeble and has been known to cause managers to pale if their MD happens to be called Smith!

9 Always remember that there are other members of your department or office team – section heads, junior executives and the like who may be called upon to receive visitors in order to relieve pressure on the manager, depending on the nature of the call.

SOURCES OF INFORMATION AND SUPPORT IN RECEPTION

The well-organised secretary will ensure that helpful sources of information and support are to hand for use in the reception context. These include:

- A regularly updated version of the organisation's internal telephone directory of extension numbers and a schedule of company personnel names, designations and locations.

- A set of local/national telephone/telex/fax directories.

- Appropriate handbooks and Yearbooks, such as: *Kelly's Directory Of Streets*, *The Municipal Year Book*, British Rail Timetables etc.

- A schedule of key telephone numbers including those for use in emergency, the manager's home telephone number, the company doctor/nurse, the duty security officer, etc.

- Details of the organisations' instructions and arrangements for emergency evacuation and assembly points.

- A first aid kit and manual.

- Duplicate maps of the organisation's premises and grounds (to help guide visitors) and maps/plans of the locality.

- Telephone/spoken word message pad and notebook to take messages and to log callers and visitors.

- A visible system to log office staff as 'in' or 'out'.

PERSONAL QUALITIES NEEDED FOR RECEPTION

As you can see, there is an art to effective reception and as with most secretarial roles, practice makes perfect. In order to minimise the practice and hasten the perfection, keep in mind the following personal qualities the good secretary-as-receptionist displays:

- **A cheerful, courteous manner** – Who would want to be met by a surly, off-hand and irritable secretary?
- **A polite but firm manner when eliciting information** – It does no harm to demonstrate that you are on top of your job and can handle people: sometimes you may need to deal firmly with persistent salesmen with no appointments, or overbearing visitors presuming upon a brief acquaintance with the manager.
- **Diplomacy and tact** – Always remember that no one likes to lose face or be exposed by 'being put down'. Comments like 'I'm very sorry that Mr Brown is unable to see you today, but he would be glad if you made an appointment for early next week ...' help to let disappointed visitors down gently.

Fig 2.15 Example of completed message using a pre-printed message pad

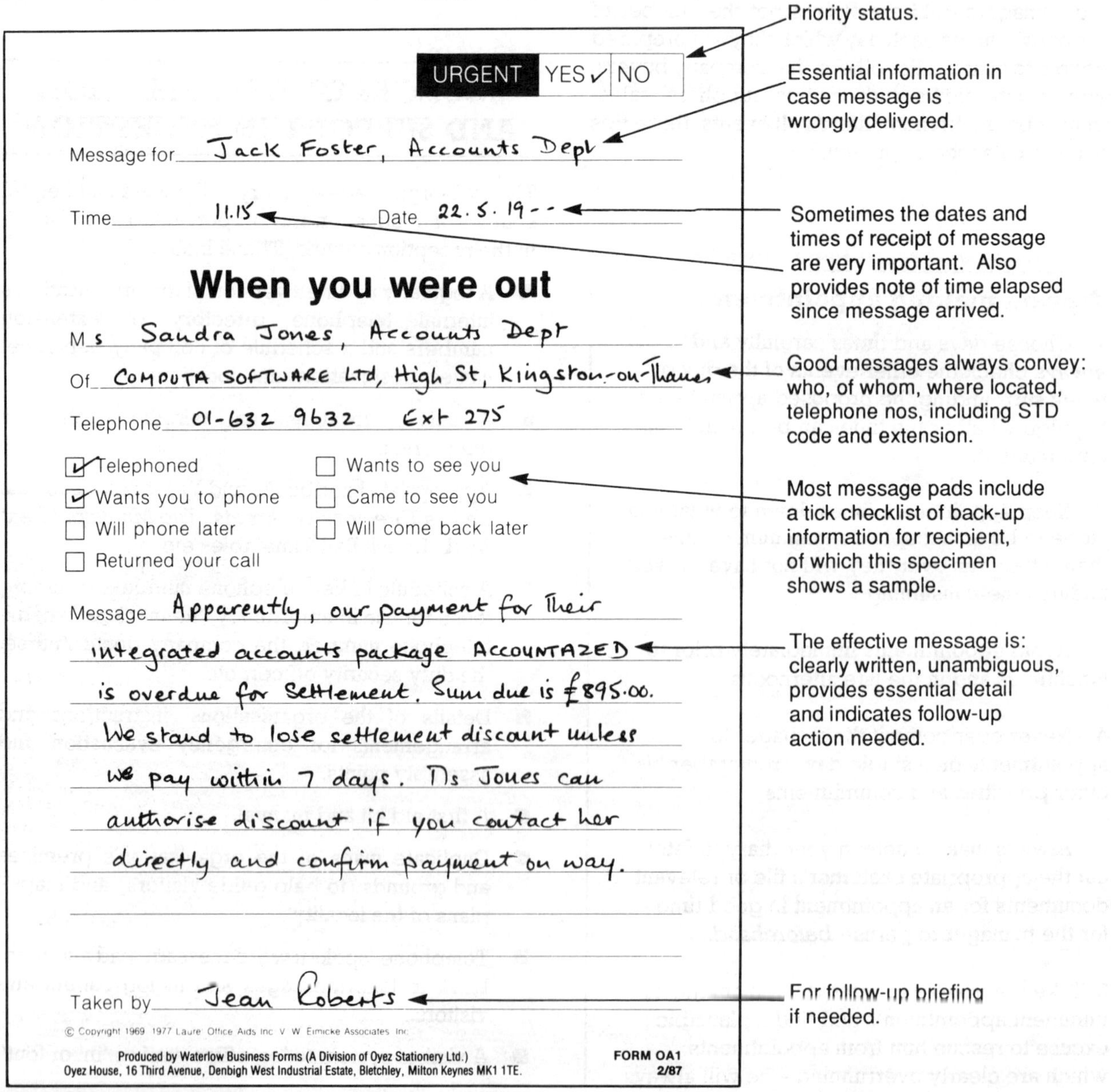
URGENT YES ✓ NO
Message for Jack Foster, Accounts Dept
Time 11.15 Date 22.5.19--
When you were out
Ms Sandra Jones, Accounts Dept
Of COMPUTA SOFTWARE Ltd, High St, Kingston-on-Thames
Telephone 01-632 9632 Ext 275
✓ Telephoned
✓ Wants you to phone
Will phone later
Returned your call
Wants to see you
Came to see you
Will come back later
Message Apparently, our payment for their integrated accounts package ACCOUNTAZED is overdue for settlement. Sum due is £895.00. We stand to lose settlement discount unless we pay within 7 days. Ms Jones can authorise discount if you contact her directly and confirm payment on way.
Taken by Jean Roberts
© Copyright 1969 1977 Laure Office Aids Inc V W Eimicke Associates Inc
Produced by Waterlow Business Forms (A Division of Oyez Stationery Ltd.)
Oyez House, 16 Third Avenue, Denbigh West Industrial Estate, Bletchley, Milton Keynes MK1 1TE.
FORM OA1
2/87
Priority status.
Essential information in case message is wrongly delivered.
Sometimes the dates and times of receipt of message are very important. Also provides note of time elapsed since message arrived.
Good messages always convey: who, of whom, where located, telephone nos, including STD code and extension.
Most message pads include a tick checklist of back-up information for recipient, of which this specimen shows a sample.
The effective message is: clearly written, unambiguous, provides essential detail and indicates follow-up action needed.
For follow-up briefing if needed.

(Reproduced by kind permission of Waterlow Business Forms)

Information processing in the office

- **Efficient organisational skills** – Close attention to detail always repays in reception duties. Both visitor and manager alike will have good reason to take you to task if carelessness results in a double appointment booking or the arrival of a visitor with an appointment when the manager is out.

THE OFFICE ENVIRONMENT

Architects, construction companies, office furniture and equipment designers, air-conditioning manufacturers and work study experts are all having to pay much more attention today to the needs of employees working in multistorey **open-plan** offices.

The plight of office workers falling sick with disturbing frequency in some office blocks has aroused journalists' attention and has been given the initials SOS, standing for 'sick office syndrome'. Investigations revealed serious shortcomings in air-conditioning systems – instead of fresh air being regularly introduced, stale air was being recycled! Unpleasant background odours – a blend of electrical, disinfectant, cigarette smoke and cleaning fluid smells – were found to be increasing, sapping energy and causing distraction. Office lighting tended to be either insufficient and poorly located or glaring and causing headaches. Desks and chairs were often badly matched, resulting in aches in the neck, arm and back. Noise from equipment inside the office combined frequently with that of outside traffic to undermine concentration and cause mistakes.

All too often, routine office safety precautions were being ignored by staff, or given too casual a profile by management. Staff were being crammed into dreary office surroundings in need of renovation which contributed to absenteeism, prolonged sick leave and high staff turnover.

Given the woeful state of offices as described above, it is little wonder that there is an urgent need for office designers and fitters to review from the bottom up the cause of stress, pressure and illness rooted in poor office environments and to improve their plans, layouts and systems accordingly.

Good office design

Fortunately, many companies and government agencies take a lead in improving such matters by appointing office environment managers, in-house office designers and information systems experts. Similarly, the science of **ergonomics** is being much more extensively applied to office furniture and equipment to allow for individuals' needs, sizes and work operations.

Fig 2.16 Open-plan office

(*Courtesy of IBM UK Ltd*)

The British Standards Institute has laid down specifications for lighting, VDU screens and noise levels in offices, and the 1974 HASAW Act has done much to make office managers more aware of design factors which promote output and minimise accidents.

Indeed, in the past decade there have emerged companies which, like shopfitters, undertake the complete fitting out and equipping of offices. Electrical and telecommunications contractors now 'plumb in' wires and flexes within pillars and skirting boards so as to avoid trailing wires. 'Systems furniture' designers have introduced suites purpose-built for the IT office age. Landscape office designers have improved former failings like noise, lack of privacy and poor ventilation, which spread colds and 'bugs', all of which made open-plan offices unpopular among employees.

Playing an active role in sustaining your 'life support system'

As a secretary, you should maintain a vigilant attitude towards the office environment in which you work, by actively discouraging antisocial behaviour, such as smoking, and encouraging responsible and caring attitudes among colleagues sharing an often busy and sometimes crowded floor area. Indeed, if your office is situated on the 24th floor of a high-rise office block, the comparison between your 'life support system' and that of a space-roaming astronaut is not so far-fetched!

The following checklist identifies major aspects of good office design and maintenance for you to consider and discuss with your fellow students.

Features of good office design

- Satisfying current legislation: toilets, restroom, room-space per employee, adequate heat and light, etc.
- Consideration of personnel work flow associated with moving around the office area so as to avoid congestion and possible accidents.
- Setting up work groups or teams in clusters; optimising access between staff who work closely together.
- Standardising on equipment to simplify procedures and staff training and to reduce costs.
- Allowing for privacy and confidentiality – enclosed interview rooms may form part of an open-plan design.
- Catering for aesthetics by creating pleasing visual and tactile effects with colour, fabrics, surfaces, materials, etc.
- Minimising noise problems with acoustic ceiling-hung baffle panels, acoustic screens and covers.
- Ensuring that the installation is flexible – panels and screens may be re-sited to provide for a fresh layout in the light of changed needs.
- Giving employees an opportunity to impose a personal identity on work areas through photographs, brought-in flowers, ornaments, etc.

This checklist – not exhaustive – proves a tall order for employers to satisfy when the constraints are considered:

- Meeting legal requirements.
- Minimising costs of floor-space rental, heat, light and rates bills, etc.
- Affording the 'high-tech' equipment of current electronic office technology.
- Coping with the status and hierarchy structures within the company.
- Avoiding customers and visitors overhearing either confidential discussions or being embarrassed by heated exchanges among staff.

In the context of office design, and the evolution of open-plan offices, the needs of the staff and the overall costs of maintaining offices are not easy to reconcile. For example, the traditional self-enclosed office box – four walls, a door and a window looking out over the car-park – minimised the stress of working as part of a group since the occupant could determine whom he saw and who saw him, and could hold confidential discussions without having to use a *sotto voce* level of conversation. On the other hand, such office boxes did little to promote effective communication face-to-face among personnel, who tended – especially if managers – to become isolated from the daily doings of the work-place, ie the general office.

In some open-plan offices, the trade-off is reversed in that, while communications and involvement may improve, the qualities of privacy, confidentiality and control of who takes up an individual's time may worsen.

Some **'turnkey' office systems** have attempted to resolve this problem by supplying both shoulder-high partitions and plastic corner windows affixed to them, as well as more traditional roof-high partitions to form offices for senior staff, training and conference rooms and so on.

Perhaps the most encouraging trend in the development of modern office layouts is that the lines of demarcation, such as seniority and status, which separate staff as a whole are becoming much more blurred. Both senior and junior staff now occupy the same open access areas within a complex, either as offices, restaurants, or social/rest areas.

DISCUSSION TOPIC

How do you think design is likely to evolve in the future? What changes would you like to see? Why?

Information processing in the office

QUICK REVIEW QUIZ

1 What steps does a firm take to ensure security when receiving visitors?

2 What helpful resources would you expect to find in a well-run reception area?

3 What categories of essential information should a well-designed message pad provide space for?

4 Draw up a checklist of the features of good office design.

5 List the advantages and disadvantages of landscape/open-plan offices for employees and management.

6 How would you handle a visitor in reception whose appointment has been delayed?

RESEARCH AND REPORT BACK ASSIGNMENT
Office layout and design

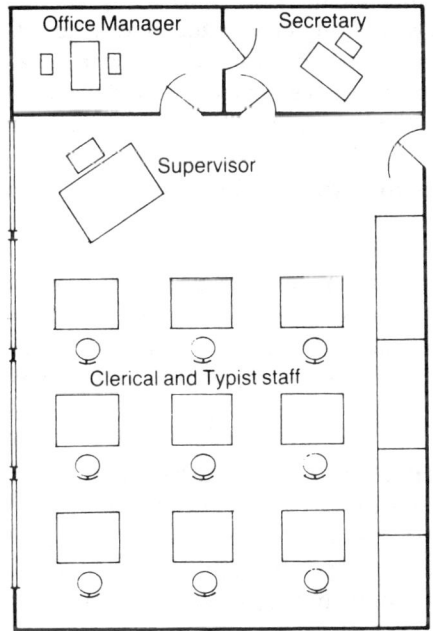

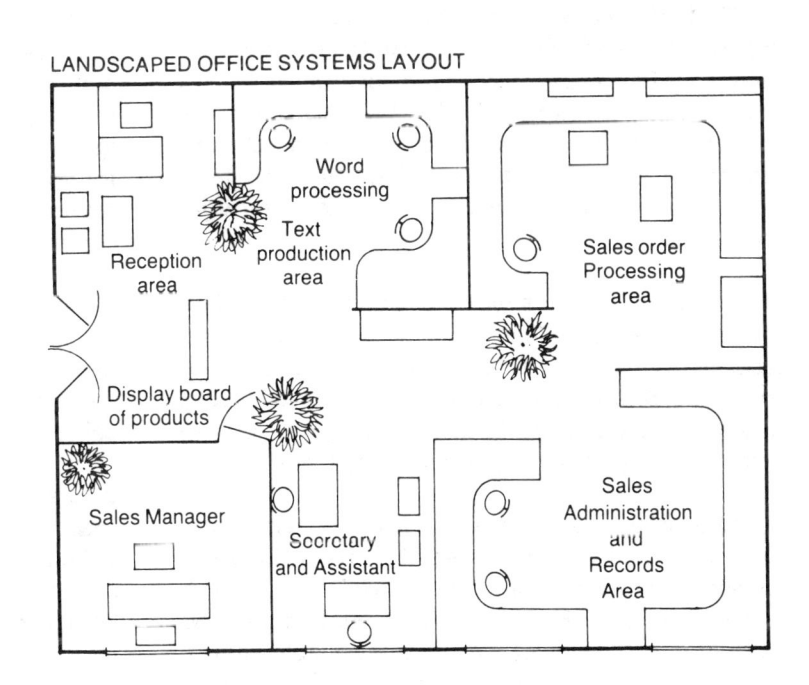

TRADITIONAL OFFICE LAYOUT

LANDSCAPED OFFICE SYSTEMS LAYOUT

Arrange in groups of three to four to visit local offices which are set out along landscape/systems office lines. Interview staff in order to find out what working in such an environment is like, what changes have resulted from IT systems installations and what advice they can give to make the best use of such work areas.

Discuss your findings with your fellow students, highlighting instances of good design, layout and work systems you discovered.

Unit 2
Summary of main points

1 **The office as an information processing centre.** Essentially, offices take in, process and store and then distribute information, while securing regular feedback as to its effectiveness.

2 **Today's secretary uses a range of IT equipment and systems for routine tasks.** Fax, telex, CABX, answering machines, desktop PC, scanner, viewdata terminal, LAN/WAN networks etc. in which computerised systems have replaced more traditional paper-based ones. Fax, telex and telephone answering machines will store overnight messages.

3 **Specific routines exist for sorting incoming mail efficiently.** Checking envelopes for missed enclosures, keeping related papers together, date stamping, prioritising, sorting into sequenced stacks (most important item first), advising manager/executives **directly** of any important/tricky matter.

4 **Outgoing mail options.** Inland – first-class, second-class; Royal Mail Special Delivery, Datapost sameday/overnight; railway airway letters; motor-cycle couriers. *Note*: recorded and registered delivery services for important/valuable items. Overseas: Datapost International, Swiftair, Express Delivery.

5 **Establishing effective diary routines.** Ensure either that there is *one* manager/secretary diary, or that regular checks to keep both fully in accord are made; manager and secretary should use the same codes/abbreviations; ensure that enough information is entered so as to be understood at a later date; have daily diary conference meetings.

6 **Key features of an electronic diary.** Calendar year display and five-year rolling diary; scanning by page, week and month; flagging up of memory joggers at required dates; search facilities for next available meeting time of executives; notepad feature for fuller details of a meeting/appointment scheduled; blocking out of time for uninterrupted work etc.

7 **Effective management of time.** Always plan ahead; use diaries, year planners, databases, etc, to record data you cannot be expected to remember; develop time-saving aids, eg abbreviated telephone number directory on CABX switchboard, often-used names and addresses on PC database; plan text processing and work filing around manager's absences when possible; use bring-forward systems as memory-joggers, set up systems for periodic routine jobs, eg reordering stationery; delegate what you can for your manager to departmental staff and tell him; review regularly what you are doing and why; drop superseded routines.

8 **Systems for classifying information.** Dewey Decimal System; hierarchical/branching database; decimal point reference system; alphabetical/numerical sequencing; chronological or geographical arrangement.

9 **Factors influencing the design of records management systems.** Time of records' currency, volume of records, speed of access needed, length of active life of record, type of medium the record is held in, cost of storage, and legal requirements to be met.

10 **Filing on disk – important factors.** Making detailed records of contents of files with file names; 'saving' frequently while processing data and copying files and disks regularly for security 'back-up' purposes; storing files/disks securely from fire or unauthorised access.

11 **Types of application software for processing/storing data.** Word processing – text, number, (and graphics if part of integrated package); spreadsheet – number manipulation and calculation; database – files of information, like paper forms, which can be interrogated and specific data extracted; graphics – for designing graphs, charts, diagrams and presenting statistical information (see also Unit 4); information management integrated packages for merging information created. The Data Protection Act 1984.

12 **Filing systems**. Computer-based cabinet and cupboard: vertical – paper files dropped into wallets arranged in sequence; lateral – files slotted into hanging wallets from outer side; mobile/rotating systems – files are held in containers which can revolve to provide access; free-standing pillars – files slot into a column which can be walked around; visual filing systems: year-planners, T-card systems, strip indexes, wipe over whiteboards, desktop card-index drums.

13 **Microform storage media**. Roll film, micro jackets, microfiches, aperture cards – all miniaturised photographed documents on film for recall on a reader-printer. Note also: computer output microform (COM), computer input microform (CIM) and computer aided retrieval (CAR) in which computers work with microform processes to find and display archives at high speeds.

14 **Important features of an effective reception area**. Clean, comfortable furniture, thoughtful lighting, up-to-date reading material, available refreshments, access to a telephone/fax, discreet decor/decorations, fresh flowers, plants; good security and reception techniques – visitors' book, name badges, staff to receive visitors, sufficient directories and references including regularly updated internal staff directory.

15 **Effective message-taking**. Always obtain name, designation, organisation address details of unknown visitors or telephone callers; note time and date of telephone messages and for whom, indicate if urgent; write down message clearly and unambiguously and sign it, make note of telephone number(s) where caller can be reached; make sure message-receiver is told of message's arrival promptly – note the value of electronic mail here.

16 **Factors involved in good office design**. Individual 'living space', ventilation/air-conditioning, temperature/humidity control, lighting, ergonomically designed seating and furniture, personal hygiene facilities (restrooms, lavatories), workflow arrangements, decor and decorations, noise minimalisation, privacy/confidentiality, concealed wiring and water/heating plumbing, room for personal items.

17 **Advantages/disadvantages of open-plan offices**. *Pluses* – more economic use of floor space; easier access to people; improved communications and group work; lower fuel costs, more cost-effective use of equipment through sharing – for support staff also; installation of unified systems furniture enhances appearance. *Minuses* – office areas more crowded, lack of privacy and confidentiality, increased noise levels, tendency for infections to spread more rapidly among staff; sharing equipment leads to delays.

Further sources of information

Information Processing, E Mullins, Pitman
Office Skills, T Foster, Stanley Thornes Publishers Ltd
The Electronic Office, Chaudbury and Agley, Edward Arnold
Information Technology at Work, D Davies, Heinemann Educational Books
Telephone and Reception Skills, Stanley Thornes Publishers Ltd
Office Technology Terms, E King, Chambers Commercial Reference
Business videos: *The Sunday Times* in association with Taylor Made Films
  Word Processing
  Spreadsheets
  Accounts
  Databases
  Communications
  Desktop Publishing

ACTIVITIES

**From traditional secretary to communications officer – by way of a computerised office system!
A case history**

by Alison George, Communications Officer, Personnel Department, IBM UK Limited Havant Plant

Having taken a secretarial course at school, I set out as a 'traditional secretary'. To me, the word 'traditional' meant everything from making the tea, taking shorthand, making carbon copies in threes, producing Banda and wax stencil copies, typing on heavy machines, relying on erasers for corrections, using a large folder as my bring forward system, and doing a massive amount of paper filing.

Having only used a computer system on a few occasions – mainly for storing information, rather than working with it – I met my first computerised office system at IBM. At that time I was personal secretary to the Plant Director with only six months experience of working with a computer-based office system.

There were a dozen or so Functional Managers reporting to the Director and Assistant Plant Manager at that time, with nearly two hundred managers reporting to them. Consequently, the flow of information was vital in such a situation – and what an asset I found the office system to be!

The system with which I work is connected through a

network which joins all IBM locations worldwide. Havant's own system provides three main menus, one specifically designed for secretarial work, one for managers, and a third which offers various extra facilities.

The computer-based office system is an extension of the various facilities I work with which gives me an opportunity to be more efficient. The basic rule is to be methodical. If you always tackle tasks in a similar way, you will always be able to search for and find information in the system.

Let me mention some of the ways in which my 'PROFS' (Professional Office System) system has helped me to improve my capabilities.

The electronic diary

There are a number of advantages in using an electronic system diary as against its traditional bound-book counterpart.

For example, a meeting can be arranged and 'booked' in several managers' diaries simultaneously at a time and date suited to all. Such meetings may be booked with ease throughout the year. Also, both secretary and manager can view the same diary and events or appointments may be very simply copied from one person's diary to another's. Periods of time – a week, a month – may be readily scanned and sections printed as needed. Moreover, notes and memory-joggers can be added and identifiers included with every type of meeting entry.

It is difficult to think of any disadvantages of the electronic diary, save that once having deleted an entry, you cannot even see any clues to where it once was, like the indentation marks of a pencilled note! This being so, we tend to add the words 'cancelled' or 'moved to an entry rather than deleting it altogether.

Different secretaries and managers have evolved their own ways of working with the electronic diary, but my usual routine as a secretary was to leave a print-out of the next day's meetings etc. on my manager's desk for his attention before leaving each evening, as he might wish to use the diary before my arrival the following morning.

Document storage – filing

There are a number of ways of accessing a document which has been filed onto your **mail-log**. An identifier may be added to it – three letters identifying its subject. Alternatively, a search may be set up for it using a 'key word' identifier – a word which will distinguish it from other documents, like 'appraisal' or 'induction'. Again, the document may be found by effecting a search by date or subject-matter or its author.

Effective searching requires care in selecting the search 'definers'. An important rule-of-thumb here is: 'The less you put in, the more you get out'. In other words, it is essential to key in a definer word or phrase as close as possible to the item sought. For example, supposing you were to search for a document entitled: MANAGEMENT DECISIONS. All would be fine, provided that you remembered its exact title. If, however, you set up a search of MANAGING DECISIONS, you would not find the sought-after document, if all you did was to initiate a search based on 'MANAG'. Instead, up would come a host of document titles on managing or management!

Document sequencing – the electronic staple

As you will be aware, many documents tend to be created in sequences. For example, a two-way correspondence between, say, your manager and a Mr Smith may well be filed together in a chronological sequence within a vertically filed wallet inside a filing cabinet. With a computerised office system, your manager could display any one item of the correspondence on his VDU simply by keying in its document reference number on his desktop PC!

Such a simple and quick procedure may be used to view an entire set of correspondence in sequence, which is, in effect, electronically 'stapled' together!

The management system and bring forward procedures

Being responsible for coordinating a range of activities involving both managers and their secretaries, it was essential that I had a system which I could use to establish the status of a project – what had been achieved, to progress chase as necessary and to respond to mail through managers' secretaries.

So, when sending a document for action through the system's electronic messaging channels, it was customary for a 'buckslip' to accompany it, which requested that action be taken by a specified date. Once despatched, a note was made on the mail-log under 'AR' – Action Required. This followed by the initials of the person responsible for the action to be taken and a 'by when' date, as well as the initials of the document's originator:

As secretaries may well work for more than one manager, it is important to identify their work clearly and to keep it in separate storage areas.

On the day identified as the action deadline, the mail-log entry will arrive back in your electronic 'IN BASKET' with the date highlighted. Then it is normal practice for the secretary to phone the person concerned to check progress and chase if necessary. It is not uncommon for a senior secretary to be handling a number of such items at any given time. And so she may elect to set up a weekly or monthly bring forward searching system to check up on any Action Required activities set up by any one of the managers for whom she works. Once an item has been carried out, it is recoded 'AC' for Action Complete. This has the effect of removing it from the search string.

Telephone directory and notes

The office system also includes a facility to enable telephone numbers and addresses of staff to be located on a worldwide basis. Often, a full set of data is displayed in this regard which includes the secretary's telephone number, electronic mailing location, system ID (identity) and NODE (electronic address), as well as details of those staff reporting to the manager and his or her telephone number. Once again, effecting a search in such a directory requires care. If you are seeking an OSBORN and you enter OSBORNE, you'll wait in vain for OSBORN to come up on the screen!

But if you simply enter SMITH, you'll end up with a list of them all!

Information processing in the office

It is possible with the system to write a quick note to someone simply by using their electronic address. And a number of helpful features exist to aid the user. For instance, if a code '.ak' is used with an outgoing message, it will electronically return an acknowledgement slip to your own IN BASKET which confirms that your message has been received. I found this particularly useful when corresponding with a member of staff in the United States, since I was able to note that he had arrived at work and read his incoming electronic mail. Then I was sure I could reach him by telephone! Another amazing feature of the system is its speed. On one occasion I sent a message to a manager in Japan and received an acknowledgement within ten minutes.

These are just a few of the features of the particular IBM office system in the plant in which I work. Others include setting up 'things to do' in a list which can have its priorities sequenced by date or level of importance. Also, the system offers a central information database available to all users.

I have now been promoted from secretary to Communications Officer for the Havant Plant, based in the Personnel Department, and though I now use it differently, I still find the system a very useful tool. I use it to set up sub-processes and routines which help me to gain time and coordinate my project work more effectively.

A computerised office system really is an asset and well worth the time taken to learn to use it well. And the pace of change in office technology today is likely to require all secretaries in the near future to know how to 'drive' one!

CASE HISTORY DISCUSSION TOPICS

1 What particular challenges do you think Alison experienced in moving away from a paper-based administrative system to one much more reliant upon electronic communications and records storage?

2 Is there a danger of 'electronic mail overload' in a system which makes Email messaging so swift and easy? What sort of 'house rules' would you introduce to minimise trivial and unnecessary messaging?

3 In what ways do you think the interglobal communications network which Alison describes is likely to be most useful to the office work of a multinational like IBM?

4 What instances of good secretarial practice can you identify in the Case History?

5 What advantages does the PROFS System provide in your view in comparison with traditional paper-based office systems?

Reliable Employment Bureau
Four case studiettes

You are the secretary of Miss Sara Durham, who manages a busy Employment Bureau in Birmingham's city centre. You work in an outer office which is connected to Miss Durham's own office by a single door and telephone system. On the opposite side of your office is an entrance door giving on to the first floor landing of the block in which your bureau is situated.

1 It's 10.30 am and Miss Durham is engaged in a lengthy discussion on her telephone with a local personnel manager seeking several office employees. The entrance door opens:

'Ah, good morning. I need to see Sara pronto ... No, don't bother, I know where she lives!'

says a tall man in his middle thirties, making as if to walk straight into Miss Durham's office.

What do you say? What do you do?

2 Later that day, a head pops round the outer door and a voice says:

'Good afternoon Miss, I take it this is the Reliable Employment Bureau? Thought so. Now I've got just the thing that will make your life a whole lot easier! Parkin's the name,' says the man, as he moves into the office, carrying a bulky briefcase, 'and Microplex Software's my game! This latest miracle of microprocessing will solve all your client records needs – it'll even tell you which side they sleep on at night! I'd like just a minute or two of your boss's time to save you hours of *yours*!'

You say: 'I'm very sorry but Miss Durham's tied up just now, can I make an appointment for you to see her next week?'

He says: 'That's all right, love, I'm in no hurry. Last call of the day. I'll just sit mesself here and rest me legs for a bit. Mind if I smoke?'

What do you say? What do you do?

3 Next morning, Miss Durham has blocked out 10 am–12 noon to finish a report for head office which includes some complicated calculations. At 11.15 am the telephone rings and a voice says:

'Good morning. Would you put me through to Miss Durham directly please. The name's Hilary, Charles Hilary. She'll know who I am, there's a good girl!'

What do you say? What action do you take?

4 A few days later, Miss Durham calls you into her office and says:

'We've had a windfall of £1 500 from head office for redecoration and refurbishment. I want to use it to give the outer office reception area a thorough facelift! As you know, we frequently have two to three clients waiting to see me and I know they have to wait for some time on occasion. I'd like you to draw up a design for the reception area (which is approximately 3.5 metres long by 3 metres deep) which will improve the lighting, do away with the tired old chairs and table and generally smarten it up. Oh, and while your at it, let me have a list of the reference books you think we need and any subscriptions we should take out. You'd better provide some accompanying notes to be on the safe side.'

The Henry Perkins Legacy
A case study

Henry Perkins (Builders) Limited was a private building company which was established in 1932 in Dilchester, a thriving market town in the middle of a rural area. The district was much favoured by wealthy couples buying retirement properties, London commuters looking for week-end cottages to acquire cheaply and renovate, and, because of its proximity to ports and the motorway network, young industrial companies in the field of electronics and light engineering.

Until recently, the company had been controlled by the iron grip of the 'Old Man', Henry Perkins, a staunch traditionalist who believed that 'the old, tried and tested ways are best,' disliked things he called 'newfangled' and stood no nonsense from his family or employees.

The workforce currently numbers 52 site employees, with some 30–40 self-employed sub-contractors, depending on the number of contracts with work in progress, and an office staff of 13, which is organised as shown in the diagram below.

Three months ago Henry Perkins died peacefully in his sleep at the age of 72, leaving his two sons, David and Andrew and his daughter Julie as directors of a prosperous business run on distinctly old-fashioned lines. At a recent meeting of directors, David, eldest son and now managing director gave this report:

'As we agreed, I've spent the past week reviewing our administrative procedures and, broadly speaking, this is the picture. We have at any given time about 100 active account customers, 30 or so large concerns and 70 small works customers. We're kept busy on the accounts side, which is virtually a paper-based system, because we have to maintain careful costing records of jobs over several months or more and because a lot of our purchase ledger work is involved in keeping track of frequent orders, even though some are quite modest.

'Our accountants do our payroll every week, but I can't say they're as cheap as they were. And we're getting, more complaints from the site men about mistakes in their payslips and their bonuses and what have you.

'On the stock control side, we still seem to be losing money on materials which just seem to disappear. We need a better system for controlling what leaves here and what unused materials ought to be coming back! And our filing system could do with a complete overhaul. I spent half an hour yesterday looking for the Robertson contract, and eventually found it in the Robinson and Parker file. There must be some better way of handling contracts we are regularly referring to while they're active.

'Then there's our company image. If you look at our letterheads and stationery, we look as if we're still in the "jobbing builder pulling handcart age", instead of doing most of our work for the council and the business park. And don't forget that a lot of the people moving into the area have worked for big outfits. I don't think our existing electronic typewriters and vintage copier can deliver the quality of text processing we need now, never mind the time taken to get a mailshot out.

'Lastly, there's what I think the experts call our "informational database". We're always getting in each other's way, or kicking our heels to get at our reference files, suppliers'

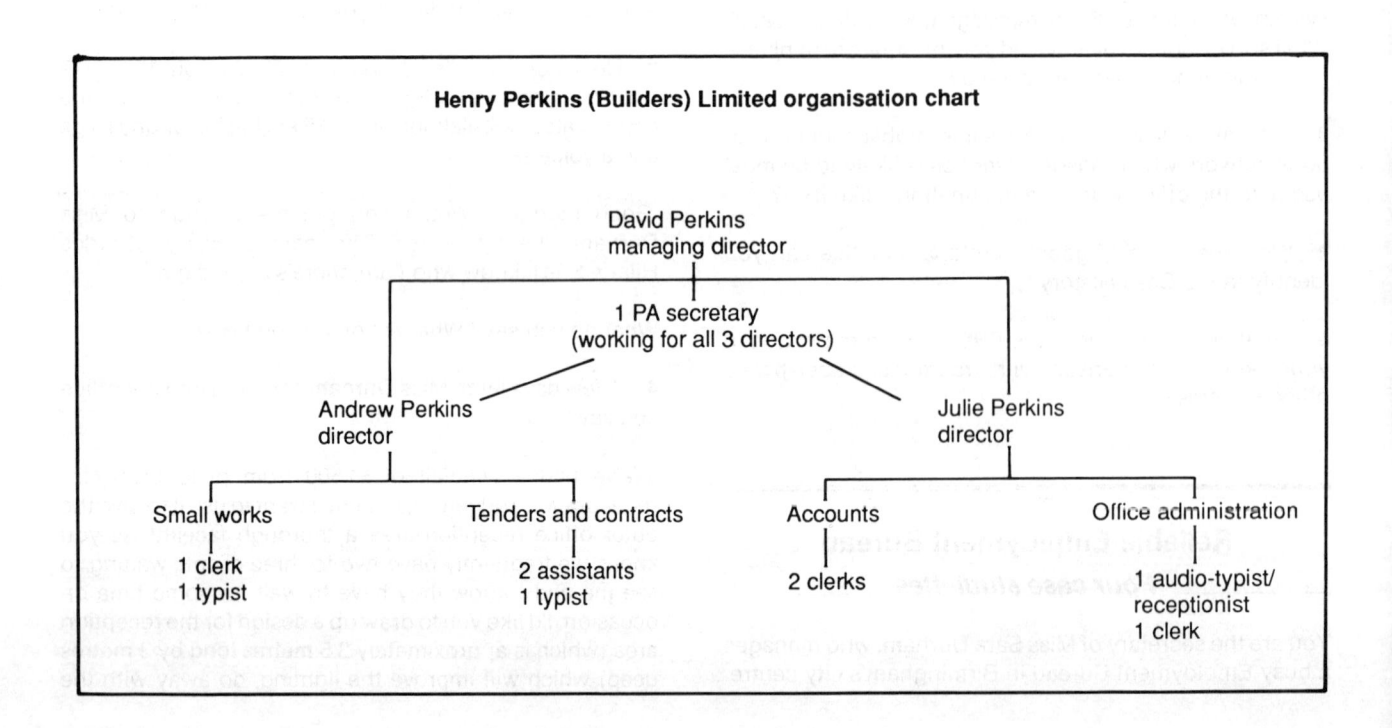

Henry Perkins (Builders) Limited organisation chart

```
                     David Perkins
                   managing director
                           |
                    1 PA secretary
               (working for all 3 directors)
                    /              \
          Andrew Perkins        Julie Perkins
             director              director
           /         \            /          \
    Small works   Tenders and  Accounts   Office administration
        |         contracts        |              |
     1 clerk         |          2 clerks    1 audio-typist/
     1 typist    2 assistants                 receptionist
                 1 typist                      1 clerk
```

price lists, contract stipulations, stock sheets and so on. We ought to take a fresh look at how we could organise this aspect better – we're not only wasting time and money, but getting under each others' skin at times.

'Well, that must be enough for starters. Dad did us proud in his way and we've him to thank for seeing us through some sticky times. But time doesn't stand still. If we're to remain competitive, we must undertake a root and branch overhaul of our administration, and be prepared to take a few chances with computers and information technology before our competitors steal a march on us – especially with our tendered contract work increasing.'

CASE STUDY ASSIGNMENT

Divide into groups of three to four. Re-read the case study and make notes of any area which David Perkins has surveyed where your studies lead you to believe improvements could be made in the firm's administrative practices. In a group discussion, decide what information processing systems you would introduce into what office section and why. Include any changes you consider may be necessary in the organisational structure of the office. Then prepare an oral presentation, supported by AVA, of some 5–10 minutes duration on your group's conclusions and recommendations. When each group has given its presentation, decide which supplied the best approach and why.

WORK SIMULATION ASSIGNMENTS

1 'Carol, I think it's time we got rid of the old four-drawer vertical filing cabinet. I'm fed up with having to kick the thing to get at the bottom drawer files! Would you obtain three quotations for me, including 15 sets of wallets for each drawer with plastic flag and card inserts and so on. I'm not fussy about colour, but don't want to pay an arm and a leg.'

Use you initiative to provide Mr John Cartwright, Office Administration Manager, with three currently correct quotations indicating suppliers and set out your findings in a memorandum to him.

2 A recent mailshot resulted in ten new customers responding and asking to be put on your firm's monthly newsletter for 'Great Wine Buys!' In order to enter them on to your mailshot listing, you need to sort them into alphabetical order following accepted filing procedures:

Rev James Arbuthnot
Jane Archer
Messrs Atkins & Pearson, Chartered Accountants
John Abbot
The Abbey Restaurant Limited
ABC Publications Limited
Archer, Quiver and Bow, Solicitors
Lord and Lady Abingdon
Mr John Henry Archer
Miss Jean Abbotson
Abdul Akram

3 You work as secretary to Mrs Georgina Lawson, Office Administration Manager of Sentinel Alarm System Limited, a company which specialises in burglar alarms and which has some 56 branches nationwide. A board of directors decision has been recently taken to update branch administration equipment by installing dual disk drive PCs for a range of uses such as processing local mailshots, keeping details of local office records such as petty cash, stock data, turnover records and so on. As you are currently pursuing a course at Middleton College of FE on office applications software, Mrs Lawson has asked you to compose a draft memorandum of about 500 words to be despatched to each branch which will achieve the following:

Set out guidelines of good practice in using a desktop PC and in floppy disk good housekeeping and security procedures.

4 You are the personal secretary of Mr James Kirkpatrick, Managing Director of North Eastern Insurance Limited, a family company based in Newcastle selling a wide range of insurance policies – life, motor-vehicle, house contents, holiday, endowment, etc. The company has grown over the past twelve years from a sole trader operation into a private limited company employing five salesmen, eight office staff and three counter assistants. Currently the firm's records of customers' policies, renewal dates, cover notes etc and the particulars of the nation-wide insurance companies which North Eastern deals with (policy specifications, costs, etc) are all held in a series of lateral and vertical filing cabinets which are taking up too much office space.

This morning Mr Kirkpatrick, on arrival at the office, says to you:

'My mind's made up! I've read an article over the week-end in *Insurance Monthly* all about microfilming paper records and operating a reader-printer to access documents as needed. We can't afford more office space, so we'll simply have to bite the bullet and convert at least some of our records to this microfilm or form system. I'd like you to look into it for me. Find out how it works and what sort of system would best meet our needs. We'd also need to establish the costs of installing a system and its running costs. Oh, and of course, which of our records would be best to start the conversion process with.

'When you've done your homework, I'd like you to make an oral presentation to the office staff on what you've discovered. Then we can all discuss whether we should make the change. After all, they'll have to make it work! Afterwards, you can draw up a brief report for me highlighting the main points.'

5 Make arrangements to research the various ways in which the organisation you are attached to manages its filing and records systems, and the equipment/media it uses to do so.

Write a report on your findings, which explains why particular systems were adopted to share with your group. *Note*: your Attachment Supervisor in the organisation must see your report first to clear it from a security point of view.

6 Ask several secretaries to explain to you their particular approaches to handling incoming and outgoing mail, and make a note of the useful tips and guidelines to share with your group.

You may wish to carry out a similar survey with regard to diary appointments and bring-forward practices.

7 Find out what arrangements and standing orders are in force to ensure that computer files are kept secure and not lost. Find out also what policies the organisation has introduced to give staff selective access to stored information. For example, who is entitled to have access to staff salary details? Who can access product costings, personnel records, customer accounts records, etc.

Draw up a checklist of what category of staff is authorised to access what type of data.

8 Find out what procedures the company has adopted to receive visitors hospitably while maintaining security. Make notes of what you discover to share with your group.

9 Arrange to interview the manager responsible for office design and layout. Find out what aspects are considered most important in providing a 'user-friendly' working environment. Report back orally to your group, basing your talk on the notes you have made.

10 Your manager, George Roberts, has come into the office and only just remembered that today is his wife's birthday. Use a copy of your *Thomson Local Directory* or *Yellow Pages* to find out your nearest florist with delivery service.

11 Find out what computer application software packages are being used in your department/organisation. Firstly make notes and then write an account of what software is being used for what purposes. Secondly, select a particular package in use in your immediate working area and investigate in detail what it is used to produce and what advantages it provides. Present your findings orally to your group, having first cleared your material with your Attachment Supervisor.

12 Find out what kinds of telephone numbers and addresses the secretaries keep in their personal databases to call upon to provide support services – both inside and outside the company.

13 You have recently been appointed as departmental secretary of the business and secretarial studies department of the college of technology, situated about five miles from where you live. Mrs Leila Fahrsi, head of department, wants to improve her mailshot and records facilities. Accordingly, she has asked you to obtain the names of the head teachers and the addresses of all the ten secondary schools nearest to you. She also wants to have the following information set up on a record of each school:

The number of pupils on the roll
Whether it is 11–16 or 11–18
Whether it is boy or girls only or mixed
Whether it is private or public sector
Whether the department recruits students from the school.

(a) Install the list of head teacher names and school addresses in alphabetical order using WP application software.
(b) Using a database application package, set up the records for each school (or, say, for five of them) creating the fields which will classify the information indicated above.

14 Part of your duties as secretary of the business and secretarial studies department is to keep a record of the purchases of materials for student use. These include: reams of file paper, A4 bond and bank paper, photocopying paper, typewriter ribbons, toner cartidges for photocopiers, audio-tape cassettes, offset-litho cleaning fluid, staples, banda spirit duplicator masters and paper, video-tapes, OHP foils in boxed sets, ring-binders and box files. These items are used to varying degrees by four departmental sections.

Mrs Fahrsi wants to know at the end of the academic year what each section has spent on such materials, and, during the year, would like to be able to access monthly a running total of the expenditure for each section.

Design a spreadsheet application which would meet this requirement.

PRACTICE QUESTIONS FROM PAST EXAMINATION PAPERS

1 Your name is Jane Robinson and you are employed by Praxiteles Textiles as secretary to Mr Roy Mitchell, Marketing Director. The company is concerned with weaving, spinning, dyeing and printing fashion and furnishing fabrics. The company is

about to launch a range of fabrics, information about which is confidential to a limited number of staff. Mr Mitchell has left you the following note:

> Jane,
> I found a confidential word processed report on the photocopier. We obviously have a problem here Jane. Staff are generally becoming too careless with confidential information. I shall suggest to the Managing Director that he sends a memo to all office staff and WP operators reminding them of how to ensure confidentiality of material in the office.
> Prepare a list for me, please, of practical points which staff should remember if dealing with such material. I'll include the points when I speak to the MD.

(RSA Secretarial Duties Stage II)

2 During this week and next, Mary, a student from the local college is with you on work experience. She is quiet and seems to be lacking in confidence. She also seems to be confused when speaking to visitors. Next week she is to spend 2 days in reception and Mrs Pritchard [Personnel Manager] is concerned that she will not create the right impression so has asked you to talk to Mary and to give her some helpful advice.
Prepare a clear outline covering the advice you will give Mary concerning her duties and behaviour. (RSA Secretarial Duties Stage II)

3 You work as secretary to the Resident General Manager of the newest Praxiteles Residential Leisure Centre at Esher, Surrey, which was opened in 1983.
One of your morning duties is to check the Reception Desk records to obtain a list of guests leaving the Centre and those arriving, plus any details of the day's special events. You find on checking today, that there has been a telephone-call from Mr David Jones, the Group's Managing Director, to say that he has left his briefcase in one of the Centre's rooms. It contains papers required for a meeting to be held this afternoon in London. He left your Centre yesterday. The briefcase is at present in the Lost Property Office. List the steps you will take and what information and services you will use in this particular matter.
The Group's administraive headquarters address is: Hamilton House, 27 Robinson Road, Bristol BS2 4HU Telex: 56780, and your Resident General Manager's name is: Mr Richard Thomas. (RSA Secretarial Duties Stage II)

4 Your name is Janice Perry and you are employed as secretary to the Head of the Business Studies Department, Mr Thomas Ruppin at Fotheringay College of Further Education and you work in the College Office. As secretary you are responsible for all correspondence to and from the Head of Department and for the arrangements of all his meetings and interviews with prospective students and other persons.
You have been asked to give a talk to the College secretarial students on the importance of diary keeping, with particular emphasis on your own diary and that of your chief, Mr Ruppin. Draw up a list of ten points that you could use to expand on when giving your talk on this subject. (RSA Secretarial Duties Stage II)

5 Briefly discuss under the following headings what you consider to be the benefits and problems of using franking machines

Type and volume of mail
Efficiency of the operator
Distance of organisation from nearest Post Office
Features of machines available

(LCC PSC)

6 Write notes for your new junior on how to handle the opening and sorting of incoming mail
List the items of equipment which would improve the efficiency of this task. (LCC PSC)

7 You have noticed that in management papers the term 'database' frequently appears:

(a) what do you understand by the term database?
(b) describe uses of a database which would be helpful in the efficient working of the organisation

(Comlon International PLC (Entertainments Group) with international interests in Europe and Australasia covering sport, leisure, drama, music, sponsorships, exhibitions, competitions, opera and concerts.)

8 Comlon International PLC manufactures and markets a range of office equipment products. You work for Mr Brown, Director of Office Design Division. Explain the different methods of storing information on microform and whether it could be of use to your organisation, bearing in mind that the Company is thinking of buying a series of microcomputers. Give your reply in the form of a memorandum to Mr Brown. (LCC PSC)

9 As the Managing Director's secretary you have been asked to suggest a plan for refurnishing the Board Room. This room is also used by other senior executives from time to time for various conferences. Write a memo responding to this request, stating the

basic furniture and equipment you would recommend, and why. (PEI Secretarial Practice Intermediate)

10 Your firm's telephonist will be away ill for the next four weeks. You decide to temporarily promote a clerk with no experience.

(a) What qualities and skills would you look for in the girl?
(b) Apart from switchboard, desk and chair, what other items would you make sure she had on hand?
(c) What would you advise her to do if the person to whom the caller wished to speak was not available?

(PEI Secretarial Practice Intermediate)

11 Filing in your firm is carried out by various clerks, as and when they have time. As a result, files are lost, papers misfiled and the system is generally unsatisfactory. It is now to be revised under your direction. State the advantages from using any ONE system and give general rules for filing. (PEI Secretarial Practice Intermediate)

12 What would you do to try to ensure that your premises and staff were as safe as possible from fire hazards? (PEI Secretarial Practice Advanced)

13 You have recently been promoted to the post of assistant to a team of four managers and you have been asked to share their fairly small office. At present the desks are arranged in the middle of the room, allowing no privacy, with the filing cabinets next to each desk, making access difficult. There is one large window.

Describe what could be done to make better use of the space, giving privacy to everyone, reducing noise and giving better access to the files. (PEI Secretarial Practice Advanced)

14 Your firm has just engaged an inexperienced filing clerk. Explain:

(a) why your firm uses numerical filing,
(b) how to prepare documents for filing,
(c) exactly what is meant by the claim that it is easier to expand a numerical system than an alphabetical one.

(PEI Secretarial Practice Intermediate)

UNIT 2
Glossary of terms and phrases

automated office records systems and equipment
Today many organisations store records either as electronic computer files, on microfilm, or as paper files which may be summoned by activating automatically rotating shelves, etc. Such systems are termed 'automated'.

bring forward systems
Both managers and secretaries use systems which act as memory-joggers, so that an item to be dealt with is not forgotten; most bring forward systems are based on electronic or paper diaries, the former making clever use of pulsing the cursor to catch the eye.

BT Gold Email
British Telecom supply this service to customers, which enables them to route electronic mail messages from one computer to another over large distances, using BT's telephone-line based wide area network and relay computers (see also modems).

company WAN networks
WAN stands for Wide Area Networks, which follow the LAN principles but interconnect national/international users who are linked by telecommunications systems.

Computer Aided Retrieval (CAR)
CAR techniques link both microform and computer systems so that data stored on microfilm may be promptly located and screened or printed out; CAR is extremely useful in large-volume records storage systems.

Computer Input Microform (CIM)
CIM techniques allow data stored as microform to be transformed into a computer-readable medium, thus allowing it to be readily scanned and distributed.

Computer Output Microform (COM)
This term describes the process through which documents created on a computer are directly produced as microform, for example as microfiches, instead of as paper printout.

decision-tree system
This term describes a means of classifying data by computer which is accessed as the user makes a series of choices; as these are made from a set of displayed menu options, so the user progresses into more detail and along a series of branching pathways to the specific information sought.

DOS
Short for Disk Operating System – all computers need a set of electronic rules governing their operations to be installed before they can accept software applications – hence the need to 'boot up' a PC with a DOS disk.

electronic file creation
A term which describes the production of data as a distinct and individual record – a file – which is created by computer and kept on a computerised storage medium such as a floppy or hard disk. Electronic files may be scanned on a VDU or printed out onto paper.

electronic notepad facility
A number of software packages, such as electronic diaries, information management and databases, include a feature much like a paper notebook, on which memory-joggers, extra details, briefings, etc, may be stored; such notebooks usually cross-reference to diary/database entries, etc.

ergonomics
A word which describes the study of human move-

ment in working environments; tables, chairs, VDUs, filing cabinets etc are designed to help people work comfortably safely and efficiently.

file directory
In the course of operations, a user will create and store a number of files on a soft or hard disk; in order to check what is being retained 'on file' the user summons the list of files – the file directory – onto the VDU (with the command, say, B>dir).

floppy disk
The information which a computer accesses as an application package, or which takes the form of data 'written' onto a work disk, may be stored on a floppy disk; this is either 3.5 or 5.25 inches in diameter and protected by a thin plastic casing – all being 'bendable' or floppy; the computer reads and writes to floppy disks as required (see also **hard disk**).

HASAW
Short for Health and Safety at Work – in 1974 an Act of Parliament laid down laws and procedures governing an employee's responsibility for his/her and others' safety, and the practices employers had to adopt to maintain a safe working environment.

imprest petty cash system
(see unit 6) This system may be in either a computer spreadsheet or on paper forms; an initial sum of money is allocated to fund short-term small value purchases which are recorded on petty cash vouchers; the allocation is renewed as it nears exhaustion.

internal LAN
LAN stands for Local Area Network – by which computer workstations and allied equipment are linked, thus enabling users to send each other electronic mail, or computer files, and to access software; data is routed around the network by file servers which often take the form of hard disks and electronic operations circuitry; LANs are usually internal and located in a building or complex (see also WANs).

log on
A term which conveys the process of obtaining access to a software application, especially on a network; the user first keys in his or her network name and then a password which is confidential and only displayed as a set of asterisks.

mail-log
This term is used to describe a checklist of electronically mailed messages which are still active and need to be progress-chased; a mail-log entry displays essential details such as from, to, date sent, content synopsis, action needed.

manual/automatic collators
Collators are machines which hold stacks of sets of pages – say of a report – which need to be collated or bound in numeric page order so as to provide sets of individual documents; manual collators are hand-operated while others perform automatically – being electrically driven.

microfiche film
A medium available in the microform range; sets of photographed and miniaturised images are stored in any required series or sequence on a sheet of film about the size of a postcard; individual images may be located and then perused by using a reader-printer.

microprocessor
Much current computer and telecommunications equipment relies on tiny electronic circuits which are built up in layers and anchored to silicon wafers – silicon chips to make a microprocessor; different microprocessors are designed and joined together so as to enable computers to carry out various functions at high speed.

open-plan
Many offices today are not divided by floor-to-ceiling partitions, but by 2 metre-high acoustic screens, plants and furniture; such offices are referred to as being open-plan in design.

optical disk storage
Until recently, data being processed by computers was stored on magnetic tapes and disks, using a material similar to that employed in audio-tapes; optical disks are made of plastic and able to store very much more data, which is read by a laser light beam.

optical scanning equipment
A scanner is a piece of equipment which uses a light-based (optical) technology to 'read' photographs, drawings and diagrams, converting them into electronic files. These files may be accepted by a computer to produce, say desktop publishing masters. (See also **optical character recognition (OCR)**, through which *text* printed on paper may be scanned and converted into electronic files stored and accessed by computer.)

RAM
Stands for Random Access Memory and usually refers to the stored data held in created files as a result of applications software having been loaded into the computer and worked with; RAM-created files may be readily edited or deleted.

ROM
Stands for Read Only Memory – usually ROM refers to programmed operations/procedures permanently

stored in the computer, which the user may access and use but not delete or change.

PC
Stands for Personal Computer, a term coined to describe the micro or desk-top computer which nowadays is either stand-alone or linked to a network or mini/**mainframe** host computer.

scroll
This word is used to describe the computer function of moving text or data up or down or right or left on a VDU screen by means of keyboard or mouse-driven cursor commands (see also **mouse**).

software application package
The correct term used to describe the 'software packages' with which a user is able to interact through the computer's electronics to process text, design graphs, use a spreadsheet, etc.

telecommunications systems
Today information is transmitted nationally and globally through a network of telephone lines and cables, satellite transmitters, radio and TV broadcasting via telephones, telex, fax, radiopagers, etc; such networks are termed telecommunications systems.

tractor-fed
Computer printers are often used to provide drafts printed on rolls of continuous paper which are fed through the printer by two sprockets which grip the paper at its edges; the traction-fed edges are torn off along serrated lines once the paper emerges from the printer.

turnkey office systems
Sets of desks, cupboards, accoustic screens etc which are modular and inter-link to furnish entire office floors.

VDU display
VDU stands for Visual Display Unit – the TV-type screen or monitor on which computer applications like word processing are displayed (see also CRT – cathode ray tube); VDUs display data either in colour or monochrome.

windows display feature
A growing number of software applications packages now include a feature called 'windows' in which data drawn from different parts of the package, or from other stored files, may be overlaid on any screen of information; in this way the VDU acts much like a manager's desk, strewn with overlapping sheets of information which may be referred to.

UNIT 3
Information handling: how to use the equipment and systems effectively

OVERVIEW

So far, we have studied the activities and structures of organisations and have examined a range of daily routines that secretaries undertake, many of which have been made easier and more effective with the introduction of IT applications.

Unit 3 provides a detailed survey of the computer-based office equipment, systems and telecommunication networks which have developed with incredible speed since the commercial introduction of the first microprocessor or 'silicon chip' in 1971.

Firstly we shall consider the concept of convergence through which various items of equipment – computer, printer, scanner, facsimile transceiver etc – are linked together to provide instant access. Also explained are the networked clusters or interconnected honeycombs of computing equipment termed local and wide area networks – LANs and WANs. Developments in software application packages are also included and integrated management information packages like SMART are examined.

The principal items of electronic office and telecommunications equipment – fax, telex, viewdata, videotex, Public Automatic Branch Exchange (PABX) and Computerised Automatic Branch Exchange (CABX), mobile phones, pagers, printers photocopiers and desktop publishing systems – are also surveyed and their value to secretarial work highlighted.

The important contribution of electronic memory typewriters and audio-dictation systems is not forgotten, but you will almost certainly be using them and examining their applications elsewhere in your course.

While working through Unit 3, it is important for you to concentrate on the basic principles of each piece of equipment or system and to consider how they make secretarial work more efficient. Inevitably, you will be faced during your career with new models, upgradings and 'add-ons', and occasionally quite new developments as ingenious business equipment manufacturers devise new ways of applying electronics to industry and commerce.

Also, it is essential that you get rid of any self-defeating thoughts about 'not being very good with machines!' Information Technology lies today at the very

heart of secretarial work and right at the centre of your course of study is the opportunity to gain ample hands-on practice and experience. And remember:

> **TALKING POINT**
>
> 'Information technology is changing office procedures so fast these days that *everyone's* a learner!'

3.1 Networks

The media of office information, information handling in the automated office; the local and wide area networks.

At the outset of this unit, it is useful to consider the media or means by which office staff process information. Naturally, man's ability to transmit, receive and interpret messages is still limited to his five senses and what they can pick up and understand. Even so, the rapid growth of information technology is stretching these senses – particularly sight and sound – in all directions. Indeed, a major challenge facing today's office worker is to develop a coping approach in the face of a rising torrent of informational stimuli rushing into organisations' offices. These may take the form of telephoned, faxed, telexed, emailed or radio-paged messages, appear as printed words and numbers in all kinds of document formats or as the many orally delivered messages from colleagues and clients moving around or visiting the office block.

The following table provides an illustration of the major means by which information is generated and relayed in the office environment today:

Media for handling office information

1 Face-to-face, direct communication
Face-to-face (one-to-one) conversation
Face-to-face dictation for shorthand/audio transcription
Meetings: face-to-face multiple intercommunication
Live talks, presentations, lectures, seminars, conferences

2 Spoken word, aural communication
Telephone aural communication, including cellnet and radio-phones
Answerphone aural messages
Aural teleconferencing (networked telephone conference)
Audio-dictation
Voice mail (system of message-leaving/accepting via telephone service)
Speaking computers (still in early development)

3 Reproduced audio/visual communication
Video-taped audio/visual communication
Video – or teleconferencing (multiple hook-up via closed circuit TV)
8 mm 16 mm 35 mm film
Tape/slide presentations
Closed circuit television (for training and making presentations)
Interactive video for training sessions

4 The written/printed word and number
Text produced via:
handwritten note, typewriter, word processor, teleprinter, facsimile transceiver, intelligent photocopier, computer-linked printer, desktop publishing system, Email LAN or telex systems, microform cameras and printer-readers, radio-pager with LCD display, etc.

Text viewed via:
scanner to VDU, viewdata (eg Prestel and private subscription services), Teletext (eg Ceefax and Oracle) VDU from computer file, microform, etc.

5 The visual graphic representation
Graph, chart, diagram, table
Line drawing, sketch
Photograph in colour or black and white
Slide transparency
Overhead projection foil/transparency
Symbolic/coded representation (eg ikons on computer menus)

6 Non-verbal communication
Human attitudes, responses or emotions transmitted via:
Expression, posture, gesture, non-verbal utterances (see also 1 above)

Office equipment used to compose, transmit and receive information employing the above media

Typewriter ☐ dedicated word processor ☐ personal computer/workstation terminal ☐ Computer printer ☐ photocopier ☐ text/image scanner ☐ facsimile transceiver ☐ telex system ☐ CCTV camera, recorder and monitor ☐ film and video cameras and monitors ☐ microform equipment ☐ Desktop publishing systems ☐ offset litho printer ☐ computerised private automatic branch exchange (CABX) ☐ Radio-pager ☐ intelligent photocopier (linked direct to computer)

Telecommunications systems used to relay office information

Internal/external telephone lines sometimes with modems to convert computer data into electronic waves during transmission along telephone lines.

Local area network cabling connecting equipment joined on to the LAN into a 'ring' which may extend over multistorey floors and company sites.

Wide area network links (WANs) system of interconnecting remotely spaced LANs via telephone lines, or radio telecommunications.

Packet switched services systems for transmitting at very high speeds computerised data either via telephone lines or radio signals using satellite telecommunications.

International radio signal transmissions increasingly used with telecommunications satellites for transglobal message routing.

Transoceanic underwater cables undersea cables carrying telephone lines were laid extensively in the first half of the twentieth century to interconnect the continents.

Laser-beam lines used experimentally to relay messages along an intense beam of light, and now part of the new fibre-optic telephone line technology.

The above table and checklists provide an initial overview of the incredible sophistication which IT has brought to office communications and amply illustrate the amazing inventiveness of IT and telecommunications researchers and scientists.

Fortunately, there are many organisations manned by technical experts able to service and maintain the IT equipment in daily office use, and many of the systems indicated above – like video **teleconferencing** – are provided by British Telecom experts or in-house technicians.

Nevertheless, this checklisted information does emphasise the astonishing speed at which technology is transforming office communications procedures and stresses the need for today's effective secretary to be computer/telecommunications literate, and confident in using much of the equipment itemised above!

INFORMATION HANDLING IN THE ELECTRONIC OFFICE

Since the early 1980s, there have been various terms and labels devised to describe the impact of information technology upon the office. An early and premature catch-phrase was 'the paperless office' which, once the deluges of computer paper print-out had been experienced, was prudently modified to the 'less paper office'! More accurate was the label 'electronic office' which implied that all the information being handled was acquired, stored, processed and distributed by a computerised equipment and electronic pulses. Yet this concept was also felt to anticipate events, given the parallel creation, storing and circulation of traditional paper documents which was occurring in many offices other than the innovative leaders of the pack. A term originating in the USA, 'the automated office', is perhaps the most happy, since it describes an evolving situation in which a great deal of the information processing taking place is being done automatically – by the stringing together of various stages or sequences without the need for human intervention.

Convergence—the meeting of the ways

As we have already discovered, the introduction of IT in office administration has gone through an evolution which started with the single, stand-alone piece of equipment – computer, word processor or photocopier occupying a corner of the office. While operators could interact with such items of equipment, they had to physically transport their output to other colleagues and offices. Indeed, in the early 1970s a common sight outside many head offices was the laborious unloading of literally trolley-loads of tractor-paper print-out, the spawn of mammoth computer printers, for luckless clerks and managers to have to wade through manually.

It therefore became rapidly apparent that it would be infinitely more convenient to leave the data in a centrally located computer and to enable remotely located users to access only those parts of it that they needed through an electronic means of data transmission. And this is indeed what took place, once the widespread introduction of desktop personal computers among managers and clerical staff had been

Information handling: using equipment effectively

Communications flow in the 'less paper' office environment

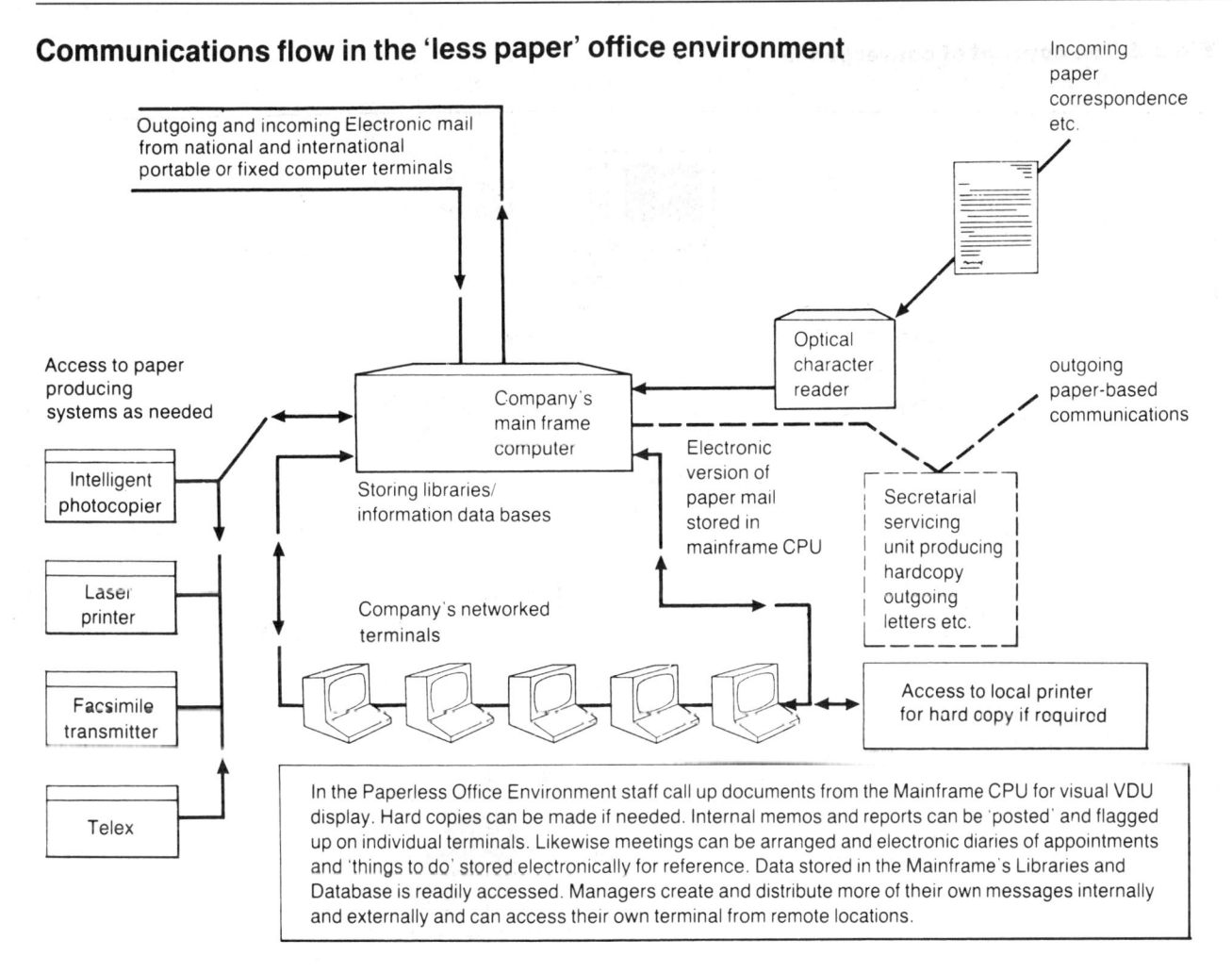

[Diagram showing communications flow with the following labeled elements:
- Outgoing and incoming Electronic mail from national and international portable or fixed computer terminals
- Incoming paper correspondence etc.
- Access to paper producing systems as needed
- Intelligent photocopier
- Laser printer
- Facsimile transmitter
- Telex
- Company's main frame computer
- Storing libraries/information data bases
- Optical character reader
- Electronic version of paper mail stored in mainframe CPU
- Secretarial servicing unit producing hardcopy outgoing letters etc.
- outgoing paper-based communications
- Company's networked terminals
- Access to local printer for hard copy if required]

In the Paperless Office Environment staff call up documents from the Mainframe CPU for visual VDU display. Hard copies can be made if needed. Internal memos and reports can be 'posted' and flagged up on individual terminals. Likewise meetings can be arranged and electronic diaries of appointments and 'things to do' stored electronically for reference. Data stored in the Mainframe's Libraries and Database is readily accessed. Managers create and distribute more of their own messages internally and externally and can access their own terminal from remote locations.

Fig 3.1

effected between 1975 and 1985. Such personnel had at their disposal – literally at their elbows – the means of interrogating mainframe computers for specific data without the need for time-consuming and costly print-outs being transported from, say, Birmingham to London. The technology which made this possible linked the mainframe computer to its many terminal users through the existing telephone-line network. A piece of equipment called a '**modem**' – short for '**modulator-demodulator**' – converted information encoded in computer digital language into waveform signals which could be carried at high speed along telephone lines to be reconverted with the aid of a modem back into computer language at their destination.

The 'me-too!' response from other office equipment users

Once the idea of transmitting data requests and answers over long distances had proved practical – and remember that telex international transmission has existed for many years – office equipment manufacturers quickly developed systems to enable computers to 'talk to each other' and to communicate with remotely located photocopiers and printers, etc.

Prompted by information-hungry users, the manufacturers realised that it would be very helpful, for example, to despatch electronic files of text to a remotely located printer for printing, collating and binding into multiple copies, perhaps as a report or manual, without the need for human intervention in between.

In a similar way, text and image scanners could be used to convert printed text, pictures or images into signals which a computer could accept and transform into an electronic file for VDU display and manipulation by **mouse** or keyboard. Also, with the help of modem technology, telex messages could be created on the desktop computer and routed directly into the national telecommunications network without the need for a special teleprinter as a stand-alone item of equipment. So, by the same means could **teletex** and Email messages be created and distributed from the same keyboard with the aid of specialised software.

What in effect transformed office information handling methods in the 1980s was a new technology which enabled items of office equipment and telecommunication systems to be joined together, or to use the technical term, **to converge**. This meant that messages composed on one desktop PC could be routed simultaneously to several other workstations,

Fig 3.2 The concept of convergence

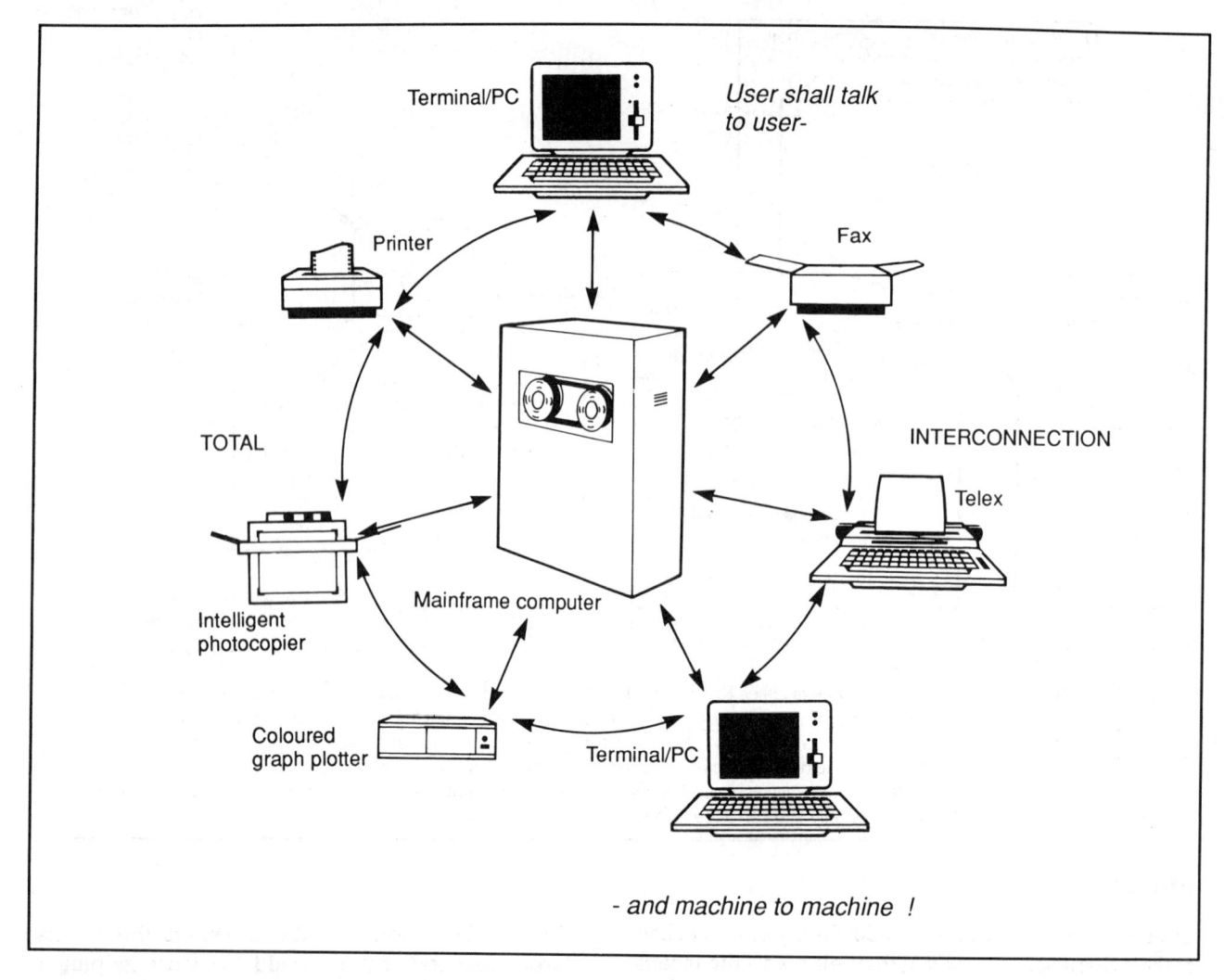

User shall talk to user—

TOTAL

INTERCONNECTION

Terminal/PC, Printer, Fax, Telex, Mainframe computer, Intelligent photocopier, Coloured graph plotter, Terminal/PC

— and machine to machine !

sent to a printer for printing, or despatched to an intelligent photocopier for duplicating (and sometimes binding) while at the same time being archived.

THE ARRIVAL OF THE LOCAL AREA NETWORK (LAN)

By the early 1980s computer and telecommunications technology had overcome the problems of developing a circuit or network and allied computer components which were capable of transmitting data or electronic messages from terminal to terminal connected together in a kind of ring or circuit. To look at, the ring of the LAN appears very much like the coaxial cable which is familiar in every living room. The LAN ring, on to which each terminal – whether PC workstation, printer or scanner – is hooked, is continuously sending a 'token' around the ring on to which electronic messages may be attached and routed to their chosen destination, which, if the message is in Email, would be another terminal, or if text for printing, would be the network printer. Thus one type of LAN is that of a 'token ring', or means of loading electronic messages on to a sort of continuous conveyor-belt for off-loading wherever instructed. (Actually, each workstation looks at each message with extreme rapidity and if it is not for that terminal, passes it on to the next – much faster than an operator can be aware of – until the rightful destination is reached.) Note: some LANs operate by means of 'bus' or 'star' interconnections (see p. 92 of Unit 3)

Major attractions of a LAN network

The attractions of a LAN for larger offices – say spread over many floors of a multistorey building – are as follows:

- ease of intercommunication between users,
- speed of message/data transmission and feedback confirmation of receipt,
- very high standards of user security – even during the shared access of software packages,

Information handling: using equipment effectively

Fig 3.3 How a Local Area Network enables people and their equipment to intercommunicate

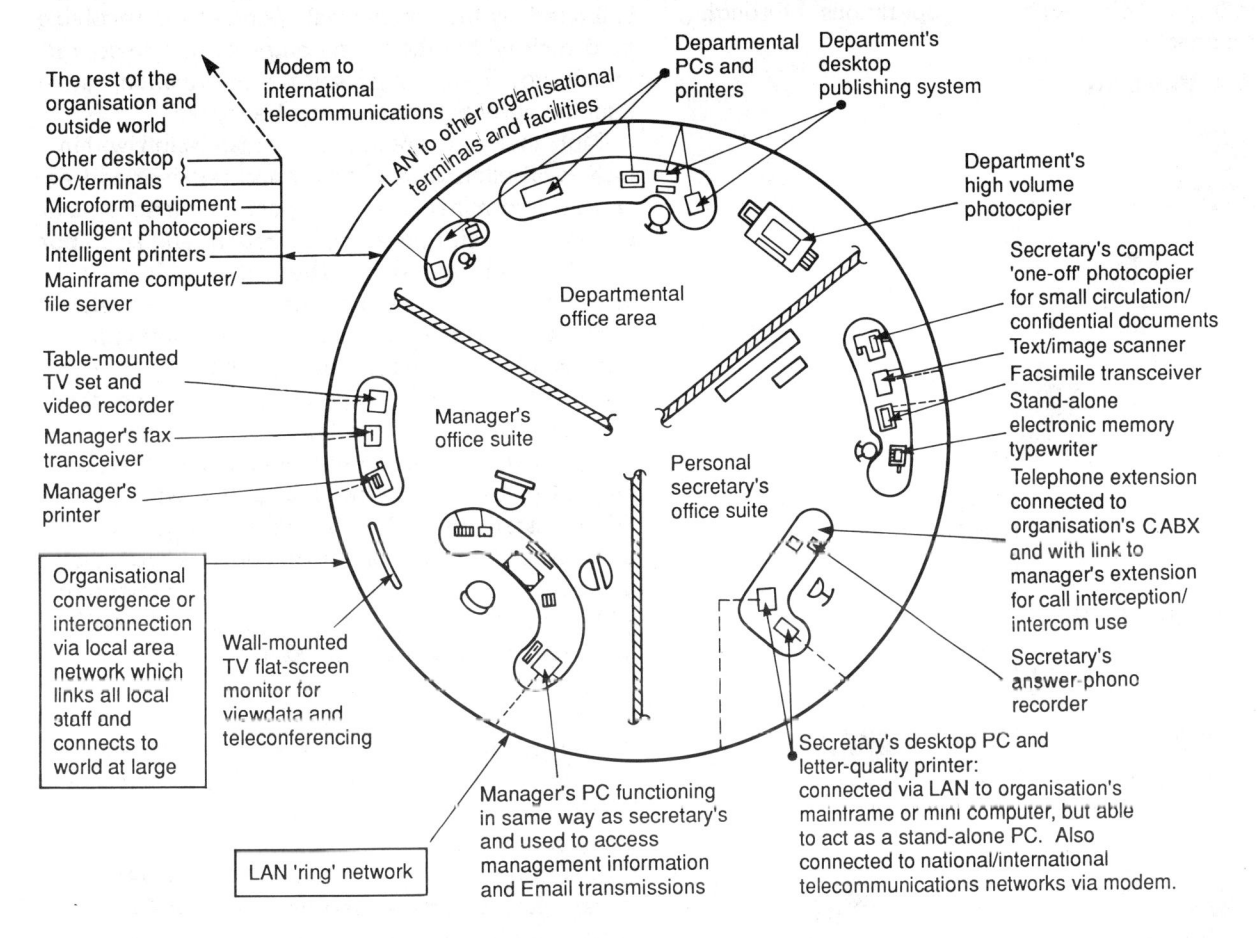

Labels around the diagram:

- The rest of the organisation and outside world
- Other desktop PC/terminals
- Microform equipment
- Intelligent photocopiers
- Intelligent printers
- Mainframe computer/file server
- Modem to international telecommunications
- LAN to other organisational terminals and facilities
- Departmental PCs and printers
- Department's desktop publishing system
- Department's high volume photocopier
- Secretary's compact 'one-off' photocopier for small circulation/confidential documents
- Text/image scanner
- Facsimile transceiver
- Stand-alone electronic memory typewriter
- Telephone extension connected to organisation's CABX and with link to manager's extension for call interception/intercom use
- Secretary's answer-phono recorder
- Secretary's desktop PC and letter-quality printer: connected via LAN to organisation's mainframe or mini computer, but able to act as a stand-alone PC. Also connected to national/international telecommunications networks via modem.
- Manager's PC functioning in same way as secretary's and used to access management information and Email transmissions
- LAN 'ring' network
- Wall-mounted TV flat-screen monitor for viewdata and teleconferencing
- Organisational convergence or interconnection via local area network which links all local staff and connects to world at large
- Manager's printer
- Manager's fax transceiver
- Table-mounted TV set and video recorder
- Departmental office area
- Manager's office suite
- Personal secretary's office suite

- availability of secure personal filing 'cabinets' within hard disk storage system,

- organisational savings – only *one* printer or scanner needed for extended cluster user groups on network,

- instant access to a worldwide network of telecommunications services and to other LANs via modem interfaces – hence links to wide area networks (WANs),

- access to international computer databases via **gateways** in, for example, **Prestel's viewdata** service,

- access to up-to-the minute and real-time computerised data and records stored on the organisation's central mainframe computer,

- capability of each PC terminal to act as a stand-alone desktop computer using floppies or built-in hard disk drive,

- user-friendliness: ikon menus and window overlays enable the user to consult several application packages at a time on the VDU and to transfer work from one package/file to another.

As a result of increased international cooperation, standards for LAN designs have been agreed by major authorities to ensure problem-free transmission across the world.

Design features of a LAN

While in Unit 3 a LAN has been referred to as a ring for the sake of straightforward description – a ring on which terminals are 'strung' like beads – a LAN may also take the form of a sort of string of two twisted wires to which terminals are connected at intervals; such a LAN message routing system (properly called a toplogy) is termed a 'bus'. Some LANs are created in the shape of stars with messages travelling from a central terminal to terminals at points surrounding it, placed as it were on the tips of a wheel's spokes. In a similar way, interconnection devices called 'multistation access units' enable a LAN to be expanded in series of eight terminals at a time.

At present the 'tokens' circulating the LAN ring, bus or star are transported in cables of varying thicknesses which are carried up, down and across office blocks just like plumbing pipes or electrical wiring, and architects today need to include such circuitry in their designs and provide conduits to carry the wires safely. Thin cable can extend a LAN at present up to about 200 metres and thick cable to about 500 metres. Star LANs can operate up to an individual maximum of some 200 feet but can be linked to fellow stars, thus extending their area of operations through interconnection.

Fig 3.4 Bus LAN

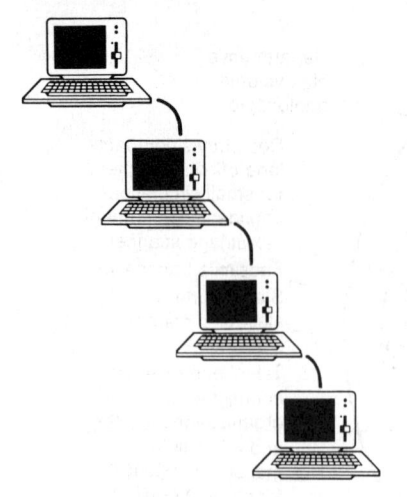

Fig 3.5 Ring LAN

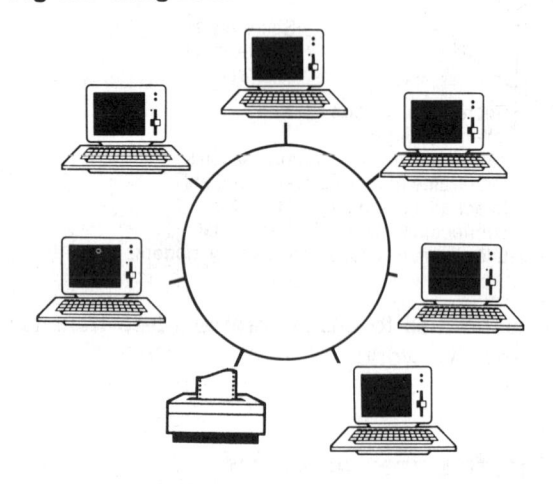

Fig 3.6 Star LAN

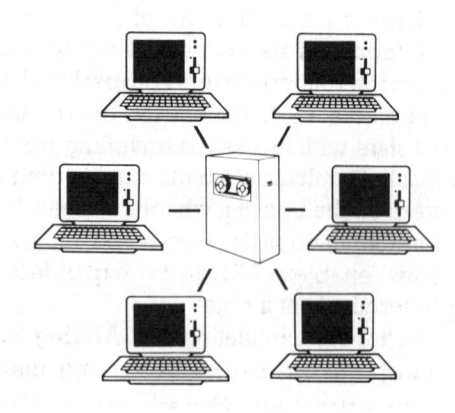

The speed at which electronic signals travel around a LAN is phenomenal. No less than 10 million pulses (10 megabits) per second travel along the wire (a bit is the basic unit of computer data expressed as a 0 or a 1), and the speed of the system is limited by the mechanical speed of the revolving hard disk within the main computer or 'file-server', which stores and organises the information, rather than the speed at which it can be routed.

Each message created for transmission within a LAN is labelled with a sender and receiver address and each terminal acts like a post-box. It accepts all messages, deciphers each, but retains and acts upon only those addressed to it. The rest it passes on to the next terminal. At the same time a message is relayed back to the sender terminal that the message has been safely received and interpreted.

All LANs depend upon a file server to coordinate and control the network. Sometimes the file server may be a massive mainframe or mini computer, but it may also be a desktop micro PC with a hard (Winchester) disk. The file server organises and prioritises the tasks of the network. Given that a number of people (may be up to 200) are interacting with it simultaneously, this is no mean electronic feat! Such file servers are termed **multi-serving** and **multi-tasking**. In conjunction with the file server is a similar communications server which enables users to transmit messages via external telecommunications networks – like those run by British Telecom or Mercury or as private leased networks of multinational companies.

In addition, many commercially marketed networks offer a **remote network link** (RNL), which enables terminals located in managers' or executives' homes to be linked to the organisation's LAN. Thus the busy sales representative or area manager can relay orders, send electronic mail memos and reports and check his incoming Email from the comfort of his home before supper or after breakfast without having to fight the rush hour to get to his office in the middle of his weekly programme of customer calls.

Security
When dozens of office workers of varying levels of seniority all use a LAN at the same time, the security of its data is of the highest importance. Therefore LAN designers have gone to great pains to ensure that top-class security is a byword of a local area network. Each user is given his or her own personal password without which it is impossible to log on to (access) the network. All passwords may be changed at any time and are known only to the user. (Forgetting a password can be very embarrassing as the DP manager then needs to undertake a laborious procedure to 'unlock' the user's files.)

Certain files and records – such as personnel salary records – can be given a security status which restricts access to code-named users only, and each user has his own electronic 'filing cabinet' which only he can unlock. At the same time, a system of 'shared drawers' within a filing cabinet provides open access to specified users. Where a file is kept in a 'private

Information handling: using equipment effectively

drawer', only the user is able to display its contents on his VDU screen. Sometimes files can be created which other users can read but not amend, or where many may read but only a few designated staff may amend. This helps to avoid the corruption of data by the insertion of innaccurate information by all and sundry.

Not only may each LAN user control security by carefully logging on and off at the beginning and end of a day, the network also provides a 'lock up' feature which enables the user to conceal work in progress on the VDU if he or she has to leave the office temporarily.

Getting the best out of a LAN as a secretary

As we have already discovered, a LAN is a system for delivering software to a user to apply to a job in hand, a means of routing messages to office sites or more distant colleagues or customers, a means of issuing international telecommunications data and a way of accessing information held in a hard disk or mainframe/mini organisational computer.

There are, therefore, four major ways in which a LAN system can aid the secretary's work:

1 Internal/External Message Routing through Email services.

2 Access to national and international telecommunications networks via gateways and modems (electronic message routing equipment) to send and receive fax, telex and teletex messages; also access through specialised computing equipment to various international packet switched systems (a method for sending large volumes of data at high speed to a receiving computer). Many LANs are also connected to both internal and external computerised telephone systems and employ computer technology to provide a wide range of call - supportive aids.

3 Access to a wide variety of software application packages stored in the main computer or hard disk and made available by a file server. The nature and scope of these packages will depend entirely upon the work and interests of the organisation and major ones are surveyed on this page.

4 Obtaining files of data for interrogation and (if user has the authority) for editing etc. Such files will be routed to the LAN user's PC/workstation

Perhaps the best way of viewing the local area network is as a means of bringing to the secretary's or manager's desk a highly sophisticated global telecommunications tool allied to a very versatile information processing system. This can range with equal ease across text, number, diagram, chart, photograph and graphic design. A LAN thus provides the management information system (MIS) features of: creation, processing/storing, distribution and feedback monitoring of data, all within the compass of the user's keyboard or mouse! The very high connectivity potential of a LAN and its flexibility and versatility have led communications experts to view it as the biggest IT development destined to affect all kinds of office administration in the 1990s!

LAN software application packages

The following software applications are frequently offered by data processing management to LAN users:

- **Electronic mail** with in-tray and out-tray features for holding messages, a means of attracting users' attention to the arrival of important messages, and a system for sending a message to designated groups – say an office team or a group of sales representatives.

- **Word processing packages** In addition to a simple WP facility built into the LAN system, users can be given access to any one of the major word processing packages – provided it is installed into the LAN.

- **Database package** The same goes for major database packages; the LAN offers its own means of storing data in shared or personal 'cabinets', but equally, the user can readily access any highly sophisticated database on to which to insert records of information.

- **Spreadsheet** Again, the DP Department will almost certainly offer a major spreadsheet facility for accounts, marketing and production etc. users.

- **Integrated management information package** This particular application software is likely to be frequently used by secretaries, since it joins together all those features covered in Unit 2 – electronic diary, appointments scheduling, notepad, meetings scheduling, etc – with straightforward, easy to use WP, spreadsheet, database, graphics and communications components and allows the user to transfer data from one package feature to another quickly and easily: calculations made on the spreadsheet can be swiftly incorporated into a word processed report.

- **Graphics package** Many managers are frequently required to communicate statistics and data in chart, graph or other visual form. Thus most LANs will include a package capable of converting data from one format to another – for example, a manager is able to see whether his information communicates more readily and effectively as a pie-chart, bar-chart, histogram or line-graph, etc. Similarly he can select those colour combinations which give his graphic data eye-catching appeal or increased ease of understanding (see Unit 4).

- **A.N. Other package** The LAN can deliver whatever application package has been designed for networked use and so this checklist could carry on indefinitely!

Fig 3.7 LAN installed in a multi-storey head office linked to a remotely located branch office

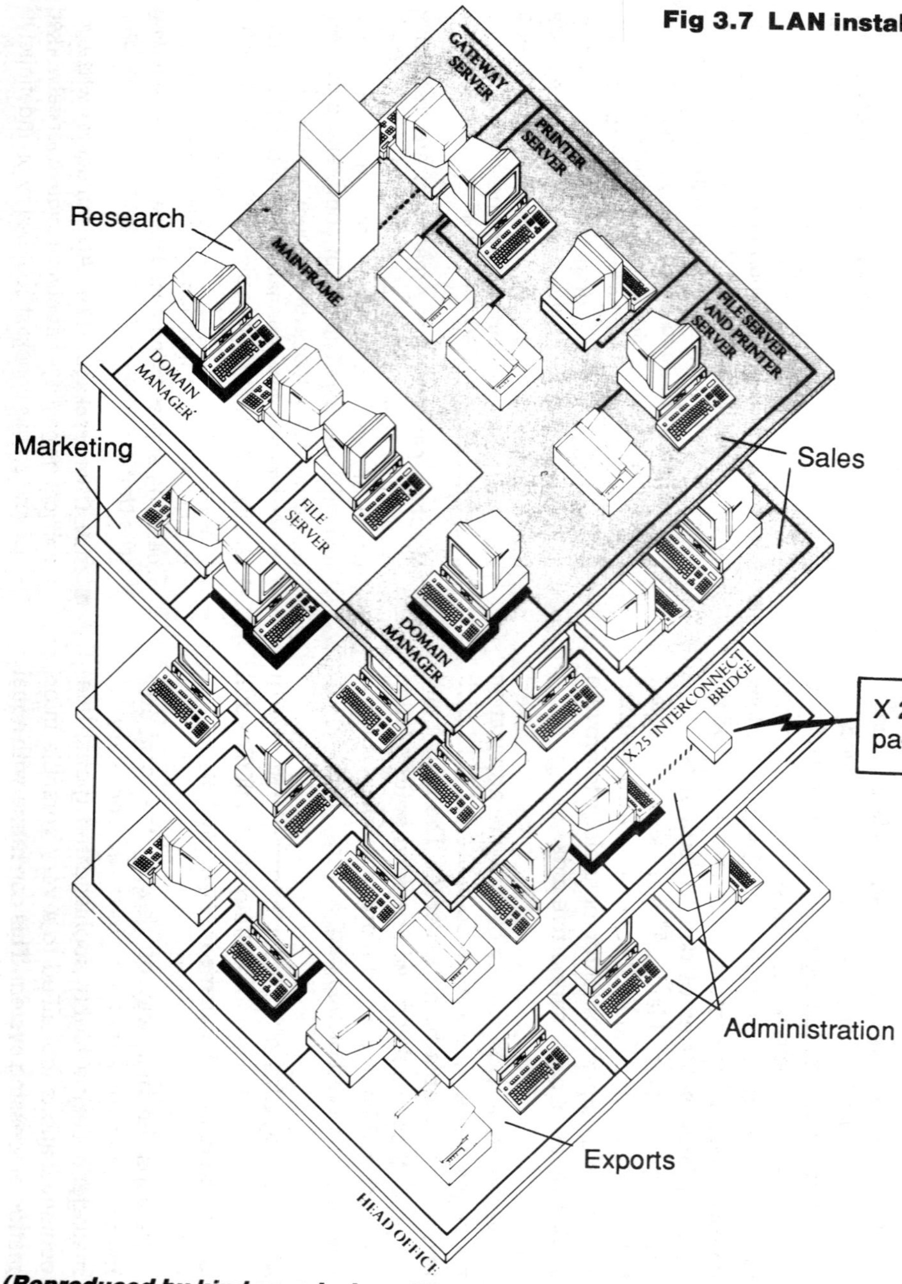

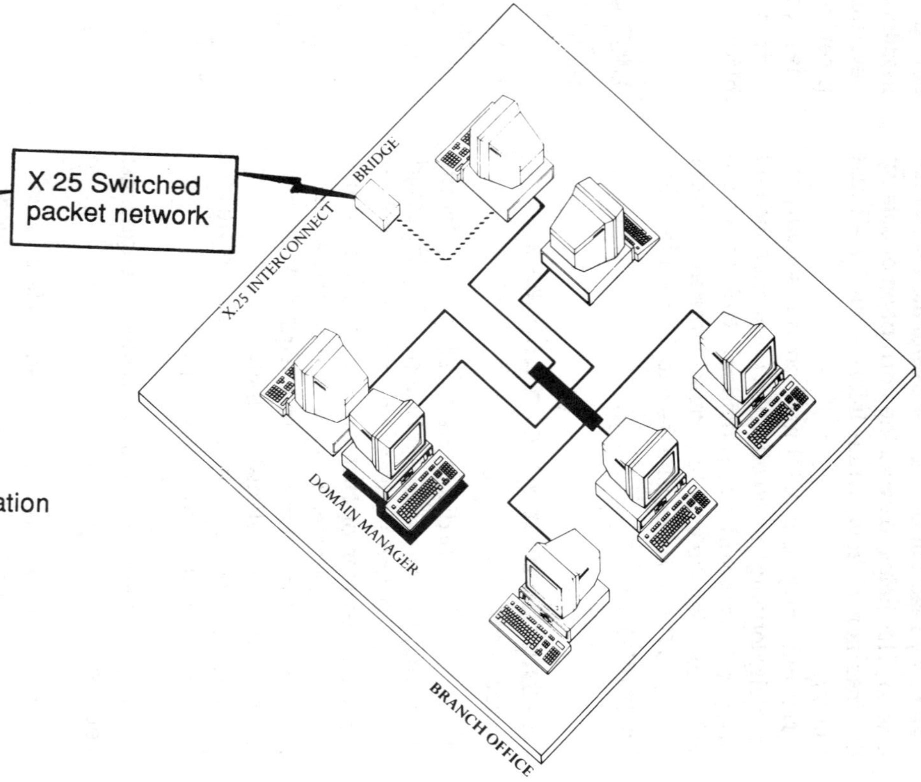

The manager station
One PC acts as a manager station holding details of the shared resources and authorised network users of the other PCs connected to it. Storing this information centrally permits changes to made at a single location and accurate presentation of available resources.

Network domains
A system of domain management is necessary if more than about 50–100 stations are involved in order to control the network effectively. Each domain is a portion of the total network representing a single department or a floor of a large building. Each domain has its own manager station.

Internetworking
The use of packet switched data networks based on the international X25 standard provides an ideal basis for internetwork links for companies based on multiple sites

(Reproduced by kind permission of Torus Systems Ltd)

LAN communications and services

In addition to the above application software features, LANs offer through modems and gateways a means of accessing these communications facilities:

- **Telephone-call making** Quick access to personal telephone directory with display of associated notes.

- **Automatic call dialling** This facility built into the LAN enables workstation users to dial calls automatically by providing, through a communications facility, direct access to the telephone network.

- **External communications services** By means of electronic routing and interconnection systems, LAN users can access:

    National/international BT telephone services,

    International fax, telex and teletex systems via British Telecom services,

    Prestel viewdata system and other European counterparts,

    Other organisations' computer databanks and databases of information via Prestel gateways services,

    National/international electronic mail services like BT Gold, Datacom, and Prestel Mailbox.

- **Internal Communications Services** Email: electronic mail systems commonly include these features:

In-coming Email

Flagging up the arrival of an incoming message, construction of a directory of incoming mail by date/time of arrival,
Indication of what mail has/has not been read by user,
Facility to store or discard incoming mail,
Facility for reading mail on VDU and to send it on to any additional LAN user, making a hard copy of message for reference outside LAN, displaying on VDU a 'flag' to indicate that an urgent Email message has arrived, while user is operating, say, spreadsheet package.

Outgoing Email

Ability to set up predetermined groups of message recipients and to send same Email message simultaneously to all – say Accounts Department Credit Control group of five staff, or all Heads of Department, or all staff working in Personnel etc. etc.

Facility to check whether the recipients of despatched mail have/have not yet read it.

All outgoing mail is electronically filed for user reference

Facility to send a created file with an Email message to another LAN user.

Ability to put a 'destroy' message deadline into outgoing mail; this is a valuable feature which erases messages directly their relevance has expired (eg information about new product launch) and prevents LAN memory being wasted.

Fig 3.8 Email in-tray list of arrived messages

```
=IN TRAY=
 Mary King                    Number of messages =      9
─────────────────────────────────────────────────────────────
 Please could you.....        *24Aug88 10:55      P.Piper
 Please can you make.....     *19Aug88 15:30      P.Piper
 Do not forget...              19Aug88 15:28      B.Whiffin
 Marketing Meeting            *19Aug88 15:26 .DOC J.Campbell
 Sales Review Meeting         *19Aug88 15:25      J.Campbell
 Please send ..                21Jan88 10:20      N.Hooper
 1988 Plan Review             *08Jan88 17:26      C.Allen
 Holidays                     *08Jan88 17:13      C.Allen
 PC User Group Seminar        *08Jan88 17:10      C.Allen
─────────────────────────────────────────────────────────────
 View Msg.   Distrbn.   Get file   Forward   Tag Delete  Archive
```

* indicates unread mail
.DOC indicates that a file is attached to the message

(Reproduced by kind permission of IBM (UK) Ltd)

This is Multi-User Smart.

System Features

- Multi-level password protection.
- Linked-window scrolling.
- Easy form fill-in for reports and graphs.
- Smart Programming Language records English commands for easy writing and editing.
- Keyboard macros and one-key "Project Processing"
- Multiple "Confidence Levels" make Smart easy to use for beginners without slowing down experts.
- On-line, context-sensitive HELP throughout the program... plus disk tutorials, training and reference manuals, Quick reference guide, and keyboard template.
- Access to operating system without leaving Smart.
- Input screen designer for creating special menus in Project Processing files.
- Personal Time Manager appointment calendar.

The Smart Spreadsheet

- Supports math co-processors for even greater speeds.
- Pages to disk to accommodate large spreadsheets.
- Up to 99 characters per cell for values and text; up to 1,000 characters for formulas.
- Up to 50 worksheets in memory at once (with on-screen windows into any number of them).
- Links models together for effortless spreadsheet consolidations.
- Custom on-screen slide show presentations.
- 8 types of calculation: math, trigonometric, statistical, financial, date, time, matrix, and regression analysis.
- 7 types of decision-making: select, lookup, case, if/then/else, and/or, Boolean, and choose.
- Goal-Seeking capability allows you to solve for any one unknown variable in an equation.
- Custom application development with "Project Processing" and the Smart Programming Language.
- Formula-locking: allows user to protect formulas from being viewed or edited.
- Sorts and organizes data.
- Full-screen formula editor.
- Built-in-format report generator.
- Iteration function that automatically recalculates a worksheet.

Smart Business Graphics

- 78 varieties of graph design, including: 3-D bar charts (horizontal and vertical); pie and cake charts; line, point, and scatter graphs; high-low charts; histograms; layer/area charts; and combination line/bar charts.
- Up to 16 color selections, 14 fill patterns, and 6 type styles.
- Fits up to 4 graphs on one page.
- Supports many popular printers and plotters.
- Automatic or user-defined scaling in Graphics.
- Sends graphs to word processing documents.

The Smart Data Base Manager

- Up to 1 million records per file.
- Custom-designed data entry screens.
- Custom applications development with Project Processing and the Smart Programming Language.
- 8 types of calculation: math, trigonometric, statistical, financial, date, time, matrix, and regression analysis.
- 7 types of decision-making: select, lookup, case, if/then/else, and/or, Boolean, and choose.
- Text manipulation capabilities include repeat, midstring, and concatenate.
- Password protection at both file and screen levels.
- Designated "read only" and "must enter" data entry fields.
- Character and numerical range verification for data entry.
- Full-screen formula editor.
- Relational file data transfers, lookups, transactions, and new file creation based on the contents of two other files.
- Complex file sorts, queries, and searches.
- Report generating to screen, printer, and disk.
- 50 on-screen windows at once, with linked window scrolling.
- File summarizations in table format for sending to spreadsheet.

The Smart Word Processor

- Pages to disk to accommodate large documents.
- Built-in mail merge.
- Wraps text around graphs, spreadsheets, and data base information.
- Custom formatting functions.
- Custom application development with Project Processing and the Smart Programming Language.
- 50 documents in memory at once.
- On-screen cut and paste: moving, copying, and other editing within and between documents.
- Draws boxes, grids, and lines on a document to create custom forms.
- Graphic character sets for incorporating custom-designed lines and boxes.
- Automatic reformatting of text after editing.
- Sorts blocks of documents alphabetically.
- 11 typestyles shown on print out.
- Full document encryption for security.
- Automatic footnoting at end of page or document.
- Automatic hyphenation.
- 80,000 word Spellchecker allows you to create custom dictionaries.
- Uses IBM Document Content Architecture (DCA) for transferring documents to other systems in format.

Smart Communications

- Asynchronous communications.
- Automatic dial, answer, and log-on.
- Automatically wraps overflow characters to left margin of next line.
- Stores commonly used setups.
- Unattended sending/receiving.
- Adds carriage returns to incoming linefeeds and transmits incoming linefeed pairs.
- Line Delay setting.
- 110-9600 Baud transmission.
- Electronic mail transfer.
- Now supports VT100 terminal emulation, plus many more modems.

Business Functions

- FUTURE VALUE of a lump sum payment at a given interest rate over a period of time.
- FUTURE VALUE OF AN ANNUITY at a given interest rate over a period of time.
- PRESENT VALUE of a future lump sum payment.
- PRESENT VALUE OF AN ANNUITY calculated.
- INTEREST RATE paid on a given amount over a period of time.
- INTERNAL RATE OF RETURN for a sequence of regular payments.
- NET PRESENT VALUE: calculates the lump sum needed to produce a given cash flow, assuming a constant interest rate.
- PAYMENT required over a given term at a fixed interest rate to equal the specified principal amount.
- PRINCIPAL that would produce a regular payment over a given term at a specified interest rate.
- TERM over which a fixed payment must be made in order to equal a principal amount.
- @TERM: calculates the term over which a fixed annuity payment must be made to equal a specified future value.
- STRAIGHT-LINE YEARLY DEPRECIATION OF AN ASSET calculated.
- ACCELERATED DEPRECIATION VALUE OF AN ASSET calculated.
- CTERM: determines how long it will take the present value of an investment to reach a specified future value.
- DDB: returns an accelerated depreciation value based upon the cost, salvage value, useful life, and term of the asset.
- RATE: returns the periodic interest rate for an investment.

Date Functions

- Converts DATE into month/day/year text format.
- Adds DATE plus NUMBER OF DAYS.
- Adds DATE plus NUMBER OF MONTHS.
- Adds DATE plus NUMBER OF YEARS.
- Converts DATE into cd-mmm-yy; dd____mmm____yy; mm-dd____yy; dd.mmm-yy; mm/dd/yy; mm.ddyy; mm/dd-yy; or mmm yy formats.
- Returns a number corresponding to the DAY OF MONTH, or NAME OF MONTH.
- Returns the name of the DAY OF WEEK, or NAME OF MONTH.
- Calculates NUMBER OF DAYS elapsed between two dates.
- Returns CURRENT DATE.
- Returns YEAR in a date expression.
- Returns the NUMBER OF DAYS passed in this century.
- Returns a DECIMAL NUMBER representing the current DATE and TIME.
- DATEVALUE: represents the number of days passed in the century.
- NOW: returns a decimal number representing current date and time.

Checklist of major features of 'Multi-User Smart' modular management, integrated software package.

Note: Package also includes sophisticated logic, statistical and search features.

Reproduced by kind permission of Innovative Software Inc.

Information handling: using equipment effectively

File management

The LAN provides users with very helpful file servicing and management facilities. Files may be introduced into the system via file-copy or scanning methods; they may be duplicated and backed up within the LAN in the normal way and displayed as a directory or index for each individual user. Various 'user-friendly' labels have been introduced – 'drawer', 'cabinet' – in conjunction with ikons which appear as drawers and cabinets to make the user feel at home with the filing systems LANs employ. Essentially, the LAN facilities are very similar to those incorporated in floppy disk PCs in terms of file creation, copying, deleting, editing and storing. What *is* different is the ability to 'post' a file to another user.

Printing services

LANS include one or more printer-servers which coordinate the printing requests of multiple users. A printer may be shared by a number of users or restricted to a designated user. Usually, expensive, letter-quality laser and ink-jet printers are shared and an ingenious electronic program minimises the time a document spends 'queuing' to be printed. On sophisticated LANs, files may be sent to an intelligent, remotely located printer for printing, collating and binding into, say, 25 copies of a report for the board of directors. Also, documents such as graphs or charts may be routed to a colour printer or plotter for multiple copies to be made.

The following diagrams (Figs 3.9, 3.10 and 3.11) illustrate some of the major ikons and screen menus through which a LAN's services are accessed.

DISCUSSION TOPIC

What dangers exist for both manager and secretary to be aware of in this era of almost instant message despatch and delivery – around the world and at all organisational levels? What approaches could a manager and secretary devise to guard against them?

Fig 3.9 LAN network 'Tapestry' - the home screen

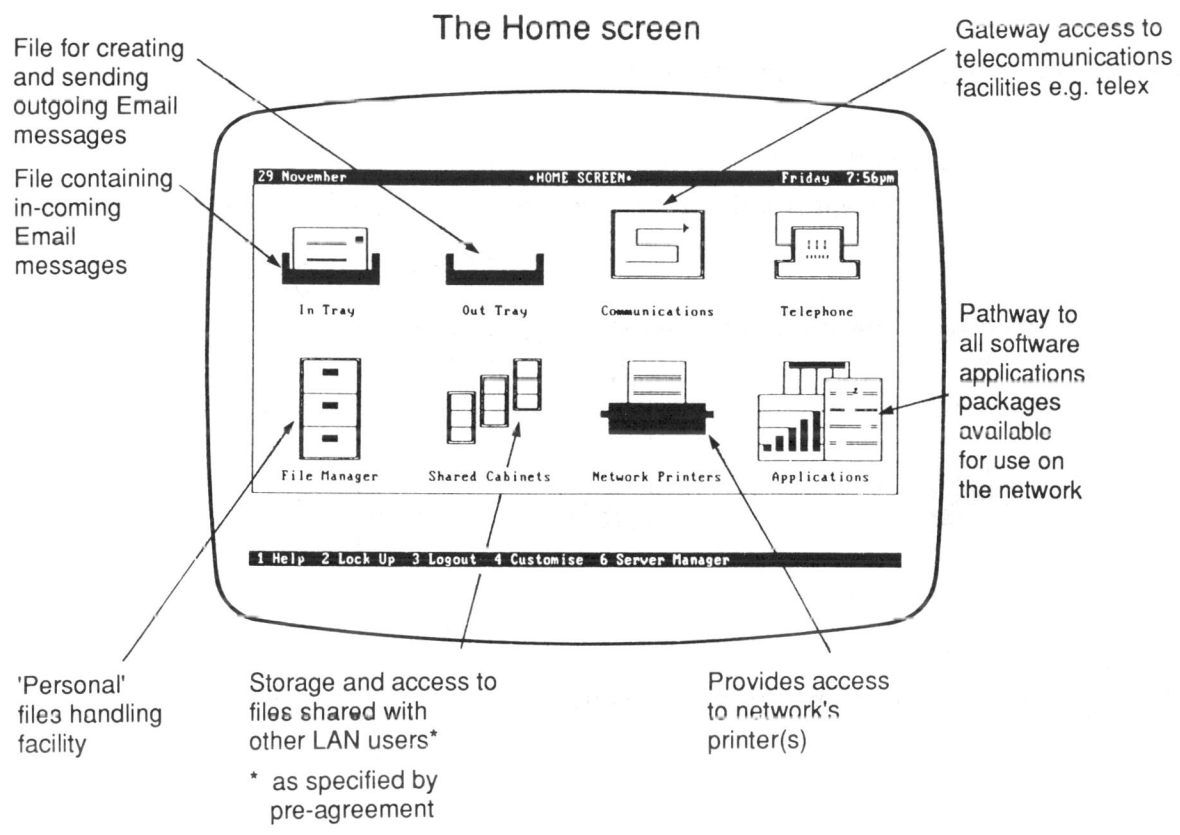

The tapestry user accesses the home screen directly after logging on. The network's facilities all begin here.

Labels on diagram:
- File for creating and sending outgoing Email messages
- File containing in-coming Email messages
- Gateway access to telecommunications facilities e.g. telex
- Pathway to all software applications packages available for use on the network
- 'Personal' files handling facility
- Storage and access to files shared with other LAN users*
  * as specified by pre-agreement
- Provides access to network's printer(s)

Screen icons: In Tray, Out Tray, Communications, Telephone, File Manager, Shared Cabinets, Network Printers, Applications

Menu bar: 1 Help 2 Lock Up 3 Logout 4 Customise 6 Server Manager

(Reproduced by kind permission of Torus Systems Ltd)

Fig 3.10 LAN Email 'Tapestry'

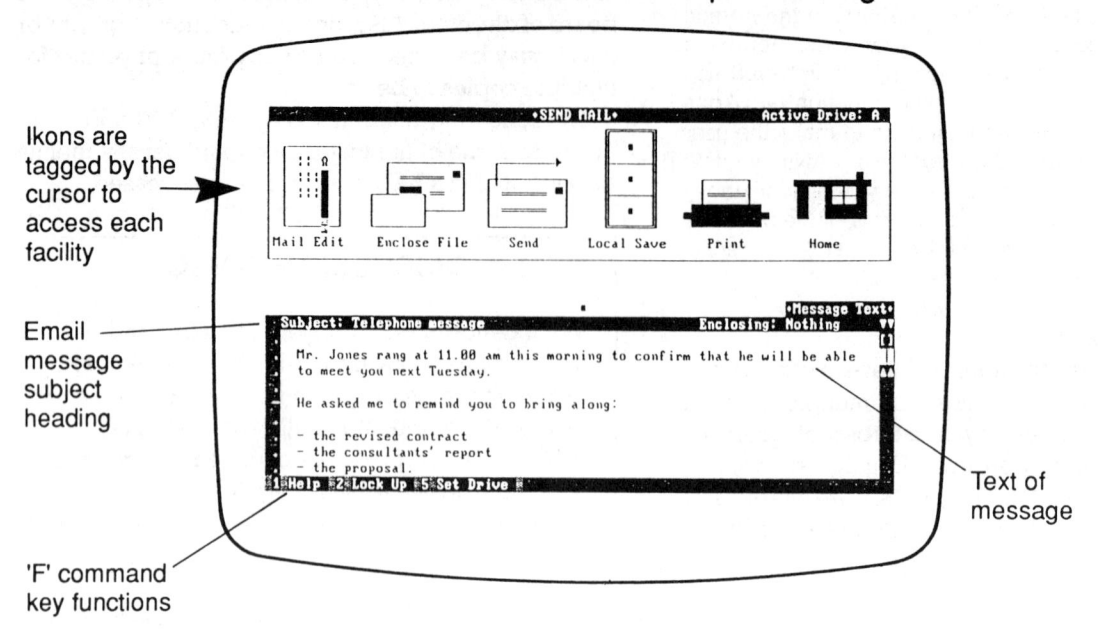

'Send mail' ikon menu and sample message

- Ikons are tagged by the cursor to access each facility
- Email message subject heading
- 'F' command key functions
- Text of message

(*Reproduced by kind permission of Torus Systems Ltd*)

Fig 3.11 LAN network 'Tapestry' - sample ikon menu

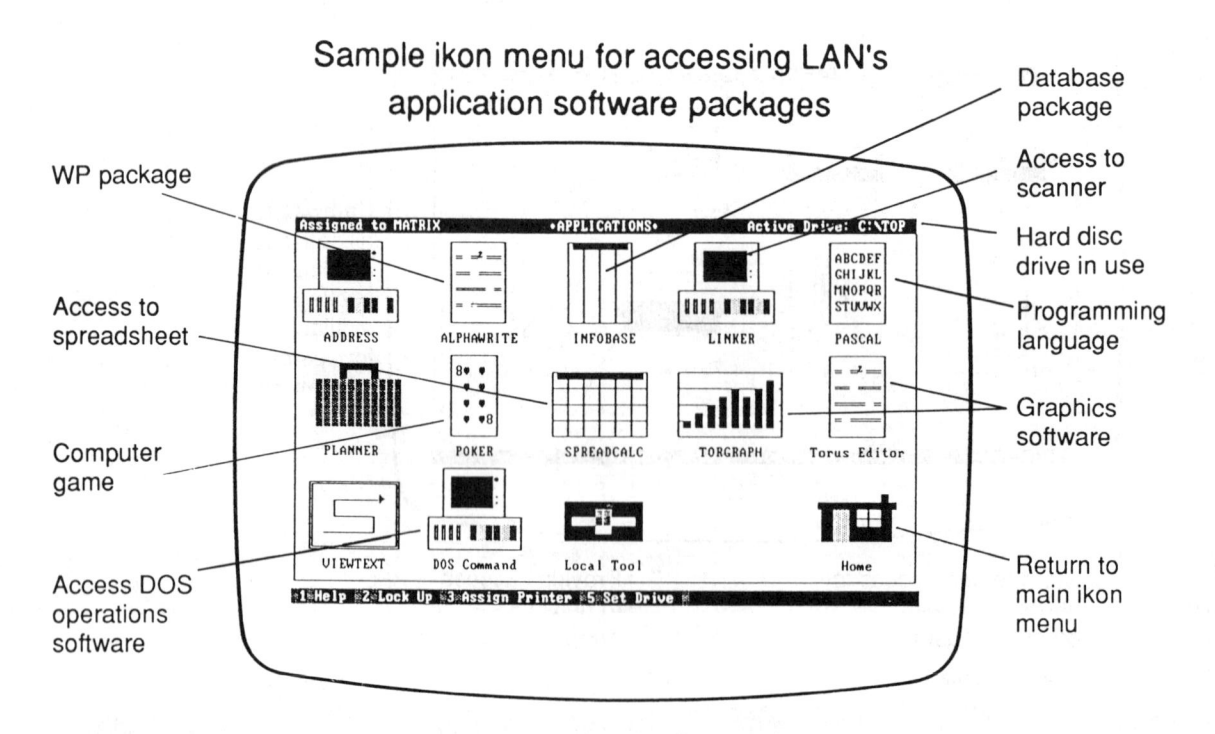

Sample ikon menu for accessing LAN's application software packages

- WP package
- Access to spreadsheet
- Computer game
- Access DOS operations software
- Database package
- Access to scanner
- Hard disc drive in use
- Programming language
- Graphics software
- Return to main ikon menu

The application menu acts like the index of a software library, providing access by means of cursor tagging to any package installed in the network.

(*Reproduced by kind permission of Torus Systems Ltd*)

QUICK REVIEW QUIZ

1 What media are available in today's office to transmit and receive printed information? Make up a checklist.

2 Explain briefly the difference between LAN and WAN.

3 What do you understand by the term 'convergence'?

4 Make a list of the main advantages to office workers of having access to a local area network communications system.

5 What major software application packages would you expect a large organisation to provide through its networked service?

6 What external telecommunications services are accessible through a LAN system equipped with an external communications modem?

7 List the principal features of an electronic mail system likely to be of help and support to a secretary.

8 What component applications would you expect to find available on an integrated information management software package?

RESEARCH AND REPORT BACK ASSIGNMENT

In a group of two to three students, establish contact with a local office which uses a LAN system. You may wish to compose a letter on departmental notepaper outlining the purposes and needs of your course and requesting a visit; or you may prefer to achieve this by telephone. Seek to obtain a demonstration of the LAN in action, particularly the sending and receiving of Email messages. Ask the office staff using LAN to give you examples of how it has changed their jobs and ask whether it has improved their information processing work.

At the same time, seek to obtain sales brochures from LAN installers describing their software products, like Tapestry II marketed by Torus Systems Ltd.

Report back to your group orally and compare notes. Then, produce a combined account of the major features you saw in action, for your class database.

3.2 Fax, telex, viewdata and videotex

Facsimile transmission; telex; viewdata and videotex

FACSIMILE TRANSMISSION

Known universally today as fax, this telecommunications system has become extremely popular with the managers and secretaries in all kinds of organisational departments, largely as a result of the speed and versatility which IT technology has given to it over the past decade. Fax can transmit to local, national and international locations all kinds of messages – hand-written notes, word processed print-out, maps, diagrams, or even photographs and can accept messages in the same range of media. Transmission is effected in the space of a few seconds or minutes, depending upon the length of the document and can be undertaken (through BT and international telephone networks or through private telecommunications circuits) directly or at cheap, off-peak times in order to minimise costs.

Fax transceivers are given a rating depending on the speed at which they can transmit. A Group 3 fax transceiver can take as little as 20 seconds to transmit or receive a typical A4 page business letter. A Group 4 series is expected to carry out the same task in about six seconds.

Feedback confirmation of the safe arrival of a fax message and the facility to transmit messages confidentially are further important features of fax.

How fax works

The way in which facsimile transmission works may be compared to the way in which a photocopier takes a copy of a document and the way a telephone line carries an oral message, which becomes an electronic signal along the telephone line and is converted back into speech at the receiver's end. In a similar way, the fax transceiver converts the text or image of the original for transmission into a series of electronic pulses or signals so that they may be transmitted over a telecommunications network of either telephone lines or satellite communication radio signals.

At the reception end (another fax transceiver), these signals are converted back into their original form, as either text, photograph or diagram etc.

The diagram (Fig 3.12) illustrates the principal routes of fax transmissions.

Sending a fax message

1 Initial checks are made to ensure the transceiver is powered up and has paper loaded.

2 The document is fed into a document feeder for encoding. *Note*: if multiple documents are being transmitted care must be taken with their alignment.

3 A test copy is taken whenever the light/shade tones of a document need to be checked prior to transmission. The fax transceiver can regulate this aspect just like a photocopier. Also, fax transceivers generally provide a dual means of document transmission (fine or standard) according to the variety of shades in the orginal.

4 The document's recipient (another fax transceiver) is contacted by dialling the appropriate fax number. *Note*: fax transceivers for extensive use incorporate a feature which provides for 50–100+ fax numbers to be accessed through abbreviated codes.

5 Transmission may be effected either automatically or after telephone verbal contact with the recipient, to talk through any relevant matters or to arrange for confidential message reception etc.

6 The fax transceiver returns to a state of readiness

Fig 3.12 Three routes for fax transmissions

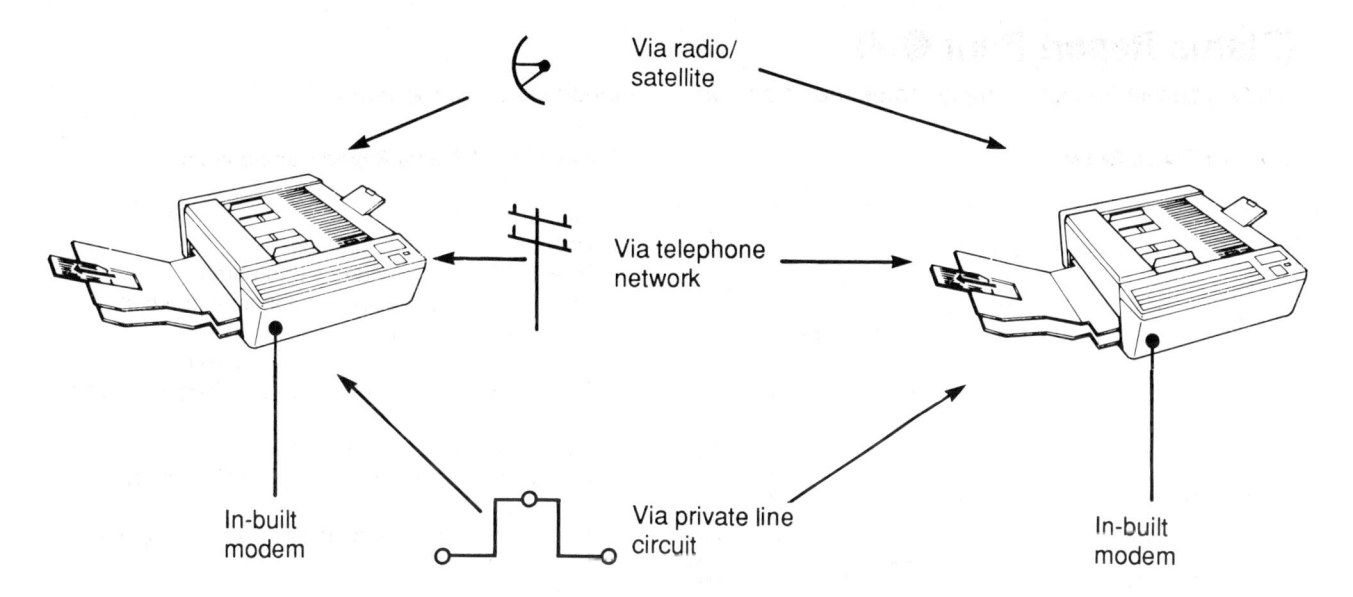

- Via radio/satellite
- Via telephone network
- Via private line circuit
- In-built modem (both ends)

(Reproduced by kind permission of Muirfax Systems Ltd)

for document acceptance once the transmission is completed.

7 A print-out of a message confirmation report detailing the date, time, transmission time, receiver machine identification code, number of pages and confirmation of the message's safe arrival may also be obtained from the transceiver.

Delayed transmission

In order to save costs or avoid busy peak transmission times, most fax systems allow the user to 'stack' a number of messages for onward transmission until a predetermined transmission time – say overnight UK time. At the appropriate moment a timer is activated to set the transmission sequences into operation. This function is usually set up at the end of the office day when no further messages are to be sent by normal means.

Status reports

A very useful feature of fax transmission is the intermittent (say after 50 transmissions) issuing of a status report which lists the number of calls made, their date, time and transmission duration, their destination and the number of pages transmitted. This provides a means of monitoring the fax bills when they arrive.

2 Receiving a fax message

(a) A check must be made to ensure that the fax transceiver is switched on to an automatic reception mode (ie AUTO RECEIVE).

(b) Care must be taken to ensure that sufficient paper is loaded into the transceiver to print out the anticipated number of incoming messages while fax is on auto receive.

Note: fax transceivers can also be set up for the manual reception of an individual message (see 5 above).

(c) At the end of each document's reception, the transceiver guillotines it and stores it in its document stacker. The date, time, and sender machine code number are printed out on each incoming message.

(d) Reception polling: this device enables the receiving transceiver to accept an incoming message once a password command has been transmitted to the sending fax, and so enables a message to be despatched and received confidentially. Polling transmission techniques also allow messages to be sent to a preselected number of fax transceivers simultaneously, once passwords have been exchanged.

Facts on fax
Specifications

All fax transceivers are built to meet international (**CCITT**) specifications and are given a group rating. Group 1 is now almost obsolete. Group 2 operates at about 5–6 minutes to process a typical A4 sized letter. Group 3 does this in about 20 seconds. Group 4 machines exist in Japan but not yet in Europe and will do the same job in about 6 seconds. Group 3s can 'talk' to Group 2s, but at Group 2 speeds only. Many fax transceivers possess a variety of resolution facilities – 'fine' for delicate work, 'standard' for normal documents and some have a 'half-tone' facility for photographic work. The size of fax rolls of paper for printing upon is a compromise between UK, European and USA paper size standards in order for respective users to be able to accept each other's documents.

Fig 3.13 Examples of status and message confirmation reports

(Status Report Print Out)

Below you will find an example status report and an explanation of its components.

Example Status Report

```
              ① STATUS REPORT
                                    ② DATE: 20/09/86 TIME: 17:24
③ TOTAL TIME TX = 00:09'  RX = 00:01'
                                    ④ ID: 0081 3 432 3211

  ⑤      ⑥       ⑦              ⑧           ⑨     ⑩      ⑪
 DATE   TIME   TX,RX-TIME   DISTANT STATION ID  MODE  PAGES  RESULT
                                                                    ⑫
 09/09  13:12   00'36"              6294        G3-S   001    OK   0000
 09/09  13:27   01'09"              6294        G3-S   003    OK   0000
 09/09  15:54   04'32"              6294        G3-S   006    OK   0000
 09/12  15:01   00'24"         03 432 1519      G3-S   001    OK   0000
 09/17  11:28   00'44"                          G3-R   000    NO   9081
 09/18  10:26   00'08"                          G3-S   000    STP  9080
 09/18  18:28   00'35"                          G3-S   000    NO   9081
 09/19  09:02   00'00"        0PPP432-1519      G3-S   000    NO   9999
 09/19  09:04   00'00"        0PPP432-1519      G3-S   000    NO   9999
 09/19  09:05   00'34"         03 432 1519      G3-S   001    OK   0000
 09/19  09:08   00'00"        0PPP432-1519      G3-S   000    NO   9999
 09/19  09:10   00'34"         03 432 1519      G3-S   001    OK   0000
 09/19  09:12   00'00"        0PPP432-1519      G3-S   000    NO   9999
 09/19  09:13   00'00"        0PPP432-1519      G3-S   000    NO   9999
 09/19  09:15   00'00"        0PPP432-1519      G3-S   000    NO   9999
 09/19  09:16   00'00"        0PPP432-1519      G3-S   000    NO   9999
 09/19  09:25   00'38"              6294        G3-S   001    OK   0000
 09/19  09:33   00'47"         03 432 1519      G3-R   001    OK   0000
 09/19  15:48   00'09"                          G3-R   000    STP  9080
```

Explanation of Status Report Components

① Title of Report
② Date and time report is made
③ Total transmission and reception time
④ TSI/CSI data (Your 9550's telephone number)
⑤ Date of each facsimile transaction
⑥ Time at which each transaction started
⑦ Time taken for each transmission (TX) or reception (RX) transaction
⑧ Identification of the remote machine
⑨ Communication mode for sending (S) and receiving (R) operations
⑩ Number of pages transmitted or received for each transaction
⑪ Result status of transaction
⑫ Four-digit code used by servicing engineer

Example codes for possible result problems:
STP (stop button pressed)
BUSY (partner fax did not answer)
NO (problem with partner machine or telephone line)

(Message Confirmation Report Print Out)

Below you will find an example Message Confirmation Report and an explanation of its components.

Example Message Confirmation Report

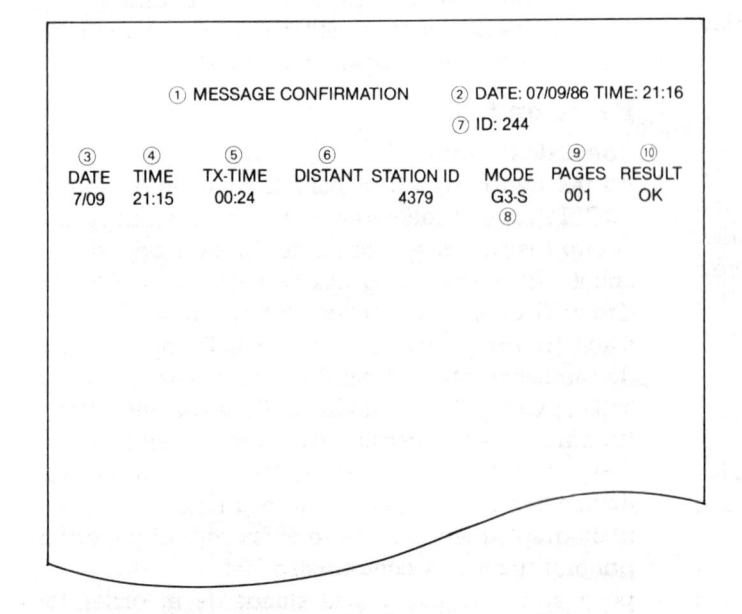

```
              ① MESSAGE CONFIRMATION    ② DATE: 07/09/86 TIME: 21:16
                                        ⑦ ID: 244
   ③      ④        ⑤             ⑥          ⑨      ⑩
  DATE   TIME    TX-TIME   DISTANT STATION ID  MODE  PAGES  RESULT
  7/09   21:15    00:24            4379        G3-S   001    OK
                                               ⑧
```

Explanation of Message Confirmation Report Components

① Title of Report
② Date and time of report
③ Date of the communication mode
④ Time at which communication began
⑤ The length of time the communication took to complete
⑥ Remote machine identification data
⑦ TSI/CSI data (Your 9550's telephone number)
⑧ Communication mode
   ("S" = Transmission, "R" = Reception)
⑨ Total number of pages transmitted
⑩ Result status of communication

(Reproduced by kind permission of Muirfax Systems Ltd)

Paper and printing

For a long time fax transceivers used thermal copying paper which did not give a particularly good copy. Currently office equipment manufacturers are developing the means of printing out fax messages to letter quality standards on laser/ink-jet printers.

Fax and the future

The future of fax looks assured. It is extremely versatile, being able to transmit handwritten notes, typed/printed text, images and diagrams and photographs in seconds. One major telephone company reckons to be able to guarantee a fax transmission to anywhere in the world within two minutes, given that there are no faults in the telecommunications network! Fax equipment is becoming cheaper to buy (machines now under £1,000) and run. Worldwide users are about to match telex in number. It is user-friendly and simple to operate. Its confidential transmission service and message integrity features are making fax increasingly popular with senior managers, and its incorporation into LAN networks is offering a versatile and express service to a fast increasing number of office staff.

A typical fax features checklist

- Storage of telephone numbers via a predetermined code
- Automatic call initiation
- High speed automatic dialling facility
- Automatic storage of last number called
- Call Progress Monitor
- Tone detection: Ring, Busy, Equipment Engaged, Unobtainable
- Repeat attempt facility
- Auto clear from originating end
- One touch auto dialling and auto polling
- Automatic copying of transmitted documents
- Delayed transmission facilities
- Reception and transmission polling
- Provision to supply status and management reports on fax transmissions and receptions

Fig 3.14 The MerlinFax HS20 compact desktop facsimile terminal with integral telephone

(*Reproduced by kind permission of British Telecom*)

TELEX

Telex, short for telegraphic exchange (of messages), has been in use for well over sixty years and its origins go even further back to the telegraph invention of Samuel Morse and his renowned morse code, developed in the 19th century. This sent electric signals along a wire for conversion into dots and dashes. In the early part of this century it became possible to convert similar signals into upper case (capital letters) words printed on to paper by a machine resembling a typewriter with a moving head printer. Such machines came to be termed teleprinters, and for the last fifty or so years, have been used to exchange textual messages internationally by means of telephone/radio signal telecommunications.

The telex system preceded facsimile transmission and it is not unusual, therefore, that it should embody features which are similar in many ways to those of fax. For example, message receivers are contacted over the telephone wire and a 'ready to receive' confirmation known as an 'answerback code' is confirmed by the receiving teleprinter – both fax and telex machines employ a kind of 'handshake' system to tell one another that they are ready to communicate. Also, telex employs many fax-type facilities such as retrying busy numbers, logging and reporting on calls and sending telexes to multiple recipients.

As by now you will have come to expect, the advent of IT gave a large boost to telex communications systems and current telex equipment resembles a desktop PC, rather than the outsize, heavy typewriter appearance of earlier teleprinters. Indeed, the user may either opt for a dedicated telex terminal or may incorporate a telex facility into a networked computer terminal. For the present, a major advantage of the telex system lies in the large number of telex terminal/system owners throughout the world. Nevertheless, the advent of fax has brought about fierce competition and telex is unlikely to continue for much longer in its present form.

Telex operations

By employing electronic text preparation and editing techniques, telex messages may be prepared, edited and checked prior to transmission by means of VDU

Fig 3.15 British Telecom's Leopard is a telex terminal with liquid crystal display, offering expandable memory, abbreviated dialling and mailbox facility, which can be linked to workstations and WPs to bring telex to your desk

or **LCD display** and microprocessor memory systems. Using features very much like those of fax transceivers, such messages may be kept on electronic file until a later transmission time and then despatched automatically. Having prepared the text of the telex, the user makes contact with the recipient by typing the telex number, obtaining a confirmatory answerback code response and providing sender identification (ie the user's own answerback code). The telex may then be despatched. Once the message has been delivered, the telex system immediately resumes a message acceptance mode, ready to receive incoming telexes, and will provide a series of print-out message status reports.

Typical telex features

A typical dedicated telex machine will be able to store and recall keyed in text and messages, provide a text editing feature very much like electronic word processing software, both send and receive telexes, despatch telexes at predetermined times, retry busy receivers, print out and log all messages and provide management reports.

Current trends and developments

In view of the rapid expansion of convergent and networked systems, telex equipment providers like BT have enabled users to access telex messaging equipment from remotely located computer workstations and typewriters, upon which telexes may be originated and then routed into the telex telecommunications system via a LAN or internal private telephone line circuit. Many telecommunications manufacturers are now able to supply circuitry along which voice, text and computerised data may be transmitted simultaneously. A few very large telex users have installed Private Automatic Telex Branch Exchanges (PATBXs) to enable a series of telex machines to intercommunicate directly and instantaneously – an invaluable asset in the world of stocks and shares.

Future trends

With the introduction of electronic mail, software has been developed which allows the operator to use telex directly from the desktop PC via the telephone line to electronic mailboxes. Thus the secretary will not need to move from her desk in order to send a telex or other electronic messages.

As an effective secretary you should ensure that you are fully proficient in handling fax and telex equipment and keep a watchful eye on IT developments and innovations which make it easier for the

Fig 3.16 Specimen telex message.

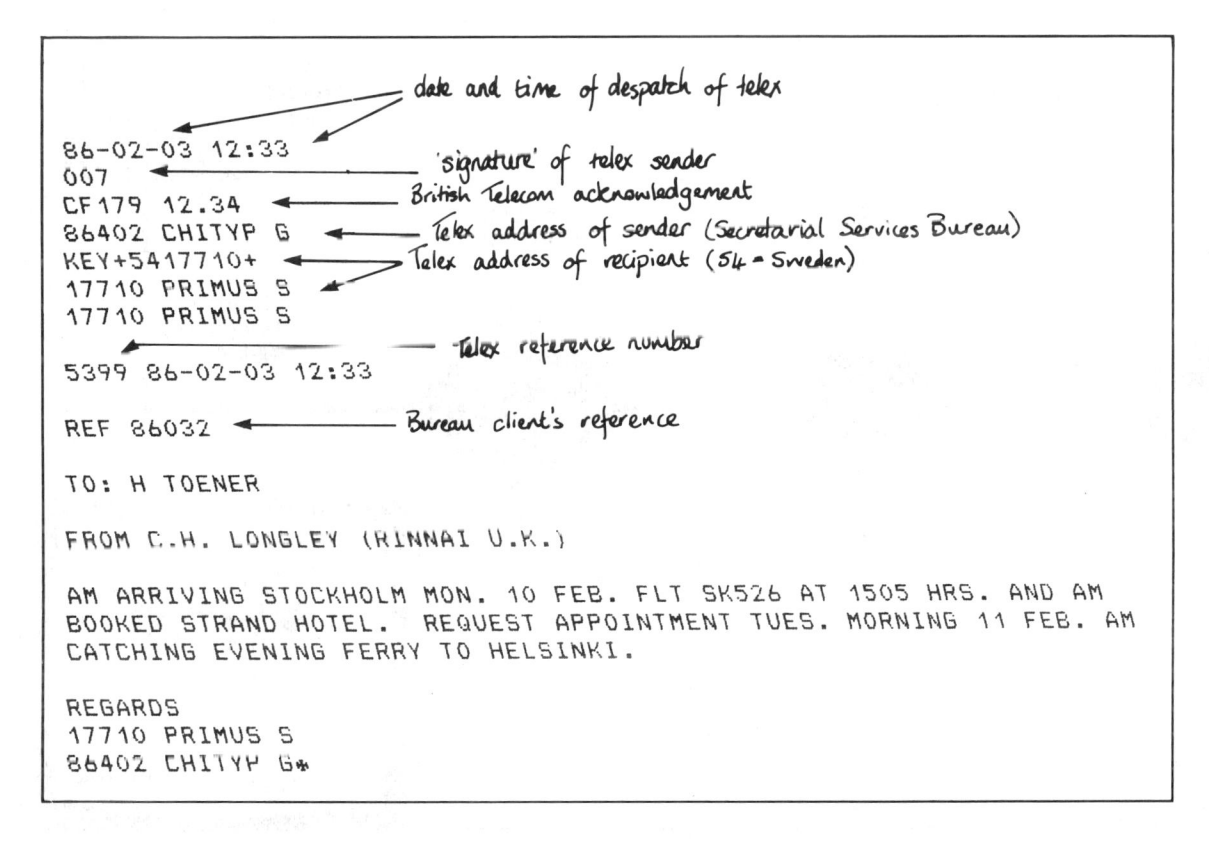

```
86-02-03 12:33          ← date and time of despatch of telex
007                     ← 'signature' of telex sender
CF179 12.34             ← British Telecom acknowledgement
86402 CHITYP G          ← Telex address of sender (Secretarial Services Bureau)
KEY+5417710+            → Telex address of recipient (54 - Sweden)
17710 PRIMUS S
17710 PRIMUS S
                        ← Telex reference number
5399 86-02-03 12:33

REF 86032               ← Bureau client's reference

TO: H TOENER

FROM C.H. LONGLEY (RINNAI U.K.)

AM ARRIVING STOCKHOLM MON. 10 FEB. FLT SK526 AT 1505 HRS. AND AM
BOOKED STRAND HOTEL. REQUEST APPOINTMENT TUES. MORNING 11 FEB. AM
CATCHING EVENING FERRY TO HELSINKI.

REGARDS
17710 PRIMUS S
86402 CHITYP G*
```

(*Reproduced by kind permission of Select Office Services, Chichester and Mr C H Longley (Rinnai UK)*)

'desktop information tool' to communicate. For the average secretary, the most useful electronic introduction for the time being is undoubtedly the facility to create a telex message on a personal workstation PC and to be able to despatch it to the outside world by means of a purpose-built telex machine within the office complex and reached through an internal network.

VIEWDATA AND VIDEOTEX

You will be forgiven for experiencing some confusion about the labels which the experts have given to various telecommunications systems. We have already learned to distinguish between telex, teletex and teletext and now have viewdata and videotex to unravel!

Actually, there is no problem here for they are both terms which are used to describe the same system. British Telecom employ viewdata to describe its Prestel service, while videotex is the internationally agreed term to label the interactive services based on a central computer, telephone transmission lines, modem, and a monitor and keyboard capable of accepting colour graphics and text.

How does videotex work?

The UK viewdata system widely in use is BT's Prestel service. At its heart are ten regionally located computers which contain a large database of information on all sorts of topics. Some of this information is provided by government and public bodies – such as data on university and polytechnic courses – and some is provided by private companies such as hotel brochures or car-hire offers.

Each Prestel user needs a VDU screen adapted to accept Prestel transmissions, a computer and keyboard to relay instructions and a modem with call-up facilities to link the computer terminal to the appropriate Prestel computer. Indeed, any desktop PC may be adapted to accept Prestel.

Prestel is accessed by keying in a customer identity number and password. Once connected, costs are incurred (see p.108) by the minute for the duration of **on-line connection**.

Prestel information is viewed and interrogated as a series of screen colour pages of information made more interesting by the inclusion of graphic diagrams and designs. Private and public organisations (Information Providers) pay Prestel a fee for having a page of data included in the Prestel database. Each page is given a unique number which is used to locate and display it on the user's screen. The Information

Fig 3.17 How Prestel works (Inset: example of a screen page)

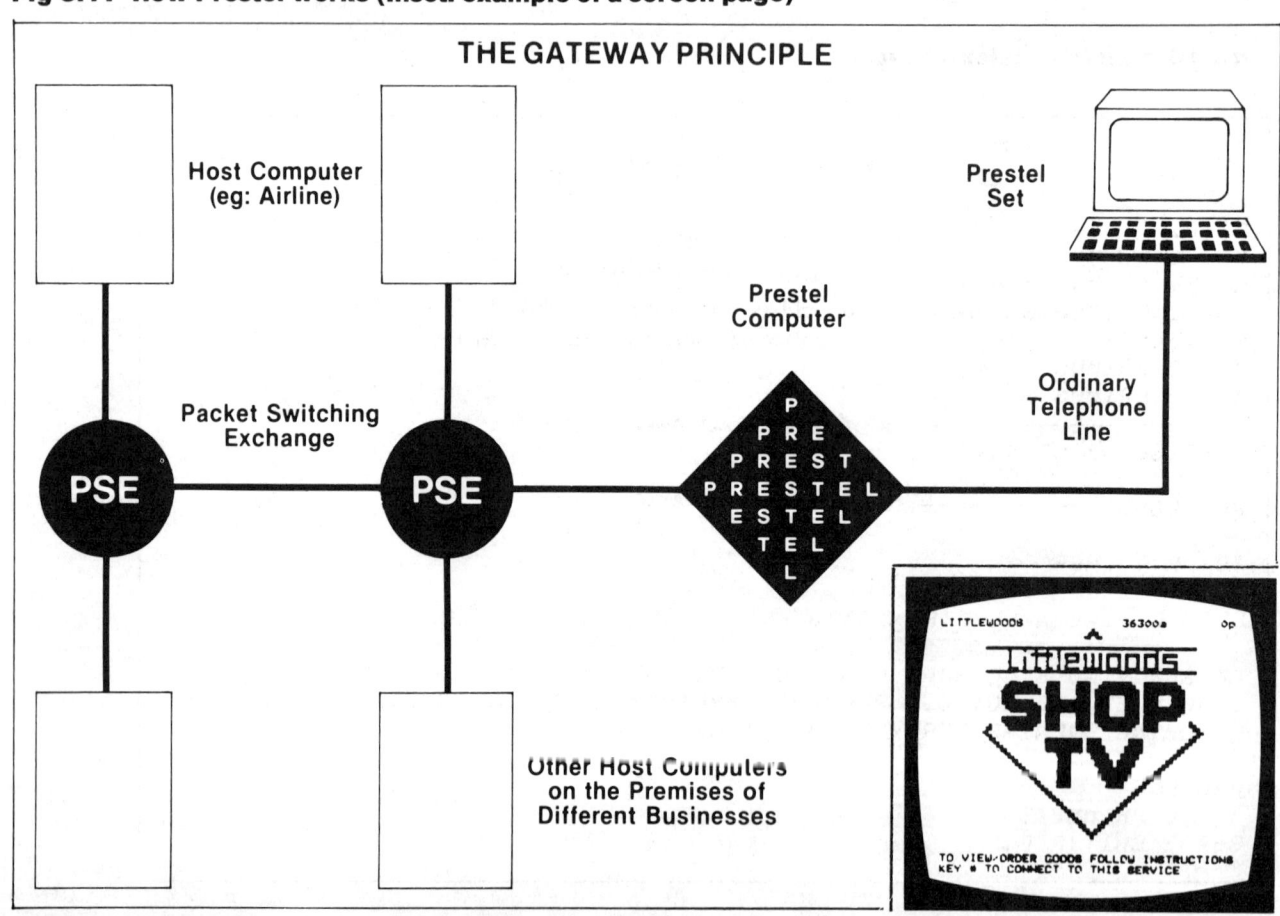

(Reproduced by kind permission of British Telecom)

Provider may update, modify or withdraw a given page by arrangement with Prestel.

At the present time there are some 360 000 pages of information available for scrutiny and the database is divided into the following sectors:

Agriculture, Banking, Education, Finance-Citiservice, Insurance Microcomputing (including a hobbyists' network) Teleshopping and Travel.

Prestel advertisers of interest to the secretary include:

air travel □ advertising rates (Press) □ bank services □ British Telecom services □ business equipment □ car hire □ cleaning services □ computer services □ employment agencies □ ferry services □ financial advice □ hotel booking □ insurance □ entertainment □ office services □ shopping services □ teleshopping □ tourist information □ What's On, etc.

Technically, the Prestel database is termed a branching or hierarchic database. The user starts at an initial menu or index listing the major sectors and then proceeds along the chosen one, branching off at will. For example, Business Information can take the user on to advertising or money markets or statistics and so on. Alternatively, a simple command will transport the user into an entirely different sector. Prestel pages are generally accessed by keying in a desired number once this is known, and the Prestel Directory lists keywords and numbers in blue and page numbers in black.

Perhaps the most important feature of Prestel for the secretary is its interactivity. The user may locate, for example, a page which lists hotels in Birmingham and there and then effect a booking for her manager. Or, she may be able to check what shows are on in London and book a musical for some visiting foreign clients. Prestel also offers such time-saving interactive facilities in banking, travel arrangements, hotel reservations, office services bureaux and so on.

A further useful feature of Prestel lies in its ability to connect the user – at a fee – to private computerised databases of information via 'gateways' – a simple term used to describe the sophisticated electronic network which links two remote computers to the user. Thus a manager in Edinburgh can browse through the menus of a United States university's database on, say, American taxation laws or registered patents on inventions!

BT also offer private versions of Prestel to larger organisations entirely for their own use. The travel industry, for example, uses a videotex system connecting tour operators with travel agents so as to reserve flight seats and hotels at the time of enquiry (subject to confirmation and deposit). City financiers also use viewdata systems to relay up-to-the-minute share prices to dealers.

Additional Prestel features include: an electronic mail system called Mailbox, which has recently been extended to link in with BT's Telecom Gold service; Closed User Groups services which link specific users privately; a means of accessing BT's telex service, and the facility of communicating with other databases through BT's gateway services.

How to operate Prestel

1 Call up Prestel, on the telephone number supplied.

2 Wait for the acknowledgement tone and then key in your ten-digit customer identification number.

3 Next key in your personal password. (*Note*: this may be changed at will.) Prestel title page appears.

4 Check if any messages are waiting in Mailbox.

5 Key in # symbol to access Main Index.

6 Follow instructions to access specific pages or key in * followed by the name of a selected sector eg *BANKING to move directly to this part of the database.

7 If the command *90# is keyed in it takes the user out of Prestel.

Useful Prestel commands

**page number#*   e.g. *221# will screen Prestel' page 221

**topic word#*   eg *TELESHOPPING# will display the Teleshopping initial menu

*00 Display that page again

*8#   Entry to telex link

*#   Go back one page

Go back two pages

*S followed by up to eight characters as a *code word#* will set up a 'pagemarker' for a selected page for instant recall. Prestel allows up to five pages to be pagemarked in this way.

**   takes the user back to a previously accessed sector

*   plus name of *gateway* eg *NERIS takes user into index of a linked computer database

*0#   takes the user back to Prestel

*333#   How to use Prestel

What does Prestel cost to use?

Given the speed, range of data, interactivity features and user-friendliness of Prestel, its costs are very reasonable to the public user. The connection charges to a Prestel computer are priced at *local call rates* and using Prestel at cheap rate times improves value for money, as does the taking of a page of data as a print-out instead of reading it while on line to Prestel. All Prestel users also pay a quarterly standing charge and a time charge which acts as a further tariff on top of the telephone charge. This charge is not levied after 6.00 pm Mondays to Fridays, nor from 1.00 pm on Saturdays until 8.00 am Mondays. Some frames or pages of information display a number which indicates an extra charge payable levied by the information provider.

Viewdata videotex and the future

Prestel originally got off to a slow start and some telecommunications experts consider that the service should have been concentrated on the business user rather than the man in the street. That the technology offers a marvellous opportunity to bring the information in reference books, research documents, encyclopaedias, timetables, catalogues, etc, swiftly and easily to the office executive and secretary is beyond doubt. That its two-way communications system offers tremendous savings in time and effort for making bookings and confirming travel arrangements and so on is also not in dispute. It remains to be seen how BT will develop Prestel so as to make its database less dependent upon the commercial interests of some information providers and more comprehensive as a public information service.

DISCUSSION TOPICS

1   With electronic mail, fax, telephone answering machines and voice mail services available to office workers, as well as the ability to work from home or remote locations through lap-top computers, BT Gold, etc, are managers, executives and secretaries likely to lose face-to-face contact? If this were to occur, would it matter?

2   How practical is the concept of 'the paperless office? What issues surround the move towards fully electronic information processing? What are its limitations?

QUICK REVIEW QUIZ

1   Explain the following terms used in facsimile transmission:
   (a) transceiver
   (b) encoding
   (c) delayed transmission
   (d) status report
   (e) reception polling

2   Briefly what are the differences between 'telex', and 'teletex'?

3   How does a teleprinter work?

4   What advantages do you think fax has over telex?

5   What type of service does Prestel offer?

6   What is a 'gateway' in viewdata terminology?

7   When is it cheapest to use Prestel?

RESEARCH AND REPORT BACK ASSIGNMENTS

1   First carry out your research in pairs, then produce a short guide for newly-appointed secretarial staff on the services which are available from facsimile transceivers and telex equipment and the respective advantages and disadvantages of each. Your guide should include a comparison of costs and provide some helpful examples which illustrate how each may be used to best advantage.

2   Find out what uses a commercial company could make of Prestel's viewdata services as follows:
   (a) As a UK national hotel chain wishing to increase its business through advertising on Prestel.
   (b) As a large company with a sales force which travels extensively in the UK and overseas.

Having done your research, demonstrate your findings to your group using a Prestel terminal if possible, or with the aid of diagrams and illustrations.

3.3 The telephone – CABX and mobile phones

Telephone services, using a CABX system; mobile phones for mobile people; how directories can help you.

TELEPHONE SERVICES IN ORGANISATIONS

Nowhere in today's office has IT brought about more changes than in the telephone systems linking in-house, local, national and international calls. Indeed, the current global network of telephone lines not only carries several hundred billion telephone calls around the world each year, but it also routes similarly huge amounts of data between computers and their users via of modems and multiplexing (a means of enabling telephone lines to transmit varying data – voice and computer language based – much faster).

It is therefore becoming increasingly difficult to view the telephone system – as it once was – as a totally distinct medium of communication. Indeed, British Telecom is currently installing an **Integrated Services Digital Network (ISDN)** in the UK which will join together voice-based telecommunications via Private Automatic Branch Exchanges (PABXs)* and the **Public Switched Telephone Network (PSTN)** with computer digital data switching networks, like BT's **Packet Switched Services (PSS)** – Datel, Satstream and Kilostream. In this way, communications in the media of voice, telex, fax, videotex, **Confravision** and digitally processed data will become fully exchangeable through a unified telecommunications network, instead of in today's piecemeal fashion in which some equipment cannot 'talk to' similar equipment of a different make and design, because they are not compatible.

While keeping in mind this trend of unifying voice and data in a single network, this section will concentrate upon the telephone system's range of services with which today's secretary must be fully conversant.

Telephone services and the office

Essentially, there are two kinds of telephone service available in any office. Firstly there is the private line which connects its user directly to the PSTN exchange which is known as a Direct Exchange Line. Some senior managers have such telephone lines connected to a personal desktop **handset** so as to be able to make confidential business calls in complete privacy.

Secondly there is the extension line which connects the user to a central switchboard. In large organisations several switchboard operators are kept busy routing incoming calls to desired extensions and obtaining telephone numbers for staff wishing to make outgoing calls. At the turn of the century such connections were made by plugging large sets of cables into a board by means of jack plugs – 'trying to connect you …' Today such arm-aching activity has been replaced by pressing touch-sensitive buttons on a desktop computerised switchboard no bigger than a ring-binder which may control as many as 50–100 extensions!

For many years small firms like accountants', solicitors' and doctors' practices used systems which linked some 8–12 handsets. Any one user could accept an incoming call and route it if need be to a companion extension. By the same token, any one user could access an outside line. Such systems, however, offered no protection from unauthorised use.

As a result, large organisations preferred to employ systems which allowed centralised control. For

---

* Note increasingly *Computerised* Automatic Branch Exchanges (CABX) are replacing their PABX counterparts.

Fig 3.18 The four stages of the telephone network

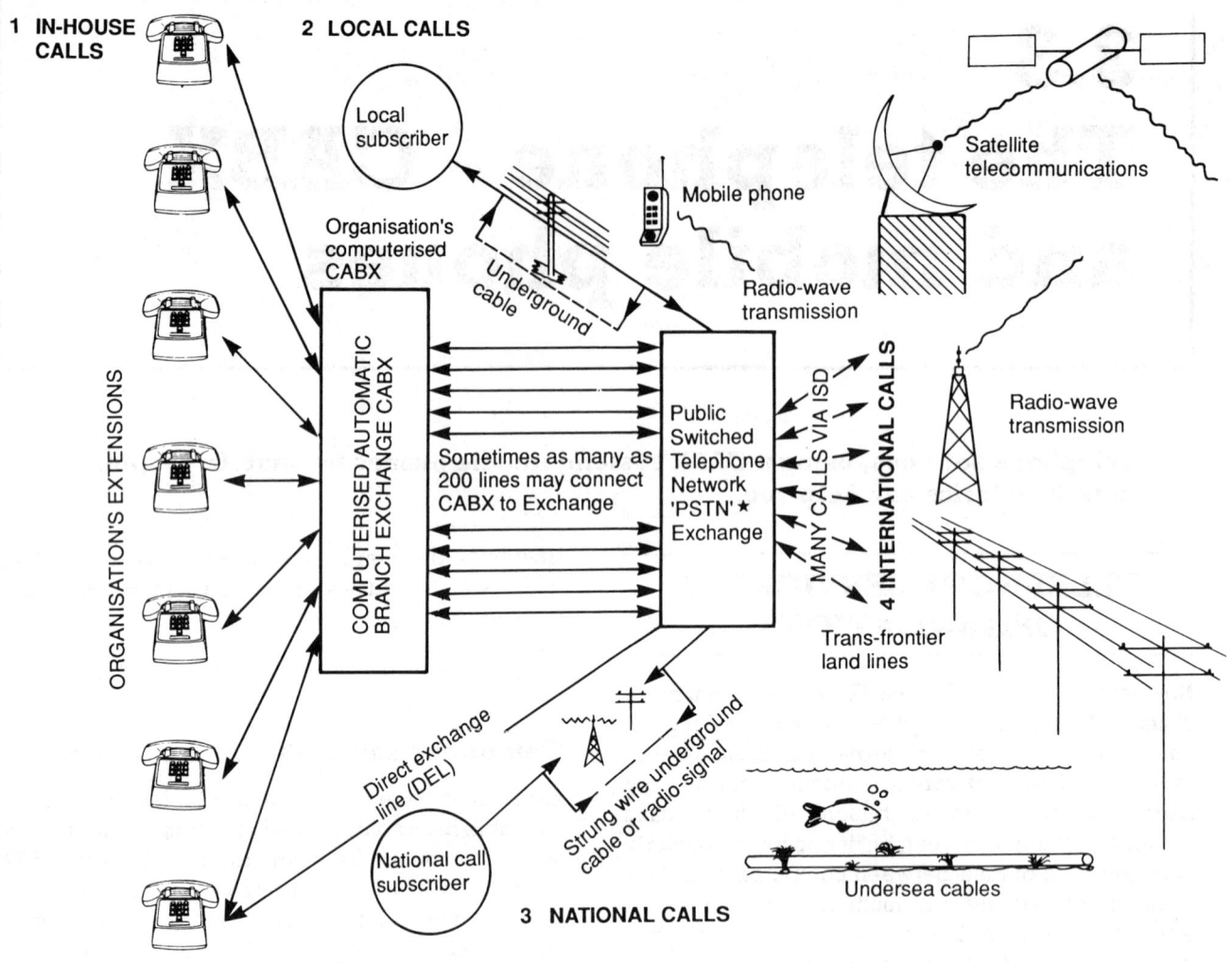

*Currently being replaced by the Integrated Services Digital Network (ISDN)

example, current computerised systems provide a number of monitoring features:

- **Outside line access limited to local call-making only**: usually by dialling 9 on any extension given this facility
- **Call barring**: outside calls may only be made through the switchboard operator or not at all.
- **Call interrupting**: audio or visual prompts are activated in handsets when calls go on for longer than a pre-arranged time (say 5 minutes)
- **Call override**: a switchboard operator or senior manager may break into a call if the caller is urgently required.
- **Call logging and reporting**: sophisticated equipment exists to monitor all incoming and outgoing calls by extension number and to calculate ongoing costs and time handset is active; such measures help to keep down telephone costs and to enable accounts departments to allocate to each department an accurate proportion of the single, all-in telephone bill it receives quarterly.

Following upon the privatisation of British Telecom a number of UK telecommunications manufacturers like Plessey and Ferranti introduced a range of C/PABX (sometimes simply referred to as PBX) computerised telephone systems capable of supplying the needs of 8–250 + extension users. Such manufacturers vied with each other to include yet more sophisticated features in order to win orders and to provide a better service. Some of the more commonly occurring ones are described on page 112.

Information handling: using equipment effectively

Fig 3.19 How ISDX is coordinating organisational telecommunications

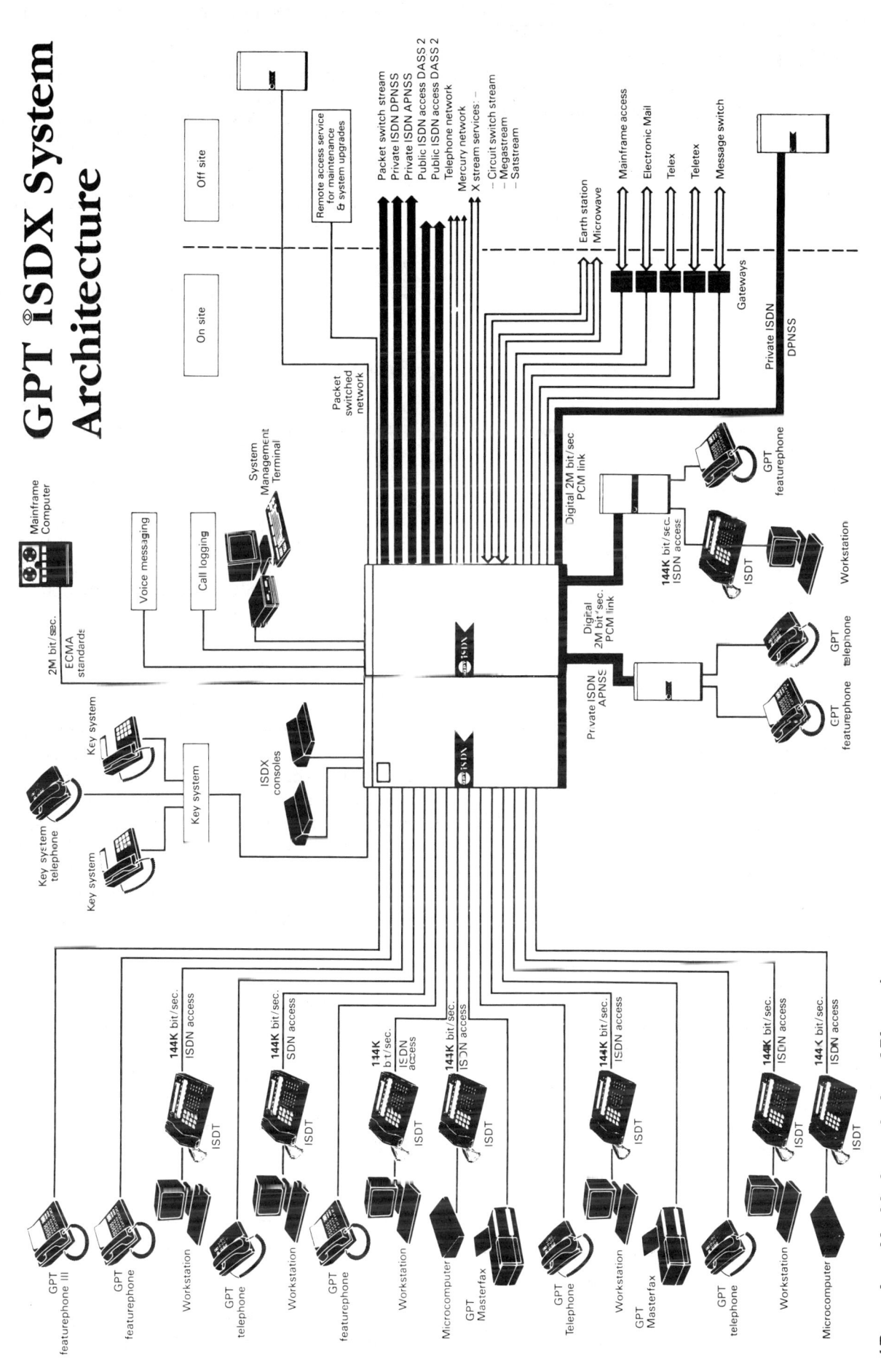

GPT ISDX System Architecture

(Reproduced by kind permission of Plessey)

Major typical features of a large CABX system

This table is based upon the Ferranti GTE OMNI System and is kindly made available by Ferranti GTE Ltd)

Some of OMNI's system features

Administration message recording – to provide usage reports
Dictation access – providing a link to dictation services
Group hunting – seeking out any one of a working team's extensions available to take an in-coming call by trying each in turn
Intercom groups – linking users via intercom speakers
Music on hold – playing a soothing tune over the phone while a caller is waiting to be connected
Paging and code calling access – ability to activate pagers used by roving staff
Standby power – facility to keep system going in event of power failure
Call barring – ability to restrict the range of connections availability on any extension

Some attendant features

Automatic recall re-dial – system keeps trying to connect to a busy number

Break in – facility to break into an active conversation in case of urgency
Call waiting – provision to alert extension user of another call awaiting attention
Camp on busy – ability to wait, having dialled a number until it becomes available and then to ring dialler's extension having effected the connection
Conference – linking of several extension users so all can converse with each other over the phone – system can also include outside callers

Some extension features

Abbreviated dialling – often used numbers are given a short 1/2 digit code to save time
Boss – secretary – direct interconnection
Call forwarding follow me – instruction for incoming calls to be routed from a customary extension to others near to a roving staff member
Call hold – facility to keep line open to caller while specific staff member located
Direct inward dialling – facility to enable incoming calls to be routed directly to selected extension by adding its number to normal organisation's number
Direct outward dialling – facility to access PSTN directly
Do not disturb – cuts phone off while meeting etc. taking place; avoids irritating interruptions
Extension to extension calling – for direct in-house phone calls

Other major features included in CABX systems are

Amplifying speech – to enable an incoming call to be heard across a room
Night service – enables incoming calls to be answered by late staying staff after switchboard staff have left
Call parking – the ability to divert an incoming call to another extension
'No answer' transfer – facility to re-route a call to another, specified extension

Note: Many of the above features of computerised switchboards are available to the general public with the introduction of BT''s System X digital exchanges.

Keysystem and CABX

In concentrating upon the CABX as the telephone system which the secretary is more likely to use in a larger organisation, it is important not to overlook the sales boost which IT has given to key system telephone networks. Essentially the key system telephone network has been around for many years in the form of the small user Post Office Telephones plans which enable any telephone extension (usually up to 8–12) to accept any incoming call and to route it to an alternative if that was where the call needed to be connected.

The key system telephone network comprises extension units linked in a circuit where each extension is able to display the status of incoming-call/extension connections which are active and this does away with the need for a switchboard operator. Any free extension user is able to answer an incoming call and usually one member of staff has this duty as a priority. Key systems are being designed with increasingly useful features for small businesses and professional partnerships, and today's secretary in training may well end up with a major responsibility for coordinating a key system telephone circuit.

Executel

A new telephone switchboard with a display unit and loudspeaker facility, storage capacity for a 20-year electronic diary, telephone number directory and reminders for external and internal calls, together with an inbuilt calculator. It may also be used as an Email and viewdata terminal for Prestel or telex via the Prestel Line.

USING A CABX SYSTEM

In order to make optimum use of a CABX computerised telephone system by means of an extension handset, it pays to have an informed understanding of

Information handling: using equipment effectively

how the system is structured and what the switchboard operator does and how he or she may be able to provide support. In many ways the CABX may be regarded as an upgraded version of preceding key and lamp PABXs but one which offers a much wider range of services both to callers ringing in and users of its internal network.

Operations at the console

The CABX at the console end embodies a noticeably slimmer and sleeker switchboard and handset for internal enquiries. The console generally possesses these features:

1 A series of panels which may be lit and made to flash in order to convey the status of each exchange line – in use or free – and a system which causes each lit panel to pulse or flash in various ways to indicate, for example, whether an incoming call is ringing on the desired extension or whether the operator has parked it while finding an alternative free extension by using the group hunting feature.

2 The CABX console will possess a numeric keypad for keying in call numbers and, usually, a number of keys – like command or function keys on a PC keyboard – which activate specific operations, like retrieving a call which has been put on 'hold' or 'park', or breaking into an active call in case of urgency, etc. Indeed, it is the wide range of such features which makes computerised versions of these systems so attractive.

3 In addition, many CABX consoles include an LCD panel on which messages are displayed to aid the operator during a series of busy transactions. For example the panel may advise that an incoming call and a specific extension number are connected, or it may display the digits of an external number as it is being keyed in on the keypad, to provide a visual check.

4 The console also features a series of ringing codes or patterns which alert the operator to an incoming call or extension user dialling the switchboard and the CABX will include a number of distinct ringing patterns and tones to convey different messages such as:

- line is busy
- there is a call waiting to be connected to your extension

Fig 3.20 Plessey's ISDX switchboard

- you are connected to an outside line
- the number you dialled is not obtainable.

5 The operator has a number of support features available at the console, including abbreviated dialling codes for numbers often used by the organisation, 'repeat last number' if connection not immediately made, and overdialling for storing the IDD prefix parts of long overseas telephone numbers in regular organisational use.

Operations at the handset

Firstly it is important to remember that all computerised systems are programmable. This means that any individual handset may be allocated a variety of permitted functions. Any extension may be programmed as a master phone with full facilities or may have a number of activities barred so that, for example, it may only make 999 calls out, or only dial local numbers direct, or only national ones.

The range of features available to the extension handset user naturally varies according to the size and hence sophistication of the system used. It is very important for the secretary to acquire as quickly as possible after appointment a thorough understanding of the organisation's system, even if this means requesting a short training course since inadequate telephone techniques such as losing or cutting off an incoming caller cause much loss of face and dent the office's image. The following features are available to the extension user on most systems:

1 Dialling out

Extension users normally access the console operator by dialling 0 and acquire an outside line by dialling 9. On many systems it is possible also to dial an extension number on the organisation's private line circuit by dialling 7 followed by the number.

2 Handling calls coming in to the extension

Remember that an important part of the secretary's role is to act as a preliminary filter of calls and to handle them accordingly. Here the computerised systems offer many useful features which may be activated (if the system operates MF4 handsets) by pressing the R button and then dialling various codes:

- Putting an incoming call on HOLD. This enables the secretary to talk without the caller hearing – for instance, to check with the manager whether he is 'in'.
- *Transferring* incoming calls to another extension – for example when it becomes apparent that another department or staff member is needed
- *Parking* an incoming call; sometimes it is necessary to keep a call in suspension while checking a matter with another extension user etc.
- *Shuttling* between an incoming call and an extension; this feature enables an extension user to move back and forth between two lines without either hearing the other and the user talking.
- *Conferencing* is a feature which permits a number of internal extensions and external lines to be linked by the extension users dialling up a code. The secretary may be expected to 'line up' such a conference for her manager.

Note: codes are available to retrieve calls put on 'park', 'hold' or 'transfer'.

In the context of taking calls, it is important to remember that most managers have the system programmed so that their secretaries' extensions intercept all incoming calls to the manager for prior screening.

3 Making calls

Outside calls may be made either by dialling 9 followed by the prefix and number needed or via the console operator after dialling 0. The following internal features are also available to the extension user:

- *Automatic ring back* allows the system to ring the user's number when contact has been made with a number which was not immediately obtainable. The user does not have to hang on to the extension receiver while waiting. This feature also comes into play if an internal extension number is busy when dialled.
- *Ring back when in* is a feature where the system notes an extension number is not being answered and then retries the user's call after it picks up the fact that the desired extension has just been used.
- *Ring back for an exchange line* contacts the extension user (the bell rings) when an exchange line becomes available if all were busy when the user wished to dial out.
- *Piggybacking* is a jargon term used to describe a feature which enables the extension user to contact other extension users on a different but connected CABX system – say of a sister company or subsidiary.

Other useful features

Most systems enable mobile secretaries and managers to have incoming or extension calls forwarded from their home extensions to other assigned extensions. For example, if you plan to spend some time in the reprographics unit, you may arrange for incoming calls to be rerouted there.

- *Call forward* diverts calls to another extension and prevents the home extension being used

- *Follow me* allows calls to be routed to further extensions as the user moves around the organisation's buildings

- *Alarm call* allows any user to arrange for a call to be made to a given handset in order to act as a reminder for, say, an important meeting. Secretaries who know they become engrossed in their work use this feature to help them remember their managers' priority appointments or overseas calls to be made, etc.

- *Night service* allows an extension user to make and take calls after the operator has gone home

- *Call waiting and intrusion* are features where the handset user is made aware of other callers queuing to talk to him/her (call waiting) and of a need for a priority user to access the line being used or to access the caller directly in an emergency (intrusion).

- *Do not disturb* allows the user of any given extension to put a bar on receiving any calls until further notice – vital if sensitive and important interviews and meetings are not to be interrupted, or if a priority task is under way.

Summary

Information Technology has made a tremendous impact upon telephone systems. The number of potential contacts – customers, government officials, organisation managers etc – who may call up the secretary has increased greatly as a result of national and international direct dialling and the extension of private line circuits. Similarly, the ways in which such callers may be handled by a CABX system have become much more sophisticated.

No two CABX or key system circuits are the same and so it becomes most important for the secretary in training to acquire a informed understanding of typical routines and features and once in post to acquire an absolutely thorough mastery of the system employed by her organisation.

Examples of British Telecom telephone services to business

Audio conferencing
Providing regional/national/international telephone hook-ups for meetings etc.

Call cost indication
Informing user of the cost of a telephone call just completed.

Citicall
Information service on stocks and shares.

Yellow Pages
1.4 million listed business services in district directories.

Credit authorisation
Acceptance of credit payment for phone calls, etc.

Pay card sales
Sale of units of phone call time via a plastic card: many public phone boxes accept this form of payment and erase time used from the inserted card (cards sold in units of 10, 40 and 200).

Freefone service
Businesses accept sales enquiries by phone and pay for the incoming calls – up to a preset time limit.

Mobile radiophone and car/train phone service
Mobile, cordless telephones connected by radio to BT telephone network; equipment is sold by Cellnet and Vodaphone for national use via BT's Cellnet system to route messages over more than short local distances.

Ship's telephone service
Long-established passenger phone service routed via radio signals and/or satellite.

Star services
Eight services provided by System X exchanges: call waiting warning signal; abbreviated call coding, up to 27 numbers' repeat last call; charge advice; call diversion; 3-way calling; call barring.

Telephone credit cards (national and international)
Internationally placed calls are accepted and placed by the operator upon the citing of your credit number; especially useful for sales representatives.

Radio paging
Individuals are 'bleeped' anywhere in UK by radio signal and asked to get into telephone contact Note: some pagers only emit certain tones, others will communicate short messages on an LCD strip.

Data sources: British Telecom and *The Telecom User's Handbook*: and Telecommunications Press

---

DISCUSSION TOPIC

What do you see as some of the disadvantages and problems of the expanding microchip-based telephone network service from a secretarial viewpoint? What personal guidelines should a secretary adopt to prevent telephone calls from becoming too intrusive and other work retarded?

> **Top secretary tips – telephone systems**
>
> 1 Maintain an up-to-date personal telephone directory of often used internal and external numbers.
>
> 2 Make use of abbreviated and central memory dialling codes.
>
> 3 Keep a checklist of the codes the system uses to activate its features – call transfer, conferencing set up etc – until you have them off by heart.
>
> 4 Make a checklist of the features and support services offered from the console and operator which can help you.
>
> 5 Ensure that whatever the system, you have a quick and simple means – intercom or other – of *talking privately* to your manager while holding or parking calls.
>
> 6 Ensure you inform your callers that you are about to transfer them or put them on 'park' or 'hold' – no one likes to feel dumped or ignored. If it takes time to sort out an intervening matter, go back to your caller to give reassurance and say what is happening every minute or so.
>
> 7 Make sure you keep at hand *up-to-date* copies of internal directories, reference books, BT charge tariffs, and other useful sources of information.

MOBILE PHONES FOR MOBILE PEOPLE

The early 1980s saw a rapid uptake among managers, executives, professionals and self-employed businessmen of the mobile phone and its 'sidekick' the radiopager.

The system developed by both Telecom-Securicor and Racal – Vodaphone under licence is called a **cellular telephone network**. As the diagram (Fig 3.21) illustrates, it enables different types of mobile telephone (powered by either car or inserted batteries) to transmit a radio signal which is, in effect, like the dialled telephone call. This radio signal is picked up at the perimeter of the cell (the area picked up by one British Telecom exchange) in which the user finds himself and relayed to a telephone exchange where it connects with the national PSTN system. As the mobile telephone user moves from one cell to another in his car, the radio signal of the continuing telephone call is relayed on to the next cell in the network.

This system is complicated and was made necessary by the lack of available radio wavebands available. As a consequence, each cell can only operate at a maximum of about 30 kilometres and must then be repeated, much like the hexagon structure of bees' honeycombs. At present the cellphone system is available to mobile car phone, transportable phone and pocket phone users. For the time being the equipment is expensive to acquire but it does offer total accessibility in the UK and its suppliers emphasise the savings to be made in time and money, where, for example, a manager can be given last-minute information as he drives to a major sales meeting or an architect on site can telephone urgent instructions about amending building plans to his office etc. The extension of mobile telephones to some trains and aeroplanes (Skyphone on British Airways) is also now taking place, so that the manager need never be out of touch with the office of the 1990s.

Radiopaging

A less expensive form of contacting mobile staff is through **radiopagers**. These are small devices, which are sometimes called bleepers, which pick up a radio signal which causes them to emit a bleeping sound. Such a signal alerts the person carrying the radiopager to telephone his office, say, from an internal extension in a large hospital, or from a payphone in the world at large if he does not possess a cellphone. The latest type of radiopager includes a LCD panel which can accept transmitted brief messages via radio signal, such as: CONGRATS! GLOBAL CONTRACT IN THE BAG! or, MOST URGENT YOU RING 01-345-9876 DIRECTLY. British Telecom offers a range of services to enable customers to transmit such messages over the UK as a whole to remotely located radiopager holders – even veterinary surgeons knee-deep in Farmer Giles' water meadows!

> **Top secretary tip – mobile phones**
> If your manager is a cellphone or radiopager user, *make sure you know his cellphone or paging number* as it is extremely frustrating, having gone to the expense of acquiring such equipment not to be contacted in an emergency. On the other hand, avoid cellphoning or paging unnecessarily. Remember that even the most tolerant of bosses go off the deep-end if they have to cope with office trivia having tramped to a distant payphone or interrupted a sales presentation to respond to a low priority matter that you could have assigned to an office team-member.

Information handling: using equipment effectively

Fig 3.21 How cellphones work

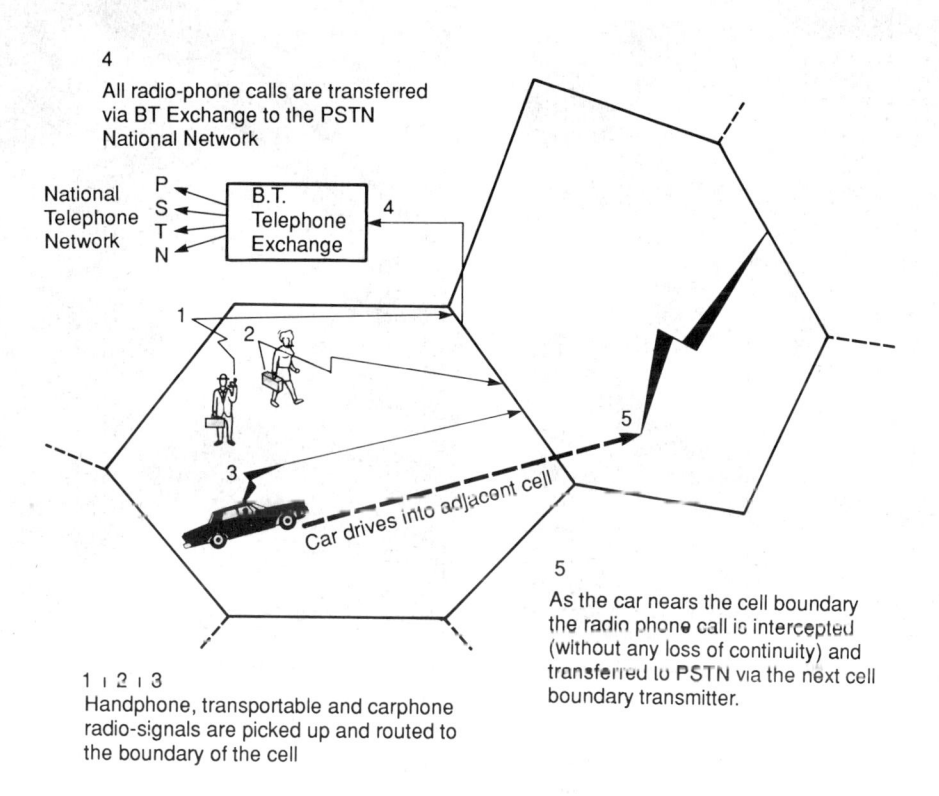

4
All radio-phone calls are transferred via BT Exchange to the PSTN National Network

National Telephone Network — PSTN — B.T. Telephone Exchange — 4

1 | 2 | 3
Handphone, transportable and carphone radio-signals are picked up and routed to the boundary of the cell

Car drives into adjacent cell

5
As the car nears the cell boundary the radio phone call is intercepted (without any loss of continuity) and transferred to PSTN via the next cell boundary transmitter.

HOW DIRECTORIES CAN HELP

When using directories for telephone work, we all tend to make straight for the alphabetical listing to find a desired number or address etc. It is a mistake, however, to overlook the extensive help and supportive information which such directories provide and the following checklist gives an overview of the many ways in which the directories we associate with the telephone can be of great help to the busy secretary:

1 The BT Phone Book

A BT Phone Book is produced for each telephone area and includes information of international, national and local relevance.

Services available by dialling 100 (the BT telephone exchange operator): booking an alarm call (your telephone number is dialled at a prearranged time for an early call etc.); advice of duration and charge for a call just finished (ADC); connecting credit charge calls, reversed charge calls, person-to-person calls, **telemessages**, ships' telephone service; conference calls, fax services etc.

Other BT services: 192 connects to Directory Enquiries (142 for the London area), 150 to Sales Service for Business Systems, 155 to International Conference Calls, and 151 to Fault Repairs Service. Note that BT offers a range of services under 'Mobile Communications' for cellphones, System 4 (BT's own direct dial radio network) and voice bank messaging service.

Information in the BT Phone Book sections
Section 1: this section contains *useful numbers* information about broadcasting stations, newspapers, local government departments in the area, hospitals, libraries and tourist information sources of information; it also provides a very useful list of places covered in the directory and their correct postal addresses.

Section 2: this section lists the *local area codes*, and details locations to which calls may be made at the 'a' rate (see BT's call charges tariff); Section 2 also lists the *national codes* which act as prefixes for national calls, eg Manchester is 061 and Birmingham 021; this section also includes the prefix codes for those parts of Eire which may be dialled direct.

Fig 3.22 A British Telecom radiopager in use

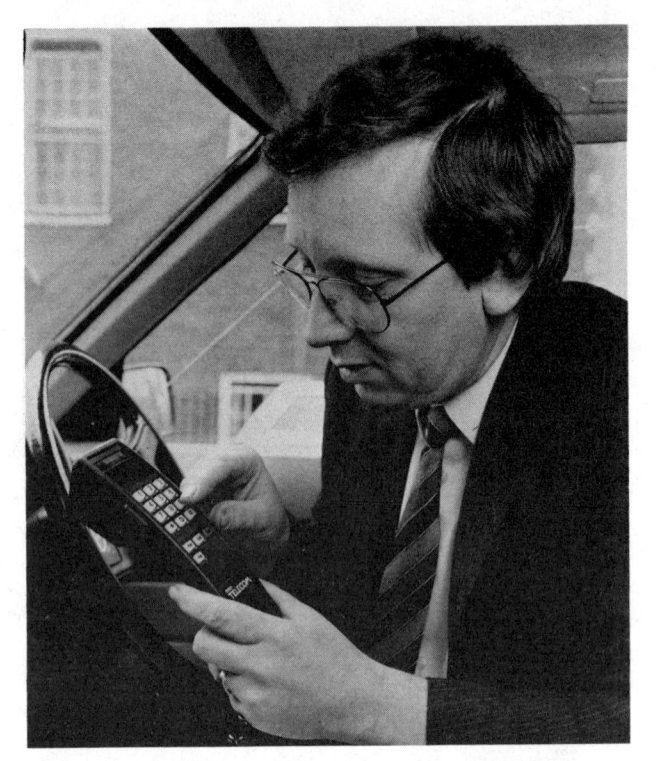

Fig 3.23 A cellular telephone from British Telecom

Section 3 in this Section helpful tips are included on making international calls via **IDD** together with a summary of BT International Services and a country-by-country listing of IDD prefixes and principal area codes; BT also include a clock diagram showing the time difference in each country and useful information on cultural/religious practices, such as a reminder about prayer times in Saudi Arabia and the working week Monday to Thursday in Moslem countries.

Section 4: advises users how to use the inland telephone service and *LISTS NUMBERS WITHIN THE BOUNDARIES OF THE AREA* of the *Phone Book* by alphabetic sequence of customers' names.

Section 5: BT include here a schedule of the Code of Practice by which they operate and advise on what to do about faults or in case of complaint. Details about OFTEL (Office of Telecommunications), a telephone consumer watchdog body, are included.

2 Thomson Local Directory

This directory is produced to cover local areas in separate editions. It provides a classified list of local businesses and services, information about airports and transport services, Citizens' Advice Bureaux, government offices, newspaper and local broadcasting addresses, travel and tourist information and leisure and help numbers and addresses. In addition, it provides helpful information on the correct postcodes of large organisations and local streets. Users will also find a checklist of last posting times to major cities from the local main post office.

3 Yellow Pages

The well known *Yellow Pages* directory is also produced in local editions and lists by sector classification the names and addresses of all sorts of local businesses and services, from plumber to tree surgeon to garage and office equipment supplier. *Yellow Pages* also supplies street maps, and help and advice sections

4 Electronic directories

Don't forget that electronic directories (databases of information) are also becoming much more readily available and include Prestel and an electronic *Yellow Pages*, accessed from the secretary's desktop PC.

Top secretary tip – your personal telephone directory

Make up and maintain your *personal* telephone directory. Every manager and office have their own specialised network of customers and contacts. Top secretaries keep a directory (on their electronic telephone database application software) of regularly used numbers and addresses and set up abbreviated call codes to dial out via the CABX system.

Information handling: using equipment effectively

QUICK REVIEW QUIZ

1 Explain what the following abbreviations stand for: PABX, CABX, PSTN, ISDN, PSS. What type of telecommunication is provided by each?

2 Using a CABX, what kind of call-regulating restraints can a central administration impose on its staff?

3 Explain what is meant by the following telephone system terms:

a group hunting *b* automatic recall redial *c* camp on busy *d* break in *e* call hold *f* call parking

4 Explain briefly the main differences between a key system and CABX facility and what kind of user would be better suited to either.

5 What type of telephone service would you expect from:

a Freefone *b* Star services *c* International conferencing

6 What action would you take if you experienced a fault on the telephone you were using?

7 What information would you find in:

a Thomson Local Directory *b* Yellow pages?

8 How does a radiopaging device aid organisational communications?

9 How does a cellular telephone system work?

RESEARCH AND REPORT BACK ASSIGNMENTS

1 Find out what a three-minute telephone call costs:

(a) At peak rates to a destination over 56 km distance in the UK
(b) To a mobile telephone (0860 numbers) at standard rate times
(c) A dialled call to Cairo, Egypt, at standard rate times
(d) A person-to-person call to the Channel Islands at peak rate

2 Find out what services British Telecom provides through its international calls service which you consider particularly useful for a secretary to know about. Compose a factsheet of the major aspects of your findings and copy it to your fellow students as a study aid.

3 Invite a telephone sales manager to give a talk to your group on the latest facilities of CABX systems and how they can help the busy manager and secretary.

4 Research the facilities offered by:

either the cellular telephone network
or radiopagers

and brief your group on your findings. Emphasise their usefulness in manager/secretary communications.

3.4 Office reprographics

B-IT: before information technology! printers; photocopiers; desktop publishing.

B-IT: BEFORE INFORMATION TECHNOLOGY!

As you already appreciate, new technologies seldom advance on a broad, even front. Usually there are advance parties of early new technology users and pockets of diehard resisters. The area of reprographics – reproducing text, number and graphic image – is no exception. At the forefront of IT-based systems are laser colour printers and colour copiers and at the rear of the field are the spirit and ink duplicators and heat-transer copiers. 'Before IT' reprographics tended to rely on three methods of reprography: either a combination of heat, light and chemically treated paper, or a means of transferring ink through a cut stencil (ink duplicating) or by transferring ink (by typewriter) on to a master sheet in a kind of embossed way so that the text thus produced could be activated by a spirit – spirit duplicated. These last two types of duplication imprint lines of text (or drawings) on to sheets of paper passing under a roller on to which the master is attached.

The technology widely known as 'plain paper copying' also preceded the IT office age but has been enhanced by IT rather than overtaken by it (see below).

PRINTERS

Electronic printers

The advent of the widely distributed desktop PC in the late 1970s meant that users either needed access to an adjacent personal printer or the opportunity to share a faster, more sophisticated and more powerful one. And to complicate matters, while office DP managers were seeking to provide a prompt and easily accessible service to managers, secretaries, clerks and WP operators, printer manufacturers were busy developing four quite different major types of electronic printer, known as thermal, dot matrix, ink-jet and laser. Each has its advantages for use in many different types of office application and the thoughtful secretary will ensure she knows which type of printer offers the best cost-effective approach for various tasks.

The dot matrix printers

This printer's name stems from the way in which it imprints characters on to paper. Early dot matrix printers possessed a print head made up of nine wires which struck an inked ribbon in various patterns so as to imprint, say, the letter A, the number 2, or the percentage sign %. A close examination of 9-wire dot matrix printing reveals the rather ragged outline made in this way:

Fig 3.24 An example of dot matrix printer

```
THE DOT MATRIX PRINTER CREATES
CHARACTERS FROM DOTS
```

The use of nine wires meant that each character was in effect nine dots high and text was printed by the printer running bidirectionally – left to right then right to left for consecutive lines of text. The 9-wire dot matrix printer could print at roughly 100–200 characters per second (cps) in what is called now draft quality typescript – that is to say with a print quality only suited for internal consumption and not up to letter quality. Dot matrix printers at the upper end of the market operated at both *draft quality* (DQ) and *near letter quality* (NLQ). The NLQ speed is appreciably slower because the print-head passes twice over each character in a slight skew to fill out its ragged edges. Dot matrix printers have proved extremely reliable workhorses for many managers and office staff. Typical ribbons last for some 3 million characters and print-heads for 100 million characters. Most low-cost dot matrix printers are used with tractor feed continuous paper which is also cheap. An additional feature of the dot matrix printer is its ability to print graphs, charts and other computer-originated diagrams. The computer directs the printing operation (as it does in the case of all electronic 'on line' printers, ie printers which accept their instructions from the computerised software program). As a result, modern software can produce very useful and flexible print-out very cheaply using dot matrix printing technology.

In 1985 some 85% of the electronic desktop printer market in Europe was dot matrix; however, the arrival of ink-jet and laser printers at more affordable prices caused dot matrix printer manufacturers to look to their laurels as users demanded a higher quality of print appearance – up to letter quality standards. As a result, a 24-pin (or wire) dot matrix printer was developed by leading manufacturers. This offered a much enhanced print appearance of letter quality and offered speeds of some 400 cps in draft mode and 50–60 cps in letter quality mode. The introduction of 24 wires improved character resolution over two and a half times. Current upper end of the market dot matrix printers embody several different types of **fount** (or font; a design of typeface) and can also accept single, cut-sheet paper inserts without tractor-fed continuous stationery having to be removed. Also, some modern dot matrix printers can accept a colour ribbon add-on and so print documents in different colours – ie vary the colour in which consecutive lines of text are printed. Thus a use of different typefaces and colour at low cost makes it possible to produce appealing sales leaflets and house magazines, etc.

While the low purchase and running costs of dot matrix printers makes them attractive, the noise of their impact printing is much less so and a market for accoustic covers to limit noise soon arose, and users need to balance low-cost with impact printer noise levels.

Ink-jet printers

These printers operate within a quite different technology. Ink is drawn up from a cartridge into a series of tubes which focus on to a central printing point. An electrical pulse ejects the ink on to the awaiting paper page which has been electrostatically treated so that the ink sticks to those parts which carry the text. The ink dries almost immediately.

While less ragged than draft quality dot matrix printed text, ink-jet text does not always convey the same high quality of appearance of either daisywheel or laser printed text. However, the quality of an ink-jet printer depends on its price and the one with 32 jet nozzles at the more expensive end of the market acts like the 24-pin dot matrix counterparts and upgrades the text to NLQ at a typical speed of 100 cps.

Like the dot matrix printer, the ink-jet can take continuous **fan-fold** paper and cut-sheet paper and generally possesses both tractor and sheet feed options. It will also accept roll paper.

Fig 3.25 An Epson printer

(Reproduced by kind permission of Epson (UK) Ltd)

Both types of printer are able to print text in the following ways:

emboldened, underscored, proportionally spaced, expanded, double height, double width and italics

all effected through keyed-in computer commands. Ink-jet printers are cheap to acquire at their lower market range and can accept normal office paper. They operate at a much quieter level than impact printers. Typical speeds are: draft quality using 10 pitch – 200 cps and near letter quality – 75 cps

Ink jet printers are currently finding a growing market as portable printers linked to lap-top computers, battery powered and about 50 cps at NLQ.

Daisywheel printers

Again, the name derives from the print-head technology. The daisywheel printer owes much to typewriter technology in that it prints by causing typescript characters connected to form a kind of wheel shaped like a daisy to strike an inked ribbon. Each character is fixed onto the tip of a plastic spoke referred to as a petal and each petal 'hammers' the ribbon in the identical sequence in which the text was keyed in on the computer keyboard. The daisy wheel thus rotates back and forth at what is now regarded as a relatively low speed about 90 cps at best. However, the daisywheel printer does produce good letter quality text.

The daisywheel printer is particularly useful for a secretary's personal use in correspondence and report work. One drawback, however, is that such printers cannot print graphs or charts nor do they offer the facility of easily moving from one kind of typeface to another, which the range of laser printer founts supplies. Exchanging one daisywheel for another can be fiddly, and if a petal is damaged, relatively expensive.

Laser printers

The laser printer is generally regarded as the very best of the electronic printers. Its technology uses a concentrated laser beam of light to transmit the computer's printing instructions (the text or image for printing) on to a cylindrical drum as a line of text or a line of a photograph or image in the making. The drum or roller moves over the sheet of paper on to which the text/image is to be printed. Those parts of the drum which have not been exposed to the laser beam's light accept the toner (black carbon dust) from a loaded cartridge and become the black printed letters or shades of black and grey in a photograph or drawing. The print resolution of laser printers is very high – 300 dots per inch, or 90 000 dots per square inch! As a result, text and images look crisp and sharp and of very good letter quality.

Also, the laser printer's print speeds are high compared to those of their counterparts. Some specialist (professional printing) laser printers can print at a rate of 200 A4 pages per minute. Typical office desktop laser printers operate at about 8–10 pages per minute, or about one A4 page every 6–8 seconds! However, this speed drops appreciably if the page for printing is complicated and includes several images.

In addition to high quality appearance, laser printers are extremely versatile – some have as many as 40 different print founts inbuilt with the facility to access others from slot-in electronic cards. Such printers provide a virtual printing house in the office!

ASSIGNMENT: FIND THE FOUNT(S) OF ALL KNOWLEDGE!

In groups of two to three find out where you can access copies of the following type founts which are in popular use today:

Univers □ Helvetica □ Old English □ Times □ Script □ Courier □ Bookman □ Zapf Chancery

Decide which fount would be most suited to what type of printed matter and compare your findings with your fellow groups. Discuss how easy access to a wide range of founts is likely to affect the ways in which a secretary may nowadays produce printed matter for different purposes and effects in various different situations.

Like its counterparts, the laser printer not only offers a very wide choice of founts, it also prints in the variations indicated above – italics, emboldened, proportional spacing, subscript and superscript, etc, and, because of its high resolution facility, can print type from very tiny sizes (printers would refer to 'four point' type) to very large sizes – say, 'eighteen points' in printers' jargon. The term point is a measurement of print height and width.

The laser printer tends to use A4 cut sheets stacked in a feeder and some models accept multisize stacking trays and can switch from A4 to envelopes or to labels directly. It also tends to be used by larger firms to produce their own forms and stationery cheaply, and its memory can retain the design of an extensive number of forms and schedules.

Line printers

It is worth noting that a high volume printer called a line printer is used in large organisations to produce computer DP printout in collated and bound report form.

Printers and paper

All the above printers will accept A4 cut sheet paper if appropriate feeders are fitted to them. Depending on their width, they will also accept continuous stationery up to some 400 mm or 16 inches in width. Dot matrix and ink jet printers accept most types of office paper, but laser printers require high quality bond paper for best results.

Printers and costs

As you might expect, there is with electronic printers a direct relationship between quality output and cost. The following factors affect such printing costs:

- Capital cost or leasing cost of the printer
- Cost of maintenance contract (can be significant)
- Renewal costs of: toner cassettes, cartridges and laser drums or black/colour ribbons or print wheels
- Cost of electricity to drive the printer
- Cost of paper used and amount used per month

Note: some printer and photocopier suppliers levy monthly charges based on the number of pages/copies printed.

When costed out at an all-in price per sheet, such costs vary considerably depending on the above factors and type of printer employed, with laser printers proving most expensive to run.

PHOTOCOPIERS

Choosing the right copier for the right job

At present there are some 175 different types of photocopier on the market and larger organisations will employ a family of photocopiers for different purposes and applications. These range from the small, personal desktop machines for very low volume 'one-off use' through middle or departmental copiers which may produce some 6000–20000 copies monthly, up to systems machines which are used in a central reprographics unit or print-room and may copy as many as 200000 pages per month. In this situation it is important for the secretary to be fully aware of the comparative costs of copying on a small copier as opposed to a systems machine – large print runs are made much more economically on large, purpose-built photocopiers and runs of 20–50 copies are very expensive by comparison on a single-sheet feed copier. Office staff tend to pay little heed to copying costs, and expect their work to be copied

Fig 3.26 The Minolta EP 870 photocopier

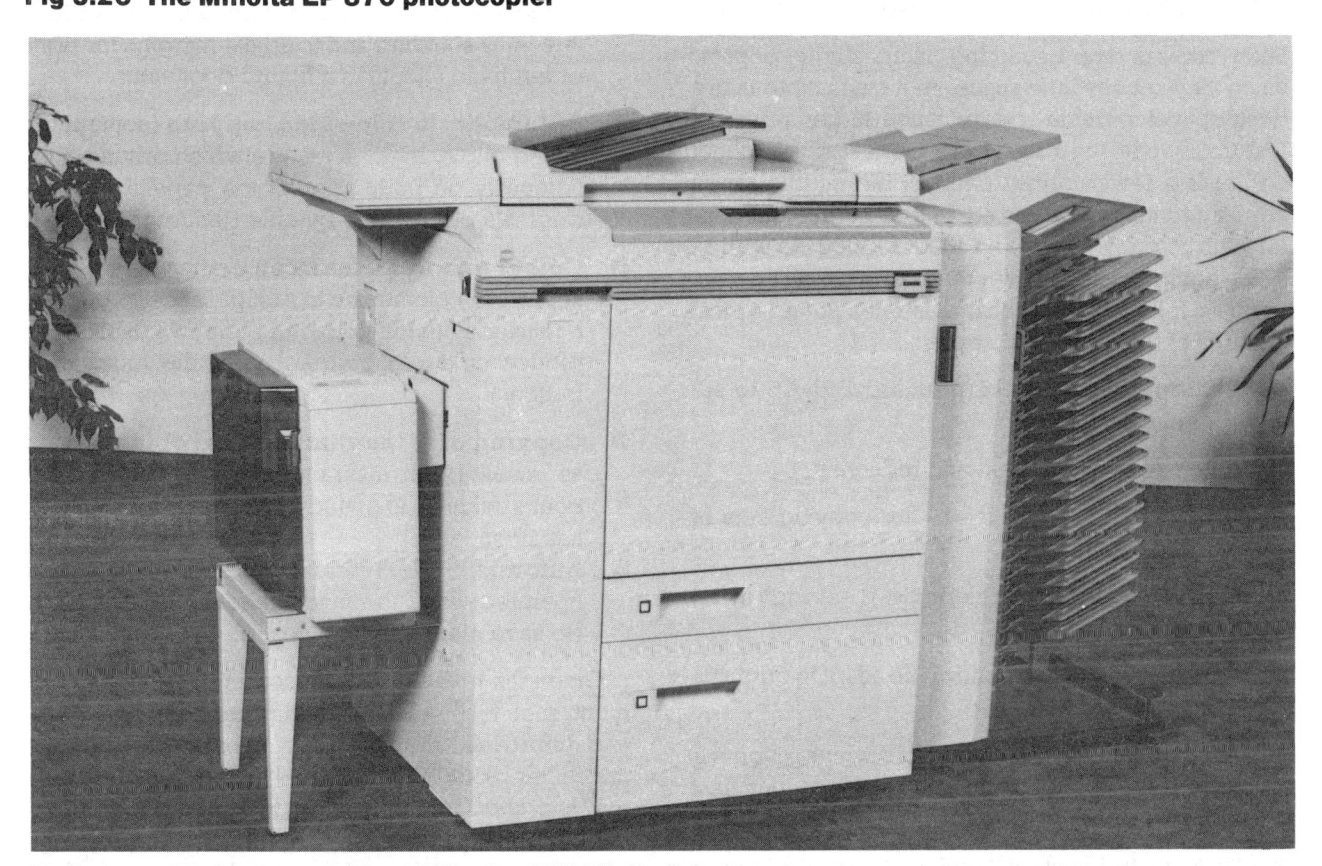

(Reproduced by kind permission of Minolta (UK) Limited)

instantly – by any machine available. Efficient secretaries control and route such reckless copying demands!

Low volume desktop copiers

The low volume desktop copier works slowly, but is reliable and cheap to buy. It is designed to handle occasional copying needs such as making a copy of an incoming letter three to four times to circulate to section heads, or to copy internal memos, notices or bulletins a few at a time.

Such copiers operate at approximately 8–15 copies per minute (cpm) and will only copy on one side of the paper at a time – to copy the reverse of a sheet requires reinsertion. The low volume desktop copier generally incorporates these features:

- hand-feeding of single sheets (a laborious process)
- light-dark adjustment to compensate for good/poor originals
- toner level indicator – to warn when toner is becoming used up
- paper jam indicator
- simple trays to hold paper passing through the copier before and after the process.

The mid-range or departmental copier

Such copiers are becoming increasingly popular since they occupy little space – not much more than a desktop yet provide a very much larger range of features. while the cost of the modest single sheet copier is a few hundred pounds, the middle range copier (sometimes referred to a departmental copier) will cost anything from £1500–£10 000. As with all office equipment, the buyer tends to get what he pays for. The following checklist illustrates some typical features of the mid range copier:

- Able to copy from A6 postcard and A5 to A3 paper sizes.
- Automatic enlargement and reduction.
- Automatic document feed – for copying sets of different originals
- Bypass feed to do a quick single-sheet copy in the middle of a long job.
- Automatic exposure control – to adapt to originals of varying quality.
- At least a 10-copy stacking bin which automatically collates copies into sets of reports, minutes, etc.
- User control system – either a security lock or insertable type of credit card which meters copies made.
- At least two automatic paper feed trays (A4 and A3) Note: some models automatically activate the appropriate paper 'cassette' tray according to the size of original.
- Capacity to hold at least 1 ream (500 sheets of copy paper) – many will hold 2000 sheets or more.
- Automatic enlargement and reduction features – both by predetermined ratios (according to paper sizes A5, A4, A3, etc, or by percentage – from, say 50% to 150% of original by single percentage steps – sometimes referred to as 'zoom magnification'.
- Emergency override switch to halt the photocopying process in the event of a mistake or machine fault.

Such is the pressure of competition to sell photocopiers – a market leader sold over half a million worldwide last year – that even the above range of features in the middle tier of copiers is being increased by such sophisticated facilities like:

- **Editing board and stylus** – rather like a computer's VDU and light-pen, this additional equipment enables the user to edit existing originals on a screen electronically and to blank out unwanted portions (image overlay), to join together parts of different originals without telltale lines showing and to adjust margins for right or left hand sheets in a bound document.
- **Automatic double-sided copying** (sometimes called duplexing) – a feature which prints simultaneously on both sides of the paper from two originals placed side-by-side (tandem copying).
- **Colour printing** – the incorporation of red, blue, sepia, etc, colours one to a single sheet (not to be confused with full-colour copiers which can reproduce colour photographs) at the touch of a button.
- **Copying of three-dimensional objects**, such as jewellery for insurance purposes and bound books without showing dark areas where light has been let in.
- **Automatic electrical power saving mode** operated when the machine is not in active use (to save electricity and costs).

Given the present pace of copier design development, such features and facilities are being extended and improved virtually every month as a new or upgraded model is introduced. Therefore the effective secretary will take steps to become fully proficient on the equipment her organisation employs and keep her eye on incoming sales leaflets and office

Information handling: using equipment effectively

equipment magazines to stay up-to-date and au fait. Local exhibitions of office equipment mounted in hotels, etc, are very useful in this respect.

The systems photocopier

The systems photocopier or print-room model will copy at speeds of 40–200 cpm and handle an output of millions of sheets per year. Such copiers will carry out all the above applications and will also:

- accept the continuous fan-fold paper for computer data copying,
- adjust to various specialist modes for, say, converting colour photo originals to black and white with good clarity,
- collate, staple/bind extensively paged documents and insert coloured chapter pages and front/back covers,
- conduct complex enlargement, reduction and automatic document reversal operations,
- handle a wide range of paper sizes – A5 to poster size from automatic feeder trays and effect runs up to 9999 copies long without stopping.

Colour copiers

Recently a wide range of full-colour photocopiers have been marketed which bring exciting design and presentation within the reach of the office manager in medium-size to large organisations.

Such machines can reproduce colour photographs and paper copies of original photographs with remarkable faithfulness, and one market leader's model can provide up to 64 tones of each major colour! Such machines operate on the laser principle and are revolutionising the quality of in-house document and quick-response sales brochure standards. Such copiers work at about 5 cpm.

Photocopying costs

The factors which go to make up photocopying costs are very similar to those for electronic printers (see page 123). Most office administration managers circulate offices with regularly updated costs per sheet according to machine used, paper size, type of copying and volume etc.

Photocopying paper varies widely in cost and the secretary with a stationery buying role should take care to select copying paper which can accept print on both sides, will not cause jams, for example, because it is too light in weight, and which is problem-free from insert to collation stage for ream after ream.

In terms of recurring photocopying costs, it is worth remembering that, while the photocopier with more automatic facilities may cost more to buy or lease, it will undoubtedly save money each month in saved personnel time – compare the time taken to hand-feed single sheets with a fully automated feeding and collating operation which may be left unattended.

Photocopiers and the future

The next phase in photocopier development is already under way with one leading Japanese manufacturer marketing a copier which is also a fax and telex transceiver and scanner! Such multifunctioning equipment is only made possible by the extensive use of reliable microprocessors and clever design.

In addition, copier manufacturers will undoubtedly want to develop further the editor board and stylus operation which resembles the kind of page creating and modifying ability fast becoming popular with users of desktop publishing equipment (see below).

We can certainly expect to see a rapid introduction of 'intelligent photocopiers' in offices with LAN networks so that text may be orginated at an individual's desk and networked to the office copier for automatic duplication according to copy commands which the user keys in at the end of the text and which instruct the copier accordingly, much like existing computer print commands. Equinox, for instance, is a new electronic system for combining the function of photocopier, word processor, laser printer, fax, modem and document scanner, with a desktop publishing system, and is also IBM compatible.

DESKTOP PUBLISHING (DTP)

Desktop publishing (sometimes referred to as electronic publishing) has been one of the fastest growing IT developments of the 1980s. Its rapid uptake was the result of a number of factors and influences, principal among which was that the equipment was already in existence – PC desktop computer with hard disk, laser printer, scanner and mouse. What was the vital additional ingredient was of course the software to do the creative job.

In a nutshell, a desktop publishing system provides its user with the means of producing page-by-page and document by-document highly attractive and well printed copy – that is a mix of:

- **text** in a wide variety of typefaces and sizes,
- **photographs, drawings, graphs and charts** all capable of being enlarged or reduced to fit a predetermined space,
- **lines, rules, shading, cross-hatching and frames** which either make reading easier or create visual appeal as part of the overall page design,

- **imported artwork from the DTP software** which can be quickly positioned on to a given page.

Previously, such printed matter had to be given to a printing house to set and print. The development of DTP, however, has had a profound effect upon the production of organisational documents and the presentation of information, as it has brought the printing house – with many of its visual and graphics devices and effects – right into the heart of office information processing.

Indeed, it is widely predicted that before the end of the 1980s some 50% of everything we read will have been produced by a DTP system!

How desktop publishing works

Perhaps the best way for the secretary in training to view DTP is as a kind of enhanced word processing and visual image combining system. Desktop publishing creates an electronic page of text on the PC's visual display screen using aspects of the mix outlined above. The text for this mix is usually orginated by means of a current commercial word processing package and, in a similar way, previously devised charts and graphs, etc, may be installed into the DTP system from a graphics software package. Photographic or drawn images are installed by means of a scanner. Once all the desired ingredients have been 'loaded' into the DTP system, the process of designing each page of the document may commence.

Desktop publishing: step-by-step

1 The mock-up phase
A mock-up of the desired page or document is created which provides the DTP editor with a clear idea of such aspects as the nature and required size of illustrations – quarter page, 3 cm x single column etc,

Fig 3.27 The screen on this desktop publishing unit shows graphics and text combined on the Aldus PageMaker system, with the mouse cursor control in the foreground

and the way in which text is to be displayed – in simple paragraphs, in columns divided by rules, with emboldened paragraph titles, or with a reversed white text in a black box, etc. The mock-up will also show the size of any required headline for eye-catching effect.

In organisations where DTP is established, the mock-up phase will also include a choice of typefaces (technically known as founts) and the respective sizes of typefaces for use in different areas of the page. The sizes of different founts varies considerably – just think of the size of some newspaper headlines and the small print of some books and documents – and is measured in points (a printer's term). The illustration (Fig 3.30) provides a clear idea of the range of fount sizes between 6 and 30 points and newspaper banner headline founts are even larger.

2 The text/graphics installing phase
The text (often called 'copy' for desktop publishing) is usually produced in organisations by departmental secretaries – as the wording for an advertisement, a handbook to set out a product's specifications, items for the organisation's house journal or as a sales brochure, etc. This copy may be produced via hard or floppy disk.

Where the text producer is familiar with the organisation's DTP system and its software is compatible with the WP package in departmental use, the WP copy may be given format/editing instructions to assist the subsequent DTP editing process, but it may fall to the DTP operator to work on the word-processed text in order to make it suitable for DTP editing (this may involve taking out underscoring or emboldening instructions if the DTP page is to be reformatted from scratch).

3 The editing phase
The text and graphics having been installed into the DTP system, the editing process may begin. In order to design each page – using the mix of typefaces and graphics outlined above a mouse is used as the DTP's control mechanism to move the cursor rapidly around the screen. It can pull down (bring into play or activate) various DTP menus of instructions – such as the shading of a space, the reversing of black on white, the 'cropping or cutting to a required size of a picture or the enlargement of the page on the VDU either to see it as a whole or to see a magnified portion of it. In addition to the mouse, the PC keyboard is used with its command keys in the editing process.

At the outset of the editing process, the DTP operator will check the mock-ups and, to save time, will select a **style sheet** (sometimes called a template) from the DTP's memory which most closely resembles the desired page design. Such a sheet is a kind of skeletal blank page with, for example, the rules and columns already set, and margins already specified etc.

The operator may then '**pull down**' the various menus which contain the instructions which he wishes to use to design the required page. These menus include:

File for loading data on to the page and subsequently storing it – simply the setting up of a file in the normal way,

View to provide enlarged or reduced displays and to check illustrative material,

Page to add page sequencing and numbering features, to set up right-hand and left-hand page alignments and to set the ongoing page structure, etc.

Frame to insert lines, rules, boxes to a desired size,

Graphic to add illustrations on to page designs,

Type to enable the operator to select the chosen fount or typeface and its size.

Note: Various DTP software applications have similar functions grouped in similar menus, and provide an extended range of instructions which the operator can select or 'tag' in order to build up the page with the desired typeface, graphics and layout. Also, for ease of use, ikon 'tool kits' are available for selection by mouse to draw lines, circles and move items around the page, etc.

4 The printing phrase

When the editing phase is completed, the printing process via laser printer is begun. The laser printer with its high quality end product and ability to print in an extensive range of typefaces (founts) and type sizes (points) is what makes DTP so incredibly versatile and useful in larger organisations. Even so, it should be kept in mind that a laser printer with a resolution of at least 300 dots per inch cannot compare for print quality with professional printing by the **phototypesetting** process in which a resolution of some 1100 dpsi is used. However, if need be, the DTP print command sequence can be relayed on to a phototypesetter.

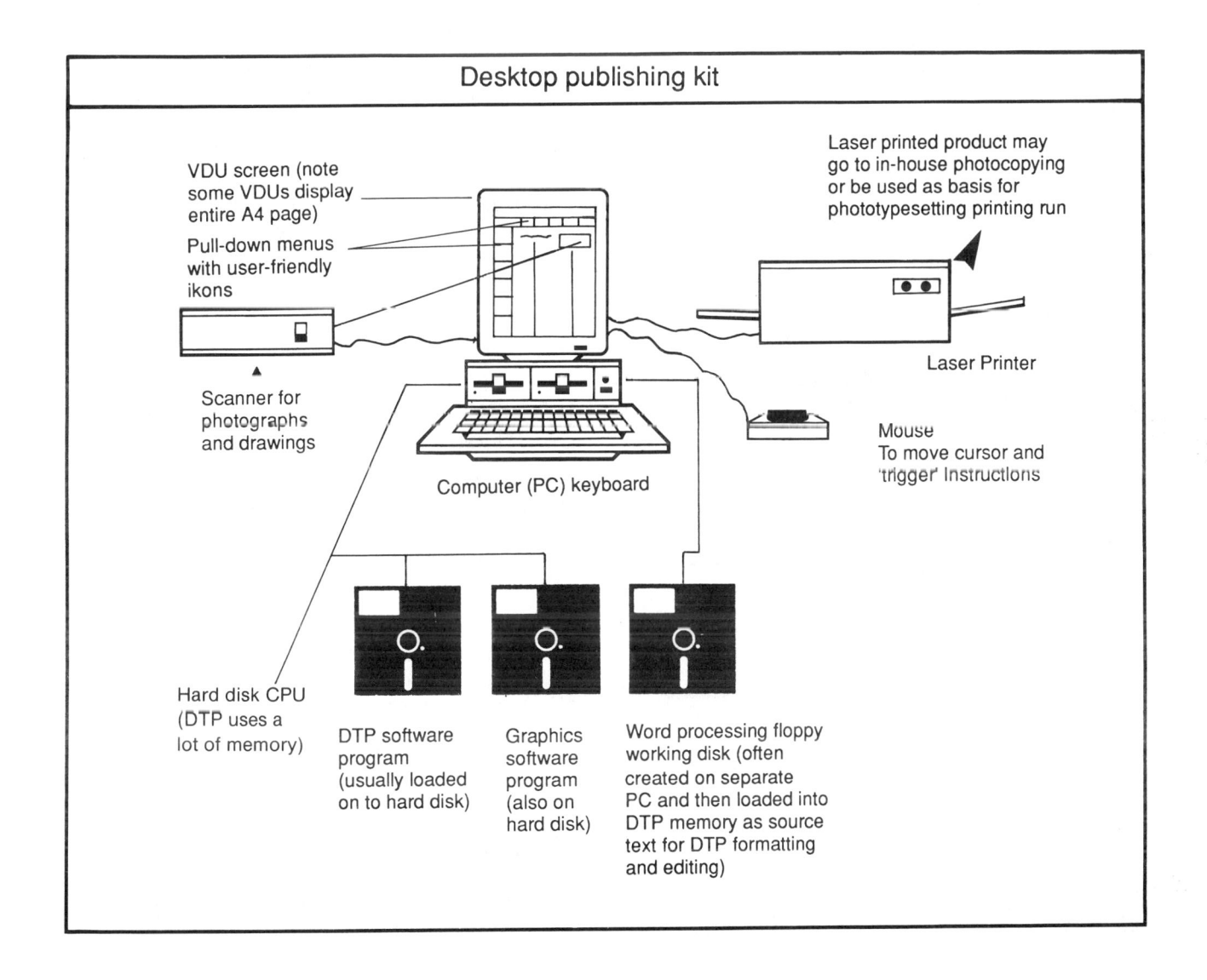

Desktop publishing kit

- VDU screen (note some VDUs display entire A4 page)
- Pull-down menus with user-friendly ikons
- Scanner for photographs and drawings
- Computer (PC) keyboard
- Hard disk CPU (DTP uses a lot of memory)
- DTP software program (usually loaded on to hard disk)
- Graphics software program (also on hard disk)
- Word processing floppy working disk (often created on separate PC and then loaded into DTP memory as source text for DTP formatting and editing)
- Laser printed product may go to in-house photocopying or be used as basis for phototypesetting printing run
- Laser Printer
- Mouse – To move cursor and 'trigger' instructions

Note: In order to achieve the best results, it is important that a high resolution VDU screen is used, together with a laser printer which is fully compatible with the DTP software – changing laser printers will change the format of the designed page.

Aldus Pagemaker in action

Fig 3.29 Examples of Aldus Pagemaker screen layouts

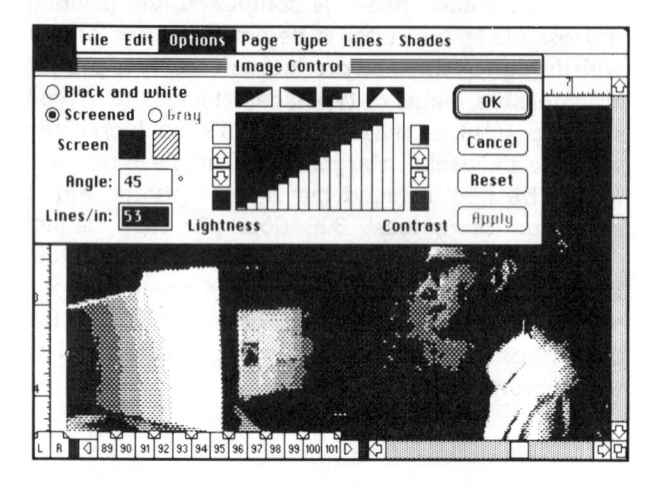

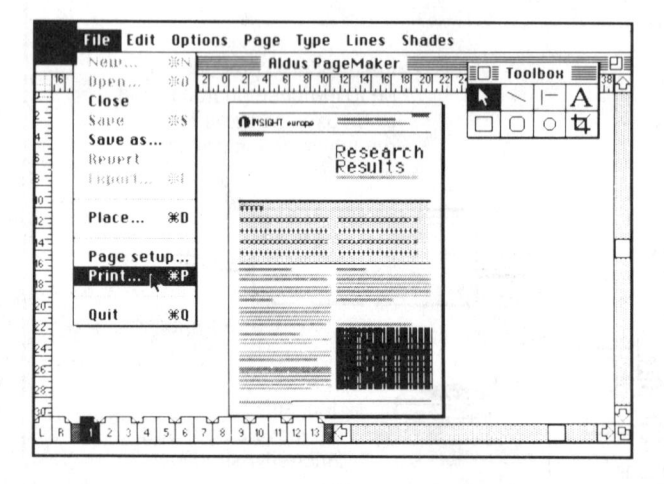

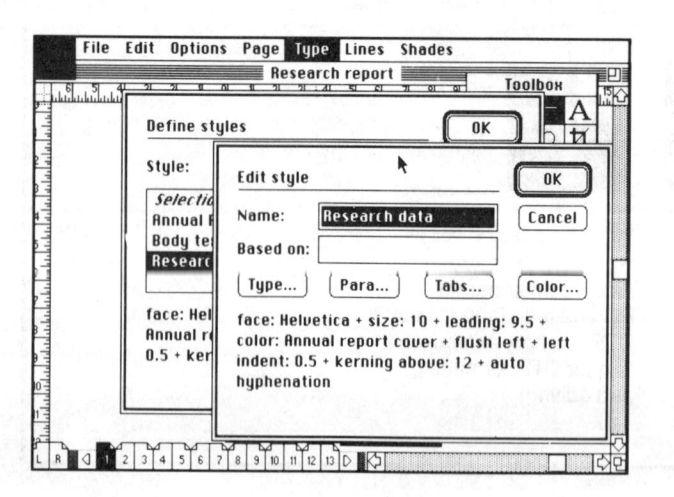

Proofreading

At each stage of the DTP process it is essential to proofread copy carefully. The nearer one approaches the end product, the more difficult and time-consuming it is to correct errors of spelling or layout.

Founts and presentation

While individual secretaries (say in an advertising department or working for a senior manager) may become expert regular users of a DTP system, it is more likely that they will originate text on their own desktop PCs for installation into the DTP unit which will be operated by a specialist member of staff working full-time in the organisation's reprographics centre. Nevertheless, it is very important for today's effective secretary to become more informed and aware than was her predecessor of elements of page design and the visual impact of different kinds of typeface and type size. For example, a Roman fount conveys a sense of respectability stemming from the length of time it has existed and been absorbed in serious publications. Alternatively, the Courier type style communicates clean, crisp modernity and Script imparts a friendly, informal message, while Old English would look quite out of place save on a fascia for Ye Olde Englishe Tea Shoppe! Given that DTP has put a wide range of founts and printing techniques at the disposal of in-house publishing, secretaries and their managers are bound to find that more is expected of them in terms of the quality and standards of the documents they produce for certain purposes, such as reports to the board of directors, circular sales leaflets and brochures to clients and AVA presentation materials for senior management, etc.

Introductory glossary of desktop publishing terms

The advent of DTP has brought into more general use a specialised, technical set of terms and expressions from the world of printing and typesetting. Here are some of the more commonly occurring terms to start your own personal checklist:

Automatic page numbering; **automatic table of contents**; **running headers and footers**: DTP programs allow the user to give the commands for the automatic sequencing of instructions throughout a document.
Automatic text flow: allows copy to move across pages when a multipaged document is being designed.
Clip art: some DTP packages include sets of artwork/graphics – say, a hand in the 'stop' gesture of a policeman to convey graphically 'Don't ...!' – which may be included in a design at will: clip art provides quick graphics for in-house documents, sales literature, etc.
Cropping: adjusting the size of an illustration so as to fit it into a given space.

Fig 3.30 Desktop publishing enables you to use a large variety of type styles and sizes

LePrint & JLaser

from

Headway Computer Products

LePrint will enhance any text and is suitable for use with Wordstar and any WP that can produce an ASCII file.

Characters can be varied in size from 4 point to 700 point (nearly 10 inches high).

A large range of Type Styles is available.

This is 12 point Old English... and this is Prestige.

Here is the Courier type style.

LCD gives a futuristic look to your documents.

All this is achieved by the use of dot commands within the text, which are recognised by LePrint. The capability of the system is further enhanced by Headway Computer Products JLASER board.

LePrint is the low cost alternative to a shelf full of font cartridges. It runs under MS DOS on IBM's and compatibles and utilises the power and versatility of the Laser Printer. LePrint will also function with a wide variety of Dot Matrix printers.

Contact HEADWAY today for more details or a demonstration of

LePrint and JLaser

This document was produced using LePrint and JLaser and printed on a Canon Laser Printer.

HEADWAY COMPUTER PRODUCTS
Headway House, Christy Estate,
Ivy Road, Aldershot, Hants. GU12 4TX.

Tel: 0252 333575 Telex: 859518 Fax: 0252 314445

(Reproduced by kind permission of Headway Computer Products)

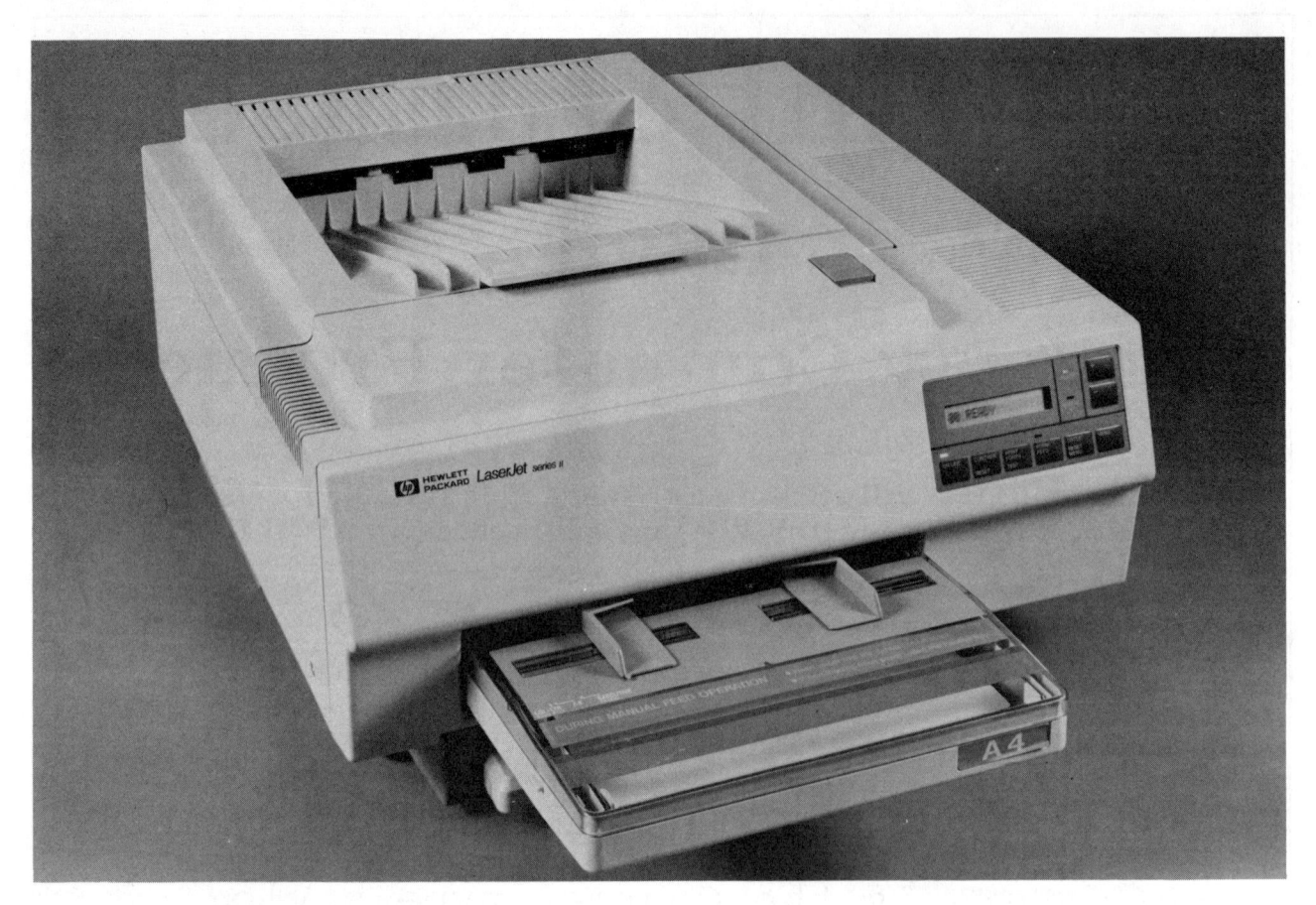

Fig 3.31 The LaserJet series II printer from Hewlett Packard

(Reproduced by kind permission of Hewlett Packard)

Kerning: adjusting the space between letters to improve clarity and visual appeal.
Leading: a term for the spacing of text line by line and the spacing between titles and paragraphs.
Left and right justification: columns or paragraphs of text may be left ragged or justified as desired.
Pica and point: are both measurements of print size: a pica is 0.1660 inches and a point is a twelfth of a pica.
Vertical rules: lines inserted between columns of text to aid the eye in easier reading.
Widows and orphans: terms for the very short lines of text at the top or bottom of a page: an orphan is an isolated word or short bottom line and a widow is a short top line; DTP can sometimes avoid the problem by modifying text spacing.
WIMP: Windows Ikons Mouse Pull-down Menus – a term to describe the 'tools' used to edit in DTP.
WYSIWYG: What You See Is What You Get – a term used to explain that a VDU page of data is exactly reproduced by the printer.

Note: A newcomer to DTP is bound to find the specialist terms and jargon expressions somewhat bewildering. But remember that, as with all IT technologies, everyone is in the same situation and the people who get on are those who are prepared to 'have a go' at grasping new ideas and techniques quickly and readily.

Applications of desktop publishing

Already DTP has revolutionised the speed and quality of in-house created documents such as:

☐ Reports ☐ Price lists ☐ Bulletins ☐ Notices ☐ Posters ☐ Social Club Announcements ☐ Catalogues ☐ Training and Technical Manuals ☐ Circular Sales Letters ☐ Leaflets, Brochures, etc ☐ AVA Foils and Handouts.

So acquiring an informed overview of desktop publishing techniques and the ability to produce WP text suited for DTP installation are essential items on the training agenda of today's secretaries!

DISCUSSION TOPIC

'All these manufacturers seem to think about is designing and selling systems and equipment which end up giving the poor old manager and secretary ever more data to read, react to and remember! Far from simplifying office life, IT's just making it much too complicated!' How far would you agree with this hard-pressed manager's cri de coeur?

Unit 3
Summary of main points

1 Principal media of office information: face-to-face; oral-aural, such as telephone, and audio-dictation; audio-visual such as closed circuit TV and teleconferencing, VDU-based, such as LAN/WAN electronic mail, computer conferencing, computer-based data processing, typewritten text processing, desktop publishing, telecommunications – fax, telex, viewdata text and image processing; viewfoil, film and slide image presentation etc.

2 Concept of convergence: previously 'stand-alone' electronic office equipment is now interconnected to link computer workstation to printer, scanner, fax, photocopier, telephone communications, etc. *Note*: transglobal messaging facilities are available through telecommunications systems from individual workstations.

3 Local and wide area networks: one of the most important IT developments for the next decade; they enable office workers to exchange electronic mail messages, share applications packages held centrally, route messages to remote locations, etc.

4 Software used on LANs word processing, spreadsheets, databases, graphics, diaries, planners, integrated information management systems, management activity support packages, self-organisation packages and desktop publishing.

5 Typical fax features: abbreviated telephone number storage, delayed transmission until cheap time rates apply, automatic call initiation, repeat attempt facility, confidential password for security at receiving end feature – only intended recipient can access, automatic copying for file of despatched documents, provision of status/management reports, including costs.

6 Telex: telex sends/receives documents internationally on 'call-up/confirmation ready to receive' basis; embodies many features of fax techniques – text editing prior to despatch, delayed transmission, high-speed transmission of batched documents, and status/management reports.

7 Viewdata: In UK service provided by British Telecom and known as 'Prestel'; some 400 000 pages of information are available, accessed by a branching database system; used to sell service and products as well as information; unlike Ceefax and Oracle, Prestel users can interact with suppliers to order goods etc. from the monitor's keyboard.

8 CABX, PABX and key system telephone service: computerised switchboard facilities are revolutionising the range of telephone services from extensions – see call barring, diverting, holding and recalling; also, call interrupt, logging and reporting; note also conferencing, camp on busy, call back when in, forwarding and 'follow me' and further invaluable features; key system telephones are interlinked to enable anyone to pick up an incoming call or access an outside line – used mainly in smaller organisations.

9 Telecommunications support directories: Local BT *Phone Books*, BT UK *Telex Directory*, BT *Fax Book* (UK Directory), *Prestel Directory*, *Thomson Yellow Pages* and *Local Directory* etc.

10 Cellular (mobile) telephones: used now in almost all UK, either hand-held or motor-car installed; calls are relayed via radio waves to the nearest BT telephone exchange; more expensive than standard telephone calls; see also Radiopagers which can receive bleeps to mean 'call us on the phone' or short LCD-displayed messages.

11 Electronic printers: mainly – thermal, dot matrix, daisywheel, ink-jet or laser; laser proving most popular for letter quality; electronic printers revolutionised the range of typefaces/founts offices can use to print text – up to 30 point print and from some 50 different founts in DTP work. Note increasing importance now attaching to presentation of documents.

12 Photocopiers: basically three versions in office use – simple desktop for 'one off' copies of, say, an incoming letter – most expensive per copy;

departmental copier for use between 5000 – 10 000 copies per month – can print on A3, A4, A5, both sides, enlarge, reduce, collate, paginate etc, often rented rather than purchased; thirdly, systems copier for large organisational use for millions of copies per year – needs specialist operators and used for bulk printing – cheapest for long runs. Note introduction of lowish cost colour photocopiers as part of in-house publishing trend.

13 Desktop publishing: DTP now prints some 40% of all available reading matter; system based on PC, printer and image scanner; pages of text can be created to taste from a series of optional founts and graphics features of the DTP software; used to print in-house leaflets, bulletins, newsletters, sales leaflets, high status reports, etc.

Sources of further information
Using an Electronic Mailbox, J Pritchard, NCC Publications
Eectronic Office Equipment, E Mullins, Pitman
Business Information Processing, D Harrison, Pitman
A Handbook of New Office Technology, Derrick and Oppenheim, Kogan Page Ltd
Getting The Message – Communications Guide for Teachers and Students, published by British Telecom
Information and Word Processing: An Introduction, King and Bone, Stanley Thornes
Information Technology in the Office, J Gaukroger, McGraw-Hill
The Automated Office, S Morris, Heinemann New Tech
Manager's Guide to Telecommunications, M Gandoff, Heinemann New Tech
Business Systems and Information Technology, R Anderson, Paradigm Publishing
Inside Information: Computers, Communications and People, J Megarry, BBC Publications Ltd
Summary of charges for telecommunications services published annually by British Telecom (details prices and charges for all types of telephone, mobile communications, telex, answering machines, etc)

ACTIVITIES

A bit of a sort out!
A case study

National Car Accessories Limited was founded in 1967 by Phil Sturrock, a live-wire entrepreneur who had begun with a single car accessory centre on the outskirts of Manchester at a time when interest in cars was booming and 'add-ons' were all the rage. In 1978, and some fifty established branches later, National acquired a three-storey building near the centre of Manchester, close to good road and rail communications. The head office building was constructed in the 1950s around a steel girder framework and each floor comprises a series of smallish offices separated by plasterboard partitions.

Today, having successfully weathered the recession of the 1970s, National has a network of 120 branches spread across southern Scotland and the north of England. Phil Sturrock remains the company's majority shareholder and managing director, and the company has the following head office departments:

Purchasing
Sales
Marketing
Accounts
Personnel
Transport
Branch Administration

The Marketing Department is headed up by Mrs Jean Watson, Director, and is situated on the western half of the top floor of the building:

The Marketing Department is currently organised as shown in the diagram on page 134

Section responsibilities
The three major sections of the Department have the following responsibilities:

Product development
Making sure that National is stocking brand-name and own brand products which are 'up-to-the minute' in design and appeal; close liaison is maintained with a large number of manufacturers, both in the UK and overseas.

Advertising
The Advertising Section is responsible for sustaining effective merchandising within the stores, and for press, promotions and exhibitions advertising and public relations. Two executives take care of these twin arms.

The Advertising Manager also coordinates the desktop publishing and reprographics work. National recently acquired a DTP system to produce its own masters for stores leaflets and sales brochures, etc. At this time, morale in the unit is low because the two reprographics assistants are being overloaded with photocopying demands from all and sundry.

Information handling: using equipment effectively

Layout of National's marketing department

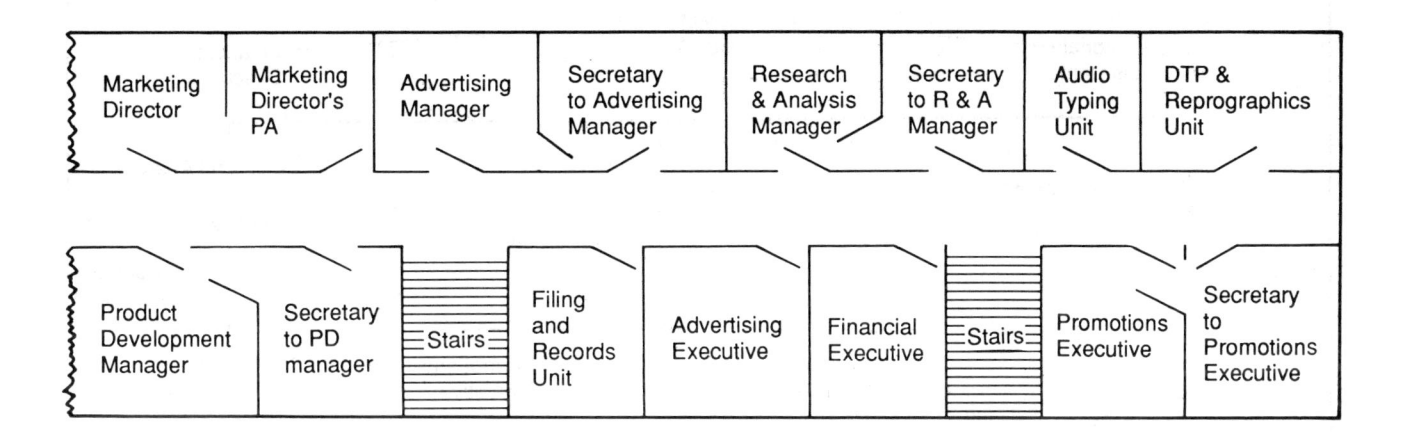

| Marketing Director | Marketing Director's PA | Advertising Manager | Secretary to Advertising Manager | Research & Analysis Manager | Secretary to R & A Manager | Audio Typing Unit | DTP & Reprographics Unit |

| Product Development Manager | Secretary to PD manager | Stairs | Filing and Records Unit | Advertising Executive | Financial Executive | Stairs | Promotions Executive | Secretary to Promotions Executive |

Research and analysis
Phil Sturrock always claims he got where he is by 'keeping a close eye on the competition and keeping one step ahead of the beggars!' So he maintains a keen interest in analyses of buying trends and product popularity and surveying what groups of motorists buy what type of products etc.

The Research and Analysis Manager is also responsible for the department's Filing and Records Unit and Audio-typing Unit. The former is really a store for past survey records and statistics and marketing data is dispersed through all the department's offices. While the Audio-typing Unit is available to everyone in theory, there is much 'behind-the-scenes' grumbling that undue priority is always given to R & A work by the typists.

Financial executive
Andrew Wilson reports directly to Jean Watson and provides advice and information on money aspects of marketing. He has to rely on the Director's PA and the Audio-typing Unit for his text processing etc and claims that his particular needs are largely underestimated.

Secretarial support staff
The Director and three managers have each a personal secretary; the director's enjoys the titles of 'PA' but the other three secretaries resent this because they consider they do just as much demanding work!

Equipment distribution
National Car Accessories Head Office has not exactly moved with the times, largely because every last penny of profit has been put into acquiring and equipping new stores. However, the success of National's rapid growth in the past five years is putting tremendous pressure on Head Office staff – with increasing staff turn-over and morale problems.

In the Marketing Department, the following equipment distribution obtains:

Current equipment distribution

PAs/secretaries to managers: 16K memory electronic typewriters (PA has fax transceiver; Product Development secretary has telex access).
DTP: scanner, PC + laser printer + 'Pagewrite' software recently acquired to do in-house masters for sales leaflets and brochures.
Copying: A3/A4/A5 departmental b/w copier
Audio-typists: pedal-operated dictation transcribers and electronic typewriters.
Filing and records: largely manual. One PC holds details of press advertising on disk and is 'stand-alone'.

Senior management have woken up to the shortcomings in providing the 'tools to do the job' – witness the acquisition of the DTP equipment and a PC installed in the Filing Unit. The following conversation took place earlier this week after a Board of Directors' meeting:

Phil Sturrock:
'You can see from my review this morning that something must be done as a matter of urgency! Over the years some of our managerial staff have been 'feather-bedded' by under-utilised secretaries, while others have had to cope as best they can on a goodwill basis by getting their work done a bit here and a bit there. It's high time we had a bit of a sort out on how we are using our secretarial and clerical support staff and on what equipment and systems they could do with to get the job done. If it's going to cost money, so be it! We'll grow no more until we get this right!'

Jean Watson:
'I think you're right. We've managed fairly well so far, but this time it's Head Office that needs investing in and not the branches. I'll set up a Task Force Team in my Department and let you have a written report and recommendations within a fortnight – well before the next Board Meeting.'

Phil Sturrock:
'Right. And while you're at it, give a thought to your Departmental layout. If we're going into this, we might as well go the whole hog!'

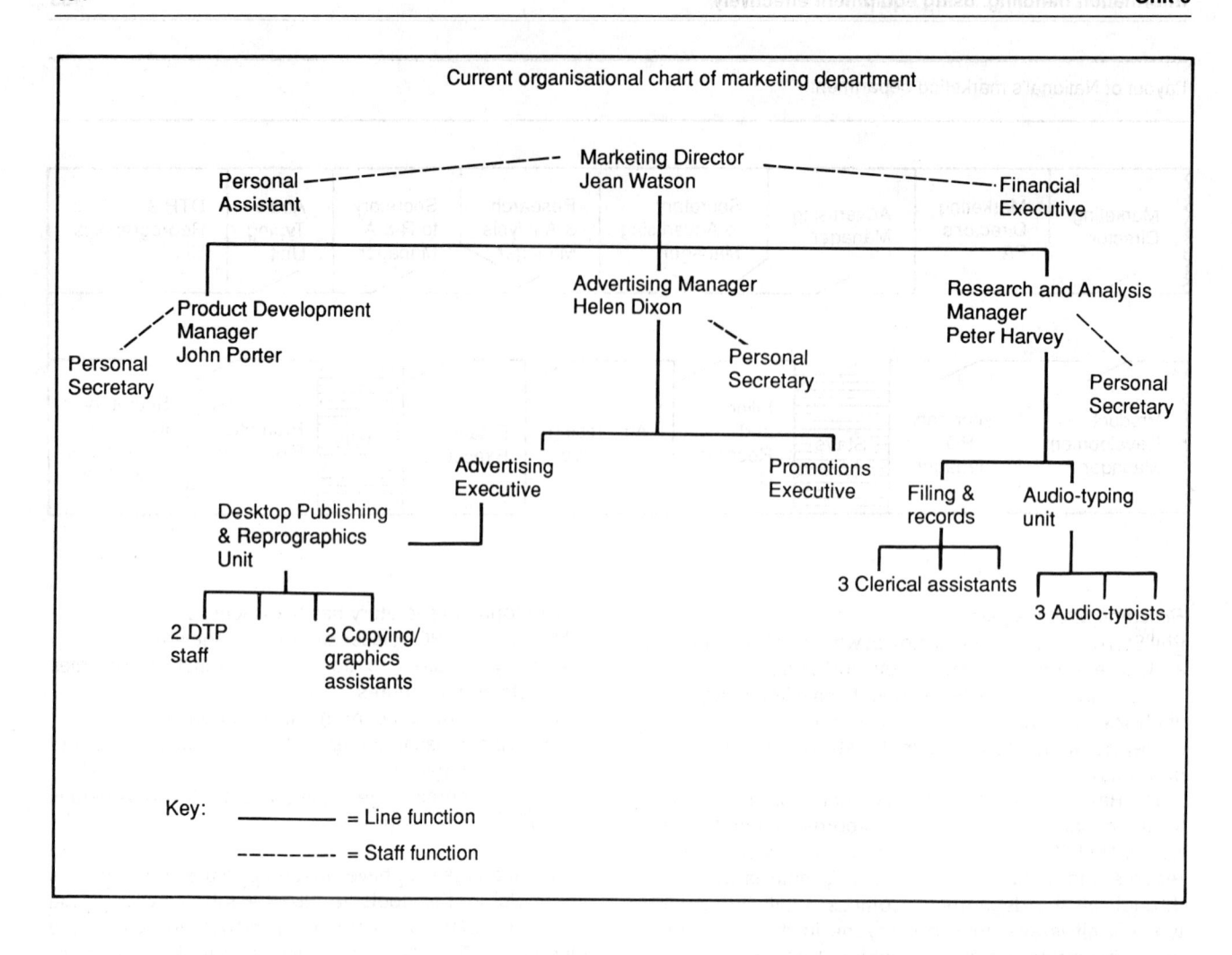

Current organisational chart of marketing department

```
                              Marketing Director
    Personal --------------      Jean Watson      -------------- Financial
    Assistant                         |                          Executive
         ┌────────────────────────────┼────────────────────────────┐
         |                            |                            |
    Product Development         Advertising Manager        Research and Analysis
    Manager                     Helen Dixon                Manager
    John Porter                                            Peter Harvey
         |                            · · ·                       · · ·
    Personal                     Personal                     Personal
    Secretary                    Secretary                    Secretary
                                    |
                         ┌──────────┴──────────┐         ┌──────────┴──────────┐
                    Advertising           Promotions    Filing &          Audio-typing
                    Executive             Executive     records           unit
         |                |                                |                    |
    Desktop Publishing                              3 Clerical assistants   3 Audio-typists
    & Reprographics
    Unit
     ┌────┴────┐
   2 DTP    2 Copying/
   staff    graphics
            assistants
```

Key: ─────── = Line function

- - - - - - = Staff function

CASE STUDY QUESTIONS

1 What problems and difficulties do you think stem from the way in which the Marketing Department is currently structured?

2 What do you think may be the human problems likely to arise in the department if the sort of changes which Phil Sturrock envisages are put in to effect? How might they be minimised?

3 What changes would you make to the ways in which the Marketing Department works in the light of the shortcomings which Phil Sturrock reviewed? How would you reorganise:

(a) the current structure of the Marketing Department's secretarial and office support services?
(b) The layout of the department so as to optimise access and ease of communications between managerial and support staff?
(c) the range and type of equipment and systems the Department should have, so as to be able to market the 120 stores and their products more efficiently?

4 Can you identify any new/additional staff needs which the department would have in your development plan? What would be the comparative advantages of advertising for new staff or providing updating training for existing staff? Which option would you take? Why?

5 What particular training needs do you think the managers and executives would need, assuming a large-scale reorganisation of work patterns and organisational structure was put into effect?

6 Where would be the best place to start in introducing a reorganisation of some 21 staff within such a department? What sort of approach is likely to prove most effective?

CASE STUDY ASSIGNMENTS

1 In pairs, draw up an organisational chart and floor layout which illustrates the changes you would make. You may assume that the building's structure would allow total flexibility within the floor space occupied by the department, other than the location of the stairs and double-swing door access to them.

2 Again, in pairs, make notes of the different types of job which your new support services structure would require. Then, select one new/modified post and design a job description for it. (See Unit 6).

3 Compose a report which specifies the new equipment/systems which you think should be introduced and give your reasons why, explaining the ways in which work processes and communications might be improved.

4 Draw up a display advertisement for a new post which your reorganisation has made necessary. It is to be a double column × 12 cm advertisement in next week's *Manchester Weekly News*.

5 Compose one of the following memoranda:

(a) For all secretarial and office support staff to introduce the new structure and equipment/systems acquisitions, outlining the advantages which will result.

(b) A memorandum to managerial and executive staff providing guidelines on what approaches to take in order to get the best service from the reorganised secretarial/office support provision.

QUICK REVIEW QUIZ

1 What major types of computer printer are in use today? How do they differ in the way they print?

2 What is the difference between a desktop, departmental and systems photocopier?

3 What major features would you expect to find on a departmental copier in the middle of the price range?

4 What criteria would you use to help you decide what type of photocopier to use for duplicating a notice to go to, say, 150 employees?

5 Explain briefly what the following stand for: (a) WYSIWYG (b) WIMP (c) cropping (d) kerning.

6 Make a checklist of *five* office tasks for which desktop publishing equipment would be particularly suitable.

RESEARCH AND REPORT BACK ASSIGNMENTS

1 Having carried out your investigations, draw up a chart to illustrate clearly the respective features and advantages and disadvantages of the following types of printer:

thermal, dot matrix, daisywheel, ink-jet, laser.

Your chart should include clear guidelines on what type of printing jobs each is best suited to provide, and an indication of costs.

2 Having researched the topic carefully, draw up a set of guidelines which illustrates the type of work and numbers of copies that are most cost-effectively produced on a single-sheet feed desktop copier, a mid-range/departmental copier and a large-volume systems copier. Show the typical comparative costs per A4 sheet.

3 When you have investigated the current desktop publishing provision, give your group an illustrated presentation on how DTP can help organisations to present information more appealingly and effectively and suggest instances when DTP would be of particular value to secretarial work.

WORK SIMULATION ASSIGNMENTS

1 You work as secretary to Mrs Carol Kingston, personnel manager of an engineering company with some 200 employees, which makes kitchen electrical appliances. Mrs Kingston has recently been given the go-ahead to install eight computer terminals and a file server in a LAN system, to administer document creation, filing and records, electronic mail and scanner-produced files of incoming paper documents, etc. The LAN installation is to serve as a pilot scheme for the rest of the company. Given your up-to-date background on LAN systems, Mrs Kingston briefs you as follows:

'I'd like you to compose a memorandum to go out to all departmental staff in my name, explaining simply and clearly what a LAN system is, what it can do and how it will help staff to do their work more easily and effectively. You can take it that our LAN software will include an integrated information management package, a good database, a spreadsheet, WP and graphics software – and, of course, an Email facility. Don't go into too much detail, but make sure you say that full training will be given. About two sides of A4 should do.'

2 Your manager, Mr Bob Croxley, is office administration manager for Sentinel Alarm Systems, which manufactures burglar alarm systems selling both in the UK and abroad. He walks into your outer office with a worried look on his face.

'I've just been looking at our fax bills for the last quarter. They've gone through the roof! Our head office and regional managers just can't be controlling the use of their fax machines at all! So, I'd like you to check out when fax messages can be sent to home and overseas destinations most cheaply, and what sort of monitoring reports, etc, our managers can access to help them keep costs down. Put it all into a set of guidelines which are user-friendly and don't raise hackles and we'll circulate it to all managers controlling fax equipment.'

3 You are the personal secretary of Mr Winston

Carmichael, export sales manager of Deepdale Cheeses Limited. Your department customarily makes some 6000 A4 photocopies each month, particularly for export documentation and sales record purposes. Mr Carmichael called you into his office this morning and gave you this task to carry out:

> 'We've just been allocated £7000 to replace our existing departmental photocopier, which is on its last legs! We have the option of buying a replacement or leasing it. If we buy, the copier will have to last for four years and be depreciated at £1750 per year. Assuming our photocopying remains at the same level, I'd like you to find out what sort of prices are currently being being asked to lease a copier equivalent to one we could buy for £7000. Take into account the costs of toner, paper, servicing, etc, and work out whether we'd be better off buying outright or leasing. It would be most helpful if you could present the comparative costs of buying or leasing side-by-side for me, and set out your recommendations below.'

4 'I've just had Ed Mackenzie on the phone from our Detroit head office. He's flying over in four weeks' time to go through the latest plans for the Essex factory. While he's here he wants to take a week's holiday in London, see some sights and take in one or two shows. Would you find out what sort of hotel accommodation is on offer from Prestel and check out location and costs. He'll want to be as near the West End as possible. Make a note of what you could book and let me see it. Oh, and find out what sort of musicals are on next month and where. I know he likes musicals.'

These instructions were thrown over the shoulder by your manager, Mr Gordon Brown, as he hastily swept up some papers into his briefcase and left the office for an appointment. Using Prestel, find out what you can which will help Mr Brown to make suitable holiday arrangements for Ed Mackenzie, a parent company vice president. Select a suitable format to brief Mr Brown on his return.

5 As medical secretary to Dr Frank Hastings, senior partner of a general practice in the county town of Midchester, you have been briefed to look into the facilities which a keysystem telephone installation could provide for the practice and what it would cost. The practice comprises eight doctors, two nurses, two administrative/receptionist assistants and yourself. Compose a short report for the partners to digest and include your recommendations as to what should be done to replace the ageing and unreliable system you are all living with at present.

6 Draw up a set of guidelines on using a CABX telephone system which will help new staff to become familiar with the system and confident about it. Base your advice on a CABX system which you have researched into or have seen in action.

7 You work for Mrs Diana Caxton, sales manager of Chique Fashionwear Limited, which sells to some 150 boutiques and stores in the Midlands, who is considering acquiring five mobile phones for your senior sales representatives. She has asked you to look into the matter and advise her of typical purchase and running costs and whether you think it would be worth the expense.

8 You work for Zenith Stationery Supplies Limited, which distributes office stationery and allied products to High Street office equipment stores.

Your manager, Mr Peter Bolton, who is responsible for the acquisition and maintenance of all office machines and equipment, thinks it is high time the firm's secretaries and reprographics staff gave more thought to the appearance of the printed word upon the page and its impact upon the reader. He has asked you to examine the appropriate uses of 10, 12 and 15 pitch type on typewriters and the typefaces and founts commonly used on daisywheel, ink-jet and laser printers. You are to draft a memorandum which offers advice to the staff in question on the sort of pitch and typeface which would be suited to:

(a) Individual letters to customers
(b) Reports to the company's directors
(c) The text of sales literature and leaflets
(d) The company's in-house newsletter
(e) Company product technical specifications

Mr Bolton has suggested you include a schedule of examples with your memorandum to illustrate your advice.

WORK EXPERIENCE ASSIGNMENTS

1 Find out what use of fax and telex is made in the organisation. Obtain permission to observe the transmission of messages and, possibly, to take part in the operation yourself.

Write a short report on what kind of equipment is being used, detailing its major features. Draw up a chart to contrast costs and time taken in using fax/telex as against conventional postal services.

2 Find out either: what LAN/WAN networking is in operation, or: which C/PABX system is installed. Then interview staff using the system to discover their views on how it helps them in their work and the various ways in which they make use of it. (Note: Find out if the organisation uses mobile telephones and radio-pagers, and if so, for what purposes.)

Deliver your findings as an illustrated talk or written account to your group.

3 Make arrangements to visit a local organisation which has a CABX telephone network installed.

   (a) Find out from the staff operating the switchboard console what advantages they have found in using CABX.
   (b) Find out from secretarial and management staff how CABX facilities aid their daily work.

PRACTICE QUESTIONS FROM PAST EXAMINATION PAPERS

1 As a secretary in a medium-sized company you have access to both a facsimile machine and a telex machine. Explain the factors you would consider in deciding whether to send a document by either telex or facsimile. (LCC PSC)

2 You have overheard the marketing executives refer frequently to spreadsheets and graphics:

   (a) State what you understand by the terms 'spreadsheets' and 'graphics'.
   (b) Describe uses of a spreadsheet and of graphics which would be helpful to Comlon.

   (Comlon is an international company manufacturing dresses and haute couture collections for sale at home and overseas)
   (LCC PSC)

3 The Board of Comlon International plc is anxious to reduce telephone call charges by introducing the following:

   (a) out of area lines
   (b) call barring
   (c) extension group hunting
   (d) telephone credit cards
   (e) call logging

Define each term clearly and then explain how each contributes to reducing call charges. (LCC PSC)

4 You work for Mr John Brown, Director of Office Design Division of Comlon International plc, which designs, manufactures and markets a range of office equipment and stationery products.

The company has decided to centralise its reprographics facilities at Head Office and offer a variety of machines, although any large amounts of printing will be carried out by Printing Division.

   (a) What are the advantages and disadvantages of such centralisation?
   (b) Describe how modern photocopiers could help the company.

(LCC PSC)

5 Comlon International plc (Entertainments Group) provides a number of leisure/arts services, including theatre ownership.

The Director of the Entertainments Department (Jack Martin) wishes to keep in close contact with Michael Deacon (General Administrator, Comlon Theatres) who visits Comlon Theatres, some of which are less than 16 km from the office. Mr Martin's staff work in different parts of the office building. Describe briefly how contact can be made. (LCC PSC)

UNIT 3
Glossary of terms and phrases

bus
An electronic term describing the circuitry which moves information around a computer's *central processing unit* (CPU) or LAN network.

CCITT
An international body, the International Telegraph and Telephone Consultative Committee, which draws up universal standards and practices for the telecommunications industry.

cellular telephone network – cellnet
Cellular mobile telephones transmit their messages through making radiowave contact with telephone exchanges situated at the edge of the 'net' they are being used in – much like a honeycomb; as a car drives from one cellnet into another, the next telephone exchange takes over the transmission of the telephone conversation going on, passing it into the national network.

closed user groups
A term defining 'clubs' or private users who intercommunicate in a viewdata or LAN/WAN network in which membership is restricted.

convergence
A term which is used with **connectivity** to describe **networked** hardware and software in which computers, fax, scanners, telex, telephones, printers, intelligent photocopiers, etc, are all interconnected and accessible by network users; note international convergence by means of **WAN** and telecommunications systems.

CABX
Short for Computerised Automatic Branch Exchange. This term stands for the installed network of telephone extensions linked to a central switchboard which routes and monitors all incoming and outgoing calls and which utilises computer-programmed features to aid communications.

database package
A database package is, in essence, an electronic filing cabinet; it holds details on any topic entered on to it and sorts them by a system which holds data in selected *fields*; thus a created database on, say account customers may be interrogated to display total sales each month, the most popular product, etc.

facsimile transceiver
Popularly called *fax* today, this piece of office equipment uses scanning techniques to 'read' a photograph, diagram or text, which is then converted into electronic signals capable of being transmitted over international telephone networks; fax numbers are keyed in much like telephone numbers to activate the fax machine to receive the incoming message, converting the message back into its original form.

file server
LAN networks require a kind of master unit which is used to drive the network and hold software packages to be accessed and work files to be stored.

founts
A fount is a term to describe an alphanumeric set of characters in a given style of design which may be used on daisywheels, in laser printers or ink-jet printers; contrasting founts are often used in desktop publishing to provide appeal and variety.

gateways in Prestel
Give access to other information stored on the information providers' own computer systems.

graphics package
This software is used to convert inputted numbers into line graphs, pie charts, bar charts, etc, or to allow free artwork design; the displayed end product may also be printed as either an *OHP transparency foil, colour transparency or coloured paper printout.*

hierarchic database
Increasingly information is being stored in computer database software which is located by the user moving along a series of branching pathways; the route taken is determined by opting for one of a number of choices offered in displayed menus. According to the choice, the VDU displays the appropriate data.

IDD
International Direct Dialling: a system by which international telephone calls may be dialled up without the intervention of the operator.

ISDN
Integrated Services Digital Network is a network which is capable of carrying telephone communications, fascimile/telex/packet-switched transmission, LAN/WAN computer messaging, etc, all through a single 'wire', cable or radio transmission.

ikon (icon) menus
Many software packages are designed so that the user may access a particular feature by 'touching' with either the cursor or other means an image displayed on the screen; for example, to delete a file no longer wanted, the picture (ikon) of an open dustbin is 'touched'.

integrated management information package
These packages interlink WP, spreadsheet, database, graphics and communications features and allow the user to incorporate a spreadsheet table or a graph or a record into a single word processed document – an 'all-in-one' flexible application package.

intelligent photocopying
Today photocopiers may be linked electronically to printers and computers so as to accept text in an electronic form and convert it into duplicated printed paper documents.

lap-top computers
Are compact machines which are either battery or mains driven and used by 'business people on the move'; they can interact via modems with their office-based counterparts.

management information system
Known also as **MIS**, the term describes a computer network which holds software on which essential information needed by managers is stored; a '**real-time**' MIS system is kept constantly up to date by adding, deleting and modifying the data held.

modems
Short for **modulator-demodulator**, the modem is a piece of equipment (sometimes designed to convert the binary coded computer message into electronic pulses which can be carried to a distant receiving computer by telephone line; the receiving computer's modem converts the signal back into a computer-acceptable form.

mouse
A device used with PCs to move the cursor around the VDU screen, using a handheld box containing a ball rolling over the work surface, the cursor on the VDU screen moving in the same direction as the ball.

multi-serving and multi-tasking
File servers need to be able to serve the needs of a number of users simultaneously who are also carrying out various tasks on *different* software packages.

on-line connection
In order to be able to operate any equipment which is driven by the computer's software commands, the equipment (eg a printer) must be connected to the computer in an 'on-line' mode.

packet-switched services
Telephone companies like BT provide services for the transmission of computerised data at high speeds over long distances via telephone cables or satellites in 'chunks' or 'packets' to receiving computers; used especially by multinationals and financial sector organisations.

photosetting
Very high quality printing on a phototypesetter: today the text and graphics are inputted by computer and computer-edited prior to printing.

points
A printer's expression describing the size of founts or typefaces.

Prestel viewdata system
BT offers its Prestel service nationally to users, who need a Prestel-accepting TV monitor, keyboard and CPU; the monitor receives 'pages' of information (some 400000 are on offer) about all kinds of topics and many users also communicate with page displayers to book hotel accommodation for example, or hire a car, by means of a modem, giving two-way contact.

PSS
Packet Switchstream Service: the name of the technical process of transmitting 'packets' of computerised data over long distances at high speed – see also *International* PSS (IPSS); some multinationals rent

private lines from telephone companies for this purpose.

PSTN
Public Switched Telephone Network: the title of the national system used to transmit telephone calls, modem-relayed messages, BT Gold services, etc.

pull down
A computer term – a pull-down menu is one which offers options activated by 'tagging' or touching the required feature, such as 'crop' or 'rule'.

radiopager
These small boxes pick up radio signals and either simply emit bleeps so that the carrier is alerted to use the nearest telephone to call the office or, in sophisticated versions, also display limited textual messages transmitted over the airwaves for reading off a **liquid crystal display (LCD)** screen built into the pager.

real-time computerised data
see management information system.

rules
A DTP term to describe the vertical and horizontal lines or boxes used to separate entries.

spreadsheet package
A spread sheet stores numbers in '*cells*'; the cells may be arranged in columns and all kinds of instructions – *formulae* – may be keyed in so as to obtain running totals, reducing balances, etc; also, if one entry is amended, all linked totals are likewise modified; in this way spreadsheets are used to aid accountants and marketing staff.

style sheet
Many DTP software packages include pre-designed page layouts (style sheets) to aid the user.

teleconferencing
(see also BT's trade name **Confravision**) This term defines the telecommunications process of linking groups of people in remote locations by means of a closed circuit television network, by which discussions and presentations take place live involving all linked participants.

telemessages
BT provides a service by which spoken messages given to an operator over the telephone are relayed to the desired recipient in printed form within fast, prescribed times.

telex
A telecommunications medium developed in the 1920s/1930s to send text and pictures 'down the wire'; only text may be transmitted by **teleprinters**, which both send and receive, once having established contact by means of an '**electronic handshake**'.

token ring
A specialist term describing the electronic circuit of a type of LAN in which created messages or files are sent round the network (like a metal washer along a wire) until the intended receiver is identified; the token 'drops' the message into the appropriate terminal and carries on round the LAN; this is a very simple explanation of a complex electronic process continuing at almost the speed of light!

UNIT 4
Creating and presenting office documents

OVERVIEW

A large part of your secretarial day is likely to be taken up with the important task of creating and presenting office documents of many kinds – letters, memoranda, reports, agendas, minutes, factsheets, itineraries, leaflets, brochures press releases, etc.

This unit provides extensive practical advice and guidance in producing the most frequently created documents: the letter, memorandum, written report and purpose-designed form. It also examines the important factors of cost-effectiveness and presentation when deciding the medium and format in which to produce an office document.

Fortunately, an impressive array of IT office equipment is available in many offices – sophisticated WP software, laser printers, desktop publishing systems, colour photocopiers, etc. These enable secretarial and reprographics staff to produce top-quality products. But, as a result, managers, and especially senior managers, have come to demand very high standards for the documents which go out from their offices, or which they receive from within the organisation.

It is therefore important that, from the outset, you set yourself high standards of quality in all the documents you produce. These qualities include choosing the most effective means of producing a given document. Not only is this in terms of cost and time taken, but also in visual appeal – easy-to-absorb layout, use of colour and print variables in paper and typescript, binding and covering, use of graphics and illustrative material. There must also of course, be an absence of errors and unsightly corrections, and helpful references and pagination to aid the reader.

Always remember: once in print and out of your hands, the documents you produce will either be a credit to you and your office, or a source of dismay and disappointment – neither of which you will be able to change! Other people will form value judgements and opinions about your office and organisation as a result of your work.

4.1 Letters

Choosing the best medium for a document; major applications of the letter; effective letter presentation; checklist for effective letter creation.

CHOOSING THE BEST MEDIUM FOR A DOCUMENT

Today's manager has a wide range of routes and media available through which to communicate, the written word:

■ letter ■ memorandum ■ report ■ notice ■ leaflet ■ minutes ■ press release ■ factsheet ■ formal invitation ■ telex ■ fax

The medium chosen for the message will depend upon the interplay of a number of features, and which of them is considered to be most important. The section below sets out the major features which affect the choice of document, and every good secretary keeps in mind such factors *before* rushing into print.

Factors affecting type of document selected for message

Urgency
The value of many business messages depends on their arriving within a given time; thus the higher cost of a faxed message will on occasion be justified by the speed of its delivery.

Time to produce
Complex and schematically laid-out formal reports are time-consuming to produce, but they invariably contain important information and the time and care taken will be fully justified if layout and presentation aid good top-level decision-making.

Complexity
Some topics are simply too complicated to be properly dealt with on an **A5** memorandum and may need a multipaged **A4** memo or report; thus the manager and secretary must weigh up what document medium best conveys a given message, depending on how complex it is.

Security
Some office matters are highly sensitive and must be conveyed securely and confidentially to their intended recipient(s); envelopes usually cater for this situation but the secretary must keep alert and *think* in advance of any possible problems which could attach to open message forms like notices. It may be that the extra time and cost of distributing individual memos in sealed envelopes is justified by the nature of the message.

Time/cost to deliver
Perhaps the most frequent trade-off is between the cost of, say, a large **mailshot**, the promised delivery times of tiered postal services (express post, first and second-class mail, etc) and the status of the message. For example, it may well prove cheaper for a company to contract with the Post Office to deliver 10 000 leaflets over a period of days than to incur added envelope and postage charges which only save a few days.

Legality
Every secretary should be aware of the legal status of given documents; while letters, invoices and telexed messages are accepted as a proof of a transaction in law, at present faxed messages are not, and so should not be used if there is any likely connection with a contract, agreement or other legally-binding relationship involved.

Impression and acceptance
Communication research has shown that as much as 25% of a document's impact and acceptance depends upon its visual appearance and feel to the hand. Gold-edged, multi-inked letterhead logo and particulars and top-quality bond paper will tend to communicate the solid financial status and respectability of the sender (even if it is not justified!) and tells the receiver that he is highly valued. Ink duplicated or photocopied circulars do not compete in this respect!

Durability
A low status inter-office memorandum with an expected active life of 24 hours may well be produced on inexpensive paper and even in handwriting. However, legal documents like contracts and leases will often need to last for very many years and care is rightly taken to use good quality text production equipment and paper which will not fade or disintegrate easily.

Top secretary tip: choice of document
Make it a habit to stop and *think* about factors like those outlined above *before* starting a task.

MAJOR APPLICATIONS OF THE LETTER

Letters are, of course, composed and produced to meet the needs of countless situations. Some situations are unique and others recur frequently. The following checklist illustrates those types of letter with which secretaries should be familiar:

- **Enquiry, acknowledgement and response**
  Enquiries for information, assistance or services come in, are acknowledged if time is needed to obtain the information for a reply and responded to *with a minimum of delay*!

- **Complaint and adjustment**
  Customers, purchasers or service users may complain about shortcomings in goods bought or work done and these need to be investigated promptly and matters put right in a suitable reply, in order to keep goodwill.

- **Orders, estimates, tenders**
  Order letters specify the details and agreed prices for goods; *estimates* detail proposed fees or charges for goods or services; and *tenders* offer to provide goods or services at very specific prices as the prelude to a contract being awarded. (Note here the term 'errors and omissions excepted' (E&OE) which sometimes still appears on such documents and which used to protect the writer against unspotted errors in prices quoted, though now no longer of legal significance.)

- **Sales, advertising, promoting**
  Selling goods and services by means, of the letter is very big business today and many letters are highly specialised, with personalised **salutations** and references – '*Yes, you, Mr Evans of 121 Sloane Square, have been selected to ...*'

- **Financial**
  This includes collection, credit requests, financial status enquiries and credit rating enquiries. Account customers who are slow payers are reminded of payments which are overdue by a series of collection letters which become increasingly terse. Businesses are constantly seeking to purchase goods or services on credit and providers need to reassure themselves by checking the creditworthiness of new or expanding customers. Those giving credit seek references from the requester's bank or an existing credit giver.

- **Job application, reference, job offer and acceptance**
  A range of letters is produced in order to fill a job vacancy – to apply for a post, to ask for a confidential report or reference, and to provide it from a current employer, and those which formally offer and accept a new appointment.

- **Invitations, congratulations, thanks, sympathy, etc**
  The world of business relies heavily on the maintenance of goodwill and personal contacts. Thus managers often write letters to thank a host after a party or dinner, to offer condolences on the death of a colleague or associate, to congratulate a friend on a promotion. Letters of invitation may be very formal – to a director as notice of a board meeting, or informal – to a customer to come to a sales presentation.

- **Disciplinary, legal, procedural**
  The letter is also used to communicate a formal warning to an employee being disciplined as part of a process required under industrial law. Other letters may be written by companies or their solicitors in civil disputes, perhaps over contracts or defects in products. Local and central government despatch millions of letters each year in order to carry out the duties legally required of them, for example, to respond to a planning application to extend a shop's premises.

- **Specialist letters**
  Many letters occur in highly technical and specialised fields such as the work of solicitors, insurance, medical, scientific, engineering and export documentation. Here, the secretary will need to have a similarly specialised background in order to give competent support (eg legal or medical)

- **Circulars, form letters, mailshots**
  In addition to the 'one off' letter, secretaries also have to produce masters for letters which are posted to many recipients simultaneously. With the aid of word processing software, files of names and addresses may be automatically merged or inserted in sequence into such letters with standard messages, and a run of addressed envelopes or labels may be similarly printed.

Top secretary tip
Take the trouble to study incoming letters from all sorts of sources and cast a critical eye over their layout, presentation, English and style; also, study copied letters from other internal departments. In this way you will very quickly pick up specialised terms and an appreciation of the work of a wide range of firms and their departments which will aid you in your letter production work!

EFFECTIVE LETTER PRESENTATION

Undoubtedly companies and public service organisations are judged – quite critically – by the standards of the letters they produce and send out. All the coloured inks and top quality letter paper that money can buy are of no account if the letter's typescript is messy and spoiled by careless errors! Use the following checklist as an aid to ensure that you keep constantly aware of the impact of your letters upon their recipients:

Features of effective letter presentation

1 The letter's frame
'Every good picture deserves a good frame: make sure the typed elements of your letters are *always* eye-catching because they stand out from ample margins; avoid carrying on too far down the page before starting a continuation sheet, and remember to use the rule around your typewriter's cylinder to check the depth of your text, or the line counter at the head of your VDU screen.

2 Techniques of display
Keep always in mind the facilities which your typewriter or word processor/printer offer you to make your letters visually appealing and easy to absorb:

- **centring**: decide in advance when to centre to your paper width or your text width; remember to use tabs for columns and to inset/indent key paragraphs or bulleted lists etc.

- **white space**: always leave sufficient white space around your headings and paragraph titles, etc. so that the reader's eye cannot miss their message.

- **emboldening**: today, electronic typewriters and printers provide a wide range of emboldening options to highlight key headings and words or phrases which thus become attention getters. (But beware of overdoing it *within* paragraphs, because it can become *very* irritating!)

- **choice of typeface/fount**: first golf-ball typeheads and then daisywheels gave secretaries the facility to vary the appearance of text on the printed page, today electronic printers have extended enormously this aspect of text presentation. When you have a spare moment, practise with the typefaces available to you and discuss with your teacher which kinds of typeface are best suited to the range of documents you are producing. The same goes for the pitches of print available to you.

- **initial capitals and underscoring**: these features offer a useful alternative to emboldening, especially in sub-headings:

  1 Use of Initial Capitals and Underscoring

- **capitals and double spacing** also offer an alternative means of catching the eye:

  LIST OF DELEGATES

- **simple, single-spaced capitals**:

  Dear Sir

  ABC COMPUTERS LAUNCH A NEW LAP-TOP!

  The latest top-quality yet inexpensive ...

  and,

  Yours sincerely
  ABC COMPUTERS LIMITED

- **progressive indentation**:

  CHECKLIST OF PRESENTATION FEATURES

    1 Aids To Typescript Appeal

      The following aids are recommended:

        1.1 **Emboldening**

          Used sparingly ...

- **indented and hanging paragraphs**:

      Some letter writers like to indent the first line of each new paragraph as a means of indicating a new topic to the reader.

  In the United States, by contrast, the
      hanging paragraph – like this one   is
      used as an alternative.

- **leader dots**: the use of leader dots may be very helpful if a letter contains items which are priced – especially where a list is long and closely spaced:

  Staybrite Varnish:

  Matt £1.45
  Gloss £1.55

- **section numbering**: occasionally long letters include data which needs to be numbered for reference and to aid the reader's understanding; the guideline here is to prefer the simple and unfussy:

  4.3.6
  is preferred to
  IV C (f)
  in referring to the sixth point of the third paragraph of section four. Again, use techniques of spacing and indentation to give the number references visual impact.

- **positioning of information/status items**: many letters include important items of information such as CONFIDENTIAL, PERSONAL, For the attention of, encs, cc and so on; make sure these are given due prominence according to current layout conventions

- **right and left justification**: remember that creating letters with WP software makes right and left margin justification of text quick and simple; the effect is clear and pleasing to the eye. Also, desktop publishing printing techniques are making letter readers far more aware of techniques of professional text presentation and the impact they make.

3 Letters and security

A number of techniques are used in letters to maintain their security; the effective secretary pays particular attention to the following points in letter creation:

- **status of the letter**: always check carefully whether a letter is to be PRIVATE, STRICTLY CONFIDENTIAL, CONFIDENTIAL or PERSONAL and mark envelopes correspondingly.

- **letter references**: these are vital: double check to make sure you quote 'Your ref' accurately and sequence your 'Our ref' file references correctly. It does no harm in the opening sentence of a letter to slip in (inside brackets or between commas):

    ... (your reference EFG/KG/AX23 refers) ...

    in order to tie up with related correspondence.

- **the date**: remember that in the UK the conventional sequence is day – month – year and never type 14/4/19--

- **attention lines**: used on both letters and envelopes help to ensure the letter reaches its desired recipient as quickly as possible – especially in large organisations.

- **recipient's name and address**: *always* make sure you get the recipient's style (Lord, Sir, Dr, Miss etc) right. Use Ms if the writer of an incoming letter just signs herself as, for example, 'Patricia Williams' with no clues as to her marital status. Also, make sure you are using the correct job title/designation of your recipient and whenever in doubt telephone the organisation's receptionist or the recipient's secretary to check. Attention to this particular area matters a great deal! As the psychologist said, 'There is nothing more important to someone than his or her name.'

- **enclosure references**: stick to the house style in use and remember that --- or *** or / in the lefthand margin, supported by enc, encs enclosure(s) below the subscription will ensure that accompanying documents are not missed; remember that the Post Office's letter-sorting machines do not like staples or paper-clips, even inside envelopes!

- **continuation eye-catchers and sheets**: some managers like to see:

    / continued ...

    or,

    / continued over ...

    at the foot of first pages or wherever a further sheet follows. If such references help to avoid sheets of a letter becoming separated they are worth including; by the same token, the customary reference at the head of each continuation sheet is a must and should include: recipient's name – page number – date.

- **subscriptions/complimentary closes**; avoid leaving your manager a cramped space in which to sign his name; if you have to sign in his absence, then there are a number of options open:

    Yours faithfully

    Fiona Sanderson

    pp John Wilson
    Sales Manager

    where pp stands for 'per procurationem' or on behalf of. Much to be preferred in the author's view is simply:

    Yours faithfully

    Fiona Sanderson

    for John Wilson
    Sales Manager

    and the wordy:

    Dictated by Mr John Smith and signed in his absence by Fiona Sanderson

    sometimes seen across the bottom of letters seems like overkill!

- **copy references**: a number of acceptable versions of indicating the despatch of copies are acceptable:

    CC   cc   copy to: etc.

    remember to include these on the letter and flimsy(ies) *except* where your manager has asked for a blind copy to be sent. This occurs when the author of the letter does not wish its recipient to know that a third person has received a copy of it. It might happen in a situation where a copy of a sensitive letter (or memorandum) from a line manager to a member of his staff is sent confidentially to the firm's personnel manager or managing director. Such copies are marked usually 'bcc' on the copy but, obviously, *not* on the letter itself!

- **envelopes**: come in a wide range of sizes and shapes; only circulars and bills should be despatched in manilla envelopes – good quality white banker envelopes are customary for personal mail; remember that typing the town in capitals and the postcode as a last, separate line helps postal sorters, and aids prompt delivery.

- **window envelopes**: are used a great deal in firms which send out mass mailings (water boards, electricity boards, etc for billing) and save time since the notepaper or bill includes a bordered space in which to type the recipient's name and address once only; however, such envelopes have a low priority/acceptance status and usually end up at the bottom of a stack of mail for scrutiny.

Fig 4.1   SPECIMEN 'ELECTRONIC LETTER' PRODUCED ON IBM'S PROFS SYSTEM FOR EXTERNAL RECIPIENT

```
Mr J Smith                                      15 September 19XX
XX High Street
Havant
Hants


Dear Mr Smith


SUBJECT  :  YOUNG ENTERPRISE SCHEMES


Thank you kindly for supporting our group meeting last week.  Your input
and suggestions were favourably received.

I enclose a copy of the minutes for your information and would offer again
an open invitation to visit us whenever you are in the area.

Thanks again,

Yours sincerely




Alison George
Communications Officer
Personnel Dept
D.220     26/32     721-4943
AG:sj

ATTACHMENT
```

Note: The fully blocked letter layout is produced automatically by the computer program as the inputs are keyed in.

(Reproduced by kind permission of IBM (UK) Ltd)

1 **Pitman Publishing**

128 Long Acre **3**	Telephone 01-379 7383
London WC2E 9AN	
2 **4**	Telex 261367 Pitman G
5	Cables Ipandsons London WC2
6	Fax 01-240 5771 Pitman Ldn

7   CONFIDENTIAL

8   Your ref   JG/PD

9   Our ref   AG/NL/ 4

10 15 April 19--

11 Mr J Green
    Appletrees
    Windmill Lane
    Peppard Common
    READING
    Berks
    RG24 3PC

12 Dear Mr Green

13 PROPOSED TEXTBOOK ON SECRETARIAL ADMINISTRATION

14 Following upon our telephone conversation of Tuesday last, I am pleased to confirm that our Project Committee met yesterday, and that your proposal was fully considered. As a result, Mrs Jean Simpson, Publisher, Secretarial Studies Division, wishes me to offer you a contract to publish your text early next year.

May I take this opportunity to offer my personal congratulations with the sincere hope that your first textbook will prove a resounding success. I should also like to assure you that your manuscript will receive my careful attention in the coming months, so please do not hesitate to let me know if I may help in any way.

15 I enclose a copy of our standard Agreement form for your information and shall contact you shortly to arrange a convenient date to finalise contract details.

16 Yours sincerely

17 *Ann Grant*

18 Ann Grant
    Editor Secretarial Studies Division

19 enc.

20 Pitman Publishing. Division of Longman Group UK Limited Registered Office 5 Bentinck Street London W1M 5RN Registered number 872828 England

Creating and presenting office documents

Format of the fully blocked letter

1. Company logo and trading name.
   Five company addresses:
   2. Postal, including postcode
   3. Telephone number
   4. Telex address
   5. Cables address
   6. Fax number and address

7. Prominently placed letter status indicator.

8. Your reference is that of the letter's recipient, John Green (JG) and his assistant, Pat Dawson (PD).

9. Our reference is that of the letter's sender – here Ann Grant as the writer (AG), and Nicola Lawson, secretary (NL). The number 4 indicates this is the fourth letter written to John Green and is a helpful filing reference.

10. Date: expressed as day (number), month (word) and year (number) and *never* as 15/4/19–.

11. Recipient's full postal address: note town in capital letters and postcode on its own line (whenever practicable).

12. Salutation: Here the less formal 'Dear Mr ... Yours sincerely' is used, as opposed to its formal counterpart 'Dear Sir ... Yours faithfully'.

7–12. This letter's layout conforms to the conventions of blocked format and open punctuation; in blocked format all lines commence from the pre-set left-hand margin as all punctuation (outside the body of the letter) is omitted.

13. Subject heading prominently displayed in capitals with good space around it; subject headings should convey briefly the letter's theme or subject.

14. Body of the letter: note that points are made succinctly in brief paragraphs and that the chosen style is informal without becoming over-friendly or familiar.

15. Eye-catching enclosure symbol: note that *** and/are also sometimes employed.

16. Appropriate subscription for 'Dear Mr, Mrs, Ms or Miss, etc'.

17. Sufficient space allotted for writer's signature.

18. Typescript confirmation of writer's name and job title (Note: some female letter-writers include Mrs, Ms or Miss after their names).

19. Further confirmation of an enclosure included; see also 'encs', 'enclosure', etc.

20. All business letters must include the address where the company is registered and its registration number to comply with the Companies Acts.

Format of the fully displayed letter

1 Logo

SCIENTIFIC CONFERENCE ORGANISERS LIMITED

14–16 Wokingham Road, Reading, Berks RG2 OR14.

Telephone: 0734 96241–5.   Telex: 496111 SCICOL.
Fax: 0734 949000 Telecom   Gold Mailbox: 48 ARG 71434

Registered Office 14–16 Wokingham Road, Reading, Berks, RG2 OR14
Registered Number 4146049 England

2 Date
(placed right of centre-line)

Your ref:

Our ref: CGB/WT   12 May, 19--

3 Fully punctuated
(also termed 'closed punctuation')

Dr. A. D. Vickers,
Chief Scientist,
Excelsior Laboratories Ltd.,
Science Park,
Coventry Road,
LEICESTER,
Leics.   LE4 6AJ

4 Salutation

Dear Sir,

THIRD INTERNATIONAL CONFERENCE ON GENETIC ENGINEERING

5 Indented paragraphs

    As you will be aware, Science Conference Organisers Limited has been privileged to coordinate the First and Second International Conference on Genetic Engineering held biannually. The First Conference, held in Helsinki in 1986, was generally considered to have been a signal success, bringing together as it did leading scientists of international repute from both western and socialist countries.

    The Second Conference, which took place in Geneva in 1988, demonstrated the significant advances which had been made over the ensuing two years, particularly in gene splicing technology.

    As an acknowledged field leader in molecular genetics, I should very much like to invite you to present a paper on 'D.N.S. Sequencing: Recent Advances'. We have it in mind for this paper to be presented from 11.00 a.m. - 12 p.m. on the first day of the Conference, Tuesday 28 June, 1990.

    The Third International Conference will take place at the University of Chicago, Illinois, which is renowned for its conference facilities and hospitality. Conference speakers will be the guests of the University from 26 - 30 June with all travelling and accommodation expenses paid, together with a Conference Fee of £700.00.

    I very much hope that you will be able to accept my invitation and look forward to hearing from you.

6 Subscription

Yours faithfully,
SCIENTIFIC CONFERENCE ORGANISERS LIMITED

Colin Brown

C. G. Brown,
Conference Organiser

CHECKLIST FOR EFFECTIVE LETTER CREATION

Do

- *Take a particular pride in your correspondence work.* Your letters are each and every one ambassadors for your manager and office!

- *Give every attention to detail.* Transcribing correctly names, dates, quantities, telephone or order numbers, is vital and one mistake could prove very costly.

- *Do your preparation work thoroughly.* Before typing or word processing, read your shorthand dictation through carefully or listen to your audio tape for the whole letter in advance (if you have time) so as to anticipate such aspects as:

    Is A4 or A5 paper needed?
    Is **portrait** or **landscape** display better?
    How many copies are required?
    Are there any amendments or instructions in the *last* paragraph which also affect the *first*?

    (If you train your manager in good techniques of dictation much of this preparatory work will have been already done!)

- *Master your paper and VDU screen sizes.* Control fully the text and its relationship with the paper.

- *Anticipate pressure times and 'rush-jobs'.* If you take carbon copies, keep some **collated** letter paper, carbon paper and copy sheets to hand to save time. If you spot an important incoming letter in the morning's post, fetch out the relevant file *in advance* so it is to hand for your manager's dictation and your own reference.

- *Discreetly help your manager's dictation.* It is not always easy to find the best word or phrase while composing and speaking simultaneously, and sentences can become tangled and ungrammatical. But never change the meaning of the dictation so that the letter becomes yours rather than your manager's!

- *Seek to keep all letters brief and with short paragraphs.* Without cramping or spoiling the look of the letter, keep to a single page whenever possible.

- *Take every care with proofreading your work.* If you have an LCD memory typewriter, read your typescript closely before printing; if you use a word processing package, do not just rely on the **spellchecker** – how does a WP spelling disk know whether 'principle' or 'principal' is right in the context of your letter?

- *Let your conscience guide you in **mailable copy** decisions.* Deep down, you will always *know* whether a letter with corrected errors is really up to being received well by its recipient.

- *Be alert for security.* Never leave a partly-completed letter in your typewriter for all to see if it is confidential and you are called away. By the same token, always remember to 'lock-up' your VDU if leaving it temporarily.

- *Give priority to your correspondence work as far as possible.* Letters are expensive to produce and distribute and usually important; managers expect them to go out on the same day they are dictated or drafted.

Don't

- *Process text in a rush!* Typing/WP errors are easily made and cost time to put right.

- *Allow yourself to be distracted by interruption.* Easier said than done, but close your office door or put up your 'Out of Bounds' sign whenever you have to process top priority work

- *Mix styles – in layout of punctuation.* Follow your organisation's **house style**, but try to follow your manager's lead if he or she has a preferred letter ingredient or format quirk. After all, it *is* your manager's letter rather than yours.

- *Mar your work by sloppy standards.* Never overtype on text, make holes in your letter paper, allow messy corrections to go out in letters or copies, fold letters carelessly, try to stuff too much into too small an envelope, create 'hills and dales' with correction fluid, etc.

- *Use headed notepaper for continuation or copy sheets.* Such practice is the mark of the cost-careless and lazy secretary!

- *Allow a letter to go out which you think your manager should see again and have second thoughts about.* Even though your manager should read outgoing post carefully before signing it, there may be pressure of time or other distractions. If you think the letter too curt, too casual or ill-judged in any way, suggest so tactfully and say you will not at all mind typing it or word processing it again if the manager wants to have second thoughts.

- *Leave an urgent letter for the afternoon post which could be despatched via a morning mailroom collection.* Help your mailroom and the Post Office to help you by anticipating the afternoon rush of collection and sorting whenever possible.

- *Waste precious time looking for names and addresses of regular letter recipients.* And do not rely on keeping them in your head. Maintain a handy electronic name and address database or card index, with postcodes!

- *Send out a letter without having taken a copy*. This letter will inevitably be the one which the Managing Director needs an urgent copy of directly!

- *Delay in filing copies of despatched letters*. While the correspondence is fresh in your mind you will more easily remember to insert filing cross-references and to collate correspondence in sets, etc.

- *Delay in despatching copies of letters to internal departments and staff*. It is irritating for your manager's colleagues to be telephoned about the contents of letter which state that they have been informed about their contents, when the informing file copies are still in your out-tray!

Top secretary tip

Explore all the advantages which information technology has brought to letter creation – ease of correction, instantly accessible file copies, printers which accept notepaper, copy paper and envelopes at the touch of a button and which produce immaculate end products, etc. Determine to master and use these advantages whenever you can, even if it means persuading your manager to purchase some new equipment. You will undoubtedly save your time and the organisation's money in the process!

QUICK REVIEW QUIZ

1 Describe the factors which affect the type of document selected to communicate a given message.

2 Explain briefly the kind of message conveyed in:

a a letter of adjustment, *b* a collection letter, *c* a status enquiry, *d* a letter of condolence.

3 Make a checklist of the major features of effective letter presentation.

4 Explain the meaning of: *a* emboldening, *b* indentation, *c* hanging paragraph, *d* leader dots, *e* justification, and how each aids letter presentation and readability.

5 List the currently accepted ways of indicating that a letter is accompanied by an enclosure.

6 What accepted ways are there for a secretary to indicate that a letter has been signed on behalf of the manager?

7 What do the following stand for?

a pp *b* bcc *c* encs.

8 Outline the principal format characteristics of:

a a fully blocked letter; *b* a fully displayed letter.

RESEARCH AND REPORT BACK ASSIGNMENTS

1 Find out how the use of scanners with optical character recognition (OCR) and LAN/WAN networks are changing the ways in which documents are created, stored and distributed in organisations. Compose a factsheet on the trends you discover, for your group's database.

2 Start up a portfolio (a collection of good examples and specimens) of letters, memoranda, reports, factsheets, forms, etc, which you are able to obtain through your network of relatives, friends and neighbours who work in offices. Draw interesting instances of format, style, structure and techniques of presentation to the attention of your class.

4.2 Memoranda

Components; major features of structure how to handle memoranda effectively.

COMPONENTS

The memorandum carries out functions very similar to those of the letter, save that it is restricted to **internal** organisational use. Thus many of the tips and guidelines you have picked up in studying the format, presentation and structure of the letter may be applied to the memorandum. There remain, however, a number of features of effective memorandum creation and distribution to be mastered.

Pre-printed components

Just as the letter contains a number of pre-printed letterhead items, so the memorandum is generally printed either in A4 or A5 single sheets or in pads with the following components in general use: memorandum (heading), to, from, subject, date and reference.

The order and location of such components varies according to preferred house style but sufficient space is allocated for the identity of the memorandum's recipient(s) and author to be inserted, as well as the date and a subject title for the memorandum. A memorandum with the 'memohead' components entered in typescript is shown on page 154.

Typescript components

Just as there are conventions regarding forms of address in letters, so there are in memoranda. Again, these vary according to custom and practice in different organisations and the degree of formality of the memorandum:

Addressing the recipient

It is common practice to address a memorandum's recipient by his or her job title only, such as managing director or south east regional manager or assistant personnel officer. Sometimes authors include the person's name as well: John Brown, managing director. But this approach can become too long, given the limited space in which to type in a memohead. Some memos are sent to 'Susan Williams, Accounts Department', where the recipient has no obvious title, but is one of, say, eight accounts clerks.

Many memos are sent to groups or teams of staff – 'To All sales representatives' or 'To Production department personnel'.

Author's styles of title

The same approach is used for the insertion of the author's job title – perhaps with name – 'From Public Relations Manager' or 'From Jean Robinson, Marketing Manager'.

The date and subject-heading

The conventions of entering the date on a memorandum are just the same as those for the letter, and so also for the memorandum's subject-heading, with the proviso that it is always a help to provide a reference if appropriate, eg 'SUBJECT OFFICE EQUIPMENT REQUISITION: ORDER NO HA14362'. This allows the recipient to cross-check quickly to an original requisition order. Similarly the author/text creator reference is useful in a subject-heading: 'Subject Resignation of Miss Carol Peters (HJK/AWC 3 June 19--). It is always good practice in letter and memorandum subject-headings to keep them short, while communicating clearly and accurately their content.

Enclosure, copy, circulation

For showing enclosures, copies, circulation, **continuation sheets** and references, the same conventions apply as for the letter and will vary according to the house style preferred. An important point to note in copying a memorandum is that **all** interested parties must be given action or information copies. Executives feel they have lost face if left 'out of the picture' (however accidentally), having been omitted from a copy list. So make it a habit to check at the point of dictation or transcription that your manager has not forgotten a likely copy recipient, by asking if 'X' is to be included.

The body of the memorandum

A fully-blocked or indented paragraph format may be employed (but consistently) and the same guidelines about paragraph titles appearing either blocked or centred, with initial capital letters and **underscoring**, etc, will apply.

Here, a useful guideline is to keep paragraphs short and to aid the reader with 'summarising headings' if the memorandum's message is long and wide-ranging. (Some reports may be set out on A4 memorandum paper with continuation sheets and incorporate a suitable report format.)

Fig 4.2 Memorandum checklist of components

A4 memorandum

```
                COURIER TRAVEL LIMITED
                       Memorandum

STRICTLY CONFIDENTIAL

To      Personnel Manager            Ref   CW/VF

From    Home Sales Director          Date  24 October 19--


Subject  Miss Kay Parkinson, Sales Department

Miss Parkinson has been employed by Courier Travel for just over three
years, during which time she has proved a loyal and conscientious
employee.  For the past two months she has been reporting to JIM
WEAVER, our Adventure Holiday Coordinator.

From the outset, there has been a regrettable clash of personalities
which I have been unable to resolve.  Today Miss Parkinson requested a
personal interview with me to express her unhappiness with the current
situation, and I promised I would do all I could to put matters right.

I should therefore be grateful if you would kindly arrange to see Miss
Parkinson as a matter of urgency in order to explore the possibility
of a departmental transfer or other opportunity from which she and the
company might benefit.

Also, I should be grateful if you would find an early opportunity to
discuss with Jim Weaver how he is finding his new post, as I am
beginning to think that the problem with Kay Parkinson may be
symptomatic of difficulties he is experiencing but not admitting to.

I enclose a copy of the appraisal recently carried out for Kay
Parkinson, and you will see that the agreed summary shows her in a
very good light.  I should be most sorry if the company were to lose
her services.

enc


cc Marketing Director
```

1. Memohead components: from, to, date, reference, subject,

   Check names, job titles and references are correct

2. Ensure subject heading is sufficiently clear and detailed

3. Memorandum body (keep A5 messages short and avoid going too far down A5 sheets)

4. Check before despatch for manager's 'OK to issue' initials

5. Remember enclosure references

6. Ensure all who are supposed to receive them are sent copies. Check if any blind copy is required and indicate who received it on manager's retained file copy as 'bcc'

7. Do not forget continuation sheet reference on A4 memorandum if a second page is required

HOW TO HANDLE MEMORANDA EFFECTIVELY

There are a number of good reasons why memos are created and distributed within organisations:

- **Written records**
  They provide a written record – to act as a memory-jogger on a person's desk, to be stored for future reference, or to convey information which needs to be absorbed and returned to at intervals.

- **Communication aids**
  They help (through the copying system) to keep team members or interested staff informed of decisions and developments.

- They act as devices through which to issue instructions simultaneously to groups of often widely separated personnel.

- **Feedback channels**
  They provide feedback to managers by confirming, for example, sales for the month of July, the acquisition of a major new client or the success of a programme of staff development.

Top secretary tip
Always remember – the memorandum, once in print and despatched, (like the letter) cannot be retrieved for second thoughts, because it should not be as curt, impatient, grudging or sarcastic, etc. So be on your guard to protect/support your manager, who may be working under stress, by diplomatically inviting a second go *before* it is too late!

Tips on effective memorandum handling

As you can see, the memorandum is a very important item in the organisation's communication toolbox. As an effective secretary, you should therefore absorb these tips into your daily memorandum-handling routines:

- **Transcribe the memorandum promptly.** Just because memos are an internal form of communication does not mean that they are never urgent.

- **Always provide current and correct names and job titles of recipients and room/office locations** – a sloppy approach here may cause a vital message to become lost or delayed. If you work in an organisation which produces internal personnel directories at regular intervals, make sure you receive your copy and make the time to scan it for changes.

- **Adopt a helpful filing method.** For example, some organisations employ various coloured copy papers where a given colour will convey:

  For action, For information only, Departmental **file copy**.

  Also, where the manager is likely to want to follow up and progress-chase a despatched memorandum, make sure you include it in your bring forward system *well before a given deadline* and don't always wait to be asked to do so.

- **Avoid leaving copy memoranda for filing in a growing stack of papers.** It is irritating and time-wasting to have to search for such a file copy when a senior executive is on your manager's telephone wishing to discuss its contents!

- **Always ensure draft memoranda are so labelled and clearly dated and numbered**, eg Draft 3 and that your office's staff are all working on **current** drafts.

- **Never despatch a sensitive memorandum without first giving your manager a chance to see it in print after an elapsed interval.** Its content may have been dictated in a fit of impatience or frustration and second thoughts are often the best ones. Many managers – and their secretaries – have got on by knowing which memoranda were exercises in venting frustration, etc, and best consigned to the shredder! In this area some secretaries and managers operate a system where the manager initials each memorandum before despatch as part of the post-signing routine. If file copies also display such initialling, then there is no room for doubt as to whether the manager wished the memorandum to go out.

- **Make it a habit to ask if a given memorandum is to be designated confidential or personal.** And use envelopes accordingly. Never deliver such memoranda as open versions for all to read.

- **Message as notice or individual memorandum to group?** Help your manager to decide which is more appropriate.

- **Provide dated deadlines for required actions and responses.** Avoid including action requests in a memorandum like:

  'Please let me have your completed returns *as soon as possible*:
  or 'I shall be pleased to receive your response *in due course*'

  For some staff such indefinite action requests tend to be translated as 'mañana' and we all know 'tomorrow never comes!'

Fig 4.3 Specimen Email memo sent to Mr Smith over a LAN office system (IBM's PROFS)

```
Unclassified              Page 1                    7 April 19--


   FROM :      ALISON GEORGE

   TO:         M R SMITH

   SUBJECT:    MANAGEMENT SUPPORT MEETING


   Following the meeting on 5 April 19XX, although your area has no specific
   actions due, I should be grateful if you would continue to attend the
   meetings for a further two months until we are sure problems will not
   recur.

   Thank you.


   ALISON GEORGE
   Communications Officer
   D.220   26/32 extn 721-4943
   HVTVM2(AGEORGE)

   AG:JS
```

Note: Entries are keyed in against displayed 'prompts'.

(Reproduced by kind permission of IBM (UK) Ltd)

Fig 4.4 How to structure effective letters and memoranda

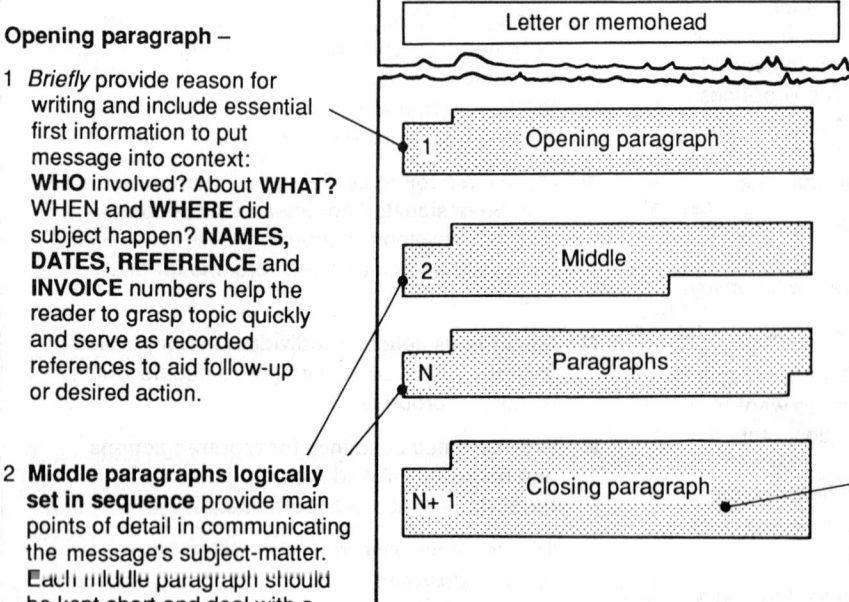

Opening paragraph –

1 *Briefly* provide reason for writing and include essential first information to put message into context: **WHO** involved? About **WHAT**? **WHEN** and **WHERE** did subject happen? **NAMES, DATES, REFERENCE** and **INVOICE** numbers help the reader to grasp topic quickly and serve as recorded references to aid follow-up or desired action.

2 **Middle paragraphs logically set in sequence** provide main points of detail in communicating the message's subject-matter. Each middle paragraph should be kept short and deal with a single main item of detail.

Letter or memohead

1 Opening paragraph

2 Middle

N Paragraphs

N+1 Closing paragraph

'N + 1' = The final or closing paragraphs
'N' = Any number of middle paragraphs – depending on complexity of topics

Middle paragraphs: typical structures
- Major →minor details
- Chronological order of events
- A–Z cover of known facts
- Logical progression –
- because this . . . so this . . .
- Balancing of pros & cons
- Analysis in logical steps, etc.

3 **Closing paragraph**
Most typically a closing paragraph states **briefly** and **positively** (but courteously) what action is desired from the recipient. It is good practice whenever possible to insert a 'by when' deadline for a response and to insert copies of messages into a bring-forward system.

Memoranda and electronic mail

Increasingly memos are being created in the medium of electronic mail messages which are instantly despatched to the workstations of intended recipients.

The normal trend in offices is for such messages to be keyed in very much like the spoken word:

'OKI DOKI! I'll check into it and come back to you in a jiff!'

Such electronic mail 'notes' tend to be very short-lived and are wiped off a networking system after a few days or a month as a matter of custom. Sometimes, however, electronic mail messages are important and are kept on electronic file for a considerable time.

It is therefore important for the effective secretary to be conscious all the time of the status of various Email messages and to adopt a suitable style and tone. Also, where paper memos are in use, it is much easier for a secretary to give the manager time to reconsider a memo and to destroy it unsent. The speed of electronic mail delivery – and its potential for instant reading and wide distribution – make it vital to avoid sending ill-considered or aggressive Email notes or messages!

DISCUSSION TOPICS

1 Is the trend towards electronic messaging likely to bring about a decline in the standard of document creation and presentation?

2 What topics would you include in a secretarial training course aimed at improving document creation and presentation skills and why?

Top secretary tip
HOW TO STRUCTURE LETTERS AND MEMOS EFFECTIVELY

Sooner or later (but most probably sooner!), your manager is going to be in a tearing hurry and drop a letter onto your desk with the words:

'Tell them no, but nicely! Must dash!' or

'Say I'll come if I can, but can't promise ... or perhaps I should go, Johnsons are a large account ... Leave it to you! Got to fly ...!'

Or, a brief jotted note on the top of an incoming letter may require similar action: 'Say too dear – might be interested if can improve terms. JG 5/4.'

At all events, secretaries need to know how to compose business letters which satisfy all kinds of needs and desired outcomes on behalf of a busy or absent boss. It therefore pays to know how to go about it, and the diagram (Fig 4.4) provides a series of helpful tips on structuring effective letters and memos.

Remember: Practice makes perfect! So make sure you gain sufficient practice in composing a range of letters and memos before doing this for your manager.

4.3 Reports and forms

Major applications of the written report; reports: components and structure; referencing, typography and presentation; pre-printed forms and documents; effective document presentation; summary.

MAJOR APPLICATIONS OF THE WRITTEN REPORT

Basically, there are two kinds of report:

Investigatory
Reports which are 'one-offs' and tend to investigate situations or problems and offer solutions for acceptance and implementation.

Routine
Reports which either cover routine events, like an inspection report on a factory's press or milling machine, or which are made in the event of situations occurring a number of times over a year, like monthly reviews of work in progress, or accident reports.

For 'one-off' reports, certain conventions of presentation and structure exist which organisations tend to adopt, much like a house style in correspondence. Such reports are set out on blank sheets of bond paper and it is for the secretary to control layout and **typography** so as to aid the report's impact and ease of absorption and understanding.

Routine reports, on the other hand, tend to be set down on pre-printed forms and much depends (to obtain all needed information) upon the skill and foresight of the form designer.

Effective secretaries need to become proficient in producing the 'one-off' investigatory report, usually from handwritten or word processed drafts, and also in designing report forms which obtain information simply and briefly yet without omitting important data.

Typical report structures

1 The long, formal report

Cover/front page
Displays: Report's title, author name(s), date and **circulation list** (may include company's technical library reference

Sources
Reference books, papers, sources of data, etc, are acknowledged

Table of contents
Displays: section by section headings and sub-headings and appendices/bibliography with page numbers shown

Report sections
Typically, this sequence is followed:

1 Terms of reference
2 Procedure
3 Summary of entire report
4 Findings
5 Conclusions
6 Recommendations
7 List of references
8 Appendices and/or specimen documents
9 Bibliography/sources of further information

Note: Sometimes a report provides only an analysis of a problem or situation and no recommendations as to the best solution are asked for; if so, item 6 is omitted.

Terminology

Title
Should be a clear and accurate summary of the

report's terms of reference, eg: Reasons for absenteeism at the Grassvalley Pit and proposals for its reduction

Circulation
List of those individuals and organisations which receive a copy of the report

Sources
List of books, magazines, journals photographic libraries, etc, from which data for the report was obtained. Key access references like Dewey decimal and **ISBNs** (book numbers) are included

Table of contents
Displays in a sequenced list headings and sub-headings etc of the report's units

Headings/sub-headings
Reports are typically structured in numbered sections and sub-sections which are given helpful explanatory headings or titles:

1 **Terms of reference**
The person or organisation commissioning (asking for) the report sets out the particular aspects which are to be reported upon and also indicates whether or not recommendations are required

2 **Procedure**
Formal reports explain the ways in which the report's author(s) set about obtaining the information

3 **Summary [of entire report]**
The main parts of the report (Findings, Conclusions, Recommendations) are summarised so as to highlight the main points. This section is located early in the report for those not wishing/needing to read it all

4 **Findings**
The areas of investigation are structured in a series of sections which proceed in a logical order. This main body of the report is referred as its findings

5 **Conclusions**
The major items of discovery/investigation are repeated in a brief form

6 **Recommendations**
If requested, the report's authors will set out a series of suggested actions which in their reasoned view will put right the problem(s) they were asked to investigate

References
Some formal reports will indicate in *superscript* a supplied reference thus:

'Mines and Factories Acts[12]'

(where '12' is an item in a reference list comprising the full titles of the Acts of Parliament referred to). This practice keeps the report's data moving on, without lengthy listings at frequent intervals

Appendix/appendices
A term which stands for a document or set of additional information of some interest or relevance to the main report which the authors felt was worth including.

Bibliography
A section at the very end of the report which lists in detail other reports, books, papers, articles etc. which are relevant or connected to the report (from the Greek for 'book').

Footnotes
Some formal reports include superscript numbered references which take the form of *footnotes* at the bottom of each page instead of at the rear of the report.

2 **The short, formal report**
Many situations arise in business and the public service in which a shorter form of the formal report is appropriate. Such reports will generally deal with simpler subjects and their overall status and importance will be lower. Nevertheless, they incorporate a similar structure:

1 **Title page** or heading (like a memohead)
2 **Introduction**/background to report (which includes a 'terms of reference' statement)
3 **Findings**/analysis of problem (sometimes called 'information')
4 **Conclusions**/summary (such a section will also include recommendations if these were asked for)

Note: There is no single correct way of titling the sections of such reports, which lies at the discretion of the author.

3 **Brief informal reports**
At their simplest (say two sides of A4 memorandum paper), reports may be constructed in three logically sequenced parts:

1 Introduction (to problem)
2 Analysis (of problem)
3 Solution (proposed means of solving problem)

Such short reports will have titles of sections geared to their subject-matter. For example:

1 Background to high levels of staff turnover in South Kensington branch
2 Analysis of causes of high staff turnover
3 Proposals for reducing staff turnover to acceptable levels

Specimen short formal report

CONFIDENTIAL

FOR: P J Kirkbride, Managing DirectorREF: HTD/SC/FWH 4

FROM: H T Dickens, Chairman, FlexibleDATE: 14 February 19—
Working Hours Working Party

REPORT ON THE PROPOSAL TO INTRODUCE A FLEXIBLE WORKING HOURS SYSTEM IN HEAD OFFICE

1.0 TERMS OF REFERENCE

On 7 January 19— the managing director instructed a specially set up working party to investigate the practicality of introducing a system of flexible working hours in all head office departments, and to make appropriate recommendations. The report was to be submitted to him by 21 February 19— for the consideration of the Board of Directors.

2.0 PROCEDURE

In order to obtain relevant information and opinion, the following procedures were adopted by the working party to acquire the information in the report:

2.1 Current office administration literature was reviewed. (Appendix 1 Bibliography refers.)
2.2 A number of companies were visited which have adopted flexible working hours systems and the views of a wide range of staff were canvassed.
2.3 Current departmental working loads and practices were observed and evaluated.
2.4 Soundings of likely staff responses were obtained from departmental managers and senior staff.
2.5 The cost of introducing a flexible working hours system was considered.

3.0 FINDINGS

3.1 Principles of the Flexible Working Hours System

The essence of a flexible working hours system consists of establishing two distinct bands of working hours within a weekly or monthly cycle and of ensuring that staff work an agreed total of hours in the cycle.

3.1.1 Core Time Band

During this period (say 10 15 am to 3 45 pm) all staff are present at work, allowing for lunch-time arrangements.

3.1.2 Flexi-time Band

Periods at the beginning and end of the day (say 7 45 am to 10 15 am and 3 45 pm to 6 15 pm) are worked at the discretion of individual staff members in whole or part, allowing for essential departmental staff manning requirements.

3.1.3 Credit/Debit Hour Banking

According to previously agreed limits and procedures, staff may take time off if a credit of hours has built up, or make time up, having created a debit to be made good. Most companies require that the agreed weekly hours total (in the case of head office staff $37\frac{1}{2}$ hours per week) is reached but not exceeded, though some firms adopt a more flexible approach, which permits some time to be credited/debited in a longer cycle.

3.1.4 Recording Hours Worked

In all systems, it is essential that logs or time-sheet records are kept and agreed by employee and supervisor for pay and staff administration reasons.

3.2 Discussions with Departmental Managers

Most departmental managers were in favour of introducing a flexible working hours system, anticipating an improvement in both productivity and staff morale. The sales manager saw advantages in his office being open longer during the day to deal with customer calls and visits. Reservations were expressed by both the office administration and accounts managers arising from the likelihood of increased workloads to administer the system.

3.4 Cost of Introducing a Flexible Working Hours System

The increase in costs of heating, lighting and administration of the system would be offset to some degree by a decline in overtime worked and the cost of employing temporary staff to cover for staff absences, which may be expected to reduce. (Appendix 3 provides a detailed estimate of the cost of introducing and running a flexible working hours system.)

4.0 CONCLUSIONS

In the working party's view, the advantages of introducing a flexible working hours system outweigh the disadvantages. Head office service to both customers and field sales staff would improve, staff morale and productivity are also likely to rise. Administrative costs do not appear unacceptable and senior staff have the necessary expertise to make the system work. Of necessity, the working party's view was broad rather than detailed and the introduction of any flexible working hours systems should allow for the particular needs and problems of individual head office departments to be taken into account as far as possible.

5.0 RECOMMENDATIONS

As a result of its investigations, the working party recommends that the Board of Directors gives active consideration to the following:

5.1 That the introduction of a flexible working hours system be accepted in principle by the Board and staff consultations begin as soon as possible with a view to establishing a time-table for implementing the change.

5.2 That all departmental managers be requested to provide a detailed appraisal of their needs in moving over to a flexible working hours system and of any problems they anticipate.

5.3 That a training programme be devised by personnel and training departments to familiarise staff with new working procedures and practices.

5.4 That a code of practice be compiled for inclusion in the company handbook.

5.5 That arrangements be made to inform both field sales staff and customers at the appropriate time of the advantages to them of the introduction in head office of flexible working hours.

> **Top secretary tip: Report structures**
> Many managers owe their success to developed expertise in a specialist field such as biotechnology or production engineering. They are sometimes not very good at (nor very much like) creating reports or similarly extensive written documents. So they will be glad to have a secretary who is really 'clued up' on how reports are structured, referenced and set out. If you provide invaluable help in such ways, the chances are that when your manager is promoted, so you will be or that your own progression will occur faster.

REPORTS: REFERENCING, TYPOGRAPHY AND PRESENTATION

The only effective report is the one which is read and fully grasped!

No matter how crucial it may be to the future of the organisation, if a report is poorly set out and visually difficult to absorb, then it is doomed to failure.

Also, good reports rely on fact and reasoned analysis to make their points. This being so, a way has to be found of displaying each major (and minor) stage of the report with suitable techniques of layout and referencing. As a result, the following features have become widespread in presenting reports for reading:

1 A logical system for dividing the various parts of the report into sections and sub-sections according to the type of report and the topics dealt with.

2 The use of letters and numbers to act as references for such sections and to enable report readers to cite particular items in follow-up memos, etc.

3 The use of typeface features of the desktop publishing system, word processor or electronic typewriter to provide visual impact by means of such eye-catchers as:

- Varied typefaces (via founts or daisywheels, etc) such as italic, bold, Courier.
- Change of pitch: eg **elite, pica, condensed** etc
- **Emboldening** [or enlarged print computer printer features]
- Use of illustrations: graphs, charts, photographs, diagrams, etc.
- Use of line spacing and 'white space'
- **Progressive indentation**
- Use of graphic symbols, eg bullets, asterisks, leader dots.
- Underscoring
- Use of capitals: double spaced, initial capitals (sometimes underscored)
- Use of boxes to enclose key data
- Use of *reverse printing techniques* via DTP

> **Top secretary tip: IT and report presentation**
> The resources available to the secretary for creating an effective means of presenting a report in typographic terms were once limited to what a typewriter could do. The advent of word processing electronic printers and desktop publishing has revolutionised the facilities the secretary can access. Reports can be made much more professional in their printed appearance and many more visually arresting features are available (see above).
>
> Top secretaries make it their business to grasp fully the possibilities of these techniques of document presentation and to master those most useful.

Binding and laminating reports

One of the effects of IT upon report creation and presentation is that managers and directors now expect reports to be of a much higher standard of appearance than those of only a few years ago.

This being the case, the secretary must learn what resources are available to aid the production of reports, for example from a helpful reprographics unit.

- High speed collation
- **Bonding**/binding and stapling
- **Lamination** of front/back covers and transparent loose-leaf covers
- Choice of coloured card/paper for cover, contents, etc
- Graphic illustrations – photographs, line drawings, 30+ point print for title pages and major section **frontispieces**, etc
- Available **clip art** – pre-drawn artwork of items like diamond shapes, company products, large pound or dollar signs – some more suited to newsletters than reports – used in DTP document creation

Fig 4.5

A SPECIMEN FACTSHEET LAYOUT

THE DEVELOPMENT OF THE OFFICE

1 **HISTORICAL BACKGROUND**

   1.1 **2600 BC Ancient Egypt:** early form of office – site managers' supervision of pyramid construction.

   1.2 **750 BC – 500 AD Ancient Greek and Roman Civilisations:** development of offices to administer government and trade and transcribe written orders etc to far-flung governors.

   1.3 **500 AD – 1000 AD Dark Ages In Europe:** offices situated in abbeys and monasteries to aid manuscript transcribing and management of farms and lands etc.

   1.4 **1000 – 1485 Medieval Feudal System:** offices employed by Norman barons and abbots (and their successors) to administer taxes and work of tied peasants.

   1.5 **1485 – 1800 Expansion of National/International Trade:** the modern office has its roots in the counting houses of 16th century merchants and the blossoming of international trade via merchant trading companies using sailing ships.

2 **DEVELOPMENT OF THE MODERN OFFICE**

   2.1 **Influencing Factors**

   The following factors influenced the development of the modern office in the 19th century:

   2.1.1 Increase in world trade following the Industrial Revolution.

   2.1.2 The invention of shorthand (1837) by Sir Isaac Pitman.

   2.1.3 The improvement in general literacy as a result of Victorian educational reforms.

   2.1.4 The invention of telegraphy (also 1837) by Samuel Morse and of the typewriter (Scholes 1868 and Remington 1874).

   2.2 **Activities of The Early 20th Century Office**

Note: 1 Use of emboldening, indentation, initial capitals and *optional* use of numbered references, use of white space etc.
  2 The neutral style and emphasis on names, dates, and *brief* 'to the point' statements.

A GOOD FACTSHEET IS CLEAR, STRAIGHTFORWARD AND EASY TO DIGEST

Logical systems for referencing reports

Written reports are generally used in organisations as important sources of information which are frequently referred to in later memos, minutes or correspondence. It is therefore necessary for the manager and secretary who produce such reports to have a clear appreciation of the acceptable ways of providing written reports with logical reference systems.

There is no single, acceptable procedure to be adopted, and set out below are some of the most generally employed.

Major sections of the report

Formal reports will be divided most probably into several sections and the referencing options available for referencing each major section are:

	A	B	C	D	E
or	I	II	III	IV	V
or	1	2	3	4	5

The choice of referencing notation for the major sections will have a bearing on what further referencing is given to related sub-sections. For example, sub-sections of the third major section of a report might be referenced as: C(a), C(b), C(c); or as III(i), III(ii), III(iii); or as 3.1, 3.2 or 3.3.

Thus some reports might have 'sub-sub-sections' referenced as: C(a)(ii), III(i)(b) or 3.1.2

Of recent years there appears to be a general preference for the elegance and simplicity of this last method, **decimal point referencing**, because it is simple, visually appealing and capable of referencing the most complex report structures. An example of this system is given in the specimen factsheet on page 163.

DISCUSSION TOPIC

Are written reports worth the fuss people make over producing them? What techniques might make their production easier?

ASSIGNMENTS: FORMAL REPORT PRESENTATION

In groups of two to three, research the following areas and report back to your class on your findings:

1 What equipment and materials are currently on the market to aid the effective presentation of reports?

2 How might the presentation of the report illustrated on flexible working hours on pages 160–161 be enhanced if it had been produced on a laser printer?

Tips on producing reports

1 **At the outset** make a project plan which times the completion and circulation of the report shortly *before* its due deadline. Make sure your manager(s) and you stick to the key dates for first, middle and final drafts, etc. Most reports end up on the desks of senior managers who have no time for late submissions!

2 **Always** key in drafts if possible on a word processor to aid subsequent draft revisions.

3 **Remember** to number each draft and to ensure that managers/executives work on the *latest* version; collect in superseded versions whenever possible.

4 **Plan ahead** and start graphics/illustrative work as soon as a report structure is available from your manager.

5 **Help** your manager to decide what reference/source material is necessary and draw up a checklist of items you can hunt up in the times your manager is out of the office, ie *plan your use of time cleverly*.

6 **Be ruthless** in cajoling/persuading managers to stick to agreed deadlines for data submission – one disorganised contributor can throw the whole project way behind and cause a log-jam!

7 **Make sure** your managers and you devote enough time to scrupulous proofreading; human nature being what it is, a typographical error can make more impact on a board of directors than the major point surrounding it.

8 **Always remember** the importance of top-quality visual presentation and seek to produce the best presented reports your resources allow.

9 **Double-check** with your manager that you are absolutely sure about matters such as:

The report's status, eg Strictly Confidential
The agreed circulation list – prompt for anyone left out by mistake.

PRE-PRINTED FORMS AND DOCUMENTS

To some hard-pressed secretaries and managers, processing endless forms and schedules may seem like a nightmare, preventing them from getting on with what they see as their real jobs! Indeed, many large organisations do require extensive sets of forms to be used – to order supplies, monitor time-keeping, calculate sales representatives' expenses, control stocks issued, and so on. Efficient organisations

Fig 4.6 Examples of bought-in forms for daily and regular events

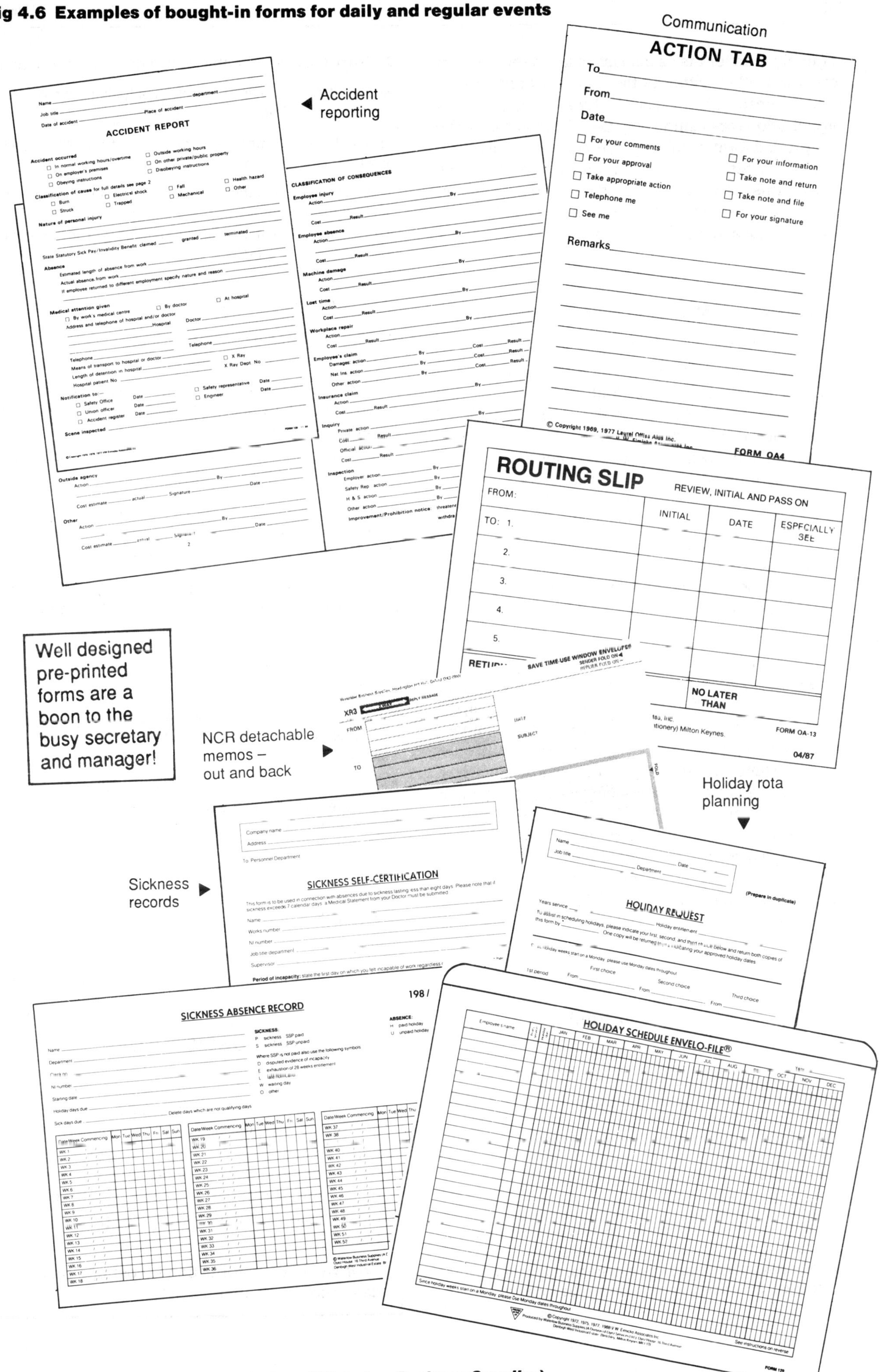

Accident reporting

Well designed pre-printed forms are a boon to the busy secretary and manager!

NCR detachable memos – out and back

Sickness records

Holiday rota planning

(Reproduced by kind permission of Waterlow Business Supplies)

regularly monitor the usefulness of and need for their forms and either withdraw those no longer needed or revise those still required. Even though many organisations are using computers for most tasks, the pre-printed form is still employed very extensively to obtain, process and store information, and in fact, many forms are being designed on in-house desktop publishing systems and printed on demand by the reprographics unit's laser printer.

Examples of pre-printed forms in common office use

Job application ■ interview notes record ■ personnel records ■ accident report ■ lateness record ■ sickness self-certification ■ sickness absence ■ job appraisal ■ performance evaluation report ■ holiday request form ■ holiday rota schedule ■ suggestions form ■ memorandum NCR forms ■ message forms ■ expenses claim forms ■ sales report forms ■ petty cash vouchers ■ purchase requisition forms ■ stock requisition forms ■ delivery notes ■ invoices ■ statements of account

---

Indeed, different organisations devise forms and schedules to meet the particular needs of a vast number of quite different routines, depending upon the nature of their activities. And the term 'routine' needs to be emphasised, since forms tend only to be worth the time and effort spent in creating them if they meet the needs of regularly-occurring situations, such as those described above.

To be an effective secretary you need to make a point of mastering the techniques of good form design, as this will certainly save you and your manager valuable time in administering many routine office tasks.

Tips on effective form design

1 Take time to consider in detail:

Why is the information needed?
When is it needed? In what time cycle?
Who needs it? And *from whom*?
How would the information be best presented?

2 Then, make up a checklist of all the parts and pieces of information needed, eg:

full name, address, telephone/fax/BTGold/telex numbers, age, date of birth, sex, nationality, personnel reference number, payroll number, qualifications, education, work experience, full driving licence, disabilities, health record, etc.

3 Next, consider how the form might best be structured:

Should it move down chronologically like a history from old to current time?

Should the most important parts come first? What *are* the most important parts?

What items in the initial checklist are trivial and not really needed? What items are crucial in the eventual collating and comparing which will happen when the completed forms are gathered in?

Seek to put your checklist of items into a running order or sequence which you will reproduce in designing the form.

4 Then draw a mock-up of the form in rough – either in longhand, on your typewriter or database software.

Always ensure your boxes or lined spaces into which responses will be inserted are large enough for the response required.

Check that your questions or instructions are: *short, simple, clear and unambiguous*.

Make sure you have not omitted any important question or data requirement and that your instructions on what must be done with the completed form are clear.

5 Produce a test model of the form. Try it out on close colleagues first. Ask them to criticise it constructively. Make any necessary amendments.

6 Print the form for use and check the first users' responses:

Did they understand what was needed?
Were any parts left uncompleted?
If so, why?

Acid test: Did the form produce the data needed – in the form expected, within the required deadlines, in a manner which permitted analysis and summary, from all those issued with it?

7 Lastly: Don't forget to monitor your forms from time to time. Events sometimes overtake regular routines, so always ask:

'Is this form *really* needed?'

If it isn't, ditch it! You will gain much valuable time and many friends!

DISCUSSION TOPIC

How many paper-based forms could be replaced by converting them into computerised databases with a resulting improvement in the speed of recovering desired information? And also, in sorting into fields (sorted categories of data like, 'List for me all those secretaries who can speak French'.)?

How would the information be put into such databases in the first place?

Creating and presenting office documents

The secretary and the account sale cycle

Virtually every secretary comes into contact with the monthly cycle of account sales – even though payments are handled by the firm's accounts department. This is usually because accounts staff need to be reassured that goods ordered have arrived and are in a satisfactory condition *before* they pay for them. So, many offices either use a form for computer input or hold a rubber stamp with a message above a box for signature and date.

Fig 4.7 The diagram below outlines the cycle of accounts documentation and you should ensure you are fully familiar with it. (See also the model invoice illustration Fig 4.8)

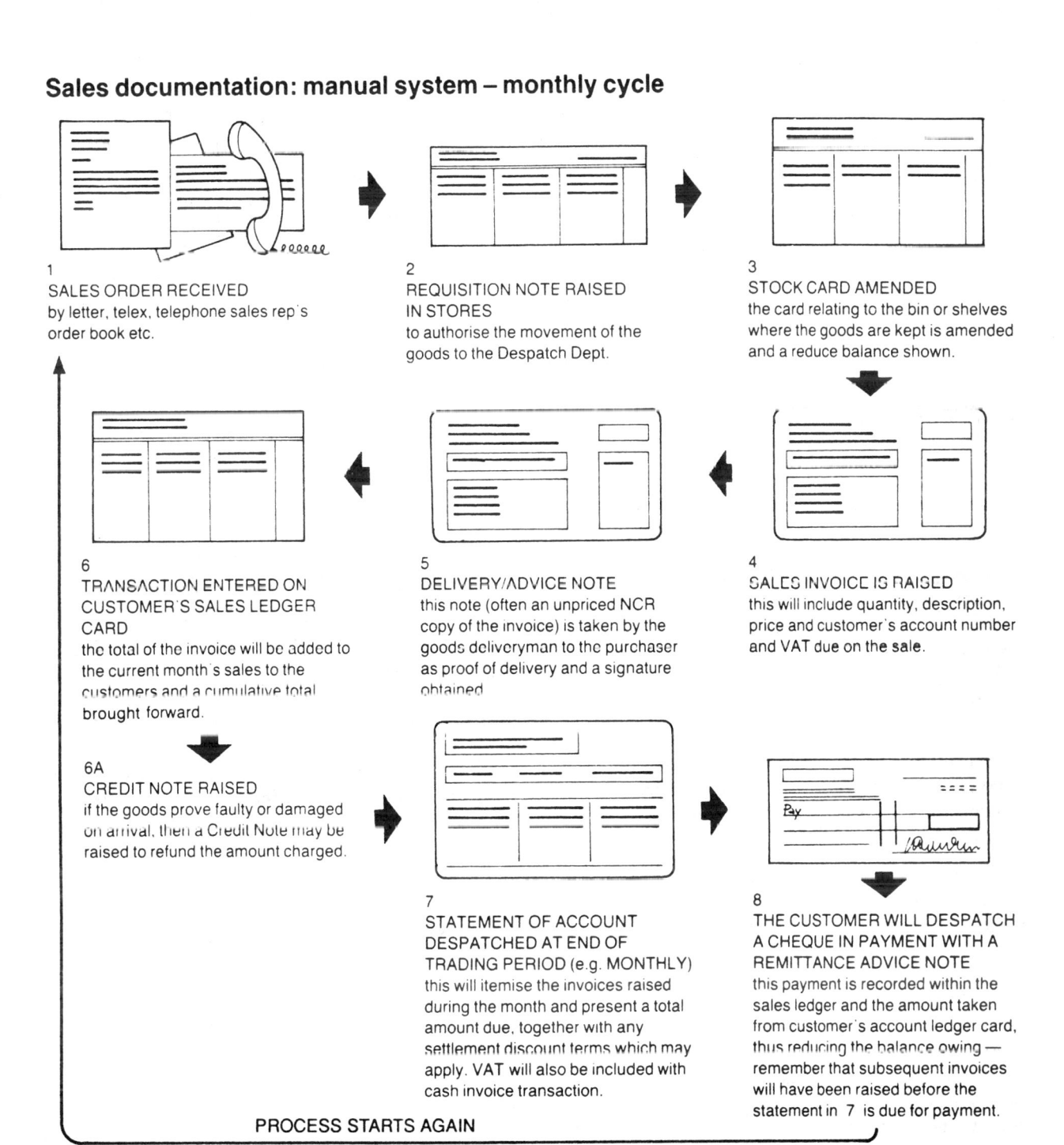

Sales documentation: manual system – monthly cycle

1 SALES ORDER RECEIVED
by letter, telex, telephone sales rep's order book etc.

2 REQUISITION NOTE RAISED IN STORES
to authorise the movement of the goods to the Despatch Dept.

3 STOCK CARD AMENDED
the card relating to the bin or shelves where the goods are kept is amended and a reduce balance shown.

4 SALES INVOICE IS RAISED
this will include quantity, description, price and customer's account number and VAT due on the sale.

5 DELIVERY/ADVICE NOTE
this note (often an unpriced NCR copy of the invoice) is taken by the goods deliveryman to the purchaser as proof of delivery and a signature obtained

6 TRANSACTION ENTERED ON CUSTOMER'S SALES LEDGER CARD
the total of the invoice will be added to the current month's sales to the customers and a cumulative total brought forward.

6A CREDIT NOTE RAISED
if the goods prove faulty or damaged on arrival, then a Credit Note may be raised to refund the amount charged.

7 STATEMENT OF ACCOUNT DESPATCHED AT END OF TRADING PERIOD (e.g. MONTHLY)
this will itemise the invoices raised during the month and present a total amount due, together with any settlement discount terms which may apply. VAT will also be included with cash invoice transaction.

8 THE CUSTOMER WILL DESPATCH A CHEQUE IN PAYMENT WITH A REMITTANCE ADVICE NOTE
this payment is recorded within the sales ledger and the amount taken from customer's account ledger card, thus reducing the balance owing — remember that subsequent invoices will have been raised before the statement in 7 is due for payment.

PROCESS STARTS AGAIN

Fig. 4.8 Specimen sales invoice

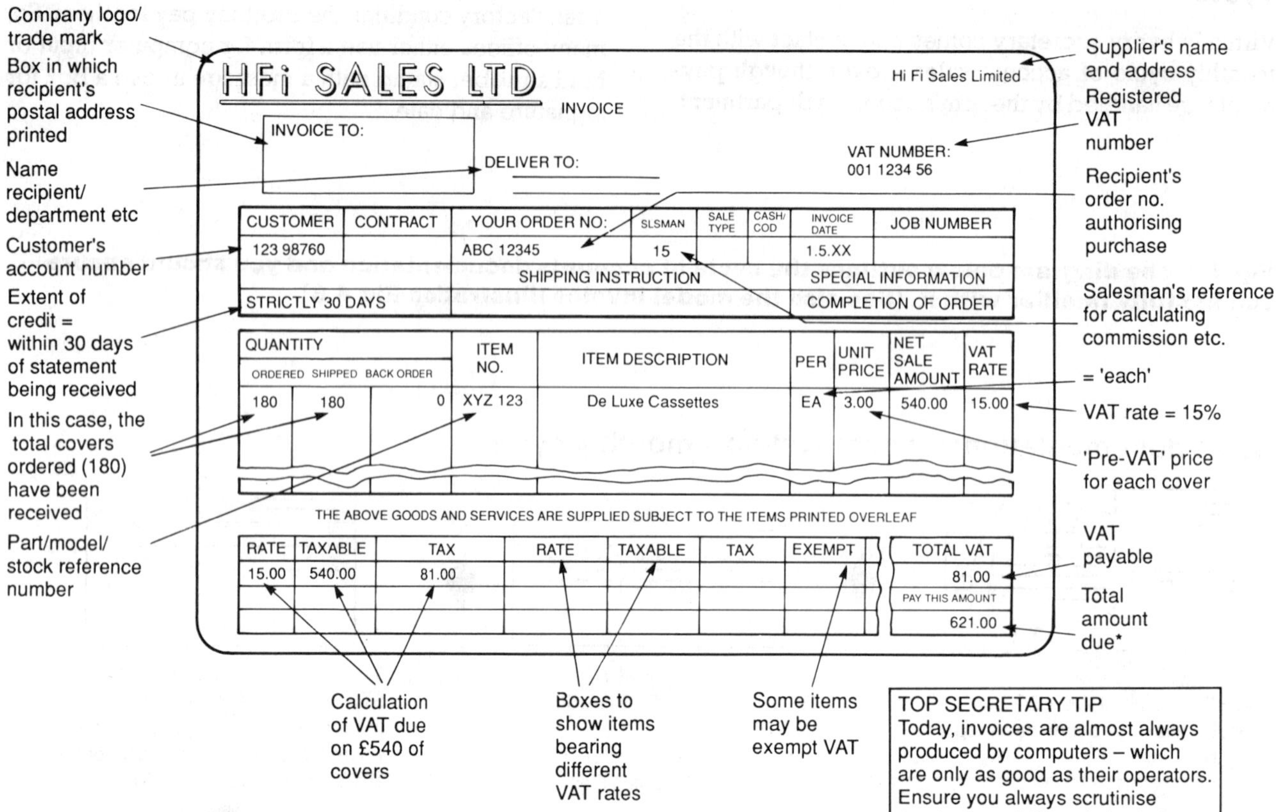

Company logo/ trade mark
Box in which recipient's postal address printed
Name recipient/ department etc
Customer's account number
Extent of credit = within 30 days of statement being received
In this case, the total covers ordered (180) have been received
Part/model/ stock reference number
HFi SALES LTD
INVOICE
Hi Fi Sales Limited
INVOICE TO:
DELIVER TO:
VAT NUMBER:
001 1234 56
CUSTOMER
CONTRACT
YOUR ORDER NO:
SLSMAN
SALE TYPE
CASH/ COD
INVOICE DATE
JOB NUMBER
123 98760
ABC 12345
15
1.5.XX
SHIPPING INSTRUCTION
SPECIAL INFORMATION
STRICTLY 30 DAYS
COMPLETION OF ORDER
QUANTITY
ORDERED SHIPPED BACK ORDER
ITEM NO.
ITEM DESCRIPTION
PER
UNIT PRICE
NET SALE AMOUNT
VAT RATE
180 180 0
XYZ 123
De Luxe Cassettes
EA
3.00
540.00
15.00
THE ABOVE GOODS AND SERVICES ARE SUPPLIED SUBJECT TO THE ITEMS PRINTED OVERLEAF
RATE
TAXABLE
TAX
RATE
TAXABLE
TAX
EXEMPT
TOTAL VAT
15.00
540.00
81.00
81.00
PAY THIS AMOUNT
621.00
Supplier's name and address
Registered VAT number
Recipient's order no. authorising purchase
Salesman's reference for calculating commission etc.
= 'each'
VAT rate = 15%
'Pre-VAT' price for each cover
VAT payable
Total amount due*
Calculation of VAT due on £540 of covers
Boxes to show items bearing different VAT rates
Some items may be exempt VAT

TOP SECRETARY TIP
Today, invoices are almost always produced by computers – which are only as good as their operators. Ensure you always scrutinise invoices carefully and check the amounts for any errors of addition or multiplication.

* Note: If purchasers pay their accounts within the specified 30 days, they may be entitled to deduct a 'settlement discount' (say 3.75%) off the total due.

Based upon the invoice of MAR-COM SYSTEMS LTD

Top secretary tip: Creating form letters and forms

Stand-by form letters and forms, flexibly designed and well presented are a real boon in helping busy managers to obtain and interpret information.

Techniques of word processing supported by laser printing can save valuable time and produce top-quality form letters and forms which can be reprinted, re-edited and updated on demand.

It therefore pays to become fully expert in WP skills like creating **non-document files** to merge data such as names, addresses, numbers and sentences into pre-produced form letters and also to know how to use (drive) software which draws boxes and panels for use in designing forms.

Then, when more copies are needed, they are only a disk-boot and a few keystrokes away from being ready for printing!

EFFECTIVE DOCUMENT PRESENTATION

Today it is generally accepted that as much as 25% of a document's acceptance, among those who read it and are influenced by what it says, stems from the way in which it is presented.

There are many features which affect a document's presentation and the following checklist summarises the major ones:

1 **Quality of materials used**

- Bought-in folders, binders, plastic wallets, conference wallets, presentation albums, laminated cards and sheets, etc
- Type and weight of paper used to display data, quality of photographic paper, etc

  Note: There are some 220 different types of paper available.

Creating and presenting office documents

2 **Type of binding used**
- Ring-binder, plastic spine clip, grip binder, spiral plastic binding, **thermal-action adhesive binding**, etc
- Use of laminates or plastic envelope inserts

3 **Equipment used for printed text graphics**
- Lettering machines to produce a variety of type sizes, founts and colours
- Daisywheel electronic typewriters, ink-jet and laser printers (note also 24-pin dot matrix printers produce virtual letter-quality)
- Desktop publishing systems for quality presentation, from office report to commercial printing of top-quality fashion magazines in full colour!
- **Graphics plotters** and printers for reproducing graphs, charts, etc. via computer software packages
- Integrated desktop software for combining graphics and word-processed text with laser printer output

4 **Use of colour to maximise visual impact**
- On covers and frontispieces
- Varied use of coloured papers to reinforce chapter/unit structures

    Note: One leading paper supplier markets paper and card in some 40 different coloured pastel/strong tints and shades for document presentation purposes.

- For section headings and key paragraphs and summaries
- In graphs and charts, etc, via colour printers, plotters and photocopiers

5 **Use of photographs, diagrams and drawings**
- To aid visual appeal and immediacy, perhaps the most striking advance lies in the capacity of DTP to enable document creators to include **half-tone** black/white photographs and drawings very inexpensively into newsletters, sales brochures, office communication bulletins, etc

    Note: Upper-end DTP systems incorporate colour printing and artwork – at increased costs, of course.

SUMMARY

The thinking secretary then, needs to weigh up and trade-off these factors when determining how to present a given document most effectively:

Is there enough **time** to manage the production of the document to the highest levels of presentation?

What would be the **cost**, given the number of people receiving the document?

To what **level of personnel** is the document going?

Will the document be going to **customers/clients**?

What is the **status of the information** in the document – highest, high, medium, low-level?

Does the document need to survive **hard use/reference over a long period**?

The answers to such questions will help the secretary, in consultation with her manager, to judge the levels of effort, time, cost and attention which the document's presentation merits.

The well-created and presented document 'says':

- 'I represent my organisation to all who read me and I have been created with pride and care and consequently look good and convey an image of reliability, flair and efficiency!'
- 'The format I have been put into makes me easy to read and remember and draws attention to my most important parts.'
- 'My structure is logical and generally proceeds from the more to the less important in crisp and logically connected paragraphs.'
- 'The language I am expressed in is free from grammatical and typographical errors and conveys a tone which is well suited to my purpose, whether I am informing, persuading or disciplining.'
- 'The reason for my taking on the form of a letter, report or telemessage is not accidental – careful attention has been given to making me as effective as possible, given the nature of my message and any need for security, speed of communication or number of people needing to digest me!'

QUICK REVIEW QUIZ

1 List the typical major sections of a long formal report.

2 Explain what information would be included in:

a terms of reference b procedure c an appendix d a bibliography.

3 What is the function of a footnote in a report?

4 List the typical parts of a brief, informal report.

5 In what ways are the main sections of a formal report commonly referenced?

6 What procedures would you adopt in supervising the production of a formal report by a given deadline?

7 What techniques can the secretary call upon to aid good formal report presentation?

8 What would you identify as features of good factsheet design?

9 What features are important in the effective design of pre-printed forms?

10 Outline the components you would expect to find on a computerised invoice.

11 Make a checklist of points which aid efficient memorandum production and distribution.

12 What are the typical features of letter/memorandum structure?

RESEARCH AND REPORT BACK ASSIGNMENTS

1 In pairs, make arrangements to visit a large organisation with a developed office administration. Interview a senior secretary and manager about the major features of the house style which they use in creating documents. Aspects which you should prepare questions on are:

- company livery and logos and how these are used on company stationery;
- accepted letter layouts;
- what types of paper and envelopes are used for what purposes;
- how reports are prepared and what equipment is used in the process;
- how they go about designing and abstracting information from forms, etc.

Try to obtain specimens of non-confidential documents and give an illustrated briefing on your return of what you found to be current good practice. you can add the examples you acquire to the group's portfolio.

2 First carry out your research, then give a 5–10 minute talk to your group on the ways in which internal Email messaging is replacing conventional memoranda production, storage and distribution. Give examples of current practice in your locality if possible.

3 Having researched the area. produce a short briefing for your group on the ways in which an information management software application package (like Smart) can help with the production of reports. If possible, illustrate your briefing with sample printouts.

4.4 Computer graphics

Applications of graphics software in the office; driving the software; graphics and the secretary.

The use of graphics application software packages in information processing has grown rapidly in the past few years. This is partly due to the widespread use of spreadsheets, and the ability to convert **spreadsheet** data into graphics data in many integrated packages. It is also partly because of the heightening of expectations among senior managers of having data presented to them in high quality graphics form – as coloured tables, charts, graphs, maps, etc.

Colour and resolution

Today VDU screens are produced with a high number of pixels per square centimetre. **Pixels** are a measurement of colour density and resolution. For instance, it is now possible to display Old Master paintings on computer VDUs with a faithful reproduction of the originals' colours! By the same token, high-quality colour printers and plotters are able to print out VDU graphics displays with anything from 8 to 156 (or more) colours and tones available.

Graphics media available in a graphics package

Table
Sets of figures in columns for analysis and comparison

Pie chart
Parts of a total arranged in pie 'wedges'.

Line graph
Display of joined points plotted against vertical and horizontal scales

Bar chart (clustered, stacked or 3-D)
Amounts depicted as 'slabs of area' set against each other for comparison

Histogram
A means of displaying a total which is distributed into component parts according to, age, size, etc

Map/contour diagram
Geographic maps, contours and shapes (say of car body designs) which may be shown on the VDU in 3-D and rotated

Symbol chart pictogram
Eye-catching symbols are used to show comparative volumes or sizes in order to make statistics more interesting and memorable

APPLICATIONS OF GRAPHICS SOFTWARE IN THE OFFICE

Naturally, graphics software may be used for any number of communication purposes, depending on the topic and the user's imagination. However, set out here are some of the major uses which are made of graphics in business and public service activities.

Graphics applications

Accounts	To show profits by product, breakdowns of costs, money owed by account customers, salary costs, etc
Production	To show percentage of rejects in output, to monitor loss of production times, to show operator costs per unit of production, to display computerised designs, etc
Sales	To compare sales turnover by region or shop, to compare sales to target, to monitor new calls made by sales reps, to show sales by product, etc.
Marketing	To compare shares of the known market, to indicate competing prices, to provide statistics on consumer demand and product specifications, etc.

Fig 4.9 The new desktop Vectra personal computers from Hewlett-Packcard Company offer IBM industry-standard compatibility. The PC family includes (*left to right*) HP Vectra Publisher PC; HP Vectra RS PC, the most powerful and expandable member of the family; the HP Vectra ES PC, an enhanced version of HP Vectra PC with performance equal to the IBM PS/2 Model 60; and HP Vectra CS PC, the entry-level unit.

(*Reproduced by kind permission of Hewlett Packard*)

Personnel	To show the age of the workforce, to illustrate pensions investments, to indicate labour turnover rates and trends, etc
Project management	To monitor the progress of large-scale projects visually – like building a shopping precinct
Presentations	To provide (either from monitor screen or colour printout) paper sheet or transparency presentation material for top management perusal

Production

It is no idle boast of major graphics software houses that their packages provide an 'in-house art studio' for users. In fact, many companies are now producing their own colour brochures and informational literature to high standards, having developed a staff member into a graphics technician, able to operate both graphics and DTP software expertly. Thus colour tones, half-tones, cross-hatching and shading, as well as multiple founts and images accessed from scanners, now form the components of an exciting 'graphics palette' from which to create arresting and appealing documents.

DRIVING THE SOFTWARE

Data in graphics packages may be manipulated in a variety of ways. The points, for instance, which go to make up the **line graph** for a given subject may be inputted by means of keying them as separate numbers – 2345, 6543, 5678, etc. The software does the rest and positions each point correctly on the X–Y axis of the graph. Alternatively, a set of figures may be produced on a spreadsheet and, thanks to the foresight of the programmers, be converted into the components of, say, a **pie chart** by means of a simple function command! Again, charts may be plotted by the use of a mouse to draw lines or bar chart slabs on to a pre-installed scale. The use of windows software may also be brought into play to overlay different graphics material for visual effect.

Creating and presenting office documents

Most graphics packages contain resident graphs and charts – line graph, stacked or clustered **bar chart**, 3-D contouring, etc – which are readily summoned up as 'frames' in which to insert data. Moreover, some graphics packages enable the user to switch installed data from, for example, a line graph to a bar chart to assess which medium offers the better means of communication. Also, colours, tones, shading, hatching, etc, can be tried out and altered at will on any given graphic display until the most appropriate is devised. Then it may be printed on to paper or OHP transparency.

One of the most useful features of an integrated information management package from the secretary's point of view lies in the facility to design a graph or chart with the graphics software and then to 'swap' it directly on to, say, a report which is being word processed. And, correspondingly, to install a set of calculations using the spreadsheet software, and to convert, say, the resultant costs of various aspects of a project into an instant pie chart by 'swapping' the calculations into the graphics software.

DISCUSSION TOPICS

1 What particular equipment do you think a secretary should have access to which would make it possible to produce high quality documents quickly and with the least effort.?

2 What contribution could a secretary's manager make to aid good quality document production?

3 Is it reasonable to expect a secretary to become proficient in operating DTP application software? How might an organisation ensure it got maximum benefit from the installation of a DTP system?

GRAPHICS AND THE SECRETARY

As you have already judged, graphics software is extremely flexible and useful as a means of converting what may be dry number data into visually appealing and interesting information. Managers are always busy and therefore welcome information presented to them in ways which make it simple and easy to digest. There is therefore no doubt that as an effective secretary of the 1990s you will possess a developed expertise in graphics software as part of your 'toolkit', of highly marketable skills.

The following section explains simply the principal features of graphs and charts used in software graphics packages.

The 'exploded' pie chart

Pie charts are made up of a set of data which goes to form a *known* total. Here, the known total is 12.5% or £62.5 m for Comfort; 23% or £115 m for Melia; and £322.5 m has been identified as the market taken by other manufacturers. The technique of showing the wedge of pie in 'exploded' form helps to emphasise it.

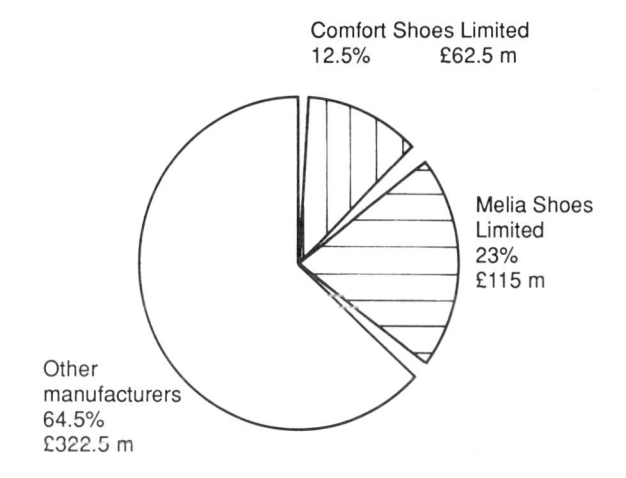

Comfort Shoes Limited
12.5%   £62.5 m

Melia Shoes Limited
23%
£115 m

Other manufacturers
64.5%
£322.5 m

Total market value = £500 m

The bar chart

The bar chart supplies a means of comparing several items which are common to a number of subjects. Here, the different products of the company are being compared in terms of the number of each which has been sold in the month of August. Note the need for a key to explain the shaded items. Sometimes bars in such charts are 'stacked' to include several items within each bar.

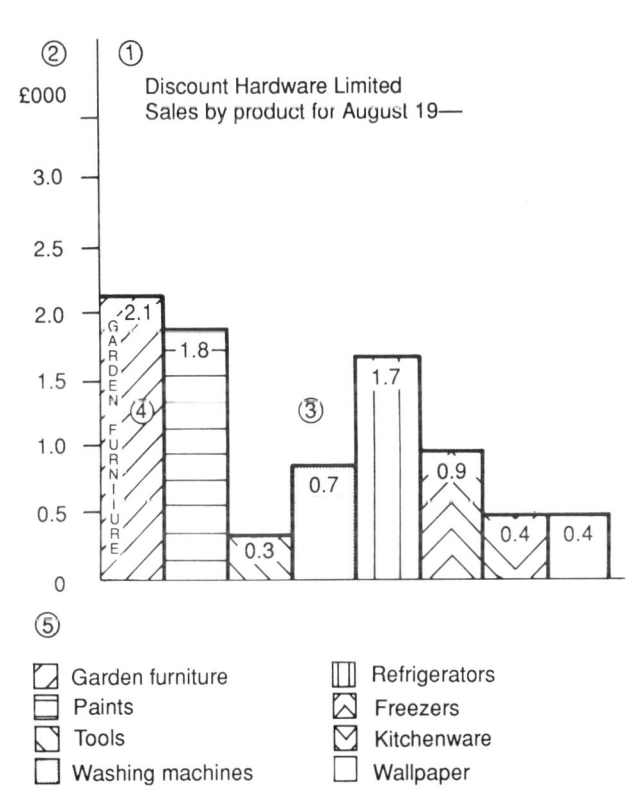

Discount Hardware Limited
Sales by product for August 19—

☐ Garden furniture   ☐ Refrigerators
☐ Paints   ☐ Freezers
☐ Tools   ☐ Kitchenware
☐ Washing machines   ☐ Wallpaper

Clustered 3-D bar chart
The bar chart is very much like the line graph – it is used to compare items – but instead of displaying connected points as lines, it sets blocks of area (the 'bars') side-by-side for prompt comparison. The bars are usually coloured differently or given varying cross-hatching to make them stand out from each other.

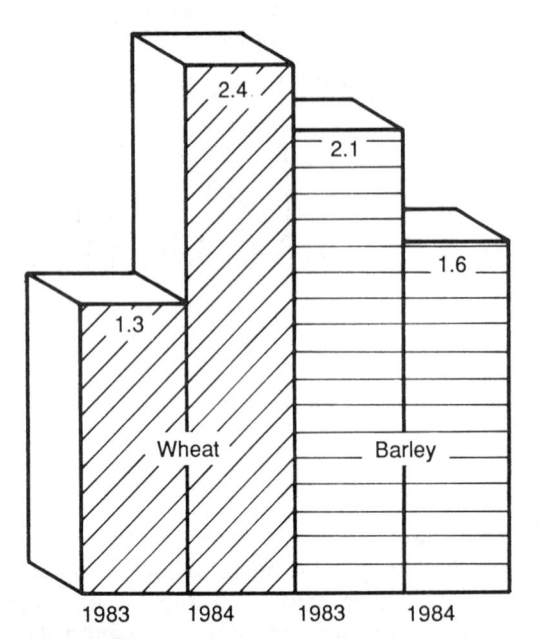

Production of wheat and barley in millions of tonnes

The X-Y axis line graph
Here, amounts are plotted against two known variables. The vertical X axis often provides a scale for amounts and the Y horizontal axis for time – in this case, showing the comparison between thousands of pounds worth of products sold in years A and B, plotted against each month of a year. Line graphs may display four or five items being compared in this way, each being easily distinguished with the aid of colour.

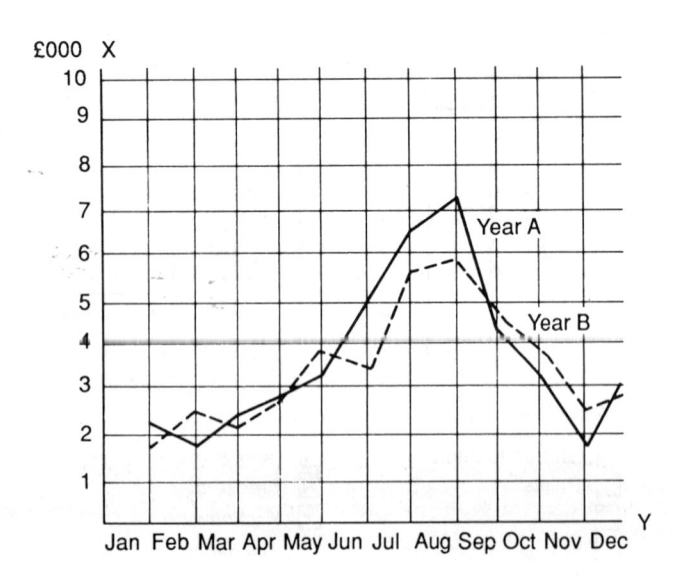

Symbol chart or pictogram
Graphics packages and DTP software usually include pre-drawn objects (called clip art) which may be used to aid graphic communication eg cars, houses wheatsheaves. Or the user may draw them freehand with a mouse. Such symbols are used to help give a set of figures or statistics more impact and appeal, as a symbol chart or **pictogram**.

3-D contour map
This technique is particularly useful for the designer, draughtsman and scientist, since it enables items to be viewed as if in three dimensions. Uses include the design of products like aeroplanes, cars and buildings.

Map
Many graphics packages include sets of maps as outlines which may be coloured and annotated according to the user's requirements.

Examples of how charts, graphs, etc, can be displayed on screen using graphics software are shown on the opposite page.

Fig 4.10 Examples of the use of graphics software to display charts, graphs and maps on screen.

'Exploded' pie chart

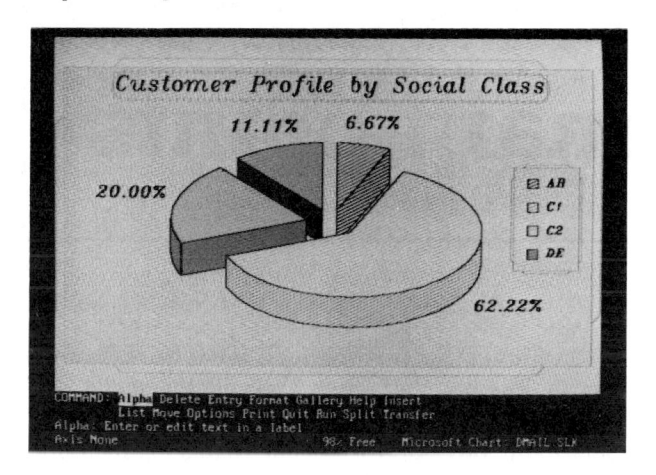

x-y axis line graph

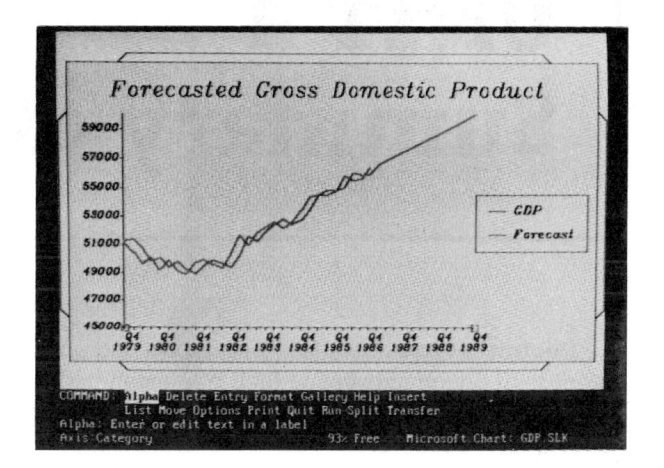

Bar chart

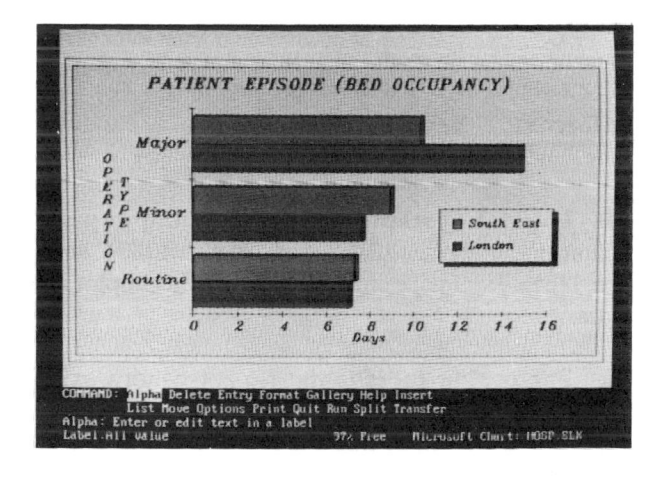

Map

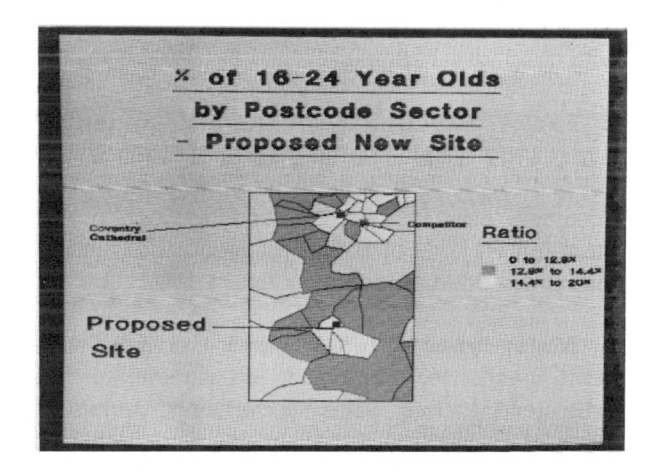

(*Photographs by Mike Taylor*)

RESEARCH AND REPORT BACK ASSIGNMENTS

1 Using your network of contacts with relatives, friends and neighbours in office work, collect some 8–12 blank forms which are used in a variety of situations in private and public sector organisations. In a class group discussion, select those you think provide interesting examples of good (or not so good) form design and explain the reasoning behind your selection.

2 Find out how firms with large invoicing operations create delivery and advice notes, invoices and statements, and make out a checklist of the information they include on each and why. Also, find out how computerisation has changed the documenting of sales transactions and brief your group about your discoveries.

3 Research into the current range of materials and equipment that office equipment and stationery suppliers are marketing which aid the attractive and effective presentation of organisational documents. You will find sales catalogues helpful here. Produce an illustrated guide which could be circulated to secretaries in a large organisation as a handy reference.

4 What do you consider to be the ingredients of effective and visually appealing document presentation?

UNIT 4
Summary of main points

1 **Document presentation**: The impact and effectiveness of documents lies in their presentation. Use top-quality paper for high-status documents, with letter-quality printers; set high personal standards for 'mailable copy; avoiding messy erasures; use your text processing equipment features (emboldening, variable typefaces, decimal point tabulation, etc); employ binding/presentation wallets and folders when appropriate and label all documents clearly and with good visual appeal.

2 **Factors affecting the choice of document for a message**: These are the degree of urgency, time needed to produce it, degree of complexity of the document, need for security, need for a legal record, the required level of status and acceptance, and the duration needed of the document.

3 **Major types of letter**: Enquiry, acknowledgement, response; complaint, adjustment; orders, estimates, tenders; sales, advertising, promoting; financial (collection, credit, status enquiries); job application process letters; disciplinary, legal contractual; circular, form, mailshot; invitations, thanks, etc.

4 **Features for creating well set-out documents**: Setting ample margins, centring, intelligent use of white space, emboldening, underscoring, initial capitals, capitals, double spacing, indenting, leader dots, number referencing, justification of text, varied use of typefaces/founts.

5 **Currently accepted letter layout formats**: Fully-blocked, fully displayed, semi-blocked.

6 **Typical components of the memorandum**: Memorandum (heading), to, from, subject, date, reference, copy(ies) to (cc), blind copy(ies) to bcc), enc(s).

7 **Accepted styles for memoranda senders/receivers**: To managing director, From sales manager, or To John Smith, From Peter Jones.

8 **Typical structure pattern for letters/memoranda**: The opening paragraph sets the scene, provides the context and essential data; second paragraph develops essential points of message; closing paragraph sums up and makes clear what action is required from the recipient, relays thanks, etc, where appropriate.

9 **Typical formal report structure**: 1 Terms of reference, 2 Procedure, 3 Summary, 4 Findings, 5 Conclusions, 6 Recommendations. For **the informal report**: Introduction, Findings, Conclusions.

10 **Logical systems for referencing reports**: either decimal point (3.1.2, etc) or mix of 1234, abcd, etc. **Note**: Decimal point system is much simpler and tidier.

11 **Producing factsheets**: No set pattern exists, but you should use the techniques learned in Unit 3 and aim to break up information into easily assimilated 'chunks' and use techniques of presentation and logical structure to aid the reader.

12 **Effective form design procedures**: Start with checklists of the essential information required; then list the entries needed to obtain it; adopt a logical structure, say from most to least essential; draw up a draft form; leave enough space for relevant responses; try out mock-up on a pilot group; design the form on a database application package for later possible amendment; print and distribute it.

13 **Commonly occurring pre-printed forms**: Accident, expenses, sickness self-certification, job application, holiday rota, message taking.

14 **Computer graphics packages**: Tables, pie charts, line graphs, bar charts, histograms, maps, pictograms can be produced, giving 'in-house art studio' capability on a desktop publishing system. Mixing text and pictures or presenting data in graphics form is extremely useful for both the secretary and manager.

Creating and presenting office documents

> **Sources of further information**
> *Pitman Business Correspondence*, Whitehead & Whithead, Pitman
> *A Handbook of Commercial Correspondence*, A Ashley, OUP
> *Report Writing*, van Emden & Easteal, McGraw-Hill
> *People, Communication and Organisations*, D W Evans, Pitman

ACTIVITIES

One way system
A case study

'The trouble is, we've been so preoccupied over the past year in getting to grips with the new network and motivating staff to use Email instead of paper memos and so on that we've let our communications systems master us instead of the other way around,' said Jim Turner, personnel and training manager.

'That's right,' agreed Liz Barker, home sales manager, 'and even before that, if you don't mind my saying so, Jim, we didn't really have any hard and fast rulings on document layout or style that were applied across the whole company. Individual departments just did – and still are doing – their own thing with memo, letter and report formats!'

'And it's not just the paper-based stuff. Yesterday I came across a set of Email messages which I thought went beyond bounds in terms of familiarity and slang. How can people chit-chat like this in one medium and immediately switch to formal language in another? I think this electronic mail set-up is bound to lead to sloppy standards!' observed Mitch Mitchel, production manager.

'I think you're all getting hot under the collar over nothing!' interrupted Angela Stuart, accounts manager. 'Does it really matter if one department likes fully-blocked letter layouts and another uses semi-blocked? And I'd have thought that, as long as this Email system gets the job done faster and easier, what do a few 'Cheers!' and 'Thanks Tosh!' matter?'

'No, if you don't mind my saying so, I think you're wrong, Angela,' commented Jim Turner. 'I accept the criticism about the lack of a coherent policy on house style and presentation, but as we're expanding so fast, I think it will come to matter more and more. What happens when a secretary or WP assistant is temporarily transferred to another department because of staff sickness? And what about standards? Surely it's better to have a single set of document production rules that everyone knows and can apply and monitor?'

'I agree,' responded Zena Cavendish, general manager, who was chairing the weekly departmental heads meeting of Newave Decor plc, a company which designs, manufactures and distributes modern furniture and fabrics. 'I think it's time we decided on introducing a set of simple, time-saving and clear-cut instructions on the creation and presentation of our in-house and externally mailed documents, save those which we have printed as artwork. Jim, would you act as a coordinator on this one? Talk to managers, their secretaries and our WP and reprographics staff and see what you can distil as good practice approaches which we can pull together. Shall we say our next meeting but one for your report and recommendations?'

DISCUSSION TOPICS

1 How important is a unified house style in an organisation? What advantages do you think come with it?

2 What sort of good practice approaches can you call to mind which might help Jim Turner produce his report?

3 What will be the implications for staff training, assuming that a new policy on document production in a unified house style is introduced?

4 What sort of problems do you think Jim Turner is likely to encounter in arriving at a sensible and enforceable set of policy recommendations?

5 How could IT-based office equipment help the delivery of a uniform house style?

6 In groups of three to four, draw up a set of suggestions ranging across letter, memoranda, factsheet and report production which you think would aid the creation of an effective house style.

7 Consider internal electronic mail messaging with your group. What, if any, procedural rules should a company require staff to follow? Compare notes with other groups in your class.

WORK SIMULATION ASSIGNMENTS

1 You are Veronica Jameson and work as personal secretary to Dr A D Vickers, Chief Scientist at Excelsior Laboratories (see the letter on page 150). Having read the letter from Mr Brown in his incoming mail this morning, Dr Vickers hurriedly briefs you as follows just before a meeting with the MD:

'Oh, Veronica, would you compose a letter to Mr Brown for me to sign to the effect that I'd be delighted to accept, etc. Only one thing, according to my diary I'm tied up here until 27th June with our Annual Presentation to the board. I could probably manage to get to Chicago by the morning of the 29th, but would prefer to delay giving my paper until the 30th – if that would still fit in with their programme. Say I won't mind if it can't be worked out and so on. Oh, and I'd better know for sure quickly, – you know how my diary fills up around June each year.'

Using an electronic typewriter or WP facility, compose a suitable letter for Dr Vickers to sign.

2 You work as personal secretary to Mrs Hazel Farraday, personnel manager of Eurodex Pharmaceuticals (UK) Limited, a multinational centred in the European Community. Mrs Farraday coordinates the job application interviews of some 150 applicants each year for a range of technician and postgraduate posts within the company. This morning she briefed you as follows:

'I'm not really happy with the form letter we send to applicants who are unsuccessful. It seems really rather terse and indifferent to me now. I'd like you to compose a fresh one along these lines: we were glad of their interest in the post, etc; never easy to decide when candidates applications are well put together; sorry you were unsuccessful in this instance – we're keeping your details on file; hope you won't be deterred from applying again, etc. Wish you success in your career development. Something like that. The main thing is that it doesn't come across as too much of a circular. Perhaps you can think of some ways of using your WP to make it appear more personalised. The trouble is, we just don't have the time to write to each applicant personally these days.'

Produce a draft form letter for Mrs Farraday's approval which you think meets the needs she outlined.

3 You work as secretary to Mr Alex Richardson, company secretary of Vulcan Engineering Limited, which manufactures a wide range of parts for the airline industry. Much of his work involves servicing the meetings of company directors and senior managers. This morning, during dictation, he said to you:

'You know, the directors and senior management are getting rather fed up with having to wade through reports, schedules and briefings which are becoming progressively more shoddy! There have been times when I've felt really embarrassed, especially as some of our directors sit on other company boards. It's not as if our people haven't got access to good reprographic facilities – you only need to look at our copiers, not to mention the new Documex desktop publishing system. I think that our middle managers have either become lazy or simply don't know what facilities they can expect their secretaries to call upon. You've as much experience in this area as anyone at Vulcan, so I'd like you to draft a memorandum for me to send out to all departmental managers and section leaders which draws attention to the importance of top-quality presentation and what resources they can call upon here to ensure they achieve it!'

Draft a memorandum which you consider will meet the requirements of Mr Richardson. Assume that Vulcan are well-endowed with the resources to produce good quality reports, schedules and briefings.

4 For this assignment, you should work in a group of three.

Your departmental head is conducting a review of the department's course marketing and recruitment procedures. As part of this review, he has briefed you as follows:

'I should like you to make some enquiries among the department's secretarial students aimed at finding out how they came to know about the courses we run here and what made them choose the course they're on. Also how helpful our course literature and brochures were, how useful they're finding our facilities and what constructive ideas they have on how we could improve our marketing and recruitment approaches. If they've got any practical suggestions for new ways of getting our information across or simplifying the process, I'd be glad to know.'

Carry out your investigations, and then, with a WP application package, produce a report in a structure and format you consider most appropriate for your head of department. Remember that good reports are factually centred, neutral in tone and easy to absorb. The points they make should be supported by evidence and not just take the form of assertions.

5 In pairs, design a form which would be effective in *one* of the following situations:

(a) To report either a typewriter or desktop PC which has developed a fault. Note that you have a technician able to carry out first-line repairs but more extensive faults are rectified by a firm of office equipment specialists on their premises.

(b) A form to be used by school/college leavers who wish to register with a local employment bureau for secretarial or office posts.

(c) A form on which sales representatives (who run company cars, use hotel accommodation and entertain clients in restaurants) can claim for the expenses they incur. Note: they are responsible for their own credit/leisure card bills which are paid for out of their claimed expenses. Your company needs receipts and supportive information in order to pass expenses claims.

6 Miss Alex West has just been promoted to Marketing Manager for *Girl in Town*, a glossy magazine published monthly for women in their twenties working in larger urban areas. You are feeling good as her secretary since her promotion means more interesting work for you.

One of your first jobs is to survey current techniques of presenting printed textual and graphics information smartly and with visual impact and attractiveness, as Miss West will be making presentations to the board of directors and potential advertisers etc. Make out a checklist with notes of the processes, techniques and systems that Miss West – probably through you – could employ to her advantage.

WORK EXPERIENCE ASSIGNMENTS

1 Ask a range of managers and their secretaries to advise you as to how they present various kinds of information at various levels within the organisation. For example, how is information presented for the board of directors/councillors and how for customers, and how for a departmental staff meeting, etc.

2 Find out what conventions of document layout/format are followed in the organisation and why.

3 With permission, collect specimen letters, reports, memoranda, agendas, minutes, etc, of a *non-confidential* nature to act as models and references of good practice.

4 With permission, collect some examples of the following documentation to take back for your group to examine:

(a) Examples of forms in use, designed by the organisation (note what they are used for).
(b) Specimen desktop published documents.
(c) Specimens printed by dot matrix, daisywheel, ink-jet, laser or bubble-jet printers, in black and white and/or colour.
(d) Specimens of advice notes, delivery notes, invoices and statements – both manually and computer-raised, if possible.
(e) Examples of sales letters, training manuals, in-house journals, publicity/press releases, etc.
(f) Specimens of faxed/telexed messages with annotations you have made of what each entry stands for.

PRACTICE QUESTIONS FROM PAST EXAMINATION PAPERS

1 You work as secretary to Mr Richard Thomas, resident general manager of the newest Praxiteles Residential Leisure Centre at Claremont Road, Esher, Surrey which was opened in 19X3. It is one of a group of similar centres and clubs throughout the country, with administrative headquarters in Bristol: Group Administrative Headquarters, Hamilton House, 27 Robinson Road, Bristol BS2 4HU, telex 56780.

The programme of events for the first anniversary of the opening of the Esher Centre (see below) is due to take place on Saturday 9 July 19X4 (today being 27 June 19X4).

```
CHECKLIST

ANNIVERSARY TIMETABLE      9/7/X4

Tennis Tournament          1430-1700
Swimming Gala              1430-1700
B. Lunch                   1200-1330
Dinner                     2000-
Reception                  1830-1945
                           +1900
Coffee                     1000
Tour of facilities         1100 hours
  (optional)
```

Mr Thomas has asked you to draft a standard letter to be handed to those people attending the anniversary activities on 9 July 19X4, welcoming them to the Praxiteles Leisure Centre and outlining the programme for the day, as listed in Mr Thomas's draft notes. (RSA Secretarial Duties Stage II)

2 Jack Martin, director, entertainments department, is concerned that the standard job application form is unsuitable for specialist personnel.

Mr Deacon, general administrator, Comlon Theatres, for whom you work as secretary, has asked you to draft a new form which will be used for technical staff required in theatres and concert halls.

Comlon International plc (Entertainments Group) is a multinational in the leisure and sports services market. Michael Deacon reports to Jack Martin and is responsible for the administration of Comlon Theatres. (LCC PSC)

3 Mr Rogers, director of sales for Comlon International plc, which designs and markets fashionwear at home and overseas, finds his time increasingly taken up with meetings with existing and potential customers as he deals personally with the large departmental stores' accounts. Consequently, correspondence and other matters awaiting his attention tend to accumulate.

Suggest measures to overcome this difficulty. (LCC, PSC)

4 When you arrive in the office on 25 March, the sales manager, Mr Hewitt, has left you the following note on your desk:

'I will be out all day. Please write a letter to Mr T Brown, of Speakline Ltd, 27 High Street, London, SW1 9LR, telling him I cannot call to see him a week today as arranged. Ask if it would be all right to call on the same date next month, at 3.00 pm. Enclose a copy of our new price list. Leave the letter on my desk ready for signing.'

Prepare the letter, bearing in mind that your firm uses window envelopes. (PEI Secretarial Practice Intermediate)

5 You work in the personnel department, and the directors of your company have decided to provide recreational facilities for the employees. As a start to this enterprise they have acquired a 5-acre site on which is a large building in good condition. It is proposed, eventually, to develop this site for the benefit of all employees. In the first instance however the personnel manager has asked you to prepare a short report on how the present building could best be utilised, bearing in mind that the age range is from school-leavers to near retiring. Write this report showing briefly how you think each age/interest could be covered temporarily. (PEI Secretarial Practice Intermediate)

6 Draw a bar graph using scales of 25.400 mm (1 in) = 2000 to depict the following:

Sales of books over a 3-year period

	1981	1982	1983
Fiction	2,000	1,500	1,500
Non-fiction	1,500	2,000	2,750
Technical	3,000	3,250	3,500
Other	1,000	1,150	2,500

(PEI Secretarial Practice Intermediate)

7 Your sales manager wishes to have a wall chart showing the total monthly sales for the first six months of the year, together with the monthly sales record of each of the three sales representatives. The following details are so far to hand:

		Sales	
Representative	*Jan*	*Feb*	*Mar*
T White	£200	£400	£600
L Brown	£100	£300	£200
S Green	£300	£200	£400

(a) Design an appropriate line graph and display the above details.
(b) State the advantages of such a visual display. (PEI Secretarial Practice Advanced)

UNIT 4
Glossary of terms and phrases

A4, A5
Paper sizes (see Appendix 4)

bar chart
Columns of data are compared against a vertical scale for impact and effect.

bonding
A term describing the process of gluing pages together as a form of binding, usually done using a heat process and plastic-based adhesive.

circulation list
Checklist of all staff receiving the same distributed memo, copy letter, report, etc.

clip art
A term labelling a range of pre-drawn graphics, such as logos, decorations and illustrations, stored in a DTP software package for a user to incorporate if desired into a page of text.

collated
Sheets of paper are brought together in desired sets or sequences, which are usually numbered.

condensed
A print size which gives a lot of information per A4 sheet because the typeface is small.

continuation sheets
The pages following the first page of a long letter, memo, etc (blank bond paper is used for these).

decimal point referencing
Sections of a report (or other document) are classified and sub-divided by using numbers before and after a decimal point, eg:
1.0, 1.1, 1.2, 1.3 etc
1.2.1, 1.2.2, 1.2.3, etc
1.2.3.1, 1.2.3.2, 1.2.3.3, etc
2.0, etc

elite and pica
Sizes of typeface used for many years in typewriters; elite prints 12 characters to the inch and pica 10.

emboldening
Increasingly popular as a means of giving impact to words, phrases, headings, etc, by printing them in darker, heavier print.

file copy
Almost always copies of created documents are made and retained; note storage may be as a paper file, an *electronic file copy* on computer, or as microformed copy.

footnotes
An added item of information positioned at the bottom of a printed page (indicated by superscript 1,2,3, etc, after a given term or phrase needing further exploration, a fuller reference, etc).

frontispiece
An illustrated facing page, opposite a major section of a document.

graphics plotters
Electronically driven machines in which coloured pens are computer-driven to produce graphs, charts, etc.

half-tone
A process important in image processing, in which shades of grey or colours in photographs are picked up by scanners, printers, etc, so that reproductions are faithfully made.

histogram
A chart which displays the distribution of data across a scale such as age, ability, fuel consumption, etc.

house style
Organisations set policies controlling the production

of their documents, eg *always* with open punctuation and fully-blocked; this practice simplifies work processes and supports a corporate image.

ISBN
A unique reference number given to published books so as to aid classification and identification: International Standard Book Number.

lamination
A process in which a transparent plastic sheet is fixed to a card or paper page or cover to make it more durable and easy to handle.

line graph
Sets of sizes, quantities, volumes, etc are plotted against time or other constants, eg sales over the year of three products.

logo
Usually a piece of graphic design used to identify an organisation, conveying what it is and does.

mailable copy
Copy (documents) are mailable when they appear free from production error or mess; overtyping and correction liquid 'mountains' do *not* make copy mailable!

mailshot
A large posting of sales letters, leaflets, etc, to potential customers or users; note use of *mail-merge* WP feature to *personalise* mailshots.

non-document file
A file set up by the software user (especially in WP) to store information which may be inserted into other files for subsequent printing – like a list of names and addresses of customers which will personalise a mailshot.

pictogram
A chart which uses symbols (sometimes in graded sizes) to convey volume, number, size, etc, in easily grasped relationships.

pie chart
A chart in the form of a circle (360°) which shows how a *known total* breaks down into percentage parts – 'slices of the pie'.

portrait/landscape
Describes the way notepaper is used: portrait = long side vertical; landscape = long side horizontal.

progressive indentation
Reports and schematically laid out documents often use a technique which sets out information in layers across the page (from major to minor). When each text entry starts further away from the left-hand margin this technique helps the reader to digest data more easily.

reprographics
A term covering all forms of copying and duplicating of data – photocopying, ink duplicating, scanning, OHP foil production, etc.

reverse printing techniques
For visual impact, text is sometimes printed white within a black box, or in contrasting colours, etc.

salutations
Greetings: eg Dear Sir, Dear Madam, Dear Mr Green (in letters, etc).

spellchecker
Most WP packages include lists of say, one to two hundred thousand words correctly spelled; WP files or individual words may be 'spell checked' by users and errors corrected prior to printout.

subscription
Signing off in letters: eg Yours faithfully, Yours sincerely, Best Wishes.

superscript and subscript
Small, printed numbers or letters above or below a line of text, used to signal footnotes, denote scientific formulae, etc.

thermal-action adhesive binding
See **bonding**.

underscoring
Underlining text either including or excluding spaces between words.

UNIT 5
Meetings, conferences, seminars and presentations

OVERVIEW

Unit 5 examines in detail the tasks that you may be expected to undertake on behalf of the manager(s) you work for so as to ensure that the administration of meetings, conferences, seminars and presentations runs smoothly.

Taking part in meetings is a major part of most managers' jobs, since the full and free interflow of ideas, suggestions, criticisms and proposals made round a table forms a crucial part of the decision-making process. The secretary will often organise the meetings and attend them to take a note of what has been said.

Over the years, various types of meeting have evolved, from the formal public enquiry to the informal marketing executives' brainstorming session. Certain types of meeting – public, board of directors or shareholders – are legally obliged to meet specific requirements as to their conduct, and all follow certain laid-down procedures or conventions.

Many organisations mount or sponsor conferences as a means of exchanging information and views among national and international specialists and of learning from expert speakers' presentations. On a smaller scale, teams of marketing, advertising, production or research and development staff will mount presentations in-house to directors and top managers in order to secure the go-ahead for a project or to brief them on developments.

As you might expect, information technology has made a distinct impact on meetings and conferences. For example, it is quite common for multinational executives to 'meet' together through closed circuit television (CCTV) teleconferencing, or its audio telephone-linked counterpart. Large TV screens in international conferences are used to screen, say, a live satellite transmission of a renowned speaker from the other side of the world. Equally, it is now possible for computer software displayed data such as diagrams, spreadsheets, formulae or text to be displayed on the VDU screens of executives across the five continents and for each of them to modify and interact with the display, while talking together over the telephone.

It is well worth noting before you start to study Unit 5 that managers are particularly demanding when it comes to the making of arrangements and the production of documents for meetings, conferences and seminars. When you remember that their senior managers and directors and/or clients may be in attendance, you can understand why they want the best of supportive service. So make sure you take the time and trouble to master the topics in this unit!

5.1 Meetings

Types of meeting and degrees of formality; calling meetings; the agenda; the chairman's agenda; minutes; how to take and transcribe effective minutes; specialist terms and phrases used in meetings.

TYPES OF MEETING AND DEGREES OF FORMALITY

Both public and private sector meetings are governed by legal requirements. The former by the Public Meeting Act 1908 and Public Order Acts of 1936 and 1986 and the Representation of the People Act 1983, and the latter by the Companies Act 1985, which replaced previous Companies Acts with one consolidating Act. A number of EEC Directives, resulting from UK membership of the European Community, and case law precedents, resulting from judges' decisions in the courts of law, also affect the holding and conduct of meetings.

However, not all meetings are conducted within a formal, legally specified framework firmly in the front of participants' minds. Indeed, many meetings which occur *within* organisations take place beneath an umbrella of company or local/central government law which is barely noticeable to the participants. The chart on this page provides an indication of the scope of different types of meeting and the degree of formality attached to each, of which the secretary should be aware.

Formal meetings

These will be closely governed by law and will be called by sending a written notice to participants. They will have their business set out on a written checklist of items called an **agenda**. The production of the agenda is also governed by rights given to the participants in terms of having an item they wish included on the agenda, provided it is submitted at the right time. A sufficient number of participants must attend so as to form a **quorum**, as laid down in

Fig 5.1 Types of meeting, according to formality

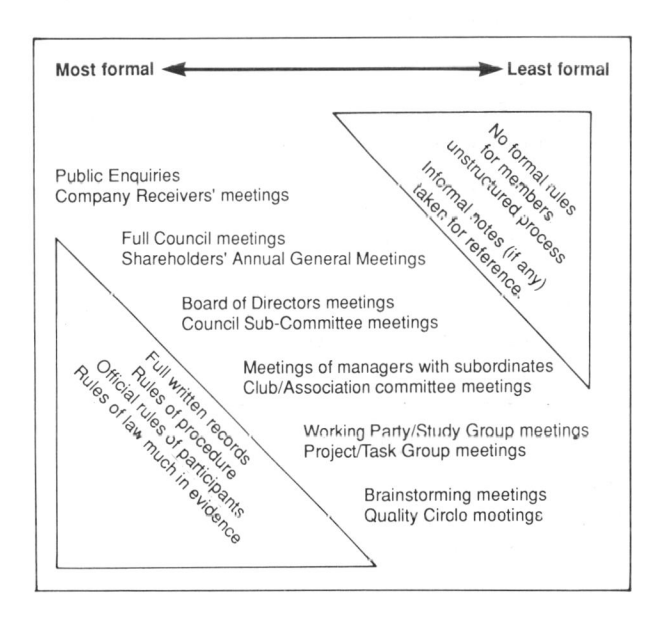

Most formal ←——————→ Least formal

- Public Enquiries
  Company Receivers' meetings
- Full Council meetings
  Shareholders' Annual General Meetings
- Board of Directors meetings
  Council Sub-Committee meetings
- Meetings of managers with subordinates
  Club/Association committee meetings
- Working Party/Study Group meetings
  Project/Task Group meetings
- Brainstorming meetings
  Quality Circle meetings

(Full written records / Rules of procedure / Official rules of participants / Rules of law much in evidence)

(No formal rules for members / unstructured process / Informal notes (if any) taken for reference)

the Articles of Association (enough participants to vote). The participants in formal meetings often have designated roles which accord their occupiers certain rights and duties – as chairman, secretary and member.

Also, the business of formal meetings will be recorded in the form of a written record called the **minutes** of the meeting. This record will either take the form of a summary of what was said, with a clear statement of what actions were agreed upon, or will simply outline what was agreed. Formal meetings also include procedures for introducing **proposals** – matters put up for debate – either in writing before the meeting, or via a set procedure during it. There are set rules in formal meetings for voting upon issues in order to arrive at a clear-cut decision agreed by a majority of the participants.

Informal meetings

Informal meetings, on the other hand, are not subject to such rules and regulations. For example, an advertising manager may invite several colleagues into the office with a spoken request such as 'I'd like to kick a few ideas around on the approach to launching the new snack bar.' In such 'meetings' the manager's secretary or PA may take notes of ideas as they occur, but no carefully constructed minutes will be produced. Similarly, the manager who called the meeting will control its direction discreetly, but it will not be structured by the running order of a pre-distributed written agenda. In a similar way, brainstorming meetings – which are called to encourage people to come up with ideas creatively – have little or no structure, since this might inhibit participants from speaking freely.

DISCUSSION TOPIC

Why are formal meetings so carefully conducted? Why do they need to have set periods of notice given to all legitimate attenders, careful written agendas pre-delivered, written records kept according to legal requirements (such as the requirements of keeping the minutes of directors' meetings) and distinct roles and procedures for members to follow?

Can you see any advantages in providing such carefully produced written records of these meetings?

Types of meeting

Statutory
Has to be held by law, eg directors' **statutory**, shareholders' and creditors' meetings.

Public
Members of the public have a right to attend, eg some council meetings, public enquiries.

Executive
The group holding the meeting (committee, working party, task force) has the authority to carry out the decisions it takes.

Advisory
The group only has the power to recommend that actions be taken – say, by a higher body with executive powers.

Annual general
The meeting held once a year by limited companies or by clubs and associations to which all shareholders or members are invited. Such meetings are called so as to give annual reports and to elect/re-elect officers.

Extraordinary general
Sometimes a serious turn of events prompts a board of directors or club committee to call a meeting of all shareholders/members in order to discuss a specific item of business, say a compulsory purchase order or threatened hostile takeover.

Command
Managers sometimes call meetings to tell staff about changes in policy or organisational developments. Such meetings do not permit discussion or attempts to change decisions.

Types of committee

As well as those committees which hold the executive and advisory types of meeting referred to, other terms are used to describe specific committees:

ad hoc
Set up to carry out a specific task: to arrange for a VIP visit or to organise a social event.

standing
Permanently set up until an executive committee decides otherwise: eg to vet membership, to organise club fixtures, to review staffing needs, etc.

policy
In the public service, in particular, policy committees make major decisions and wield much power.

sub-committee
Sub-committees are set up by and report back to main committees and are usually advisory.

Committee roles

Chairman
Heads the committee and is responsible for its activities; coordinates its work and ensures it abides by the rules laid down.

Vice chairman
A senior committee member able to stand in for the chairman.

Secretary
Administers the work of the committee and attends to the production of all arising documents.

Treasurer
Keeps all financial records and acts as steward for money held; produces financial reports on demand and annually.

Other typical posts
Membership Secretary, Publicity Officer, Social Secretary, Minutes Secretary,

Company secretary
In limited companies, the company secretary is generally responsible for servicing the meetings of the board of directors and ensuring that its proceedings meet legal requirements.

The secretary's role in administering monthly meetings

Days	Chairman	Secretary
1 ■ Meeting takes place ▽	Chairman chairs meeting. ▽ Chairman edits for accuracy, clarity, unambiguity, etc. ▽	Produces draft minutes from shorthand notes. ▽
7 ■ Minutes drafted, agreed and circulated with notice of next meeting ▽		Minutes of last meeting sent to members with notice of next; items/proposals for inclusion in agenda of next meeting requested. ▽
14 ■ Proposals, agenda and chairman's agenda prepared and circulated ▽	Draws up agenda with assistance/ consultation of other members and in liaison with secretary; checks wording of formal proposals for inclusion as agenda items; ensures members will understand what each agenda item is about, ie it is sufficiently explained in wording, etc. ▽	Produces and circulates agenda; draws up Chairman's Agenda ▽
21 ■ Correspondence checked ▽		Advises Chairman of correspondence received; sends chairman's agenda to chairman with relevant papers before meeting. ▽
25 ■ Papers for tabling copied ▽	Chairman meets/talks to Secretary before meeting to go over any potentially sensitive items, etc, and to receive an up-dating briefing. ▽	
■ Pre-meeting updating + briefing ▽		
27/27 ■ Meeting venue and papers prepared ▽		Records apologies for absence received from members; prepared for meeting – checks location/environment: heating/ ventilation/lighting in order, enough seats, water and glasses, stationery, pens, blotters, spare copies of agendas, minutes of last meeting, papers to be tabled, etc, are all to hand. ▽
28 ■ Cycle restarts	Chairman calls meeting to order ...	Takes meetings folder/minute book to meeting for reference access. Gets ready to take minutes

CALLING MEETINGS

The time-honoured way of calling a meeting is to send a written notice of its date, time and venue to the membership of the committee, board of directors or working party.

Supplying formal notice

Where directors' meetings are concerned, directors are entitled to be given periods of notice of intended meetings. Such periods will vary according to the rules under which such meetings are called. For example, a directors' monthly board meeting may require two weeks' notice – if that is what is laid down in the memorandum and articles of association. Where annual general meetings of shareholders in large companies are concerned, the rules may require that each shareholder receives an individual notice a clear 21 days beforehand, and may also require that the notice is published in a national newspaper at least one calendar month in advance. These arrangements are usually handled by the company secretary, whose office services shareholder and board meetings.

In notifying company directors, or governors of schools and colleges, a letter is frequently used. It should be stressed that protocol requires that each director or governor receives a personally typed letter, and *not* a photocopied one. Thus the merging facilities of word processing and good laser, letter-quality printer come into their own in such often-repeated tasks. Such formal letters of invitation adopt a tone which is factual and respectful without becoming cold and aloof.

Sometimes, notices and agendas are combined and set out in brief and simple structures:

Formal notice of a meeting

> THE GUILDHALL ASSOCIATION
> 75, Main Street,
> Leeds, 8.
> 20th January, 19—.
>
> NOTICE IS HEREBY GIVEN that a meeting of the Management Committee of this Association will be held at the Headquarters of the Association on Wednesday, the 6th February at 2.30 p.m. for the transaction of the business itemised in the appended agenda.
>
> (Signed) ....
> *General Secretary*.
>
> *Agenda*
> 1. Minutes of last meeting.
> 2. Consider matters arising.
> 3. Receive applications for membership.
> 4. Financial Statement.
> 5. Correspondence.
> 6. Receive reports from (*a*) Welfare Sub-Committee (*b*) Building Committee.

Informal notices

The calling of meetings of social, hobbyist and recreational clubs and groups is more informal both in terms of the periods of notice required (which will most likely depend on how busy the club secretary is at the time!) and the format of the notice itself. Pre-printed postcards are a popular time-saving medium used by club secretaries.

Within companies and public service departments, meetings will be called via the memorandum or, if they are of middle to low status, by the posting of a notice or bulletin.

The manager and secretary will need to take account of the following in maintaining an effective routine for calling meetings:

- What the law requires to be done
- The status of the meeting and its participants
- The trade-off between saving time via duplicated or pre-printed notices and according due courtesy and respect via individualised notices to high-status members.
- The need to maintain the organisation's image through its approach to administering the meeting, in this context external involvement has a greater need than purely internal.

Tele- and audioconferencing

Increasingly, information technology and telecommunications are providing new ways of bringing people together in meetings and conferences – even though they may be continents apart!

The practice of 'teleconferencing' has been in existence for some years and is marketed by a number of large telecommunications companies including British Telecom. In essence, participants either make a short journey to a local studio, or the telecommunications firm sets up an in-house studio. In the same way, the other conferencing members are provided with sound-proof studio facilities. Then, TV cameras and audio equipment are used to capture both the picture and the voices of the executives in each studio. By means of a telecommunications network using land-lines, radio-waves and satellite relaying capabilities, a television transmission is effected to each linked studio and each group of executives can see and hear their counterparts live on a TV monitor as they discuss, say, a plan to market a new product across Europe, or internationally. Furthermore, a video-tape transcript of the teleconference is usually taken to provide a record of the meeting.

At large, international conferences, it is now quite common for live televised transmissions to form part of the programme. A professor in a North American university, for example, is able to deliver a paper by means of satellite communications live to a scientific conference taking place in London, Paris or Bonn.

This televised lecture can be enjoyed by a large audience because IT can now display TV pictures on cinema-sized screens.

At a more modest level, busy managers can be easily connected by telephone in a network, so that several managers in distant regional or international locations can all take part in an audio telephone conference. In this situation, the secretary may well find herself listening to an amplified telephone extension so as to enable her to record the meeting in shorthand. Alternatively, the transcript may be made from an audio-recording of the meeting, where tape-recording facilities are part of the organisation's CABX system.

Electronic notices and agendas

Today, a number of large organisations are using management information systems (MIS) software to aid their communications. As you will by now be aware, such systems operate via LAN/WAN computer networks which interlink all the desktop workstations of the organisation. A very useful feature of such a system (which networks electronic mail and provides access to mainframe databases as well as allowing workstations to operate independently) is that the software includes a built-in means of calling meetings and communicating agendas electronically. For example the type of communication shown below may be composed (on a pre-designed format) and then relayed to all concerned via Email.

By using the electronic diary feature of the system, David Jones, who as advertising manager has called the meeting, has electronically checked that the first available day and time for all those of whom attendance is required is 11.00–12.00 on Monday 23 June. Also, the system will not only relay the notice and agenda to the participants electronically, it will also block out the meeting time on each individual's diary to avoid a subsequent clash of appointments/commitments. At the same time, David Jones will mail the

Fig 5.2 Electronic notice of meeting sent by Email to participants

```
                    NOTICE OF A MEETING

    DATE:          Monday 23 June 19--

    TIME:          11.00 - 12.00

    LOCATION:      Room C 236

    TOPIC:         Review Layout For New Sales Catalogue

    REQUIRED PARTICIPATION:  David Jones   Linda Hopkins   Adnan Farzi
                             Pat Jenkins

    OPTIONAL:                Frances Dixon   Terri Peterson

    AGENDA:

              1  Feedback on redesigned section formats            AF

              2  Finalising of colour photographic material        PJ

              3  Decision on cover layout                          All

              4  Updating on costings                              LH

              5  Report on distribution and delivery               DJ

              6  AOB/ DONM

    REFERENCES:    Please bring paste-up of catalogue and draft costings
                   schedules; PJ - proposed new photos.
```

message to Frances Dixon and Terri Peterson, but will give them the option of attending, which they will confirm when they read their electronic mail.

THE AGENDA

Refer to the agenda shown on page 191 as you read these explanatory notes.

1 Agendas are usually produced on A4 with the name/status of the committee or body holding the meetings displayed in letterhead fashion.

2 It is customary for a 'potted' version of the notice calling the meeting to be repeated above the agenda as a reminder to members of the date, time and venue of the forthcoming meeting.

3 Note the title 'AGENDA' is prominently displayed and centred.

4 Items 1, 2 and 3 are the traditional 'openers' on agendas. A meeting normally begins with the chairman asking if there have been 'any apologies for absence'. Once these have been noted, the minutes of the last meeting are referred to under item 2. Members are asked by the chairman if the minutes as circulated are 'a true and accurate record of the

Fig 5.3 Specimen agenda relayed to participants by a LAN office system (IBM's PROFS)

```
Unclassified                           Page 1


                              AGENDA
                              ------

CHAIRMAN:              ALISON GEORGE
SECRETARY:             J STREET

PURPOSE OF MEETING:    MANAGEMENT SUPPORT MEETING
DATE OF MEETING:       5 APRIL 19XX          VENUE: CONF ROOM 2
START TIME:            14:00                 STOP: 16:00

ATTENDEES:             A GEORGE
                       J STREET
                       M R SMITH

+-------+-----------------------------------------------+----------+
| TIME  |                    ITEMS                      | RESP'Y   |
+-------+-----------------------------------------------+----------+
|       |                                               |          |
| 14:00 | OPEN MEETING / CURRENT STATUS                 | A GEORGE |
|       |                                               |          |
| 14:15 | AREA 1 REPORT ON ACTIONS                      | M R SMITH|
|       |                                               |          |
| 15:00 | AREA 2 REPORT ON ACTIONS                      | J STREET |
|       |                                               |          |
| 15:45 | DISCUSSIONS AND CLOSE                         | A GEORGE |
|       |                                               |          |
+-------+-----------------------------------------------+----------+

           PLEASE BRING ALL RELEVANT BACK UP INFORMATION
```

(Reproduced by kind permission of IBM (UK) Ltd)

business of the last meeting'. Under item 2, members may only discuss matters of accuracy and suggest amendments and corrections for the chairman to approve. Once approved, the chairman customarily signs the minutes held by the secretary to the committee which are then placed in the minutes book. (Note: These must not be loose-leaf but in a bound book form for company minutes.)

5 Correspondence received traditionally appears as the next item, if there is any.

6 Item 5 illustrates how a proposal (received by the secretary to the committee in writing *before* the meeting) should be set out on an agenda. Note the set-piece structure which is generally accepted: 'That ... be ...'. This structure enables a 'yes/no' vote

---

AJAX ENGINEERING COMPANY LIMITED

STAFF SOCIAL CLUB COMMITTEE

The next meeting of the Social Club Committee will take place on Tuesday 21 February 19-- at 5.00 pm in the Training Suite

AGENDA

1 Apologies for absence

2 Minutes of the meeting of 19 January 19--

3 Matters arising from the minutes

4 Correspondence: Letter from the Managing Director confirming the £10 000 donation towards refurbishing the Social Club.

5 Proposal:

   That retiring members of company staff and their spouses be given free life membership of the Social Club.

   Proposer: Pamela Everett
   Seconder: Jack Carter

6 Repairs needed to Sports Ground Clubhouse after recent storm damage.

7 Report on progress of the Annual Theatre Visit from Jean Saunders, Chairman, Working Party.

8 Updating on Social Club funds: Angela Roberts, Club Treasurer. Financial report to be tabled.

9 Any other business.

10 Date of next meeting.

Circulation: Chairman, Secretary, Treasurer, Committee Members.

Information Copies: Managing Director, Personnel Director.

to be taken on the proposal if need be. At the meeting, the 'proposal' will be referred to as a 'motion'. In formal meetings, the proposer will speak to it first, any opponent(s) will speak second, and the seconder (proposer's supporter) speaks third. If accepted, the motion is then referred to a 'resolution'. Formal proposals generally require a proposer and seconder.

7   Item 6: It is likely that chairman and treasurer will have met before the meeting to discuss the likely costs and to be able to steer the committee towards making a sensible decision as to how much to spend and the degree of urgency, etc.

8   Items 7 and 8: Note that committee members need to be given agendas which provide sufficient information about each item to be discussed. For example, 'Christmas dance' would be much too general and lacking in informative detail. Note also that meetings frequently provide opportunities for committee members to be briefed and updated. A **'tabled' paper** is one which is distributed to members at a meeting; in formal meetings it may be noted but not voted upon. In company meetings especially, strict rules apply to ensure that directors receive papers **before** the meeting and have time to study them and take legal advice upon them if need be.

9   Item 9: 'Any other business' traditionally occurs as the last item of discussion on the agenda. It enables members to bring up any matter they feel strongly about and also provides a slot for the Chairman to introduce an item which needs discussion and which has arisen since the agenda was produced. Usually chairmen do not allow important matters to be decided under 'Any other business', but ask for the topic to be included in the next agenda. Many directors' agendas do not include an 'Any other business' item, so as to avoid matters being introduced without warning.

10 The date of the next meeting is usually negotiated as the last item of business. It will be confirmed in the notice of the next meeting sent out by the Secretary to members.

11 The inclusion of a circulation list on an agenda is optional. Here it is shown to indicate the courtesy informational copies which the Committee Chairman sends to company directors who have a legitimate interest in the Social and Welfare Clubs' activities.

Notes:
While there are no absolute rules on agenda formats, common sense applies, and the sensible use of white space, centring and indenting make an agenda easy to digest and visually attractive.

Numbering of agenda items: some agendas start each time with 1 for 'Apologies for absence' and carry on numerically until 'Date of next meeting' is reached – as the example on page 191 illustrates. Other agendas, however, carry on with a single sequence of numbers, where 1 was the very first item of the very first meeting, and 126 might be the reference number of 'Apologies for absence' of the fifteenth meeting. Thus Minutes of the meeting of ... would be 127, Matters arising 128 and so on. This system has the advantage of each item having its own unique reference number, whereas under the system illustrated, the date of the meeting relating to an item being referred to becomes crucial.

Top secretary tip: Agenda and minutes
Some committee members can prove tireless editors of agendas and minutes, so take particular care to get names, dates, numbers, titles, etc, right in the documents you produce. This will help the chairman and save costly time spent on corrections at the meeting.

DISCUSSION TOPIC

What aspects of current printer technology would be useful in printing agendas and minutes?

THE CHAIRMAN'S AGENDA

The chairman's agenda is produced by the meetings secretary, as a management tool. In essence, such an agenda is an annotated form of the one which goes to committee members and is for the chairman's eyes alone. In order for additional prompts to be included, reminders and supportive information, the chairman's agenda customarily has the format in the example shown on page 193.

Notes on composing a chairman's agenda

1   The tone of the notes written by a meetings secretary under the items headings will vary according to the closeness of the relationship with the chairman. While clearly understood abbreviations are acceptable, it is wise to avoid an over-familiar style and to make sensitive observations diplomatically, such as:

You will recall that this item is one of Charlie Smith's hobby-horses and that he is capable of talking on it at length.

Meetings, conferences and presentations

193

```
           AJAX ENGINEERING COMPANY LIMITED

             STAFF SOCIAL CLUB COMMITTEE

                    CHAIRMAN'S AGENDA

       For the Committee Meeting to take place on:
       Tuesday 21 February 19-- in the Training
                    Suite at 5.00 pm
```

CHAIRMAN'S NOTES

1 Apologies for absence

Susan Barnes' husband rang to say that she is progressing well after her car accident – he hopes she'll be out of hospital by middle of March, depending on tests, etc.

(Remember: Send Get Well card)

Derek Lawson wrote to say he will be away on a Training Course in Leeds.

2 Minutes of the last meeting

3 Matters arising from the minutes

You will remember that Susan Barnes was involved with discussions with Personnel Dept regarding the creche; I understand she was due to report back that the creche installation proposal was accepted in principle – good for recruitment, etc.

Report back for Susan Barnes

4 Correspondence

Only letter this month is from MD. This is the largest donation I can remember the Club receiving.

Don't forget to ask Secretary to write 'Thank you' letter to MD

2 If a chairman's agenda is to be of any value, sufficient space must be left down the right-hand side for legible handwritten notes to be made.

3 Your role as meetings secretary is sometimes difficult in that, while you may have the most detailed knowledge of the committee's work, it is the chairman who holds the senior post. The chairman is entitled to the best notes and pointers that the secretary can provide, in an even-handed and neutral way, so that informed decisions can be made. This is especially valid in organisations in which chairmen are often appointed as a result of their senior positions, which may prevent them from giving as much time to the committee as they would wish.

4 Remember to make chairman's agenda notes clear and capable of being understood by a vice chairman or other last-minute substitute in the event of the chairman being unable to chair the meeting.

5 As the chairman will need to refer quickly to the agenda during a meeting, it is helpful to provide key prompts in capitals and to use spacing and indentation to aid the eye.

Pre-meeting servicing checklist

Ask yourself the following questions, and make sure you have the right answers, in the run-up to the meetings you service:

1 Has every member received the notice, agenda and any supportive papers for the meeting?

2 Has a list of apologies for absence been made out for the chairman?

3 Has incoming correspondence been copied for chairman and treasurer? Should all members be given a copy of an important letter at the meeting?

4 Are sufficient spare copies of agenda, minutes of the last meeting and any supportive papers available for members who forget to bring their own?

5 Have reserved parking spaces been properly 'signalled' with name-plaques of members? Do caretaking staff know start and finish times of the meeting?

6 Does the foyer receptionist have details of the meeting so as to direct members to it? Is it posted on the electronic noticeboard?

7 Have appropriate arrangements been made for refreshments? Are these limited to serving coffee and biscuits on arrival or does the chairman need to be prompted about adjourning the meeting for a served meal?

8 Is the venue properly prepared? Note the importance of a personal check shortly before the meeting of: lighting, room temperature, ventilation, seating and table layout (this can be square, oblong, round, U-shaped etc). Is each 'place-setting' ready: blotter, notepaper, water glass, name-plaque, set of any tabled papers, ball-point pen, etc?

Does the seating plan accord with the chairman's wishes and established conventions? Have organisational staff been advised of the meeting so as to avoid interruptions? Is the venue secure in terms of ensuring confidentiality?

9 Are all the documents and papers to hand which the chairman will need: chairman's agenda, copy of the minutes of the last meeting (or minutes book) for signature, copies of correspondence received, list of apologies for absence, reminder note to welcome new members, copies of papers to be discussed, etc.

10 If audio-visual aids are to be used at the meeting, such as an overhead projector with foils, slides or videocassettes, have these been checked and equipment tried out by a technician before the meeting? Is microphone equipment required if it is a large meeting?

11 Final checks by the secretary: Minutes book or file to hand in case reference is made to a previous minute. Spare copies of documents, minutes notebook, spare pens/pencils, spare writing-paper, personal and manager's diaries available. Checklist of names of all members for reference and to check arrivals. Refreshments on hand. Assistant notified of likely absence from office and location of meeting in case or urgent messages, etc.

12 Post-meeting: pick up and dispose of papers left by members – post on to them as appropriate. Arrange for room to be tidied, switch off appliances.

DISCUSSION TOPIC

What IT-based office equipment would you seek to use to help you service regular meetings? Give reasons for your choice.

MINUTES

There are, essentially, three different formats for minutes: narrative, resolution and action:

1 Narrative minutes

Narrative minutes are so termed because they narrate or 'tell the story' leading up to decisions which are made. The advantage is that a record is made of individual members' views and underlying reasons for arriving at a decision. It is therefore extremely important to ensure that the summarised version (in reported speech) is unbiased and not partially selective. The specimen minutes on pages 195–196 of the Ajax Engineering Social Club committee meeting have been set out as narrative minutes.

2 Resolution minutes

This form of minutes records only the decisions reached. It does not record any of the discussion prior to a vote being taken. Typical use is for board meetings. Traditionally, resolution minutes are set out as follows:

> 126 Annual review of operatives' pay
>
> Resolved:
>
> That an award be made, based upon a 4.5% increase on basic rates of pay, and that rates for piece work and overtime remain the same.

3 Action minutes

Often used by committees, action minutes are written in narrative form but include a right-hand column headed 'action by'. At the point opposite the sentence of the minutes which requires follow-up action is displayed the name or initials of the meeting participant asked to carry it out. The chairman then checks at the next meeting what action has been taken.

AJAX ENGINEERING COMPANY LIMITED

STAFF SOCIAL CLUB COMMITTEE

Minutes of the Committee Meeting held on Tuesday 21 February 19-- in the Company's Training Suite

The Meeting commenced at 5.00 pm

MINUTES

Present: Shirley Johnson, Chairman, Paul West, Secretary, Angela Roberts, Treasurer, Tariq Aziz, Jack Carter, Pamela Everett, Christopher Knight, Jean Saunders, Winston Richards.

1 **Apologies for absence**

Apologies for absence were received from Susan Barnes and Derek Lawson.

2 **Minutes arising from the meeting of 19 January 19--**

Winston Richards drew the meeting's attention to Item 5: Visit to Mary Rose Exhibition. He affirmed that he had said that criticism of the planning of the visit had been 'ungracious', and not, as minuted, 'ungrateful'. The Chairman approved this amendment of the minutes which she then signed as a true record of the meeting of 19 January 19--.

3 **Matters arising from the minutes**

Item 4: Installation of Creche

The Chairman reported on Susan Barnes' behalf on the developments concerning the installation of a creche at the Company's South Road site, which had been accepted in principle by the board of directors as a means of aiding recruitment of both office and shop floor personnel.

4 **Correspondence: Letter from managing director confirming £10 000 donation to Social Club**

The Chairman read the managing director's letter to the Committee, who were extremely pleased to learn the extent of the company's generous donation. All agreed that the sum would form an excellent basis for the fund-raising series of events being planned to finance the renovation of the Social Club. Angela Roberts agreed to draft a letter of thanks for the Chairman's signature.

5 **Proposal:**

That retiring members of company staff and their spouses be given free life membership of the Social Club.

   Proposer: Pamela Everett
   Seconder: Jack Carter

In proposing her motion, Pamela Everett emphasised the increasing funds upon which the Social Club could rely and that it could well afford to provide life membership gratis to retired company staff. She added that many had given lifetimes of service to both the company and the Club.

9 **Any other business**

Christopher Knight asked whether there had been any progress in getting the fruit machine repaired, as its income was very useful. The secretary reported that Ace Games Limited had gone out of business and efforts were being made to reallocate a service contract.

The Secretary reported that the bar extension licence had been granted for the forthcoming Forties Fancy Dress Dance.

10 **Date of next meeting**

The next meeting was scheduled to take place on Tuesday 22 March 19-- at 5.00 pm in the Training Suite.

        Signed: Chairman

Fig 5.4 Specimen minutes relayed to participants by a LAN office system (IBM's PROFS)

```
Unclassified                          Page 1



CHAIRMAN:                  A GEORGE

SECRETARY:                 J STREET

PURPOSE OF MEETING:        MANAGEMENT SUPPORT MEETING
                           - MINUTES

DATE OF MEETING:           5 APRIL 19XX

ATTENDEES:                 A GEORGE
                           J STREET
                           M R SMITH

ABSENTEES:                 NIL

Further actions were agreed as follows :

1. AREA 1

It was decided to  further explore the suggestion of
upgrading section 2.

                    ACTION : M R SMITH

2. AREA 2

No actions to be taken required this month.




ALISON GEORGE
D.220   26/32
Personnel Dept
721-4943
HVTVM2(AGEORGE)
```

(Reproduced by kind permission of IBM (UK) Ltd)

> **DISCUSSION TOPIC**
>
> Why is it customary to use reported speech in narrative minutes, do you think? What, if any, are the advantages of using this system?

HOW TO TAKE AND TRANSCRIBE EFFECTIVE MINUTES

While the role of the secretary at a meeting may well be carried out by a manager or executive, as one of the committee's officials, very many meetings occur in business and the public service, where this is done by a personal secretary. It involves servicing the committee – providing the documentary back-up and care of the venue and surroundings, etc. It also includes taking minutes of the meeting and producing the draft for editing by the chairman, and then duplicating and distributing sets of minutes to members.

In order to produce effective minutes, the following guidelines should be followed:

Taking the minutes

1 Take a real interest in the work of the committee or project group. You cannot minute effectively what you do not follow or understand.

2 Get into the meeting room early and, having set out papers, glasses, water carafe and stationery, etc, be sure to note who is present and who sent apologies for absence.

3 Make sure you can put the name (correctly spelled of course!) to each face, so that you know instantly who is speaking. Use the initials of members in the margin to the left-hand side of your notes to save time. You can then use the right-hand margin to make particularly important points.

4 If you are using shorthand to take your notes of the meeting, generally avoid trying to take a verbatim transcript (ie to take down *everything* which was said). A good deal of 'waffle' or verbiage is uttered at most meetings and producing a full transcript of the meeting is a waste of time and effort. Good chairmen usually sum up towards the end of each item of business before a consensus decision is made or a vote taken. This is an important moment for the minute-taker as it will provide the salient points for noting. If in doubt, ask the chairman *before* the meeting if there is any item for which a full transcription would prove useful.

5 Get to know who are the senior decision-makers and influencers. This is not to imply 'switching off' when other members speak, but to suggest paying special attention when senior members join the debate.

6 Set down your notes in double-line spacing so that you can go back and insert a word or phrase easily if you need to.

7 Seek to pick up key words and phrases to act as triggers when you transcribe the notes:

... 25% increase in Co sales ... GB to be appointed Deputy Chairman ... decision not to go ahead with purchase of Oldham premises ... deadline of 26 May ...

8 Use abbreviations and symbols – like arrows or brackets if they help to communicate data easily and quickly, but *only* if you are sure you will remember what they stand for at a later date.

9 Make sure you note the date of the next meeting and always take your diary – and your manager's if need be – to meetings, so as to ensure that the dates fixed are suitable.

10 Most meetings include confidential items, so clear tables of any papers members leave behind, and shred as necessary.

Transcribing the minutes

1 Never defer this important task. Remember the cycle of the regular meeting, and the need to distribute minutes promptly. Also, it pays to transcribe while the meeting's business is still fresh in your mind.

2 Always use a word processor or memory typewriter to save time in producing second/third drafts.

3 Check in advance with the chairman as to the format conventions to be applied – narrative, action, resolution. Note that some meetings adopt the convention of never referring to a speaker by name but of using an impersonal construction like:

It was suggested that ...
Strong reservations were expressed about ...
A major cause of concern was considered to be ...

Make sure that you know the adopted conventions before you start.

4 Sometimes feelings run high in meetings and members say things in the heat of the moment which they would consider ill-advised in calmer moments. No one will thank you for highlighting such moments in painful accuracy:

Mr Pierce said that Research and Development wanted their brains testing if they thought this pathetic excuse for a new product would ever sell.

At such times, it is both diplomatic and prudent to convey the sentiment and not the precise words:

Mr Pierce expressed serious concerns about the potential sales appeal of the proposed new product.

5   Busy secretaries also learn how to condense lengthy and sometimes digressing discussions with phrases like:

After a general discussion it was decided to …
The committee *considered this problem at length* and the chairman in gauging the feeling of the meeting, concluded that … be actioned.
Summing up after a lively discussion, the chairman …

6   Seek to convey the important points quickly and simply: managers are busy and prefer the short to the long, provided that arguments are not distorted. Always ensure that you convey the action statement – what was decided – clearly and accurately since minutes serve as written records and you have a duty to provide a faithful transcript. If you have problems over transcribing a sensitive item, consult with the chairman and abide by his/her advice.

7   Lastly, always maintain the confidentiality of your draft minutes until the chairman has approved them.

DISCUSSION TOPIC

What routines and practices do you think likely to be helpful for a secretary to adopt who regularly takes minutes?

TERMS AND PHRASES USED IN MEETINGS

Ad hoc   from Latin, meaning 'for the purpose of', as for example, when a sub-committee is set up specially to organise a works outing.

Adjourn   to hold a meeting over until a later date.

Adopt minutes   minutes are 'adopted' when accepted by members and signed by the chairman.

Advisory   providing advice or suggestion, not taking action.

Agenda   a schedule of items drawn up for discussion at a meeting.

AGM   Annual General Meeting; all members are usually eligible to attend.

Apologies   excuses given in advance for inability to attend a meeting.

Articles of Association   rules required by Company law which govern a company's activities.

Attendance list   in some committees a list is passed round to be signed as a record of attendance.

Bye-laws   rules regulating an organisation's activities.

Casting vote   by convention, some committee chairmen may use a 'casting vote' to reach a decision, if votes are equally divided.

Chairman   leader or person given authority to conduct a meeting.

Chairman's agenda   based upon the committee agenda, but containing explanatory notes.

Collective responsibility   a convention by which all committee members agree to abide by a majority decision.

Committee   a group of people usually elected or appointed who meet to conduct agreed business and report to a senior body.

Consensus   agreement by general consent, no formal vote being taken.

Constitution   set of rules governing activities of voluntary bodies.

Convene   to call a meeting.

Decision minutes   resolution minutes are sometimes called 'decision minutes'.

Eject   remove someone (by force if necessary) from a meeting.

Executive   having the power to act upon taken decisions.

Extraordinary meeting   a meeting called for all members to discuss a serious issue affecting all is called an Extraordinary General Meeting; otherwise a non-routine meeting called for a specific purpose.

Ex officio   given powers or rights by reason of office. For example a trades union convenor may be an ex officio member of a works council.

Guillotine   cut short a debate – usually in Parliament.

Honorary post   a duty performed without payment, eg Honorary Secretary.

Information, point of   the drawing of attention in a meeting to a relevant item of fact.

Intra vires   within the power of the committee or meeting to discuss, carry out.

Lie on the table   leave item to be considered instead at the next meeting (see **table**).

Lobbying a practice of seeking members' support before a meeting.

Minutes the written record of a meeting; resolution minutes record only decisions reached, while narrative minutes provide a record of the decision-making process.

Motion the name given to a 'proposal' when it is being discussed at a meeting.

Mover one who speaks on behalf of a motion.

Nem con from Latin, literally, 'no one speaking against'.

Opposer one who speaks against a motion.

Order, point of the drawing of attention to a breach of rules or procedures.

Other business either items left over from a previous meeting, or items discussed after the main business of a meeting.

Point of order proceedings may be interrupted on a 'point of order' if procedures or rules are not being kept to in a meeting.

Proposal the name given to a submitted item for discussion (usually written) before a meeting takes place.

Proxy literally, 'on behalf of another person' – ' proxy vote'.

Quorum the number of people needed to be in attendance for a meeting to be legitimate and so commence (also quorate)

Refer back to pass an item back for further consideration.

Resolution the name given to a 'motion' which has been passed or carried; used after the decision has been reached.

Seconder one who supports the 'proposer' of a motion or proposal by 'seconding' it.

Secretary committee official responsible for the internal and external administration of a committee.

Secret ballot a system of voting in secret.

Shelve to drop a motion which has no support

Sine die from Latin, literally, 'without a day', that is to say indefinitely, eg 'adjourned sine die'.

Standing committee a committee which has an indefinite term of office.

Standing orders rules of procedure governing public sector meetings.

Table to introduce a paper or schedule for noting.

Taken as read to save time, it is assumed the members have already read the minutes.

Treasurer committee official responsible for its financial records and transactions.

Ultra vires beyond the authority of the meeting to consider.

Unanimous all being in favour

QUICK REVIEW QUIZ

1 What Acts of Parliament are related to the holding of *a* private sector meetings, *b* public sector meetings?

2 Explain the meaning of the following meetings terms:

a statutory, *b* executive, *c* advisory, *d* extraordinary.

3 What types of committee are these:

a ad hoc, *b* standing, *c* sub.

4 Make a checklist of the specific duties of these committee officers:

a chairman, *b* secretary, *c* treasurer.

5 Outline in sequence the duties of a secretary servicing a regular cycle of monthly meetings.

6 In what ways may meetings be called? Which method is appropriate for:

a a board of directors, *b* a departmental meeting, *c* a drama club committee, *d* an annual shareholders' meeting?

7 Write down in sequence the customary items on a meeting agenda.

8 In what ways may agendas be numbered? What advantages are offered by the systems you identify?

9 What are the main features of a chairman's agenda?

10 Explain the difference between narrative and resolution minutes.

11 How would you set out action minutes?

12 Set down brief guidelines on effective minute taking to be followed by a secretary servicing a meeting.

13 Make up a pre-meeting servicing checklist which you think covers the main areas a secretary should administer.

14 Explain briefly the meaning of the following:

a bye-laws, *b* casting vote, *c* ex officio, *d* point of information, *e* nem con, *f* quorum, *g* standing orders.

RESEARCH AND REPORT BACK ASSIGNMENTS

1 In pairs, find out how organisations use information management software packages to call meetings, provide agendas and create and despatch minutes. Brief your group on your findings, and display any printouts you were able to secure in your base room.

2 In groups of two to three, research into the legal requirements of:

a running company directors' meetings, or *b* shareholders' meetings, or *c* county council meetings. You will find it helpful to check out the work of the company secretary for (a) or (b)

Give an illustrated talk on your findings to your group or provide a factsheet for your group's database.

3 Having carried out your research, give your class a five minute talk on *one* of the following:

(a) the duties and responsibilities of a committee chairman
(b) a committee secretary
(c) a committee treasurer

4 Collect specimen sets of notices, agendas and minutes for your group to inspect and examine. Helpful hint: look for them in company annual reports, building society reports, papers sent to shareholders, business pages of newspapers, reference libraries.

Make a note of their format, wording and style.

5 In pairs, make arrangements to interview a manager and secretary who are involved in attending and servicing meetings. Make a checklist of questions to ask on how they operate, and what advice they could give to a secretary new to this area of office work. Produce your findings as a list of briefing points for your group.

5.2 Conferences, seminars and presentations

Organising a conference; the main stages of organising a conference; seminars and presentations

ORGANISING A CONFERENCE

Helping with the planning and organisation of a conference is undoubtedly one of the most challenging yet rewarding roles you can undertake, since it will almost certainly require all your accumulated skill and expertise!

Both private and public sector organisations mount conferences, on a local, regional, national or international basis, for a variety of reasons:

- To share knowledge and attitudes about a newly emerged topic – like information technology in the office
- To be given an expert updating on a given theme by national/international experts
- To evolve a response to a particular topic as a group of specialists

Indeed, the reasons for mounting conferences are many and varied, but all involve bringing together a large group of people – as delegates – to listen to expert speakers and to take part in arising discussions and forums.

Increasingly, conferences are taking place, both nationally and internationally, by means of telecommunications links or hookups. The following systems are now available to conference organisers:

Audio telephone conferencing National and international telephone systems are able to interlink, say, 20 executives of a multinational company so that each can hear the others clearly and converse with them, as if in the same room. Such a facility can make extensive savings in the costs of bringing such executives physically together.

Audio-visual teleconferencing Sight is added to sound by transmitting television signals (via landline, submarine cable, or satellite) so that while conversing, executives can also see each other, and any item or visual material being presented or examined. Moreover, video tapes and clips may be introduced for all to view and comment upon. Telecommunications companies are now able to set up conference studios on employers' premises for such national or international teleconferences.

Computer workstation conferencing The technology which enables digitised signals to be transmitted through telephone lines has made possible the interlinking of remotely located computer workstations. Here, a PC user may interact with a central coordinator who sends out information to a 'circle' of users – for example displayed screens of written data. Each circle member may key in comments and responses viewable by all, or may 'converse' with an individual participant of the conference circle in privacy.

This particular conferencing/communications system is proving a popular means of supplying open learning and training, while hobbyists use it as a means of keeping in touch and accessing a central bulletin board of information.

Interactive software conferencing A leading computer manufacturer has recently launched a system through which a PC user can dial up a colleague (or colleagues) across the world and, with contact

Meetings, conferences and presentations

Fig 5.5 Organising a national/international conference

A checklist of major items and their place in the Conference Project Plan

Major decisions:

When? Where? What?
Who speaks? Who comes?
What will it cost?

Vital deadlines to be met

Speakers secured programme designed and mailed bookings secured budget finalised

Attention to detail counts!

Meeting speakers' needs ensuring delegates comfort anticipating wants and needs providing good communications

Week	0 → 1	1 → 5	5 → 8	8 → 25	25 → 48	48 → 51	51 → 52	52 → 55
	'Go' Decision	Strategic Planning	Costing and conference budget	Promotion and sales drive — Finalising speakers and programme	Promotion and sales drive — Services to organise	Detail work run-up	Conference takes place	Post-conference

'Go' Decision

Form conference planning team and identify roles:
- Chairman
- Marketing
- Delegates coordinator
- Hotel and catering, etc

Strategic Planning

Decide:
- Theme
- Dates
- Duration
- Venue
- Clientele/target delegates

Map out:
- Target speakers
- Topics
- Supportive provisions
- Exhibition
- Booth/equipment display
- Social programme

Costing and conference budget

Identify cost centres and set fees for delegates
- Fees of speakers
- Cost of hotel accommodation
- Hire of suite(s)
- Catering

Specialist services:
- AVA/communications
- Decor
- Transport
- Reprography

Marketing and publicity:
- Advertising
- Programme printing
- Delegates' packs

Construct a break-even chart

Finalising speakers and programme

Produce and mail first programme

Obtain confirmations from invited speakers and:
- Photographs
- Talk synopses
- Curriculum vitaes

Market conference:
- Advertisements
- Mailshots
- Press releases
- Articles
- Letters to VIPs
- Phone calls
- Free entries in specialist journals

Set up conference administration unit and coordinator

Devise systems to process bookings

Services to organise

Produce and mail final programme

Confirm provisional venue and hotel bookings

Hire:
- AVA specialists
- Transport – coaches/minibuses
- Catering specialists
- Decor/signs/logos/backdrops specialists

Design and print day-programmes and delegate packs

Checks arrival times of speakers and VIPs

Detail work run-up

Prepare venue:

Registration/enquiry desk
- Seating
- Podium
- AVA equipment
- Cloaks
- Press room
- Speakers' quiet room
- Car parking
- Dining facilities

Finalise:
- Reception
- Procedures
- Name badges
- Parking vouchers
- Seating plans
- Social programme for spouses
- Escorts for VIPs
- Mobile phones for organisers
- Rehearsals for speakers (identify internal 'stand-by' speakers)

Conference takes place

'Think!'
- Patrol
- Monitor
- Observe
- Anticipate
- Back-up
- Maintain PR profile

Look after:
- Speakers
- VIPs
- Delegates

Post-conference

Produce:
- Conference accounts
- Pay bills
- Write thank you letters
- Hold team debriefing meeting
- Produce conference report and mail/publish it

established, transmit a screen-displayed, software application – say a graph, chart or document – which may be updated, modified or altered by any of the participants, as they converse over the phone! This particular break-through is proving a boon to designers, engineers and scientists all over the world.

THE MAIN STAGES OF ORGANISING A CONFERENCE

The chart (Fig 5.5) illustrates the main stages of conference organisation and provides a series of checklists which the team of organisers will draw up and action during each phase.

The 'Go' decision

Deciding to mount a conference is no light matter and the decision-makers will need to ensure they have the commitment and the financial and administrative resources to make it a success. A poorly organised conference will mar an organisation's corporate image.

Usually, organisations mounting conferences hope for a return on the investment made, such as making a profit, but the return is often less tangible though equally important – improved awareness of the firm's activities and products, enhanced **public relations**, acceptance as a leader in a specialist field, etc.

Whatever the motivation to undertake the highly complex and demanding task of planning and running a successful conference, the essential ingredients from the outset are:

- Creating a skilled, communicative team
- Devising and keeping to a conference project plan
- Assigning clearly understood and accepted responsibilities to team members.

Strategic planning

At the beginning of the planning period, the team must make a series of important decisions which will affect the eventual success of the conference:

Theme What will the conference be about? Are its topics likely to attract sufficient delegates by being topical and interesting?

Venue When, where and for how long will the conference take place? How long is too long? Is the proposed venue (location) easy to reach, regionally, nationally or internationally?

Clientele What kinds of delegate will the conference attract? Will the conference's proposed topics and speakers prove sufficiently appealing?

Speakers What sorts of speaker can the team interest? What fees might they require? Can they be afforded?

Extra features What supportive features should be included? A lavish evening social programme? Tours and shopping trips for delegates' spouses? Exhibitions and displays?

Costing and budgeting

Crucial to the success of the conference is the creation of an effective budget. Organisers usually approach this aspect by designing a break-even chart. Such a chart indicates:

The amount of money which will be spent on *fixed costs*: hire of conference suite, speakers' fees, early advertising, hire of **AVA**, etc.

The amount of money which will be spent on *variable costs*: additional hotel accommodation, additional covers ordered for delegates' meals, extra delegates' packs and printed conference papers, etc.

The amount of income which each confirmed booking generates.

Fig 5.6 Break-even chart

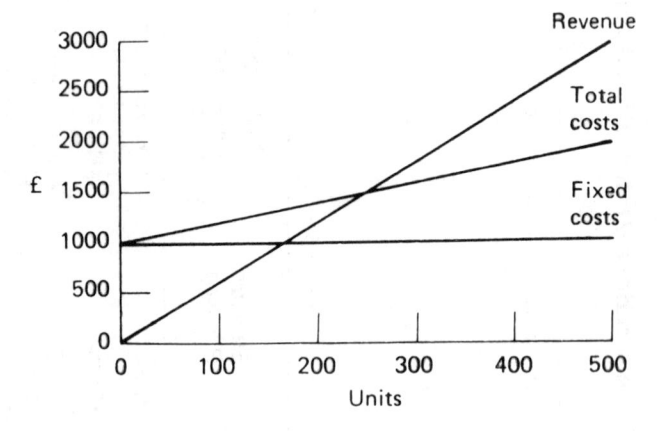

Profit at 500 units of output £1000.
Break-even point 250 units.

On the basis of charting such financial information, it is possible to project accurately how many conference places at, say, £200 per day (fully residential)

Fig 5.7 Example of a conference booking form

Second International
Information Technology Conference

APPLICATION FORM FOR DAY DELEGATES
(Fully Residential Application Overleaf)

Please reserve for me a place on the day(s) indicated, and for the evening(s) specified

at £80 for each day programme (or £210 for all three days), and £30 for each evening event.

PLEASE NOTE: AS A RESULT OF SPONSORSHIP A LIMITED NUMBER OF PLACES ARE AVAILABLE FOR BONA FIDE *
UK TEACHERS AT £40 a day (DAY PROGRAMME ONLY).
Attendance at the conference is eligible for GRIST/LEATGS funding

CONFERENCE COMMENCES ON TUESDAY 28TH JUNE FOR DAY DELEGATES

	No of Places at Conference	No of Places at Evening Events	
TUESDAY 28th JUNE			Conference Dinner
WEDNESDAY 29th JUNE			Theatre and Dinner
THURSDAY 30th JUNE			Conference Banquet

PLEASE NOTE: all day delegates conference fees include coffee, luncheon and tea
I ENCLOSE A CHEQUE/ MONEY ORDER FOR £
INVOICE REQUIRED

REMITTANCE SHOULD BE MADE PAYABLE TO "SECOND CHICHESTER INTERNATIONAL CONFERENCE (WSCC)" AND SENT WITH THIS FORM TO THE INTERNATIONAL CONFERENCE SECRETARY, CHICHESTER COLLEGE OF TECHNOLOGY, WESTGATE FIELDS, CHICHESTER, WEST SUSSEX, PO19 1SB.

SIGNED ....

NAME ....
please use block capitals

ORGANISATION / EDUCATIONAL INSTITUTE ....

ADDRESS ....
....
....

JOB DESIGNATION ....

TELEPHONE
(Please include area code)   OFFICE   HOME

PLEASE PHOTOCOPY OR SEND FOR ADDITIONAL APPLICATION FORM
* Applications must be accompanied by official endorsement from the institution

Chichester College of Technology
Telephone (0243) 774213
FAX (0243) 775783

(Reproduced by kind permission of Chichester College of Technology Governing Body)

and how many places at £120 per day (conference only) need to be sold in order to recover outgoings. Where income and outgoings meet is called the 'break-even point'. As sales climb beyond it, a profit is made.

Here it is also worth noting that conference organisers frequently seek commercial sponsors – say, equipment manufacturers, publishers or government agencies – to sponsor the conference by donating significant sums to offset costs. They, too, expect a return on their investment in terms of publicity and advertising of their sponsorship.

The principal costs centres to be considered are displayed on the chart on page 203 and include: Speakers' fees, hotel accommodation, catering, advertising and publicity costs, hiring of venue and transport, paper and printing and conference staffing costs.

Promotion and sales drive

Often the fine tuning of the conference programme is taking place during the early stages of the sales drive. Thus a first draft programme will sometimes include the phrase 'speaker to be announced' against a particular day and time. Needless to say, it is crucial to secure top-quality speakers early to ensure a successful sales drive.

Typically, conferences are advertised in specialist magazines and journals which the **targeted delegates** are likely to see. In addition, mailshots of publicity literature and proposed programmes are sent to likely participants. Frequently large volume mailshots are needed as a response rate of three per cent is typical, of whom half may actually take part. Additionally, certain potential delegates may receive personal letters of invitation, especially if they are VIPs and/or important decision-makers. The advertising account for an international conference will often amount to several thousand pounds.

Once the conference begins to be marketed and applications invited, a central unit needs to be set up to handle bookings and to act as a communications centre. At this stage, ensuring that hotel accommodation can be extended as demand grows is essential, since it is imprudent to book too many rooms too early. Many hotels operate a flexible system, provided that bookings are made sufficiently early – a central factor in conference planning.

On page 205 is a typical conference application form for day delegates to an international conference. Note the information which is considered essential: clear indications of days to be attended, whether or not social events are desired and the name, address and job designation of the applicant, with home and office telephone numbers. Note too the provision of a special conference telephone number (so as not to overburden normal incoming CABX lines) and the conference fax number – essential for international conferences.

Hiring of conference services

Provisional bookings will have been made early in the conference planning sequence and need to be confirmed some twelve to eight weeks before the start date. These include:

- The specialist company which will provide the conference audio-visual aids, such as **back-projection**, TV, lighting and sound, OHP slide projection and screen, **microphones** – lapel, **multi-directional** and roving. Such companies also stage-manage the speakers' presentations.

- The firm which will provide drapes, flowers and decorations for conference foyer, suite and reception areas.

- The catering company which will provide refreshments, lunches, post-conference cocktail receptions and banquets, etc. They will need updating on confirmed numbers of **covers** and any special dietary requirements as the conference nears.

- Printers may need to be supplied with detailed day programmes which include photographs and biographies of speakers as well as synopses of their lectures.

- Transport and drivers may need to be hired to convey delegates between hotels and the conference venue.

- The conference venue for approximate numbers, facilities and equipment needed, notices and signs required, fire regulations, etc.

The run-up to the conference

As the first day of the conference draws near, the pace quickens. During the last two preceding weeks, many practical tasks need to be carried out. Some may seem small but all are crucial. For instance, ensuring that staff running exhibitions have sufficient power points, and have not been forgotten in catering arrangements. Similarly, cloakroom facilities need to be considered and sufficient provided to avoid bottlenecks and late starts to lunches and so on. A good conference team tends to coordinate the final stages in terms of:

- Attending to speakers' needs
- Ensuring delegates' comfort and enjoyment
- Looking after VIPs
- Ensuring good press coverage
- Planning for easy access and smooth movement around the conference venue
- Ensuring the registration system will work effec-

Fig 5.8 Example of part of a conference programme

Second International Information Technology Conference

Tuesday 28 June 1988

Aims: To brief delegates at the leading edge of Computer Based Information Technology. A highly qualified team of international experts will demonstrate how information technology can enhance your profitability and keep your business one jump ahead of the competition.

Day Theme: Information Technology in Commerce and Industry

Day Sponsor: IBM (UK) LTD.

Day Chairman: **John Griffiths** UK International Information Systems Director, IBM (UK) LTD.

10.00-10.30		Keynote address by **John Cope**, MP – Minister of State Department of Employment.
10.30-11.10	**Speaker**	**Mary Ruprecht** President, Mary Ruprecht & Associates Inc, Management and Office Automation Consultants, Minnesota, USA The Impact of Information Technology on Industry and Commerce and the Training Needs Generated
11.10-11.40		Coffee served in the Exhibition Area
11.40-12.15	**Speaker**	**Jim Sullivan** Office Systems Manager, IBM (UK) Ltd The Revolution in the Office-The Integrated Approach
12.15-12.30		Panel Session for Questions Chaired by Day Chairman
12.30		LUNCH
14.00-14.45	**Speakers**	**Dr Richard Huseman** Chairman Department of Management, University of Georgia **John Schleier** Executive Professor of Management, University of Georgia and former IBM Executive **Dr Frank Hoy** State Director, University of Georgia Small Business Development Centre The Smart Office - The Future of Technology, from Electronic Messaging to Executive Information Systems
14.45-15.30		Tea served in the Exhibition Area
15.30-16.00	**Speaker**	**Harry Tuffill** Interactive Workstation Products Manager, IBM (UK) Ltd Future Application Strategy for Desktop Micros
16.00-16.30	**Speaker**	**Geoffrey Dart** Head of Information Technology, Marks & Spencer plc Information Technology Development in Retailing and Distribution
18.30 for 19.00		Dinner in the Goodwood Room, Chichester College of Technology
20.30-21.30	**Speaker**	**Dr Peter Cayan** President, State University of New York, College of Technology, Utica/Rome The Harnessing of Distance

Chichester College of Technology
Telephone (0243) 774213
FAX (0243) 775783

tively so that delegates are 'processed' quickly and numbers checked for lunches, etc. Here a computerised database system is extremely helpful, which is used from initial booking onwards. Also, different coloured day lapel stickers or badges are invaluable in helping organisers to identify speakers, VIPs, residential delegates, etc.

Post-conference tasks

Clearly there is important work to do in dismantling equipment and in tidying the venue. Also, once all bills are received and paid, a set of accounts needs to be produced which details sources and totals of income and also the various expenditure headings. Thus a residual profit (or loss) will be calculated.

In addition, it is important to ensure that visiting speakers are hospitably seen to their departure points and that they promptly receive fees and letters of thanks.

Lastly, it is very helpful to hold a debriefing meeting of planners to discuss strengths and weaknesses to be taken account of for the next conference venture. Sometimes delegates' packs include a conference questionnaire to help with this.

Top secretary tip
The global telecommunications network is extending and developing at an astonishing pace. The top secretary therefore needs to become as expert at servicing IT-based conferences as at arranging and supporting their 'round-the table' equivalents.

DISCUSSION TOPIC
How would you use computer-based information systems to best effect in coordinating the mounting of an international conference? What software application packages are likely to prove most helpful, and why?

Conference administrative documents

Set out below is a checklist of the typical documents and administrative schedules which the secretary is likely either to produce or assist in producing. Make sure you know the key features of content and format for each:

- Conference planning schedules
- Draft budgets, interim reports and final conference accounts
- Accounts rendered for goods and services supplied
- Invitation letters to speakers and follow-up correspondence or faxed documents
- Form letter to speakers requesting: photograph, biographic notes and synopsis of talk
- Form mailshot letter to advertise conference
- Display advertisement copy and publicity material
- Conference draft programme, final programme and day programmes
- Delegates' application forms, maps and factsheets
- Letters/forms to book hotel accommodation
- Computer printouts of confirmed delegates (regularly updated)
- Hiring contracts/agreements for conference services (book photographer if required)
- Draft menus, seating plans, layouts
- Listing of confirmed VIPs
- Draft/final press releases, articles, features
- Delegates' wallet documents – day programmes, talk summaries, handouts, notepads and any promotional items as 'giveaways'
- Social programme itineraries and details
- Written briefings to conference organising staff
- Name badges, car parking tickets, place cards
- Conference reports: draft and final
- Post-conference letters of thanks

SEMINARS AND PRESENTATIONS

A seminar is basically a meeting in which one or more speakers presents a series of prepared facts and figures to brief interested parties, such as colleagues, clients or training course participants, or balances a set of arguments, or proposes a point of view for discussion, etc.

The term 'presentation' is often used as an alternative to 'seminar', which is usually kept for training and educational or academic meetings. A presentation in a business context tends to be used to describe a meeting in which a team of presenters employs a range of audio-visual aids (AVA) to demonstrate an intense visual impact for, say, a proposed new advertising campaign or suggested new product to a group of senior executives, to help them in making important decisions.

The AVA support may include:

- Flip-charts and coloured jottings
- Photographic slides and taped audio commentary
- Video-taped TV programmes or sequences
- Transparencies (view foils) of data or illustrations screened on an overhead projector
- Computer program sequences on large VDU screen
- High-quality illustrated documents
- Audio-taped sequences

The secretary's role

As a general rule, seminars and presentations are mounted for middle to senior executives and the manager responsible will naturally be at pains to ensure that they run smoothly and efficiently. Moreover, clients, customers or distinguished visitors may be involved and the organisation's image will be 'on the line'. In the sections dealing with the administration of meetings and conferences you will have discovered the importance of forward planning and attention to detail. The same care must be given to the mounting of meetings and seminars. Senior managers are invariably busy, often work under much stress and tend to be intolerant of slipshod work.

Before the seminar/presentation

- Effect the same arrangements for the reception and care of visitors outlined in section 2.4 of this book.
- Check the location, as for a meeting, in terms of seating-plan, participants' papers, writing materials, name-plaques, etc.

But also:

- ensure that all TV screens, VDUs, OHP screens, flip-charts, etc, will be in full sight of *all* participants. Nothing is more irritating than being unable to read all of a *viewfoil* (transparency) or to see what is being discussed.
- Accompany the technician yourself to check that the AVA equipment to be used is working properly and correctly focussed. Keep spare plug fuses, projector light-bulbs, slide carousels, etc, *to hand in the location*. If it is your own responsibility to service the meeting, make sure you know how to replace them, and practise if need be.
- If the AVA materials are produced in-house and are your manager's responsibility, double-check that:

Transparencies are clearly numbered and in the correct sequence; ensure that they are mounted in the special OHP cardboard frames to avoid curling in the heat of the projector. (Proofread them – errors will reflect greatly on the presenter!)

Photographic slides are in the correct sequence and inserted the right way round in their carousels. (An upside-down slide may occasion instant mirth and ruin a vital presentation.)

Video and audio-tapes are wound on to the desired start point; make sure that audio-equipment is not in its safety lock travel mode and thus impossible to start at the key moment.

Desired lighting for the room is available – remember that members may wish to see to write during a presentation in a dimmed room.

Scheduling seminars and presentations

It is most important that the manager and secretary produce a timed schedule of the forthcoming presentation so that its coordinator and presenters know exactly what happens next, and so that individuals do not overrun their allocated time-slots. Also, such a schedule is essential for AVA technicians who may be activating light dimmer switches, starting video sequences and the like.

Such schedules provide the information which enables seminars and presentations to be run *professionally*.

Fig 5.9 Extract from a presentation delivery schedule

```
TIME     ACTIVITY                    PERSONNEL           TECHN SUPPORT

11.00    Introduction of             Dr Paul Rogers
         New Design for              HOD R&D
         Portable Typewriter
         Carrying Case

11.10    Cue for video of                                Start video
         design                                          Dim house
                                                         lights

11.15    Resume                         "      "         Switch off TV,
         presentation                                    raise lights
```

- Note that speakers may be supplied with electrical buttons at the end of a wire to signal cues to technicians for slide changes, etc.

- Note also that specialist firms exist to install and operate AVA systems – at a price – for conferences and high-level presentations. Large organisations will employ their own technical units, whose staff will design and make sophisticated coloured slides which provide high quality graphics and textual illustrations to emphasise key points. Such slides can be designed with the help of computer graphics software and may also be commissioned from specialist firms.

During the seminar/presentation

As organising secretary, you may be required, either alone or in turn with colleagues, to take notes of speakers' presentations in shorthand for a summary to be made and circulated later, or be needed to take notes of a questions and discussion session. In such situations, the techniques of minute-taking will prove helpful, and it is essential that you maintain concentration and do not miss a vital question and response.

After the seminar/presentation

Clearly it is important to ensure that visitors' AVA materials are safely returned to them and in-house materials filed away securely.

Arising summaries, reports, discussion papers, etc, should be promptly transcribed and circulated following the procedure outlined for meetings administration.

Top secretary tip
Pre-meeting rehearsals and equipment checks are *essential* if seminars and presentations are to go without a hitch. At such times your manager is likely to be very busy and will value your reliability in supervising this area.

QUICK REVIEW QUIZ

1 Write down in sequence the main phases of mounting a conference.

2 What is a break-even chart? How does it work?

3 How would you ensure that conference speakers are properly looked after during a three-day conference?

4 What services could you expect to obtain from external businesses to aid the mounting of a conference?

5 What impact is IT having on conferences and meetings?

6 What actions should a secretary take when responsible for the setting up and servicing of a seminar or presentation?

RESEARCH AND REPORT BACK ASSIGNMENT

Find out what services are available to organisations wishing to mount conferences in your area. In pairs, note down the sources of information, and list these services; then compare notes with what others in your group discovered.

UNIT 5
Summary of main points

1 Both public and private sector meetings are underpinned by laws: Public Meeting and Order Acts 1936, 1983 and 1986, and various Companies Acts (see consolidations of 1985); see also EEC Directives and Case Law precedents.

2 The conduct of meetings varies in the extent of formality: Formal meetings – appointed offices, required period of notice, written agenda, chairman's agenda, formal proposals and resolutions, minutes and tabled papers, etc; informal – no strict leadership, no formal records, no set procedures.

3 Types of meetings: Statutory – required by law; executive – able to carry out decisions; advisory – having to refer decisions back to an executive group; command – relaying decisions, allowing no discussion or changes.

4 Typical meetings officials: Chairman – overall coordinator and 'umpire'; secretary – factotum/administrator, vice-chairman – senior member able to substitute for chairman, treasurer – steward of finances and financial records.

5 Meetings notices: May be sent as either letters, postcards or memos, depending on the type of meeting; must convey the time, date, place and type of meeting; invitations for agenda items to be sent in are sometimes included.

6 Agendas: Basically there are two types, committee's and chairman's. The committee agenda is traditionally sequenced – apologies for absence, minutes of the last meeting, matters arising from the minutes, items for discussion, any other business, date of next meeting. The chairman's agenda follows the same sequence but allows for confidential prompts, tips and guidelines to be added.

7 Pre-meeting servicing checklist: Check venue beforehand: lights, ventilation, temperature, seating plan, name-plaques, blotters, refreshments. Check each place has relevant papers and writing paper/pens; ensure you have spare sets of relevant papers and any apologies for absence; check parking available and directions to venue; check over any AVA aids to be used. Clear up securely afterwards; send papers to absent members.

8 Tips on taking minutes: Check which format is required – narrative resolution or action. Ensure names of all the parties are known and their positions; have the agenda handy for reference; avoid trying to note everything verbatim; listen carefully to the chairman's summaries of items; note a decision exactly and the votes as taken. Use double-line spacing, identify speakers by initials, and asterisk vital points.

9 Phases of conference planning: 1 'Go' decision. 2 Strategic planning – what, where, when, who to speak, what delegates? 3 Costings and budget agreed. 4 Securing of speakers, finalising programme and printing. 5 Promotion and sales drive. 6 Organisation of support services. 7 Detailed run-up planning and briefings. 8 Conference delivery monitoring. 9 Post-conference debriefing and bill-paying.

10 AVA equipment and systems used in presentations and seminars: Flip-charts, wipe-over whiteboards, electronic boards with paper printout feature, photographic slides (sometimes with audio commentary), video cassette TV, overhead projectors and transparencies 16 mm film and screen, computer program sequences on relay monitor, teleconference hook-up, audio-taped sequences, etc.

Sources of further information
Meetings, Their Law and Practice Lawton, Rigby & Hall, Pitman M & E Handbooks
The Expotel Insiders Guide to Conference Planning, published annually by Expotel Executive Travel Limited
'Meetings, Bloody Meetings!' video, Video Arts Limited
People, Communication and Organisations, D W Evans, Pitman

ACTIVITIES

The 1990s secretary: changes and challenges
A case study

You are one of a class of students following an intensive course of secretarial study in Midbridge College of Technology's business studies department.

Your head of department, Mrs Kathryn King, has been recently involved in a series of meetings with other heads and the college principal, vice principal and chief administrative officer, aimed at drawing up a series of ideas for events to celebrate the college's forthcoming Silver Jubilee Year.

Mrs King's suggestion, which has general support, is for the business studies department to mount a two-day conference for business executives and secretaries in the region which will examine the extent and nature of the changes and challenges which may be expected in the work and role of the secretary in the 1990s.

In order to test the degree of interest in her idea, Mrs King recently contacted a number of influential people to see if they would support the mounting of such a conference. These are the reactions she obtained:

Sir Archibald Cockburn, chairman of International Telecommunications Limited, whose head office and main factory are some ten miles distant from the college:

'What a splendid idea! Of course, I should be delighted to offer my support, and I'm sure my managers and their PA/secretarial support staff will want to help in the delivery of the conference. Please come back to my PA when you want to discuss matters in more detail.'

Jennifer Rooke, chairman of the Midbridge branch of the British Institute of Management, home address: Plum Tree Cottage, Cirencester Road, Little Gatting, Midshire MS3 9LG:

'I'm sure your idea will prove a popular one among my institute's members. Only last week in a committee meeting we were thinking of putting on a similar evening event for our coming season of meetings. We could assist you with publicity and I'm sure provide you with a speaker and so on. I'll bring the matter up at our next committee meeting. Meanwhile perhaps you could let me have a schedule of your first thoughts on the conference's structure?'

Susan Vickers, secretary of the Midbridge and Castlebrook branch of the Institute of Qualified Private Secretaries, 23 Coppice Row, Midbridge, Midshire, MS2 5TR:

'The local branch and institute will be only too pleased to help you deliver such a conference. For one thing, it would give us a splendid opportunity to get across to employers of secretarial staff the rapid rate of change that technology is bringing to the secretarial role. And I'm sure that I could persuade Zoe Weissman to be one of your speakers if you wish. She lectures in administrative studies at Wolverston Polytechnic, knows this district well and has recently obtained a PhD for an examination of future office administration trends. And she happens to be a very good speaker, well able to handle any provocative questions, etc.'

Jim Goodson, chief administrative officer of Midbridge College of Technology:

'As far as I am concerned, there should be no problem in your having the Assembly Hall for two days in the last week of March for your conference. It has Fire Brigade approval for 350 seated delegates, and our resources centre should be able to stage-manage the AVA and lighting, etc. If you contact Mrs Shepherd (college refectory manager), she could tell you the cost of providing morning and afternoon refreshments and a buffet lunch per delegate. Parking shouldn't be too much of a problem. By March the new student car-park should be completed with a capacity of an additional 250 spaces. Yes, I think that logistically we could cope – provided your department does all the arranging!'

Letter from the examinations secretary of the Chartered Society of Commercial Arts and Crafts (CSCAC), Society House, Montague Crescent, London WC3E 4AJ, telephone 01-987 6543: (see p. 213).

This morning, Mrs King came into your class and discussed her ideas with you and your fellow students. Her latest brainwave was for your group to act as the conference's secretariat and to undertake a significant part of the conference's administration:

'It would be a marvellous experience for you all to carry out real work activities and to meet local employers and professional people. Of course, I shall ensure that this work doesn't get out of hand and interfere with your studies. But just think how you'd cope with a conference question in the exam!'

As a result of Mrs King's persuasive skills, you are all now enthusiastic conference administrators! Here are the tasks which you have been asked to carry out.

CASE STUDY ASSIGNMENTS

1 In groups of four to five and starting with the supportive responses outlined above, design a two-day conference programme which you think would prove most suited to the aims of the conference; which are:

To provide an opportunity for managers and secretaries alike to consider the implications of current technological and organisational trends upon the work and role of the secretary during the next decade.

Your programme should provide sufficient factual detail, while making the series of events appealing and important to potential delegates.

2 In pairs, compose a mailshot letter to be sent to likely delegates – managers, training and personnel executives, secretaries, committee members of local professional institute branches, etc – which aims to publicise the conference and to encourage recipients to send in for a conference application form.

> Dear Mrs King
>
> PROPOSED TWO-DAY CONFERENCE ON THE FUTURE OF SECRETARIAL WORK
>
> Thank you for your letter of 12 September which outlined the background to your College's Silver Jubilee celebrations, and your ideas for a conference on future trends and challenges in the work of the secretary in organisations.
>
> The Society would be pleased to participate in the mounting of such a conference, especially as it would provide a first-class opportunity for the Society to publicise its new range of personal/information assistant and secretarial examinations.
>
> Our Office Administration Studies Officer, Ms Fiona Stanshawe, would be available on the proposed dates of the Conference – 25 and 26 March to deliver an illustrated talk about our new schemes. Please contact her if you wish to make use of her expertise.
>
> Meanwhile, please do not hesitate to contact me if I may be of any further help.
>
> Yours sincerely
> Henry Jackson
> Examinations Secretary

3 Using the current range of costs and prices which exist in your college/school for food, accommodation hire, caretaker overtime rates, etc, draw up a schedule which totals the projected cost of mounting the conference. (Don't forget overnight hotel accommodation for speakers and their travelling expenses.) Having worked out the anticipated costs, decide upon a conference fee which would cover costs if you were able to attract 200 delegates. Note that your principal doesn't wish to make a profit in this instance, but simply to cover all overheads.

4 Compose a suitable letter to go to all speakers, asking them to supply a black and white photograph, brief biographical notes and a résumé of their talks, to reach you no later than 1 February 19--. Use a word processing system to produce the letter on a mail-merge basis.

5 In groups of three to four, draw up a checklist of the equipment and facilities which will need to be available to both speakers and delegates. Remember that busy managers will need to keep in regular touch with their offices and may need to contact people over a wide area.

6 In pairs, design a suitable display advertisement to promote the conference:

Either 12 cm square to go into the monthly magazine of the Midshire Federation of Directors and Employers *or* a four column × 20cm display advertisement to be published in the *Midshire Gazette*.

7 In a group of three to four, draw up a checklist of the conference duties needed to be taken care of in the college from the week preceding the conference and during it. Your schedule should clearly indicate who has been charged to do what, by when and who is overall supervisor of each task.

8 A team of receptionists (from another class) has been selected to receive delegates and register them and to staff an information point and guide service. Compose a suitable memorandum to brief them fully on their duties and overall approach, etc.

9 Half-way through the talk of the conference's second speaker, the microphone amplification system breaks down. Fortunately the speaker has a voice which carries well. However, the resources centre has no back-up equipment in college. The nearest supplier, Conference Systems Limited, is some 40 miles away in Wolverston. The next speaker is due to begin after lunch in two hours time.

Note down what actions you would take and in what order to help overcome this problem.

WORK SIMULATION ASSIGNMENTS

1 You work as personal secretary to Mrs Janet Fraser, marketing manager of Bonjour Cosmetics Limited. Mrs Fraser's job requires her to make frequent presentations and to coordinate her marketing team's demonstrations and briefings.

This morning she briefed you as follows:

> 'I think our audio-visual equipment and resources are becoming distinctly old hat! I'd like you to find out what mobile equipment is currently on the market and then to make up a shopping list, with costings of what you think we ought to purchase as essential items of a new kit. Oh, and you'd better include whatever explanatory notes you think I may need!'

Produce the schedule requested by Mrs Fraser.

2 Your personnel department is currently producing a company training manual for all office staff. You feel rather pleased because the training manager, Nick Fellowes, has asked you to produce a draft on about two sides of A4 of notes for guidance to new company secretaries on how to produce the notices, agendas and minutes for in-house meetings. He wants your notes to be easy to grasp, practical and clear.

Use a WP system to produce the draft Nick Fellowes asked for.

3 Make arrangements to take the minutes of your college/school student association committee meeting, and produce them for circulation in liaison with the chairman.

4 See if you can sit in on a staff meeting at your study centre and take down (with permission) practice notes for minutes transcription.

5 Organise a meeting within your own group on one of these topics:

(a) a review of the subject content of your course and proposals for its amendment
(b) how the social and recreational activities of your college or school could be further extended and developed and how funds might be raised to finance them.

By arrangment, half the group takes notes to produce minutes for meeting (a) and the other half for meeting (b). Make a tape recording of both meetings (which should last some 20 minutes) so that you have a reliable source to check your version of the minutes with. Having produced your minutes in *narrative form*, compare them with those produced by other group members and select the best, giving reasons for your choice under headings of: accuracy, format, style and presentation.

PRACTICE QUESTIONS FROM PAST EXAMINATION PAPERS

1 Check back to question 1 of Unit 4's practice questions (page 179) and re-read the background details. Then answer the following question:

In order to finalise arrangements for the Anniversary Day, Mr Thomas wants to call a final briefing meeting to go over the arrangements with the restaurant manager, the chef, the chief finance clerk, and the sports manager. Mr Thomas has asked you to arrange for the meeting to be held in his office next Wednesday at 10.30 am and to base it on his checklist (see question 1 of Unit 4). Draft a notice and agenda for this meeting. (RSA Secretarial Duties Stage II (adapted))

2 The programme of events for the Anniversary Activities (see question 1 Unit 4 practice questions) indicates that a certain amount of printing of cards and event sheets, etc, will be needed. Mr Thomas has asked you to prepare a checklist of the likely printing needs for the day and the internal services that will be required. (RSA Secretarial Duties Stage II)

3 Normally you yourself take the minutes at council meetings, but you were unable to do so last night. Your stand-in has handed you the following notes, which you will now need to correct, using proper terminology for the official minutes. Look at the draft and rewrite each sentence, but substitute the correct terminology where appropriate:

When the meeting began, only five members were present and the chairman said *that not enough people had arrived to start the meeting*. Just then Mr S James arrived and there were then sufficient people for the meeting to start.

Everybody present agreed that the Rev Johnson and Dr Hackett be *asked to join the committee*.

The vice chairman of the housing committee *suggested* that the meeting should accept the rate increase of 6% and Counc S Smythe also *thought this a good idea and asked the meeting to accept*.

After discussion, there were equal numbers for and against and the chariman *had to decide*. (RSA Secretarial Duties Stage II)

4 (a) Prepare a list of points to enable a junior secretary to take and transcribe minutes of a committee meeting effectively
   (b) Express the following item in minuted form:

   Matters arising – 16/8 – Mr Jones said 'I should like to report that after further discussion with the interviewing panel it was decided to appoint Mr Frankland as safety officer.' (LCC PSC)

Meetings, conferences and presentations

5 One of your duties is to prepare the draft minutes for meetings of the Association of Textile Staff. Notes from the last meeting were taken by the junior secretary, who has passed them to you, together with the agenda to prepare the minutes. (RSA Secretarial Duties Stage II).

```
THE ASSOCIATION OF TEXTILE STAFF
Executive Committee Meeting
22 June 1985 at 5.00 pm in the Staff Dining Room

AGENDA

1  Apologies

2  Minutes

3  Matters arising

4  Proposed Redundancies

5  Any other business

6  Date of next meeting
```

ATS — Exec. Mtg. 23.6.86

Present: Freda Lownes, Ken Long, Roger Peters, John Dean, Sara Riches

1. Sam Taylor
2. ~~Agreed~~
3. None
4. J.P. Reported: notification rec'd from MD that redundancies in office staff will be necessary due to computerisation. Discussion, FL put Assoc. response "that this Ass. protests at the proposed redundancies and asks the Co. to review the pos. 2nd — KL. Vote — None against — carried.
    JP to report to MD.
5. RP asked for discuss at next mtg (15.9.86) on increasing min. nos. req. for mtgs.

6   Briefly discuss how effective signs and notices can assist in the smooth running of a two-day residential conference to be held in non-purpose-built accommodation. (LCC PSC)

7   Comlon International plc design and manufacture office equipment and stationery products. As the company's work has increased, it has been agreed to invest in additional computer software for the furniture designers. You are asked to arrange a one-day training session at a local hotel for 20 designers, 10 of whom work at head office in the UK, 5 in Germany and 5 in France. List and explain the arrangements which need to be undertaken to ensure a successful day. (LCC PSC)

8   As part of a staff training scheme, the Managing Director has arranged for a Business Management expert to address all senior staff one evening. The meeting is to be held in the Board Room. What would you do to ensure that the Board Room was properly arranged, with all the necessary facilities for the meeting. (No marks will be awarded for details of invitations, agendas, notices of meetings, travel arrangements etc.) (PEI Secretarial Practice Advanced)

9   You have been appointed secretary to the Managing Director. His monthly meeting with Departmental Heads is due in two weeks' time. Explain what action you would take to prepare for this meeting, what your role would be during the meeting, and what you might be expected to do after the meeting. (PEI Secretarial Practice Advanced)

UNIT 5
Glossary of terms and phrases

agenda
A checklist of items for discussion and eventual decision-making, used to keep meetings relevant to 'the business in hand'.

AVA
Audio visual aid – viewfoil transparency, video cassette, etc, used to support presentations, seminars, talks, etc.

back-projection
A means of projecting films, videos, etc, on to large screens from the side of the screen lying away from the audience.

brainstorming session
A process by which people in a meeting 'spark' ideas off each other in order to find solutions to problems or suggestions for new products, etc.

closed circuit TV
See unit 3 glossary – teleconferencing.

cover
Catering term for each individual place-setting.

minutes
A set of notes which summarise accurately the main points of what was said and what decisions were taken at a meeting.

multidirectional microphones
Microphones which are used in question and answer sessions because they can pick up sound coming from any direction.

official receivers
Government officials who take control of companies which are bankrupt, so as to ensure any remaining assets are disposed of according to company law.

proposals
An item submitted in writing to a meeting which requires a 'Yes-no' response, eg 'That the annual subscription be increased by £10'.

public enquiry inspectors
Government officials who preside over public enquiries, say about a proposed by-pass, and who make recommendations to government ministers, having heard representations.

public relations
A specialist activity in organisations which liaises with TV, newspapers, radio, etc, to supply news items calculated to show the organisation in a good light.

quorum
An agreed number of committee members needed to be present before certain types of meeting may legally proceed. See also *quorate*.

tabled paper
A printed document given to committee members at a meeting, for perusal but *not* discussion.

targeted delegates
Those potential participants who are considered most likely to attend a conference and at whom the sales drive will be aimed.

viewfoil/overhead transparency
Clear acetate sheets or rolls on which text and diagrams may be drawn with special pens printed or photocopied for showing on the overhead projector's screen.

UNIT 6
Services and the secretary

OVERVIEW

As we have already seen, the work of many organisations depends to a large degree on a range of specialist services which may be called upon from time to time. Within large organisations, these services include: personnel, computer and data processing, work study and organisation and methods, management accounting, transport, and so on.

Similarly, many organisations rely on external agencies, bureaux and service companies to provide specialist assistance – but only as the need arises. For example, travel agencies, banks, postal and distribution agencies, printers, employment bureaux, chartered accountants and solicitors all rely upon receiving orders and instructions from other businesses or government departments.

This unit examines the extensive services which a manager and secretary can call upon to aid their work. Those services surveyed in detail are: personnel, financial and banking services, postal and private sector delivery services, and travel services. Information on further services, such as employment agencies, computer bureaux and secretarial and exhibition services, is given in Appendix 1 at the end of this book.

> **Top secretary tip**
> Wherever your career may take you, always make it a firm rule to keep a personal address database of useful services in your working locality, as well as those available nationally and internationally.
>
> When external services are needed, it is usually in a hurry! A sudden demand for an overseas business trip, a requirement to deliver a package to Frankfurt within 24 hours, or to send a card and flowers to a colleague suddenly admitted to hospital.
>
> It also pays to establish good relations with the senior staff of the agencies you use – travel, banking, delivery or secretarial – on a regular basis, so that 'when the balloon goes up' you can make effective arrangements calmly and swiftly – and provide yet another reason for your manager and organisation considering you not only indispensable but well worth that rise!

6.1 Personnel services

The functions of a personnel department; checklists of major sections of personnel forms and schedules; contents of a contract of employment.

All organisations need personnel services. Small firms cope with the demands of running their personnel services by allocating tasks like recruitment, training or pensions arrangements to various staff, whose duties are varied and very flexible. If you should join a small firm in a secretarial capacity, you may well find yourself carrying out a number of these activities. Larger companies and government agencies will almost certainly include in their departmental structure a personnel department. As the title indicates, such a department deals exclusively with matters which affect the people who make up the organisation's workforce. In Japanese companies the personnel service encompasses a 'cradle to grave' approach which literally starts with antenatal classes and ends with a company financed funeral. In the different cultures of Western Europe and North America, citizens make more private and personal arrangements, but the role of the personnel department in organisational life has increased tremendously in the past twenty years, partly because employees expect more and better services from their employers, and partly because employment law has become much more complex and demanding.

THE FUNCTIONS OF A PERSONNEL DEPARTMENT

While there is no such thing as a 'typical' personnel department, the following functions are those usually undertaken by a large department:

Recruitment

Managers in various departments will give their requirements for a new post to Personnel, who will draw up the documents which are needed to process a recruitment (see p. 222). New staff may be needed as a result of company expansion, an employee gaining promotion to another post, a resignation, and so on. The department may also conduct initial interviews, to produce a shortlist of candidates for the manager to see.

Induction

Once appointed, new staff need to be given an initial period (a day, a week, depending on the post) of training aimed at familiarising them with: company policies, company rules and procedures, an overview of the company's activities, its range of products or services, its structure and organisational systems and introductions to the new employee's immediate colleagues.

Training

A personnel department will coordinate and deliver a wide range of training courses for all employees, from instruction in operating a new piece of equipment, to techniques of supervision for new supervisors, to devising strategies for future company development for senior managers. Many personnel departments employ a training manager and assistants to perform this important role.

Career development and employee records

A personnel department will maintain and update detailed records for each employee which log his or her career development, any changes in duties and the sequence of job moves and/or promotions, as well as any training given. Such records are usually kept on computerised databases, which are invaluable when vetting an employee's application

The recruitment process

1. Need for new post identified.

2. Line manager details needs: reviews post for changes if it already exists, or lists fresh requirements if a new post is to be established.

Lists the physical, educational, experience, aptitudes, skills and personality requirements needed in the person who could do the job successfully. Prioritises requirements as 'essential' or useful'. →

3. *Personal specification* is revised or a fresh one drawn up.

← Defines: who the employee reports to and who may report to him: lists in detail the duties and responsibilities of the post-holder.

4. *Job description* is revised or a fresh one devised.

5. A *classified or display advertisement* is composed for insertion in local/national press.

← Sells the job by briefly indicating what benefits – pay, prospects, 'perks' etc are offered in return for an applicant possessing the expertise displayed as needed in the advertisement.

These may include potted history of the organisation and details of successes as well as outline of job location, duties and prospects. →

6. *Duplicated particulars of the post* and application forms are made ready for posting to applicants; the job description may be included in pack to applicants.

7. *Initial letters of interest are* received and application packs despatched

← Smaller organisations sometimes ask only for 'letters of application'; large firms want the 'full application package'.

During this period, line managers and personnel staff meet to organise interview procedures and agree who will assess what. →

8. Completed applications are received which include *formal covering letter of application, completed application form(s)* and a copy of a *curriculum vitae*.

Note: many organisations hire *employment consultants* to sift through initial applications and to propose candidates for shortlisting.

← National and international companies receive *hundreds* of applications for key posts!

9. Shortlisted applicants are sent *letter invitation* to attend *for interview.*

10. *Acceptance letters* received from shortlisted applicants.

It is common practice in private sector companies for employees to make very confidential applications for new jobs. Their references will only be taken up with the candidate's permission, and usually after an oral job offer has been made and accepted – 'subject to satisfactory references being received'. →

11. *Confidential references* are obtained from referees cited in application forms and copied for interview panel, along with shortlisted candidates' application forms and CVs.

Interview panel also provided with *interviewing schedule* on which to record impressions and ratings.

This schedule gives the interviewer a means of 'marking' the candidate for aspects like:
Appearance
Alertness
Knowledge/expertise
Potential
Rapport

(continued on page 223)

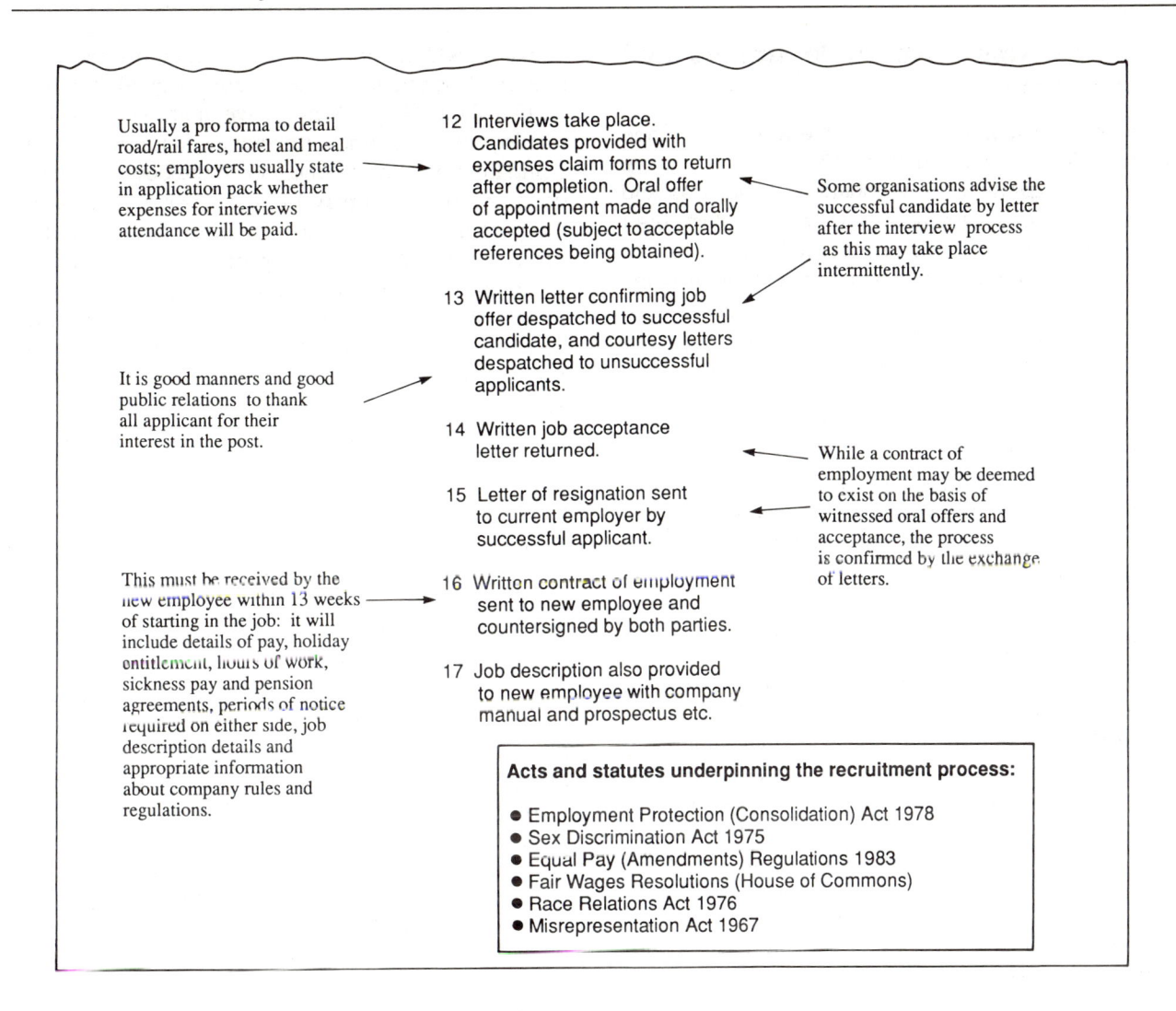

Usually a pro forma to detail road/rail fares, hotel and meal costs; employers usually state in application pack whether expenses for interviews attendance will be paid.

It is good manners and good public relations to thank all applicant for their interest in the post.

This must be received by the new employee within 13 weeks of starting in the job; it will include details of pay, holiday entitlement, hours of work, sickness pay and pension agreements, periods of notice required on either side, job description details and appropriate information about company rules and regulations.

12 Interviews take place. Candidates provided with expenses claim forms to return after completion. Oral offer of appointment made and orally accepted (subject to acceptable references being obtained).

13 Written letter confirming job offer despatched to successful candidate, and courtesy letters despatched to unsuccessful applicants.

14 Written job acceptance letter returned.

15 Letter of resignation sent to current employer by successful applicant.

16 Written contract of employment sent to new employee and countersigned by both parties.

17 Job description also provided to new employee with company manual and prospectus etc.

Some organisations advise the successful candidate by letter after the interview process as this may take place intermittently.

While a contract of employment may be deemed to exist on the basis of witnessed oral offers and acceptance, the process is confirmed by the exchange of letters.

Acts and statutes underpinning the recruitment process:

- Employment Protection (Consolidation) Act 1978
- Sex Discrimination Act 1975
- Equal Pay (Amendments) Regulations 1983
- Fair Wages Resolutions (House of Commons)
- Race Relations Act 1976
- Misrepresentation Act 1967

for a more senior post. They also help in assessing a job rating, which in some companies is directly related to pay scales – the more demanding the job, the more the pay. Thus all posts in a firm may be listed and given a reference, where the most junior job may be rated as 1, and managing director's as 35, along a continuous scale.

Employee appraisal and review

A personnel department, in liaison with respective departments, will devise, operate and update the organisation's personnel appraisal and review procedures. In brief, these usually take the form of an annual negotiation with each employee (where the job includes a degree of freedom of action and decision) to agree a set of objectives – to increase sales, efficiency or profit, or to reduce waste or employee turnover, etc – which are to be achieved within the next twelve months. At the same time, accepted changes in the employee's job tasks (**job description**, see below) may be made. During the year (at each quarter) a review interview is likely to be conducted to measure progress. Such appraisal and review procedures are linked to promotion, pay and bonuses in many firms.

Disciplinary and grievance procedures

The Employment Protection (Consolidation) Act of 1978 sets out a wide range of legal obligations an employer has to meet in order to provide employees with fair and just conditions of employment and safeguards against **unfair dismissal** and discrimination. As a result, it falls to a personnel department to administer the organisation's procedures for disciplining employees who have broken company and/or legal rules and instructions.

For example, an employee who smokes in a no smoking area of a petrol refinery is subject to instant dismissal for obvious reasons. On the other hand, an employee who arrives intermittently late for work because his wife is ill and there are small children at home may be justified in claiming unfair dismissal were he to be summarily dismissed. Because of the many grey areas in cases of disciplining staff, the law provides for a set machinery, known as a grievance procedure, to come into play which ensures a fair hearing, and ultimately, access to an industrial tribunal, a kind of employer/employee court, if matters have not been settled in the work place. Similarly, employees are entitled to oral and written warnings in any disciplinary process prior to being dismissed.

Relationships with trade unions and associations

Many organisations employ people who have joined trade unions or associations. They do so to have access to experts who negotiate their salaries and conditions of employment and who protect their interests in the event of a new technology or working practice being introduced by management, or when companies wish to cut back their workforces, and so on. Personnel departments employ staff who are expert in industrial relations and in negotiating with trade union officers. In this capacity, such staff act as spokespersons for the management viewpoint, but also relay the trade union's views to top management. While occasional strikes make the national headlines, it is the expert behind-the-scenes work of such personnel staff and their trade union counterparts which keeps the wheels of industry turning amicably.

Staff welfare and social activities

In a very different capacity the personnel department often supports and promotes the various clubs, recreational activities and social events which the employees of large organisations take part in. Enlightened companies regard this work as very important, since a workforce with a high morale works better, wastes and breaks less, and achieves higher output. In this context, a personnel department may also produce and distribute company newspapers and bulletins to keep employees up-to-date with company and staff activities.

Confidential counselling service

Many personnel departments also provide a confidential counselling service. For example, an attractive young woman working as a secretary might find herself subject to sexual harassment during the course of her work for a particular executive. In such stressful cases – and these may also include unfair and vindictive treatment of an employee by a superior, the personnel department can provide the means of offering unbiased and expert advice and of resolving the problem by prompt 'behind the scenes' action, such as transferring the secretary and thereby avoiding the loss (by resignation) of a valuable employee.

Pensions and retirement

Today, most large organisations operate pensions funds for their employees. Some firms offer non-contributory pensions where the employer funds the whole pension. Most operate a scheme which requires the employee to make a contribution with the employer. The government operates a State Earnings Related Pension Scheme (SERPS) and this is very often consolidated into the overall pensions package which the organisation administers via a specialist pensions assurance company. Multinationals like Shell, ICI or IBM may have thousands of former employees enjoying pensions funded by the company pension scheme and so the coordination of company pensions may be very demanding. Lastly the personnel department will often have responsibility for a company policy of preparing staff for retirement by reducing their workload and stress in a period of some three to five years preceding retirement. This may involve reducing the working week by a day a week for the five years prior to retirement and encouraging the development of hobbies and community activities.

Summary

As you can see, the work of a personnel department is varied and challenging. Its staff need interpersonal and communication skills of a high standard as well as expertise in negotiating and in long-term records administration. The effective secretary needs to possess an intelligent appreciation of the services offered by personnel. Access to personnel's non-confidential records may save you much time and effort, and you will gain expert support in areas such as recruitment, training and advice on handling staff problems.

Moreover, if you should join a small firm in a secretarial capacity, you may well find yourself carrying out a number of the activities outlined above, if on a smaller scale.

DISCUSSION TOPIC

Would you like to work in a company/organisation in which pay and 'perks' were linked to performance, and measured by job appraisal? If so, why? If not, why not?

CHECKLISTS OF MAJOR SECTIONS OF PERSONNEL FORMS AND SCHEDULES

Reproduced by kind permission of Waterlow Business Supplies.

Personnel requisition

Description of need
date needed:
job title and category:
recruitment salary range:
permanent/temporary:
full/part-time:

Reason for need
replacement or addition:
if replacement, give reasons:

Requirements
education:
qualifications:
experience:
other please specify:

Approval:

Date vacancy filled: Name:

Short application form for employment

Surname   Forenames
Address   Telephone Nos –
                      private/business
Date of birth   Nationality

Detail of any physical disabilities
Current clean driving licence?

Any criminal convictions other than a spent conviction under the Rehabilitation of Offenders Act 1974?

Employment:
  Position applied for:
  Pay expected:
  Would you work full-time? part-time? – state hours/week
  If offered this post would you work in any other capacity? – please detail
  Have you previously worked for us?
  On what date would you be available?

Note: An extended application form also asks for details of education, employment history, and personal/professional references.

Interview report (extract)

Candidates are rated in this way:

Poise

| Ill at ease, jumpy and nervous | Somewhat tense, easily irritated | Reasonably at ease | Self-assured | Extremely self-assured |

☐ ☐ ☐ ☐ ☐

(Interviewers tick an appropriate box)

The areas so rated are: appearance, poise, friendliness, personality, conversational ability, alertness, knowledge of field of work, qualifications, skill, experience, drive and initiative, overall.

Disciplinary warning record (checklist of contents)

Name/job/title/department/date of warning/
  expires on:
Date/time/reference of offence:
Classification of offence: eg incompetence/
bad work/abuse/lateness/insubordination/
  other

Details of offence:

Previous Warnings Not Expired Details:

Note: Such careful records need to be kept by a personnel department to satisfy the requirements of the Employment Protection (Consolidation) Act.

SPECIMEN JOB DESCRIPTION

JOB DESCRIPTION

Date: 12 January 19--   Previous Review Date: 15 June 19--

Job Title: Personal Secretary to
                    Deputy Sales Manager

Department: Home Sales Department

Location: Company Head Office

Responsible To: Deputy Sales Manager

Responsible For: Work of WP Assistant and
                    Office Information Assistant

Scope of Post: To provide secretarial services and informational support to the Deputy Sales Manager and to assist in administering the activities of the home sales force; to coordinate and supervise the work of the DSM's word processing and office information staff; to liaise with field sales personnel according to DSM's briefings and requests.

Major Responsibilities

1. To supervise the opening of correspondence and to ensure its prompt distribution according to house practices.

2. To transcribe and deliver as appropriate incoming fax, telex and Email messages.

3. To accept, transcribe (using appropriate media) and despatch DSM's correspondence, reports, memoranda and textual messages.

4. To maintain the DSM's electronic appointments and scheduling diaries efficiently.

5. To administer the DSM's paper and electronic filing systems effectively, and to ensure the security of all computer-stored data.

6. To supervise the operation of office equipment so as to maintain efficient, cost-effective and safe practices.

7. To make travel/accommodation arrangements for DSM and designated staff as required.

8. To administer the sales force expenses payment system and to maintain the DSM's office petty cash and purchases systems.

9. To maintain a cost-effective office stationery provision in liaison with the company's office administration manager.

10 To receive visitors and look after their comfort and hospitality needs.

11 To supervise the work of the DSM's office personnel so as to maintain good standards and timely completion of delegated tasks.

12 To monitor office practices and procedures and to advise the DSM on possible improvements and modifications in the light of changing office technology and information systems.

13 To ensure that office security is maintained and that confidences are not breached.

14 To promote an alert approach to HASAW matters at all times.

15 To undertake any reasonable task from time to time at the DSM's request as may be deemed appropriate within the scope of the post.

Equipment/Systems Responsibilities

Office Computer Terminals for safe operations and malfunction reporting.

Office fax, CABX extensions, photocopying and printing equipment for cost-effective and safe operations and malfunction reporting.

Office-held computer files for safe-keeping and prompt accessing and liaison with company DP manager for defect/malfunctioning reporting.

Education and Qualifications

General education to GCSE standard and vocational secretarial education to LCC Private Secretarial Certificate/NVQ Level 3.

Previous office information processing and secretarial experience essential; the post also requires developed interpersonal/communication skills and developed office applications software and telecommunications expertise as well as word processing proficiency.

Fig 6.1 Specimen form

Personnel Record update

NAME _____ DEPARTMENT _____ DATE _____

In order that we may keep our personnel records up-to-date, please show below any changes since
Date of Last Update _____ show changes only.

Address _____ Phone _____ Weight _____

Marital Status: _____

I have joined/left _____ Trade union

Number of dependants including yourself _____

Dates of birth of children born since last update _____

Have you joined/left our pension scheme? _____

Describe any physical defects you have developed since last update _____

Describe any major illness you have had since last update, explain _____

If you received compensation for injuries since last update, explain _____

Do you now have a car available for your own use? _____ Registration number _____

ADDITIONAL SCHOOLING OR SPECIAL TRAINING

Dates	School/college etc.	Name of course and brief description

New memberships in technical or professional societies _____

New professional offices or honours _____

Any other changes you would like us to note _____

Employee's signature _____ Reviewed by _____
Supervisor

NOTE TO SUPERVISOR: Describe on the reverse side any special projects or assignments which you feel have aided this employee's development and increased his value to the Company.

© Copyright 1963, 1968, 1979 — V. W. Eimicke Associates, Inc.
Produced by Waterlow Business Supplies (A Division of Oyez Stationery Ltd)
Oyez House, 16 Third Avenue, Denbigh West Industrial Estate, Bletchley, Milton Keynes MK1 1TE

Form 108
2/87

(Reproduced by kind permission of Waterlow Business Supplies)

Services and the secretary

SPECIMEN PERSONNEL SPECIFICATION FOR A PERSONAL SECRETARY

Personnel Specification

Date:
Date of previous review:
Job title: Personal secretary
Reporting to: Middle tier manager

Characteristics	Necessary	Helpful	Optional
Physical:			
20-20/Corrected vision	✓		
Good hearing	✓		
Manual dexterity for keyboarding	✓		
Good carriage and well-groomed appearance	✓		
Qualifications:			
RSA/LCC Secretarial Diploma/Certificate		✓	
Shorthand to 100 wpm	✓		
Typewriting to 40 wpm	✓		
Word processing to NVQ Level 2	✓		
Information processing to NVQ Level 2		✓	
English to GCSE A–C	✓		
French to GCSE A–C		✓	
Experience:			
Previous personal secretarial post		✓	
Coordination of overseas travel arrangements		✓	
Working under pressure to tight deadlines	✓		
Personality:			
Tact/discretion/confidentiality	✓		
Self-starter	✓		
Sense of humour		✓	
Interest/hobbies:			
Foreign languages		✓	
European culture			✓
Fashionwear/clothes		✓	
Circumstances:			
Able to start work 1.5.19—	✓		
Clean driving licence			✓
Willing to travel abroad		✓	
Willing to work late at times	✓		

Drawn up by: _____
Approved by: _____
Issue Date: _____

CONTENTS OF A CONTRACT OF EMPLOYMENT

By law, a new employee must receive a written contract of employment within thirteen weeks of starting in the job. The contract represents both the rights and obligations of the employer and employee. For the employee to work conscientiously, safely and loyally, and for the employer to pay salary/wages when due, to insure the employee and provide a safe working environment. Specifically, the contract of employment sets out the agreed hours of the working day and week, the amount of paid holiday entitlement, the intervals between pay days and the salary/pay structure agreed, as well as any arrangements for paid commission, bonuses or overtime worked. In addition, the contract will clearly set out the arrangements for pension payments and the extent and duration of sick pay. Also, agreed notice of termination of the contract on either side will be included.

The contract 'package' additionally includes clear details of the job which is to be done and any organisational rules and procedures which the employee must follow.

Note; As an employee's job and duties change, for example upon promotion or transfer, a revised job description or even a revised contract of employment should be given.

QUICK REVIEW QUIZ

1   List the major functions of a personnel department in a large company.

2   What do you understand by the term 'employee appraisal'?

3   What legal procedures are necessary before an employee may be dismissed for misconduct or breach of company regulations?

4   Make a checklist of the main activities which an employer undertakes in appointing a secretary to a senior manager.

5   Explain the difference between a personnel specification and a job description.

6   List what you consider the qualities and abilities an interviewer should assess in interviewing a secretary to work for four middle managers.

7   What are the principal features of a contract of employment?

8   What items do you consider to be of major importance in the design of a job application form for office staff?

9   How could IT aid the work of a personnel department?

RESEARCH AND REPORT BACK ASSIGNMENTS

1   In pairs, arrange to interview a personnel manager and ask what he/she sees as the most important services he/she manages and why. Find out how the personnel department organises its records management, and how it deals with staff problems and complaints, while seeing both management's and employees' viewpoints. Brief your group on your return on current personnel practice.

2   In pairs, collect a range of current display advertisements for secretarial posts from your local and national newspapers. Consider the commonly requested skills and abilities in them and what pay and conditions of service they offer. Discuss your findings within your group and how you measure up to market requirements.

3   Arrange in pairs to interview a local manager who is regularly involved in job application interviews. Ask how he/she organises personally and/or a panel of interviewers so as to be able to conduct effective interviews and what support services he/she requires from his/her secretary in the job application process. Make a checklist of your findings for distribution to your group, after having given them a 5-10 minute briefing.

6.2 Financial services

How PAYE income tax payments are calculated; payroll and pay as you earn; how to operate an imprest petty cash system; checklist of finance and accounting terms.

Small organisations, such as sole traders, partnerships and small private limited companies, frequently pay for a bank or a local firm of chartered accountants to produce their weekly/monthly payroll for their employees. Many small businesses are manufacturing or sales intensive and employ a minimum number of office staff. They therefore prefer to pay a fee to have the calculating and record-keeping associated with PAYE done for them. It is worth noting that most of the drudgery has been taken out of this work as a result of the development of **payroll software packages**. However, it is important that you acquire a sound understanding of the way in which PAYE (the pay-as-you-earn tax system for employees) is operated, since one day you may be asked to compute pay and deductions yourself.

This section also explains how an imprest petty cash system works and how it should be operated. While larger organisations naturally concentrate their financial transactions in an accounts department, it is common practice for departments to be allocated a cash 'float' from which to purchase incidental items. And again, maintaining the petty cash system may well fall to you.

Of all the external services a manager and secretary may call upon, those supplied by the major banks and **credit/leisure card** companies are in the first rank and deserve close study. This section therefore explains the various ways in which goods and services may be purchased 'on account' with different types of credit card, and then proceeds to examine the principal services of a **clearing bank** which touch most closely upon secretarial work.

While a great deal of secretarial work is concerned with words in their various applications, number work in the form of PAYE, petty cash, invoice checking, making up paying-in slips, etc, is an equally important secretarial skill to master. So, if you are more comfortable with words than numbers, you should concentrate especially hard on this area!

HOW PAYE INCOME TAX PAYMENTS ARE CALCULATED

1 New employee brings in P45 form

P45 Part 1: this is for the former employer. It provides details of the employee's total pay to date and tax paid on it; when completed to show the employee's move, Part 1 is sent by the former employer to his local PAYE tax office.

P45 parts 2 & 3: the employee gives these to the new employer. They provide details of the employee's previous PAYE reference, National Insurance Number, date of leaving last job and totals of pay and tax deducted. On Part 3, the new employer enters the new PAYE reference, starting date and particulars of the job and sends it to the local PAYE tax office.

Sometimes a new employee does not produce a P45. In this instance the employer must ask whether the employee has another job or has not worked before. The employee must then fill in a P46 and the employer complete a P15 for a code number to be obtained.

2 Tax Tables and P11 records summary schedule

In order to calculate the new employee's pay and income tax due (on a weekly or monthly basis), the PAYE clerk is provided by the Inland Revenue with two sets of tax tables, a P11 form and National Insurance tables for recording each set of payments made and deductions levied. Table A shows in a set of 52 weeks or 12 months how much pay free of tax the employee is entitled to according to his/her Tax Code. Tables B to D indicate how much tax each week or month is payable on the amount on which tax is due.

These calculations are summarised on form P11, along with the details of the National Insurance contributions paid by both employer and employee, on a sliding scale, depending on the amount earned. Also recorded are payments for contracted-out occupational pensions, any statutory sick pay or maternity pay. At the end of each tax year, the employer totals this information and sends it to the local PAYE tax office. At regular intervals, the employer pays the tax and insurance/pensions money deducted to the Collector of Taxes (in West Yorkshire).

3 Weekly or monthly payslip

The new employee is given a printed payslip (often produced by computer) which shows gross pay and net pay. Gross pay may include overtime, bonus, commission and any back pay due, as well as basic pay – on all of which tax is payable *after* deducting **superannuation/pension** contributions. As well as National Insurance contributions, other deductions may include: trade union subscriptions, social club fees, and any further deductions for previously unpaid tax.

Fig 6.2 P45 form

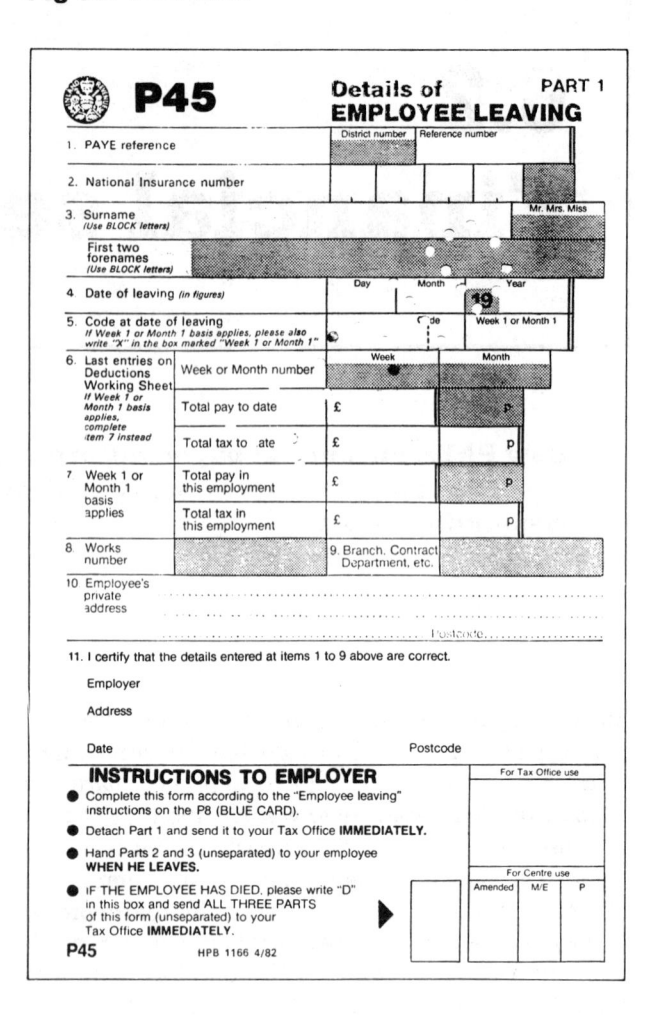

(Reproduced by kind permission of the Controller, HMSO)

4 A typical payslip looks like this

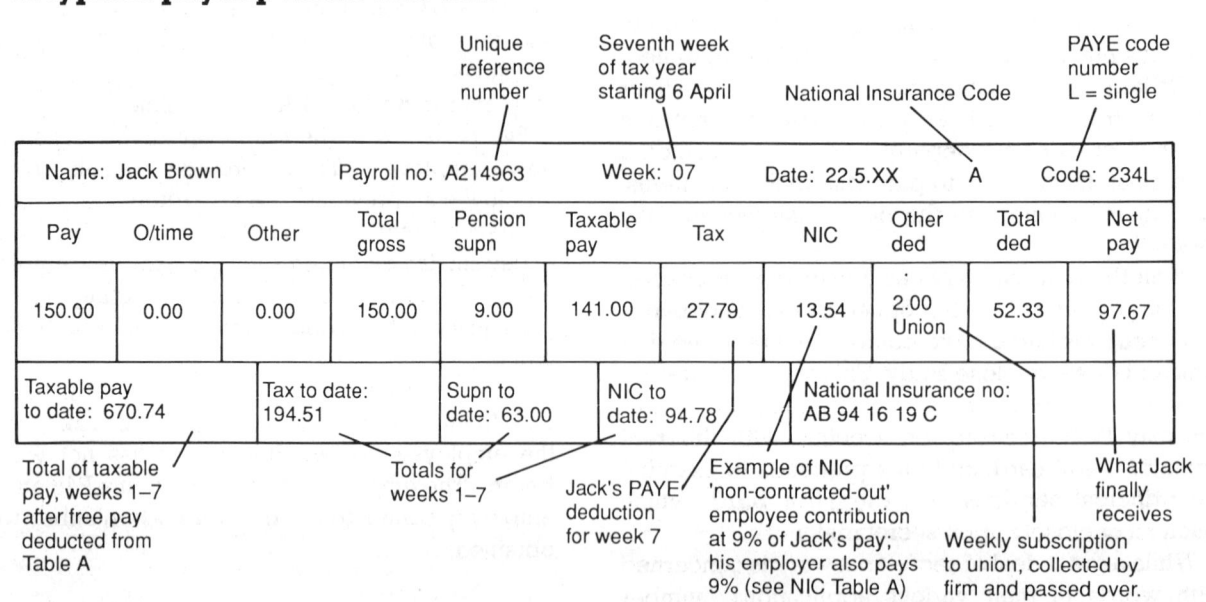

Name: Jack Brown			Payroll no: A214963		Week: 07		Date: 22.5.XX		A		Code: 234L
Pay	O/time	Other	Total gross	Pension supn	Taxable pay	Tax	NIC	Other ded	Total ded	Net pay
150.00	0.00	0.00	150.00	9.00	141.00	27.79	13.54	2.00 Union	52.33	97.67
Taxable pay to date: 670.74			Tax to date: 194.51		Supn to date: 63.00	NIC to date: 94.78		National Insurance no: AB 94 16 19 C		

- Unique reference number
- Seventh week of tax year starting 6 April
- National Insurance Code
- PAYE code number L = single
- Total of taxable pay, weeks 1–7 after free pay deducted from Table A
- Totals for weeks 1–7
- Jack's PAYE deduction for week 7
- Example of NIC 'non-contracted-out' employee contribution at 9% of Jack's pay; his employer also pays 9% (see NIC Table A)
- Weekly subscription to union, collected by firm and passed over.
- What Jack finally receives

Fig 6.3 P11 form showing tax to date

Example of PAYE section of form P11 from week 1 to week 7

Employee's surname *in CAPITALS* BROWN		First two forenames JACK DOUGLAS				
National Insurance no. AB 94 16 19 C	Date of birth *in figures* Day 19 Month 07 Year 67	Works no. etc A 214963			Date of leaving *in figures* Day Month Year	
Tax code † 234L	Amended code † Wk/Mth in which applied	6	4	19XX		

PAYE Income Tax

Week no	Pay in the week or month including Statutory Sick Pay/ Statutory Maternity Pay (2) £	Total pay to date (3) £	Total free pay to date as shown by Table A (4) £	Total taxable pay to date Ø (5) £	Total tax due to date as shown by Taxable Pay Tables (6) £	Tax deducted or refunded in the week or month Mark refunds 'R' (7) £	For employer's use
1	150 00	150 00	45 18	95 82	27 79	27 79	
2	150 00	300 00	90 36	191 64	55 57	27 78	
3	150 00	450 00	135 54	287 46	83 36	27 79	
4	150 00	600 00	180 72	383 28	111 15	27 79	
5	150 00	750 00	225 90	479 10	138 94	27 79	
6	150 00	900 00	271 08	574 92	166 72	27 78	
7	150 00	1050 00	316 26	670 74	194 51	27 79	
8							
9							
10							

Superannuation contribution of £9 per week deducted before calculating the taxable pay

(*Reproduced by kind permission of the Controller, HMSO*)

5 P60 annual summary

At the end of each tax year on 5 April, all employees are given a P60 form which confirms the total of their pay and PAYE deducted by the employer for that year; then the process starts again at week one.

PAYROLL AND PAY AS YOU EARN

In large companies, the weekly and monthly calculations of employees' pay and statutory deductions are carried out by specialist payroll accounts staff using payroll software application packages. However, in many smaller firms, secretaries may be expected to compute, deliver and record payroll details and to prepare payslips and salary/wages payments on a regular basis. This section, therefore, explains how pay is calculated and what Inland Revenue documents are used in the process.

Pay as you earn (PAYE)

In order to help employees pay their taxes and other deductions with a minimum of discomfort, both tax and National Insurance contributions (NICs) may be paid either on a weekly or monthly basis. Thus taxes due are 'paid as you earn'. The amount of income tax which an employee must pay each year is calculated as follows. Firstly the Chancellor of the Exchequer sets tax rates in pre-set tax bands. For example, someone earning up to £19,300 per annum will, at present, pay tax at the rate of 25%. Roughly speaking, one pound in four is collected as income tax. Above this amount, the tax rate jumps to 40% so that four pounds in ten are due to the Inland Revenue.

Then, the Chancellor also sets each year the earned income allowances which may be paid to the employee by the employer free of income tax. For example, the single person's earned income allowance is £2605 per annum free of tax at the time of writing, so that tax only starts to fall due on earnings beyond this amount. For a married couple, the sum is higher, at £4095 per annum. Thus an employee will pay tax on the net amount earned after the free pay allowances have been taken into account, and at the rates or bands of tax set by the Chancellor of the Exchequer according to income.

In order to calculate the amount of income tax due under PAYE arrangements, the following procedure is applied.

1 The employee must be in possession of a PAYE coding which will represent the total amount of earnings he/she is allowed to retain before tax is deducted. This code will be made up of certain allowances, such as single or married person's allowance, widows' or single parent families' and blind persons' allowances, etc. The code letter L is used to denote single persons, H to denote married persons and codes such as BR and NT stand for 'basic rate, no allowances' and 'no tax payable'. Thus a code of 260 L would mean that you are a single person entitled to the standard allowance. PAYE codes are issued or modified each year after the submission of an individual's tax return to the Inland Revenue.

2 Each year, or as required, the Inland Revenue issues tax tables to employers to help them calculate tax sums due from each employee, whether paid on a weekly or monthly basis. The PAYE tables are used as follows:

The income tax year commences on 6 April and so the tables are broken down into 52 weekly or 12 monthly periods from this date. The first table to be consulted is Table A. This table shows how much free pay an employee is entitled to on the basis of his/her PAYE code:

Week 1	Code	Total free pay to date
	234	45.18

Thus the amount of pay on which income tax is due from a person with a code of 234L in week one will be the amount of the basic pay *plus* any payments for overtime, bonuses, commissions, etc, *after* superannuation/pension payments have been deducted and also *after* that week's free pay amount (here 45.18) has also been deducted:

Basic pay	Overtime	Superannuation	Free pay	Taxable pay
200	30	13.80	45.18	171.02

As each week moves into the next, the sum of free pay allowable increases in equal stages, until in week 52, the full amount due has been allocated.

The next table to be consulted (Inland Revenue B–D) shows week by week (or month by month) the tax due on an accrued amount of pay – in other words, by week seven, taxable pay may have become £1160, on which the tax due will be £336.40.

In order to calculate the amount of tax due on a given pay week; the payroll clerk computes as follows:

1 What is the total pay due for week/month?
2 What is the total pay to date?
3 What is the total free pay to date (see Table A)?
4 What is the total of taxable pay to date?
5 What is the total of tax due on this amount (see Tables B–D)
6 How much tax has already been paid (accumulated) in previous tax weeks?

Thus: Tax due for the given week then equals the sum left after total tax already paid has been deducted from total tax due, and this tax payment is deducted from the taxable amount of weekly pay, along with other deductions.

These computations are recorded weekly/monthly on form P11 (see illustration on page 233).

National Insurance and other deductions

As well as being liable to pay income tax, the employee is also required to contribute (along with the employer) to the National Insurance scheme. This scheme funds both statutory sick pay and state pensions payments. It operates with an employee either 'contracted in' or 'contracted out'. If contracted in, then an employee will pay between nil and a small percentage of pay in a range of pay bands up to £305.00 per week and £27.45 a flat rate addition thereafter. If contracted out (which means that the employee pays into a state-approved private pension scheme) then the rates paid are slightly lower. In both 'in' or 'out' instances, the employer also makes a weekly contribution of a similar percentage. Employers also use weekly tables to compute NI contributions.

In addition, an employee may elect to pay into a personal pension scheme which the organisation operates. Occasionally the organisation may pay all the instalments but usually both sides contribute. In this case, the payments are deducted from gross pay before the taxable sum is arrived at.

As well as income tax, national insurance and pensions deductions, an employee's payslip may include deductions for a range of other items, such as a subscription to the social and/or sports club, outings or Christmas club fund and a regular trade union or association membership subscription which the firm may collect and pay over as a goodwill measure.

The employer pays the income tax and NIC amounts regularly to the local tax office and submits annual summaries of deductions levied.

Checklist of Inland Revenue 'P' forms

P1   Annual tax return
P2   Notice of PAYE coding
P7   Employer's guide to PAYE
P8   How to operate PAYE
P11 52 week record sheet for PAYE and NIC
P14 Annual PAYE employer's return
P45 Form to record PAYE details for leaving employee
P60 Form to summarise employee's annual pay and tax deducted

Methods of paying wages and salaries

Historically, millions of workers who were paid weekly received their pay in cash, together with their payslip in a sealed envelope, because the vast majority did not have a bank account. This method of paying wages was time-consuming because the cash had to be fetched from the bank and painstakingly divided into the correct amounts of notes and coins. Furthermore, the presence of large amounts of cash in transit or on employers' premises provided a significant security risk.

Today, very few employees are paid in cash. They either recieve their pay in the form of a cheque for banking in their own personal current accounts, or their pay is by **direct credit** to their bank account on a given day and only the payslip is provided at the workplace. This last method of payment is simplest and safest to operate and saves the clearing banks from having to clear millions of pay cheques each week.

HOW TO OPERATE AN IMPREST PETTY CASH SYSTEM

Virtually all departments in private and public sector organisations need to have direct access to modest sums of cash at regular intervals. The reasons are many and varied: to maintain a hospitality provision of coffee and biscuits, to make an emergency purchase of stationery between the regular supplier's visits, to pay for a junior member of staff's bus fare when delivering an urgent package across town and so on.

To meet such needs, the accounts department of the organisation provides a 'petty cash book' to each department which acts as an extension of the main cash book. The procedure for using the petty cash book is as follows:

1 The petty cash book is started up with an injection of cash from the firm's cashier. The amount decided upon varies according to the needs of the department which have been established over the year. The example below illustrates an initial injection or 'float' of cash of £50.00. The petty cash controller enters this amount in the 'Received' column and provides the cash book folio or page reference and

Fig 6.4 Example of a petty cash book

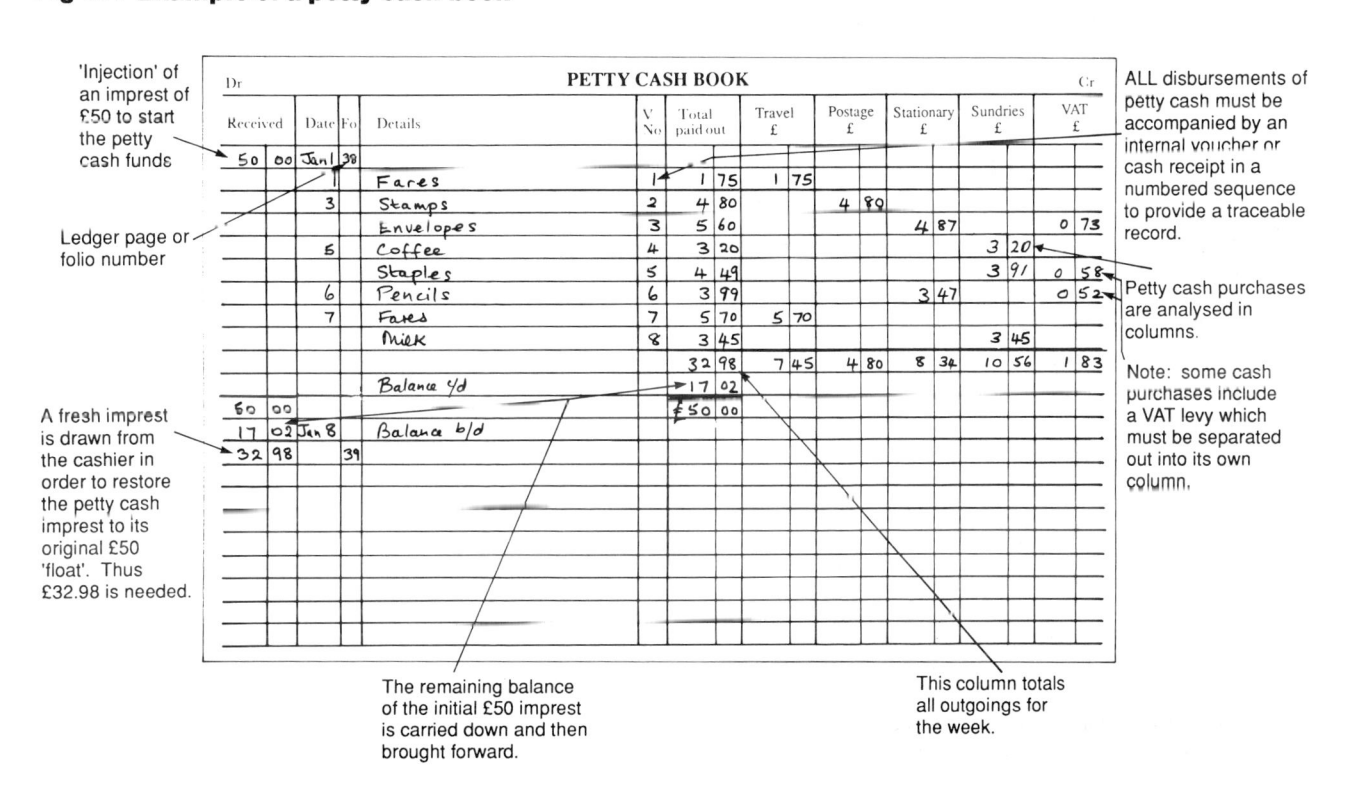

Received	Date	Fo	Details	V No	Total paid out	Travel £	Postage £	Stationary £	Sundries £	VAT £
50 00	Jan 1	38								
			Fares	1	1 75	1 75				
	3		Stamps	2	4 80		4 80			
			Envelopes	3	5 60			4 87		0 73
	5		Coffee	4	3 20				3 20	
			Staples	5	4 49				3 91	0 58
	6		Pencils	6	3 99			3 47		0 52
	7		Fares	7	5 70	5 70				
			Milk	8	3 45				3 45	
					32 98	7 45	4 80	8 34	10 56	1 83
			Balance c/d		17 02					
50 00					50 00					
17 02	Jan 8		Balance b/d							
32 98		39								

'Injection' of an imprest of £50 to start the petty cash funds

Ledger page or folio number

A fresh imprest is drawn from the cashier in order to restore the petty cash imprest to its original £50 'float'. Thus £32.98 is needed.

The remaining balance of the initial £50 imprest is carried down and then brought forward.

This column totals all outgoings for the week.

ALL disbursements of petty cash must be accompanied by an internal voucher or cash receipt in a numbered sequence to provide a traceable record.

Petty cash purchases are analysed in columns.

Note: some cash purchases include a VAT levy which must be separated out into its own column.

date. The £50.00 thus provided is called an imprest, which means an amount of money forming part of an ongoing series of allocations.

2 As the petty cash controller meets individual requests for cash – whether to buy stamps, pay for fares or replenish milk, tea or coffee, etc – a voucher, numbered in sequence, is issued and signed for by the recipient of the cash so as to provide a written record. The controller then enters the description of the purchase and the number of the issued voucher (or receipt which is given a number) into the 'paid' columns (see the example on page 235). Additionally, the amount is entered into one of a set of analysis columns so that the various headings of outgoings may be brought together for the organisation as a whole in its accounts ledgers.

3 At the end of the petty cash accounting period – or as the petty cash imprest needs topping up – the various purchases are totalled and a balance is carried down representing what is still unspent from the original imprest.

4 The petty cash controller then obtains a further imprest, being the amount of cash needed to restore the imprest to its original sum. In the example, the second imprest needed amounts to £32.98, which transaction is also recorded in the firm's cash book, or in its computer system.

In this way, a petty cash controller or responsible secretary is able to maintain a supply of small sums of cash for appropriate departmental needs for the duration of the financial year. As cash is involved, it is particularly important that due care be taken in maintaining the petty cash book and in issuing vouchers or obtaining receipts, so as to ensure that columns balance and that no sum of cash disappears from till or cash box which cannot be accounted for.

The imprest system and spreadsheet software

The recording of petty cash transactions is ideally suited to the computing and storing applications offered by even the most modest of spreadsheet packages.

The initial left-hand columns may be set up to record cash received, while the columns further to the right of the screen may be set up to detail amounts paid, voucher numbers and analysis columns in just the same arrangement as a petty cash book offers.

Additionally, the spreadsheet's ability to store numerical formulae used in repeated calculations enables the user to obtain running totals very simply and quickly. The process of carrying down and bringing forward is promptly keyed in and hard copies are available on demand, while the imprest may be speedily Emailed to the cashier for checking, along with a request for a top up!

Fig 6.5 Example of petty cash voucher

Such vouchers will be issued when staff request cash from the imprest system in order to make small purchases. The recipient of the cash signs for it and the request is authorised by the petty cashier.

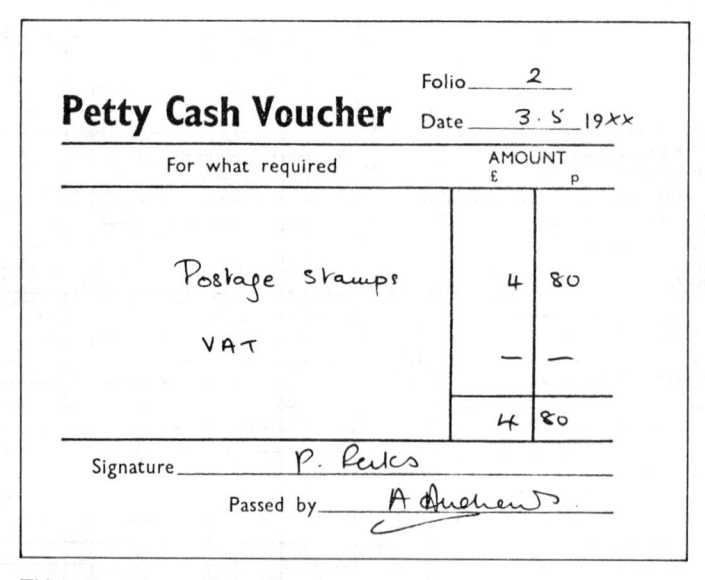

This transaction is recorded in the petty cash book.

Note: Retailer's receipts are also retained and used as petty cash vouchers in the same way.

Fig 6.6 The Smart Software System, composed of spreadsheet, word processor and database manager running under SCO XENIX V.

(*Photograph by courtesy of Wickes Associates International Limited*)

CHECKLIST OF FINANCE AND ACCOUNTING TERMS

advice note
A note which acts as proof of delivery by an organisation's driver, who retains a signed NCR copy for the accounts department; on many advice notes, the details of prices and discounts are omitted to maintain security.

assets
Valuable items such as money, goods, machinery and buildings, which are needed in order to run a business; 'fixed assets' commonly refer to plant and equipment (fixtures and fittings, buildings and vehicles, tools and machinery).

auditors
The Companies Acts require annual accounts to be vetted by authorised accountants prior to being passed on to the Inland Revenue. Public service organisations also employ auditors to monitor expenditure.

bad debt
The amount of money an account customer owes which is overdue for payment and likely to be difficult to recover.

balance sheet
An annual report which lists the various accounts a company has kept in terms of its assets and liabilities – what it owns and what it owes, together with details of shares issued if a public company.

bank reconciliation statement
A financial report drawn up by an organisation's accounts staff to compare the figures on the bank statement with its own records so as to check out any possible discrepancies.

capital
The money which is put up by a sole trader or shareholders to start a business or to inject more finance into it from time to time.

credit control
The activity of monitoring the payment of accounts by customers so as to avoid bad debts and to ensure that the organisation's cash flow (the availability of cash) is not adversely affected.

credit note
If delivered goods prove faulty or are invoiced in error, the accounts department will issue a credit note which has the effect of cancelling out a raised invoice; credit note details are included in statements.

creditor
A person or organisation to whom money is owed for goods or services received.

debtor
A person or firm owing money to the organisation for goods or services purchased.

depreciation
As machinery or equipment is used, its value decreases; depreciation is the cost of this decrease. At annual intervals accounts staff need to put on one side replacement monies to fund the purchase of new equipment, etc.

discount
A discount is a proportion of the customary sales price for a product or service which its seller is prepared to deduct – either for a cash payment or for the prompt settlement of, say, a monthly account – usually termed a settlement discount. A trade discount is applied to goods which are purchased by plumbers, builders, garages, etc, intended for retail resale.

double entry bookkeeping
A system which balances a company's books by posting all transactions into related debit and credit columns, depending on whether money is coming into or going out of the business.

drawings
When sole proprietors, partners or company directors take cash out of their organisations from time to time, these are referred to as drawings and must be accounted for.

financial reports
Senior company managers frequently require specific information on the company's financial situation and may need to know the amount of money tied up in account sales, the level of gross profit for the past quarter, the amount of money owed to creditors, etc.

folio
From the Latin for leaf, a term for a page of a ledger.

ledger
The accounts of a company were formerly kept in leather-bound books called ledgers; today the term ledger stands for a set of accounts – for purchases, sales or for the nominal ledger – which go to make up the complete set of accounts.

liabilities
Commonly monies owed by account customers, but also, in accounting terms money due to staff as pay, or to the bank as a loan.

nominal ledger
Used to record various headings of income and expenditure; sometimes called the general ledger.

purchase ledger
This ledger records all the various transactions relating to goods or services which the firm buys in or purchases: sometimes referred to as the bought ledger.

returns note
Customers unhappy with the quality of a product (eg damaged on delivery) may send it back to their supplier with an accompanying note for signature to act as a record of return.

sales ledger
This ledger records the sales transactions (of products or services) of the organisation.

statement
A listing on a particular type of accounts form of all the invoices issued to a customer using a given (usually monthly) accounting period, less the value of any raised credit note(s). The amount totalled at the foot of the statement is deemed payable, less any early settlement discount allowed.

stock card
Products which are stored pending sale are detailed and listed on cards (or on computer) and replacement orders are made when stock falls to predetermined 'minimum' levels; sometimes called a bin card.

stock requisition order
An order made out on a form to request that items be

Services and the secretary

Fig 6.7 Double-entry book-keeping

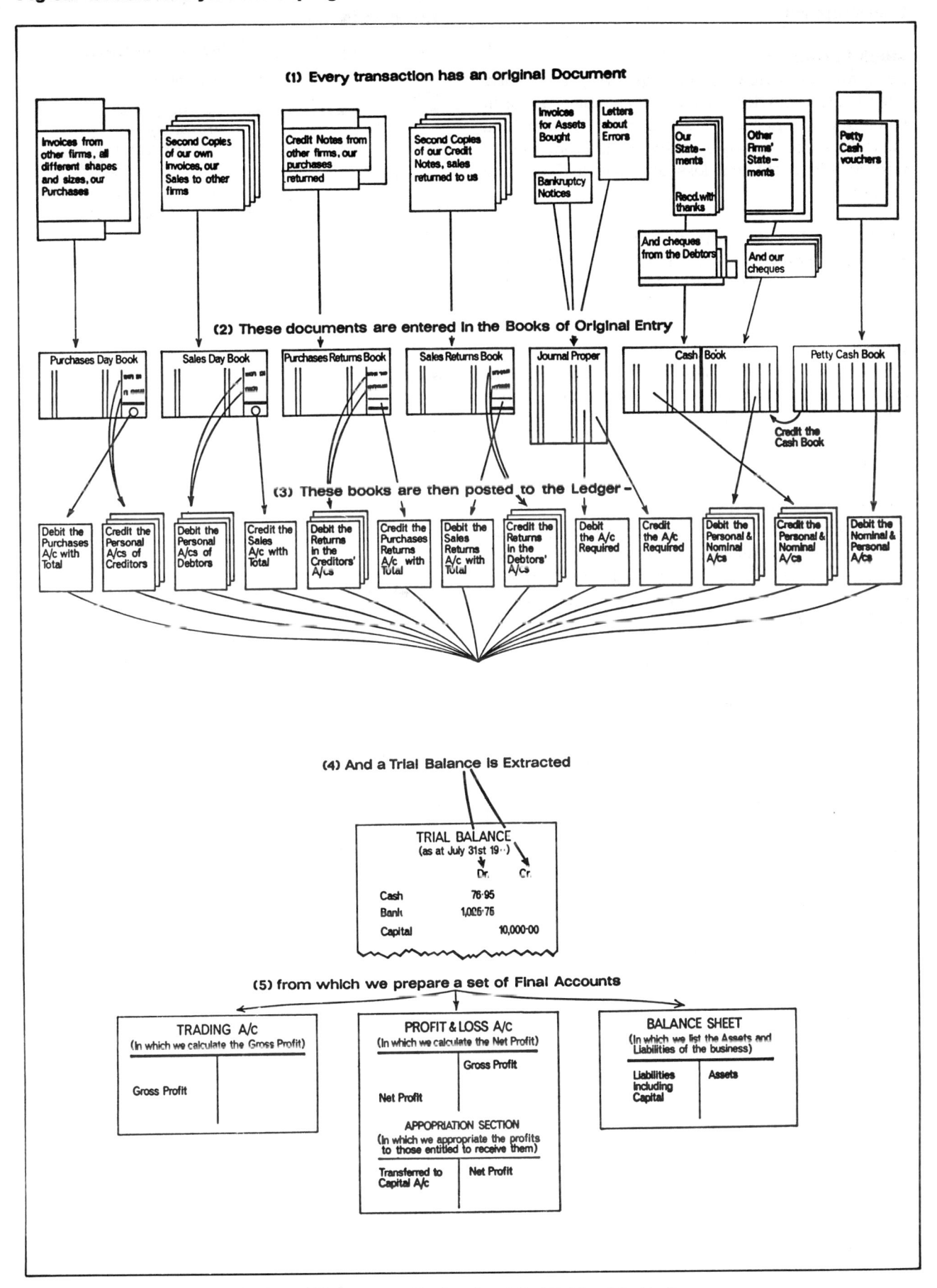

(Reproduced by kind permission of Heinemann Professional Publishing Limited)

supplied, either from existing stocks or by ordering from a supplier.

stock-taking
An operation carried out either quarterly, half-yearly or annually to check physically the amount of goods in stock and to price them, so as to know their total value. This operation is essential to the production of trading and profit and loss accounts and balance sheets.

trading and profit and loss accounts
A report drawn up to calculate the profits (or losses) a company has made, prior to preparation of the balance sheet.

trial balance
A monthly exercise carried out by accounts staff to check that no errors have occurred in compiling a month's set of accounts; the balance summarises the company's debit and credit transactions for the month.

value added tax (VAT)
A government tax which is levied at the point of sale and collected by manufacturers and retailers; it forms an added percentage of the sales value of the goods or services and is currently 15% for those items not exempted (or 'zero-rated').

Top secretary tip – financial terms
The financial aspects of business affect *all* who work in it. The above glossary sets out some of the principal terms used in accounting and finance circles. Make sure you note down fresh specialist terms you come across and familiarise yourself with them.

Specimen trading and profit and loss accounts

Trading Account

Sales		£37,500
Opening stock	£ 4,500	
+Purchases	£15,000	
	£19,500	
–Closing stock	£4,600	£14,900
		£22,600
–Direct labour costs		£10,000
–Gross profit		£12,600

Gross Profit Margin

$$\frac{\text{Gross profit } £12,600}{\text{Sales } £37,500} \times 100 = 34\%$$

Profit and Loss Account

Gross profit		£12,600
Business Salaries (including your own drawings)	£ 3,000	
+Rent	£ 1,000	
+Rent	£ 250	
+Light/heating	£ 250	
+Telephone/post	£ 250	
+Insurance	£ 250	
+Repairs	£ 1,000	
+Advertising	£ 750	
+Bank interest/HP	£ 750	
+Other expenses	£ 900	£ 8,400
–Net Profit		£ 4,200

Note for simplicity all figures shown are exclusive of VAT.

Reproduced by kind permission of Midland Bank PLC

Note
A trading account details the amount of gross profit generated from sales over a given period after allowance has been made for stocks held and purchases obtained as well as the costs during the period of direct labour (employees). The gross profit achieved in the example of £12 600 represents 34% of sales turnover.

The second account (for profit and loss) shows what further costs must be deducted from the gross profit to arrive at a sum for net profit. These amounts represent the routine costs of running the business, other than direct labour costs and purchases.

Fig 6.8 Balance sheet

Specimen Limited Company balance sheet as at 31 October 19X2

Remember that a balance sheet is like a snapshot and is only accurate for a single point in time, here 31/10/19X2

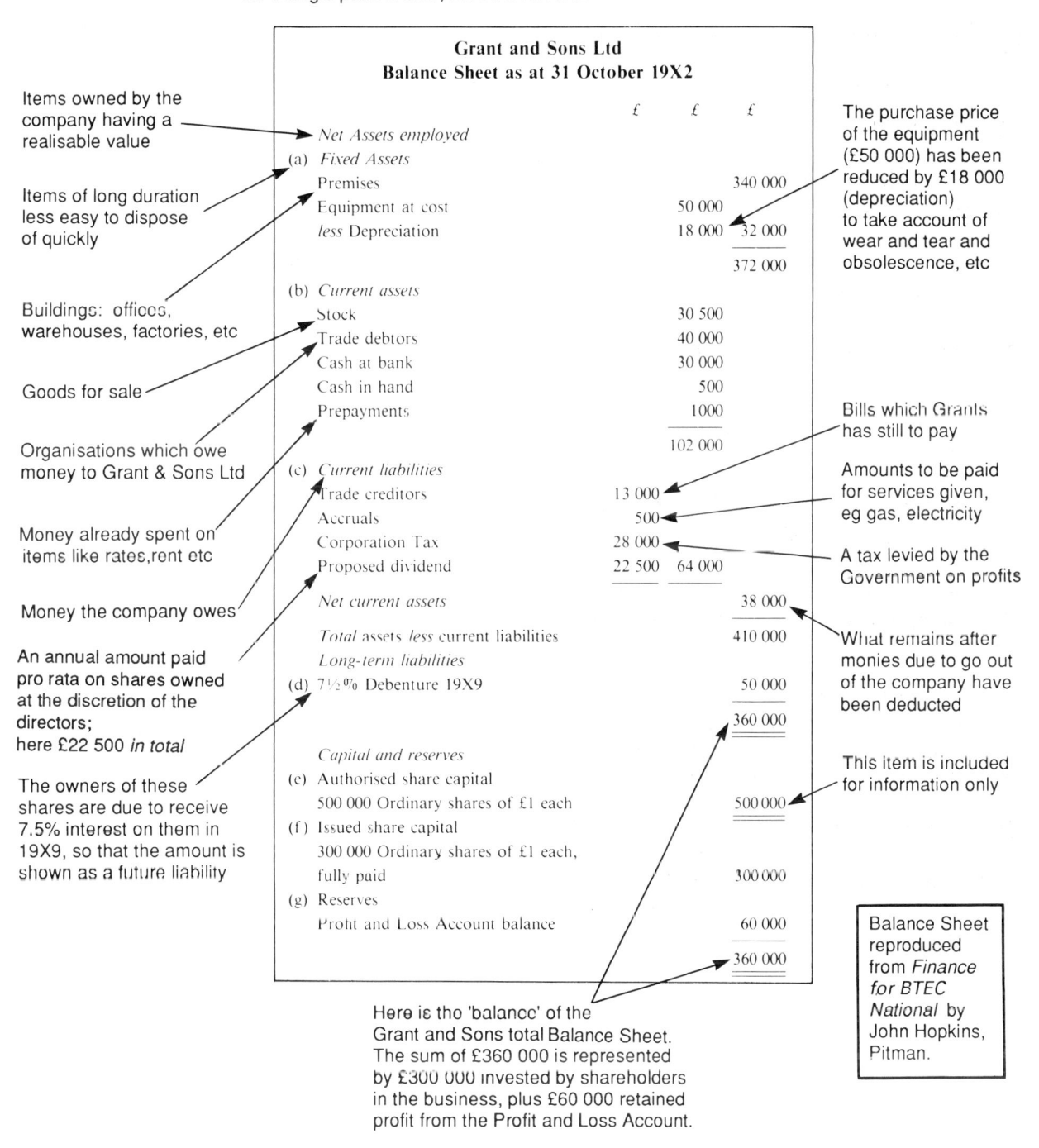

Grant and Sons Ltd
Balance Sheet as at 31 October 19X2

	£	£	£
Net Assets employed			
(a) *Fixed Assets*			
Premises			340 000
Equipment at cost		50 000	
less Depreciation		18 000	32 000
			372 000
(b) *Current assets*			
Stock		30 500	
Trade debtors		40 000	
Cash at bank		30 000	
Cash in hand		500	
Prepayments		1000	
		102 000	
(c) *Current liabilities*			
Trade creditors	13 000		
Accruals	500		
Corporation Tax	28 000		
Proposed dividend	22 500	64 000	
Net current assets			38 000
Total assets less current liabilities			410 000
Long-term liabilities			
(d) 7½% Debenture 19X9			50 000
			360 000
Capital and reserves			
(e) Authorised share capital			
500 000 Ordinary shares of £1 each			500 000
(f) Issued share capital			
300 000 Ordinary shares of £1 each, fully paid			300 000
(g) Reserves			
Profit and Loss Account balance			60 000
			360 000

Annotations (left side):
- Items owned by the company having a realisable value → *Net Assets employed*
- Items of long duration less easy to dispose of quickly → Fixed Assets
- Buildings: offices, warehouses, factories, etc → Premises
- Goods for sale → Stock
- Organisations which owe money to Grant & Sons Ltd → Trade debtors
- Money already spent on items like rates, rent etc → Prepayments
- Money the company owes → Current liabilities
- An annual amount paid pro rata on shares owned at the discretion of the directors; here £22 500 *in total* → Proposed dividend
- The owners of these shares are due to receive 7.5% interest on them in 19X9, so that the amount is shown as a future liability → 7½% Debenture 19X9

Annotations (right side):
- The purchase price of the equipment (£50 000) has been reduced by £18 000 (depreciation) to take account of wear and tear and obsolescence, etc
- Bills which Grants has still to pay → Trade creditors
- Amounts to be paid for services given, eg gas, electricity → Accruals
- A tax levied by the Government on profits → Corporation Tax
- What remains after monies due to go out of the company have been deducted → Net current assets
- This item is included for information only → Authorised share capital

Here is the 'balance' of the Grant and Sons total Balance Sheet. The sum of £360 000 is represented by £300 000 invested by shareholders in the business, plus £60 000 retained profit from the Profit and Loss Account.

To the expert eye, a Balance Sheet is like a 'frozen frame' picture showing how healthy and wealthy (or otherwise!) a company is.

> Balance Sheet reproduced from *Finance for BTEC National* by John Hopkins, Pitman.

QUICK REVIEW QUIZ

1 What is a P45 form used for?

2 Which Inland Revenue Tables are used to compute PAYE? How do they work?

3 List the components of a typical payslip.

4 What do the following stand for:

NIC, SERPS, PAYE.

5 Explain briefly how PAYE is calculated for a weekly-paid employee.

6 What are the following used for:

P2, P11, P14, P60.

7 What does the term 'imprest' mean?

8 Explain simply how a petty cash controller records the allocation of sums of petty cash.

RESEARCH AND REPORT BACK ASSIGNMENTS

1 Arrange to visit an organisation which administers its PAYE by computer. Find out how the process is administered and report back to your group.

2 Find out what services your local Inland Revenue tax office provides to local employers and employees. Give your group an oral briefing on your findings, using any documents you obtained.

3 See what diagrams and charts you can locate which readily explain how an accounts department works and how double-entry bookkeeping is carried out. Display what you find in your base room as a memory aid.

6.3 Banking services

Customer accounts; banking services related to the account; bank travel services; checklist of banking terms in general business use; the secretary and plastic money.

When banking services are referred to in a general business sense, what used to be called the 'Big Five Clearing Banks' are usually in mind. The term 'clearing' refers to the ability of such banks to clear customers' cheques – to pass the sums due from their own customer's account to the recipient's, which may be held in another clearing bank, and vice-versa.

You may also have contact with merchant banks during the course of your work as a PA/secretary. A merchant bank is a source of finance to businesses lent out at an interest rate. The merchant bank also deals in stocks and shares and may act in this way as a company's agent.

Today the number of the clearing banks has grown, and they are now formed into a Committee of London and Scottish Bankers. Such banks arrange for the 10 million or so cheques made out daily to be cleared every morning in London by a body called the Association of Payment Clearing Services (APACS).

In addition, many millions of transactions each year are cleared between banks by means of BACS – Bankers Automated Clearing Services Limited.

UK and EEC banks are also introducing interactive banking services via viewdata and/or PC networks to enable customers to obtain up-to-the-minute balances, to amend standing orders/direct debits and to give various instructions on the handling of their accounts. EFTPOS – Electronic Fund Transfer at Point of Sale – will undoubtedly mushroom in the next decade and allow card-holding customers to purchase goods which are paid for by moving funds directly by computer from the customer's to the seller's bank account at the time of sale. Latest prices of stocks and shares are already available on various forms of viewdata system and bank customers are soon likely to be able to access this service and to buy and sell electronically through their office desktop computer networked to the bank.

The volume of business which personal and business bank accounts has generated in the past decade has grown enormously and today banks could not function without extensive computer operations. This aspect of banking will continue to grow rapidly over the next decade and secretaries need to keep abreast of the many computer-based services which are available to aid managers and staff in the course of daily business affairs.

In a nutshell, the role of a clearing bank is to keep deposited money securely, to facilitate the transfer of money between customers and their creditors, to offer expert advice on financial matters and to provide customers with accurate records of their transactions on demand. In practice, however, banks offer a myriad of services and the following section outlines those which are most central and relevant to the secretary's work. It pays to keep an eye on the banking sections of newspapers and journals for news about banking innovations and new services.

CUSTOMER ACCOUNTS

While banks administer millions of personal accounts, our interest is in the commercial accounts maintained by both private and public sector organisations. These are:

- **The current account** Used to process daily business transactions where money passes into and out of the account (interest is paid to personal account customers with sufficient balances)

- **The deposit account** Used to store money not immediately needed on which interest is paid

- **The currency account** Used to maintain money in an overseas currency (by export/import firms).

Documenting the current account

Naturally, customers and their bankers need to ensure that details of all transactions are scrupulously monitored. So various forms and documents have been developed to record each phase of the inward and outward flow of money from the current account.

The cheque book

Current account customers are issued with a cheque book with which to make payments for goods or services purchased. Business cheque books may be ordered with 50/100 blank cheques and either crossed or uncrossed (see below). Each page of the book comprises a cheque stub (counterfoil) on which to record retained details of the cheque payment, and the tear-off cheque itself (although some banks have a counterfoil form at the front of the cheque book). The cheque has to be filled out carefully to avoid confusion and possible theft or fraud. The cheque writer enters the date, the name of the person or organisation to be paid, the amount in words and figures, and signs the cheque, (see example). Many cheque writers draw lines along unused sections of the cheque so that figures and amounts cannot easily be inserted or modified.

Additionally, the cheque includes over the signature space a printed version of the official name of the account – whether an individual's name or a business trading name. Companies operate various arrangements in which one or more directors or senior managers are required to sign cheques, in order to maintain security. Many businesses use 'continuous stationery' cheques and print these on computer.

Each cheque also includes three important reference numbers:

- the reference number of the bank branch, eg 20-99-93
- the individual number of the cheque, eg 500931
- the unique reference number of the account, eg 01234567

These numbers are printed across the bottom of the cheque in a format which is machine readable, essential to the cheque clearing process and to provide ready references.

Open and crossed cheques

Some cheques are printed with a pair of vertical

Fig 6.9 The components of a business cheque

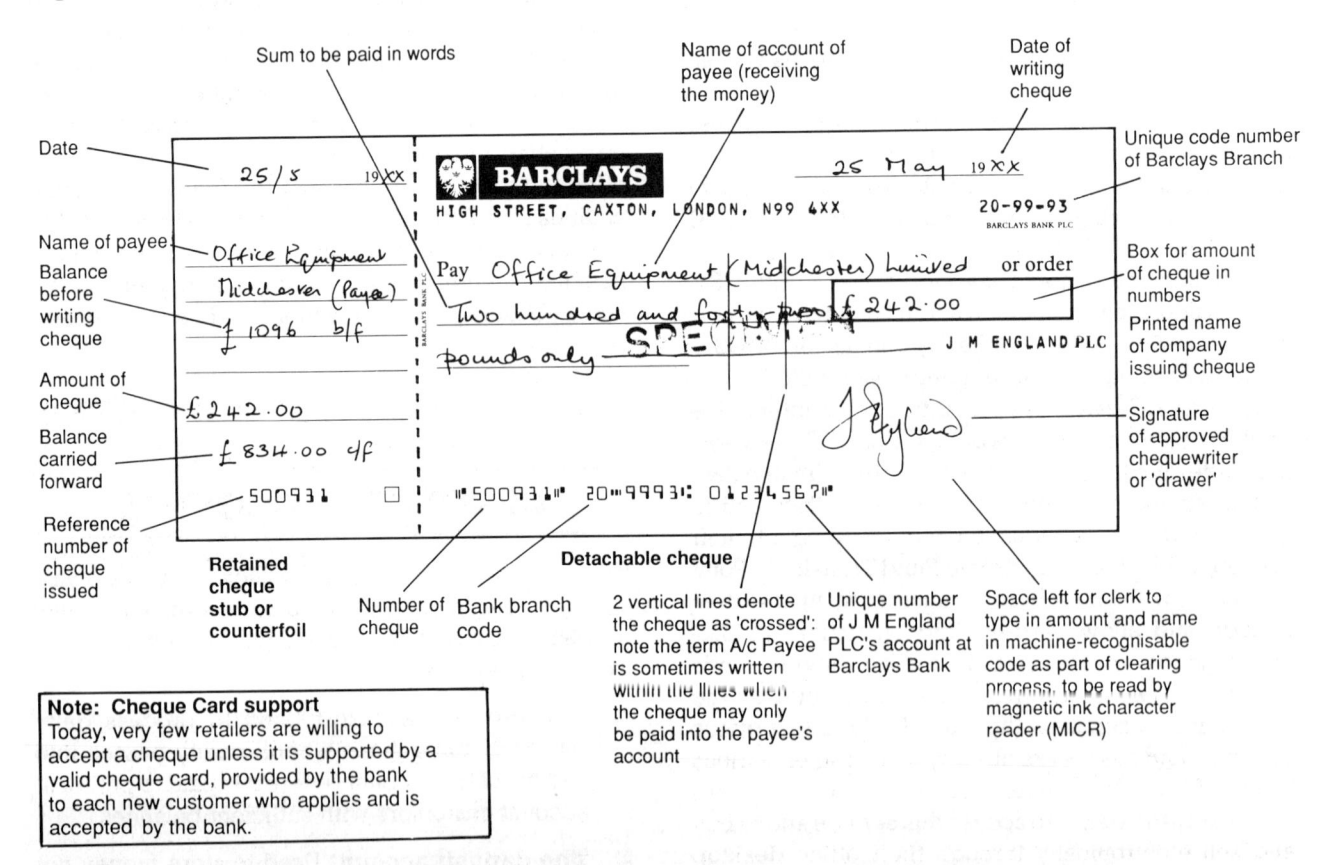

Note: Cheque Card support
Today, very few retailers are willing to accept a cheque unless it is supported by a valid cheque card, provided by the bank to each new customer who applies and is accepted by the bank.

(Reproduced by kind permission of Barclays Bank PLC)

Services and the secretary

parallel lines across the middle of the area in which the amount is written in words. They are referred to as crossed cheques. Such cheques must be paid into the recipient's bank account. This prevents cheques being converted into cash by someone illegally. Some companies write into the crossed area instructions such as:

- **A/C payee** This requires the cheque to be paid only into the account of the named recipient entered after the word 'Pay ...'
- **Not to exceed £X** This acts as a precaution to avoid more than the fixed sum specified being paid out against the cheque

Note: 'open' or uncrossed cheques are much less secure and most business cheques are crossed.

The clearing process normally takes three working days – before a company receiving payment by cheque can be sure the money has been transferred to its account. Special express clearance can be obtained on a cheque for a fee. While banks maintain personal accounts free of charge as long as they stay in credit, business accounts are charged fees which vary according to the amount of work done on behalf of the business customer. Such charges are shown as a cost on the monthly statement. Fees charged are regularly reviewed.

The paying-in slip or book

As shopkeepers and other businesses wish to secure their takings frequently, usually daily, they are issued with **paying-in books**. These take the form of tear-off slips and retained portions. Columns/boxes are pre-printed on each slip in which to total the amounts of various denominations of banknotes and coins and to enter the value of each cheque to be banked. The combined total is shown clearly. When paid into the bank, either over the counter or through a night safe, both the customer's and bank's portions of the paying-in slip are date-stamped to provide a record. All money – cheques or cash – paid in is carefully checked and credited to the current account on a daily basis, allowing for the cheque clearing period.

The statement

Normally, bank statements are compiled and posted to customers monthly, but individuals may secure alternative arrangements. Like the statement of account issued by an accounts department, the bank statement provides a record of transactions and shows a balance – in credit or overdrawn – which is correct at the time of issue.

A bank statement provides the following information:

- Name, address and account number of the account owner
- Sheet number in numerical sequence of each sheet of the statement
- Date of issue
- Type of Account, eg 'current'

The statement is divided into columns which detail the dates when cheques were cleared and posted to the statement, as well as the dates when payments into the account were received. Each cheque's number is shown, and the amount paid out is given in a withdrawal column; money coming into the account is shown by amount in a deposit column and details are also given of its particulars – a cheque paid in, a dividend from shareholdings, an automated band credit, etc. A column at the right-hand side of the statement shows a running balance total at intervals as money comes in and goes out, and a final balance is given. A number of abbreviations occur on statements, eg:

SO	Standing Order	OD	Overdrawn
TR	Transfer	AC	Automated Cash
DD	Direct Debit		(from dispenser)
EC	Eurocheque	CC	Cash or Cheques

At the foot of the statement the balance to be carried forward to the next sheet (due the following month) is clearly printed.

Note: We have already examined the process of bank reconciliation checks, and it is important to remember that the bank statement only records cheques presented and cleared; significant sums paid out may still be in the pipeline. Similarly, payments due may not have reached the statement production process. In order, therefore, for an accurate and up-to-date evaluation to be made of a company's or individual's financial position, cheques issued need to be cross-referenced (reconciled) to the statement and details taken into account of payments received after the statement was produced.

BANKING SERVICES RELATED TO THE ACCOUNT

As well as clearing cheques and maintaining a record of the account, banks also provide a valuable range of extra services.

Standing orders

Regularly occurring bills for gas, electricity, etc, may be paid automatically by making a standing order for the amount due to be paid to the creditor. On the appointed due day (each month, quarter, etc), the bank will pay the bill and amend the account accordingly. As such payments are electronically cleared, this procedure saves on time and paper.

Direct debits

Like standing orders, direct debits are authorisations given by the account customer for a bill to be paid and the amount debited from the customer's account. However, the direct debit date may vary from one month to another, and creditors may vary the amount billed without obtaining the customer's further authorisation. While this is helpful in saving time and administration, personal account customers running a tight monthly account could find themselves overdrawn by the unexpected increase of a direct debit.

Bank giro credits

A most helpful service for those in business faced with paying a series of bills together is the bank giro credit facility. The bank account number of the creditor and the amount due are made out on a pre-printed giro credit form. A single cheque is made out for all the giro credits to be paid, and is passed together with the giro credits to the cashier. The bank pays the bills by electronic clearance and details the transactions on the customer's statement. Many firms present their accounts to customers with tear-off bank giro credit forms included on the statement.

Security services: night safes and safe deposit boxes

While some businesses install their own safes to store money, most prefer to bank it at the end of each day's trading. For this purpose almost every bank branch provides a night safe facility. The completed paying-in slip, together with cash, notes and cheques, are locked into a special wallet and then loaded into the night safe's drawer. The night safe is accessed from the street and has a specially constructed drawer, opened by the customer's personal key. Open, the drawer can accept the wallet; as it closes, the drawer rolls round and releases the wallet into the bank's internal safe.

Night safe deposits are dealt with by bank staff first thing the next morning, and the paying-in book and wallet are then ready for collection and for the process to recommence.

Within the bank's vaults a number of safe deposit boxes are installed. These may be rented and documents, valuables, deeds, etc, may be kept safely in a fire-proof environment. The bank may make a charge to fetch up and redeliver items stored in such boxes.

Status enquiries

This term stands for those enquiries which banks make between themselves on behalf of their business clients, who need to ascertain discreetly whether someone wishing to open an account may be trusted and up to what amount, or whether for instance someone who is about to negotiate for the purchase of a property or its lease is reliable.

Loans and overdrafts

A large slice of a bank's profits stems from the loans it makes to its customers and from those accounts which are allowed to run on **overdraft** – 'in the red' – since interest charges are levied in both cases. An amount loaned is normally related to the recipient's ability to provide collateral – some form of security such as the deeds to your house which the bank can hold and convert into cash if repayments go by default. The interest charged on such loans is negotiable but will normally be several points above the current base rate.

Prudent customers usually give early warning if their account is likely to go into the red and secure an understanding with their bank managers about the amount of an overdraft to be carried and its duration. Overdrafts also attract interest charges and, while not inexpensive to maintain, may be cheaper than other forms of loan such as hire-purchase or credit card purchase.

Loans by banks to overseas customers and governments can be made by computer, using the SWIFT system (the Society for Worldwide Interbank Telecommunications).

BANK TRAVEL SERVICES

Foreign currency

Most larger bank branches include a foreign desk which deals with customers' overseas financial requirements. Frequently these include obtaining foreign currency ahead of foreign holidays or business trips. Customers receive the exchange rate current when the currency is made up; its value may be debited to a current account or it may be exchanged for cash. A small commission is charged for this service.

Traveller's cheques

The foreign desk will also provide traveller's cheques in various denominations. They are similar to conventional cheques but need to be signed by the user in advance; at the time of encashing at a foreign bank, they are signed again in the presence of the cashier and the signatures are compared. The reference numbers of the cheques are carried separately, and if lost or stolen, they can be directly cancelled and their value reinstated to the traveller. Traveller's cheques may be obtained in pounds sterling or local currencies or in a currency of your choice (eg US $)

but this involves paying the commission twice! Note that foreign banks usually require to see the owner's passport when the cheques are encashed, and also, as a commission is charged for each encashment, it pays to restrict these and to use larger denomination cheques.

Eurocheques and cheque cards

Some 40 western European countries accept Eurocheques supported by Eurocheque cards. These are supplied upon request just like their UK counterparts. Goods or services may be purchased in the same way and amounts made out in the local currency. Eventually the cheques are cleared back in the UK and the amount, converted into sterling, debited from one's account in the normal way.

Eurocheques are very popular since they are extremely simple to handle and used as required without forward planning. Local value added tax on goods purchased and brought back to the UK can be reclaimed at airports and border customs offices.

In addition, the foreign desk will telex money credits to overseas banks for a commission. This service is useful for those abroad who need to access funds unexpectedly.

Much of the foreign desk's work lies in assisting the exporting and importing activities of companies which need to have a range of letters of credit, bills for collection and other specialist means of guaranteeing payment and credit worthiness exchanged between themselves, their agents and customers.

Checklist of further bank services

In addition to those services detailed above, the major banks also provide specialised services in these areas:

- Drawing up of wills and undertaking **trusteeship**
- All kinds of tax advice and tax planning and pensions advice
- Stocks and shares purchase and sale for customers
- Insurance brokerage across the spectrum of business needs such as employers' liability, fire, theft, stock and motor vehicle cover
- Full payroll and computer bureau services
- Export/import advice and assistance
- Credit card business with retailers and service industries
- Provision of commercial and personal mortgages

CHECKLIST OF BANKING TERMS IN GENERAL BUSINESS USE

APR
Annual Percentage Rate – the annual interest amount (eg 26.3%) payable by monthly instalments on a loan.

bank charges
In effect a quarterly bill, debited to the customer's account for work done in clearing cheques, paying standing orders, etc. These vary and are fiercely negotiated by firms!

banker's draft
A type of cheque which the bank issues (in the name of a payee), having debited the amount from the account of the customer, who wishes to use it to pay for a transaction: it is 'gold plated' because it will not 'bounce'!

bounce
A colloquial verb used to describe a cheque which has been written (uttered is the specialist term) without enough cash in the account to cover it, and so is 'bounced' back to its receiver (payee) by the bank.

cheque card
A plastic card issued to account customers which possesses a unique reference number; this is written or stamped onto the back of the cheque and provides the bank's guarantee of payment up to approved levels between £50 and £200.

express clearance
An overnight service to obtain rapid confirmation that funds exist to cover a written cheque.

gold card
Some banks issue (for an annual fee) a card to high earning customers which provides them with extensive credit facilities and superior services like being overdrawn without incurring charges.

joint account
An account containing funds accessible by two or more people from cheque books showing the names of the drawers.

OD
Two dreaded letters which stand for overdrawn against each such sum on a statement, representing a cheque issued without enough money in the account to cover it.

PIN
Personal Identification Number, keyed into cash

dispenser keyboards as part of the process of obtaining cash. Always to be kept a personal secret!

post-dated cheque
A cheque with a future date written on it, by which time the drawer hopes to have enough funds in the account to cover it. Note that it is illegal to write a cheque knowing that you do not have enough money to support it; most retailers will not accept post-dated cheques.

refer to drawer
Another dreaded term, usually stamped on the back of a cheque which the bank returns to its payee because the clearing process has discovered that the drawer has insufficient funds to honour it. The payee can re-present it once the drawer has rectified matters.

stops
A cheque drawer can instruct the bank to stop a cheque, ie halt the cheque clearing process, if, for some reason – faulty goods or some dissatisfaction – the drawer does not wish to pay on the cheque already issued. Note: Cheques supported by cheque cards cannot be stopped.

trustee
A term to describe a person, or the bank itself, who carries out duties on behalf of someone, arising usually from a person's will; the trustee will monitor and effect a variety of transactions according to the terms of the trust.

Remember to add to this glossary the banking terms you encounter!

ASSIGNMENT: DECIPHERING 'BANKSPEAK'!

In pairs, find out what the following stand for:

CHAPS, MICR, BACS, APACS, EFTPOS.

Then, having made brief notes on each, give a five-minute talk to your group on how your chosen topic contributes to efficient banking services.

THE SECRETARY AND PLASTIC MONEY

The popular term 'plastic money' was coined a number of years ago to describe the range of credit and leisure/debit cards like Access, Barclaycard, American Express and Diners Club, which could be tendered to retailers for goods and services. Sooner or later, of course, the credit given on the security of the cards has to be backed up by the transfer of real money from the credit card user's bank account to the retailer's through the transfer services of the credit card companies. Today the term 'plastic money' has become much more generalised and used to describe a wide range of purchasing activities which do not rely upon cash or cheque payments. This section describes the various types of plastic card currently in use and considers their uses in the business lives of the manager and secretary.

Cheque guarantee cards

Firstly it is important to distinguish between a credit card and a cheque guarantee card. The cheque guarantee card was introduced in order to reassure retailers that the person paying by cheque had sufficient funds in a current account to cover the purchase. The CGC guaranteed the retailer that a purchase of up to £50 would be paid for by the customer's bank if need be. Thus the retailer was paid while the bank and customer sorted out any shortage of cash in the latter's current account. The shop assistant writes down the number of the card on the reverse of the cheque as a means of verifying the guarantee. Once this cheque has been guaranteed in this way, the bank will not stop it – even at the customer's request. One criticism of the CGC lies in its low per transaction limit. As a consequence, more and more consumers are using credit cards to make purchases and so accessing larger amounts of credit (some gold star card users may be given up to £10 000 of credit buying power), while also gaining time before payment falls due. Some banks issue cards which act as both cheque guarantee cards and credit cards.

Credit cards

Credit cards were introduced into the UK in the early 20th century as a means of reassuring hoteliers and shopkeepers that a person could sign for goods and pay up on the presentation of an account. This same principle still applies today. Both clearing banks and independent credit companies issue credit cards to individuals after careful vetting and taking up of references. The amount of credit – the credit limit – for an individual depends upon earning power or the amount of money in savings accounts, etc. At the point of credit sale, the credit card owner presents the card and its details, including the unique reference number, are imprinted upon the special receipt form supplied to record the transaction. The customer signs the receipt and keeps one copy as a record, the retailer keeps another, and posts a third to the credit card company to obtain payment. It is worth noting that the retailer pays a fee to the credit card company for each transaction, deemed worthwhile for the extra business credit cards generate. At monthly intervals, the credit card company sends a statement of account showing all the transactions made to the credit customer. The credit customer pays this account, usually by cheque from a bank account. Provided it is paid within the time limit shown on the statement, no interest charges are incurred. If, however, the customer delays payment, for say a month, another statement will be sent detailing the same charges but with an additional 1-2% of the value of the purchases added to it. It is therefore most important for all such credit card users to appreciate that an annual percentage rate (APR) applies to all credit card purchases, usually of some 22%-34%. Thus banks and credit card companies are happy for payments to be deferred or for minimum monthly part-payments to be made, since they earn money from the interest rates they then apply each month.

Where travellers purchase foreign banknotes with credit cards, the interest charges are applied from the date of purchase.

Both credit and leisure/debit cards are popular with business executives and their secretaries since they enable company and personal expenditure to be clearly divided. They allow job-related purchases, such as expenses, to be paid for in arrears separately and with each transaction fully documented. By the same token, they release the travelling manager from having to carry large amounts of cash, while providing flexibility and reassurance that unexpected expenditure can be met without embarrassment. New clients may be taken out to dinner, or cash obtained from the bank on presentation of the credit card. Furthermore, major credit card issuers have gone to great pains to ensure that their cards are acceptable in various overseas countries. In terms of comparative value, it is worth noting that some cards may be obtained gratis, while others have to be purchased by an annual subscription, and the trade off may be in the extent of their acceptance and the extent of credit authorised.

ATM/cash dispenser cards

For some years now, bank customers have been able to obtain cash from the automated teller machines (ATMs) by inserting an ATM or bank service card and keying in a personal identification number (PIN) and the amount required. The machine first reads the card's reference number from its magnetic strip and then checks on the bank's central computer to ensure that the customer has sufficient funds in the account to cover the cash withdrawal. This being the case, the requested amount of banknotes is released, together with a receipt. ATMs enable customers of major banks to access cash over a 24-hour day, seven-day week from most of their national network of branches.

Debit cards

Comparatively new, debit cards are in many ways similar to credit cards. They are preferred to the retailer and enable the transfer of funds from the shopper's bank account to the retailer's, by activating computerised electronic fund transfer in the same way as the ATM card. Problems between the major banks and retail servicing companies arose over differences as to who should bear the costs of administration, but the debit card is certain to become more widely used. However, the credit card still retains the advantage of deferring the debit of the customer's account for an extended period.

Smart cards

These are the most sophisticated cards available and include in their construction silicon chips which enable them to store as many as 800 banking transactions. Some cards embody display panels and keying in facilities and provide confirmation to both purchaser and retailer that sufficient funds exist (at the bank) to pay for a particular purchase. The card issues a unique number as a reference and this is all the sales person has to note to ensure that the customer's bank passes the sum due to the retailer's bank!

Charge account cards

Large stores and businesses now increasingly offer their own credit cards for account purchasing. These work very much like the credit cards outlined above but may embody better or worse interest charges, and credit limits, etc.

Phone cards

In an effort to reduce the robbing of coin-operated public telephones, many countries now provide card-operated equivalents. Customers purchase plastic cards issued by telephone companies in advance which contain a time value. The cards are inserted into the telephone call-box and, as calls are made, the time value of the card is erased from the card until it expires.

Telephone credit cards

National and international telephone calls may be made both at home and abroad by quoting the reference number of the user's telephone credit card to the operator. The cost of the call is monitored and, with a supplementary fee, added to the quarterly telephone bill with which the credit card is associated.

Top secretary tip – credit cards

It is extremely worrying for all involved if a manager should lose company or personal credit cards or have them stolen. A number of specialist companies (and clearing banks) now offer a completely confidential service for credit card users. They store all the reference numbers of the user's plastic cards and operate a 24-hour stand-by service in case cards are lost or stolen.

Once having received a telephone call from the card owner, such companies will promptly advise banks and credit card companies to cancel the currency of the cards, thus minimising the risk of the owner becoming liable for any purchases made on stolen cards. Some will also arrange the direct reissue of new cards.

Such precautions are well worth promoting to your manager.

DISCUSSION TOPIC

Do you think that the clearing banks and building societies are meeting the needs of business and busy office workers? What additional or different services would you introduce?

QUICK REVIEW QUIZ

1 What do you understand by the following:

bank reconciliation statement, capital, depreciation, drawings, folio, trial balance, trading account, profit and loss account, balance sheet.

2 What ledgers are typically kept in a company? Explain briefly what each is for.

3 What types of account might an import-export business be expected to hold in a bank?

4 Describe the process known as 'clearing a cheque'.

5 What essential information should a completed cheque supply?

6 What does 'crossed a/c payee' mean?

7 What do the following stand for:

OD, RD, DR, DD, CR, EC, CC, SO, AC.

8 Explain how the bank giro credit system works.

9 What service can the businessman obtain from Eurocheques?

10 What are status enquiries?

11 Makes a list of the major services a bank offers to businesses.

12 What services are provided by:

EFTPOS, SWIFT, CHAPS, ATMs, BACS.

13 What are the following used for:

a banker's draft, a PIN, a night safe wallet.

14 Explain the difference between:

a cheque guarantee card, a credit card, a cash dispenser card, a charge card.

15 What services will be available through the use of debit and Smart cards?

RESEARCH AND REPORT BACK ASSIGNMENTS

1 Invite a bank manager or one of his/her deputies to give your group a talk on what services the branch provides for local businesses. Take notes during the talk and produce from them a short account, emphasising key points for your revision notes.

2 In pairs, arrange to visit a local bank *or* building society and find out how their work is aided by IT systems and equipment. Brief your group orally on your return, and compare notes.

3 Interview a local manager and secretary who make regular use of credit cards in the course of their work. Find out what tips and guidelines they can offer as a result of their experience. Record your findings in a short account and copy it to your fellow students.

6.4 Post Office services

Mailing letters and parcels; other services.

A central part of every secretary's role is to ensure that outgoing letters, packets and parcels reach their destinations as quickly, safely and cost effectively as possible.

Equally, as an effective secretary you will need to be aware of the wide range of supportive services which external agencies like the Post Office offer in the general area of message and materials distribution.

This section outlines the principal services which the Post Office currently offers to business and public service organisations and with which you need to become fully familiar. The range and extent of the Post Office's services are always being improved and so you should make time in your working day to update your knowledge.

MAILING LETTERS AND PARCELS

Letters

The inland letter service operates on a two-tier basis of first and second-class mail. The Post Office aims to deliver 90% of first class mail by the next working day and 96% of second class mail by the third working day after posting. Currently first-class letter post up to 60 grams weight costs about 40% more than second-class letter post. There is no weight limit imposed on first-class mail, but a PO maximum envelope size is 610 mm long by 460 mm wide.

It is important to check out the latest posting times at your local main post office for UK regional centres, as this will affect the PO's ability to deliver as outlined above. It is also useful to know that post offices sell 220 mm × 110 mm pre-stamped envelopes in packs of ten for your manager's or your own briefcase for business trip use, etc. Most post offices also provide multi-denominational stamp book dispensers for quick access.

Registered letters and recorded delivery

While it is possible to obtain a free certificate of posting on request for any letter or card, the Post Office provides two services which are most useful for certain situations – for example posting a final demand for payment. Here, the sending of a final letter of collection may be effected by recorded delivery. The sender receives a receipt from the Post Office to certify posting and the recipient is required to sign for the delivery of the item.

Whenever items of value or those needing security are to be posted, it is wise to send them as registered mail. Registered envelopes may be purchased from a local post office and an additional surcharge is levied. Registered letters may also be insured with the Post Office according to a tariff of values and fees. Again, the recipient is obliged to sign for the acceptance of a registered letter.

These services are also available for overseas letters.

Compensation

Provided a certificate of posting is obtained, compensation may be applied for in the event of a letter being lost or damaged. Also, the Post Office itself pays out compensation on certain of its postal services if delivery deadlines are not met.

International letters

Letters to countries in the European Community do not need airmail stickers or to be sent in airmail envelopes, and the same first-class postage rates apply for letters not exceeding 20g weight. The Post Office offers compensation and insurance services for overseas mail like those of its inland service.

Letters posted outside the European Community region are charged at A, B and C tariffs, depending on distance and airmail costs, etc. Such letter charges increase at 10 gram weight intervals. The Post Office's annually produced *Post Office Guide* supplies full details regarding international postage rates and conditions, including what items are prohibited.

Note: Non-urgent letters and packets may be sent by surface mail at cheaper rates, but delivery takes weeks, rather than days.

Urgent delivery needs

The PO offers a range of inland services for letters requiring urgent delivery.

Special delivery: A surcharge is made in addition to first-class postage costs and, provided the item is posted before the latest posting times, it will be delivered individually if it should miss the next working day's first delivery. A certificate of posting is also provided, and such letters must be taken to a post office.

Express delivery: such letters are delivered on arrival at their destination post offices by special courier in normal working hours. Letters (or packages) must be taken to a local post office and a surcharge is made in addition to normal postal costs.

Railway letters: In some parts of the UK letters may be delivered to railway stations for despatch on the next train to another station for collection.

Datapost: Designed for packages rather than letters, the Datapost service offers 'sameday' or 'overnight' money-back guaranteed delivery. A package weighing from 1–10 kgs costs some £13 to deliver. Items are generally delivered by 10.00 am or 12.00 pm. A full informational booklet is available from the Post Office.

Overseas urgent delivery

Datapost: Also available internationally, where European and Rest of World tariffs operate on items weighing from half a kilogram upwards. Datapost packages require a green customs C1 label to be completed for business papers or a PP69 or PP70 customs declaration form for goods. Datapost provides a comprehensive booklet on procedures and delivery details, etc.

Airway letters: Some airports provide a service by which letters may be despatched on the next departing aeroplane; normal postage is affixed and the airline makes a surcharge.

Swiftair: The Swiftair service, available on airmail items to some 135 countries, aims to deliver to such countries by the next day and to be at least a day faster than normal airmail. The airmail postage surcharge for this service is very reasonable (a standard £1.50 at present). The Swiftair service is obtainable at all post offices.

Parcels

The Post Office offers an inland parcel service at two rates, national and area. Costs are tiered at kilogram intervals. The area rate is applied to groupings of adjacent counties and the term 'county parcels' is used. Currently it costs a little extra to send a parcel nationally rather than within a local area. A three-day maximum delivery time is currently advertised for anywhere in the UK. The Datapost service is also available for parcels.

The Post Office offers special rates for bulk, contract parcel senders and has introduced 'Superservice' for inland parcels, where 48-hour delivery is guaranteed and a fleet of 1000 vehicles employed. A 'Nightrider' overnight parcel delivery service is also now available.

OTHER SERVICES

Girobank

Due to be privatised, the Post Office's Girobank plc offers a wide range of banking services to users through some 20 000 UK PO branches. These services include current and deposit account facilities, personal loans, credit extension, insurance, Visa-based credit card and the LINK cash dispenser card system from automated teller machines (ATMs).

Checklist of further Post Office services

Cash on delivery
For a fee the PO will collect cash paid for delivered items.

Redirection
For a modest fee, mail will be redirected to new addresses.

Intelpost
The PO operates both a national and international facsimile service from specified centres.

Contracts and discounts
Bulk users may negotiate with the PO on terms for bulk mailshots and the use made of services.

Services and the secretary

Business reply service
Response cards/envelopes on which postage is paid in advance, which a customer may return to a business free of charge.

Postal orders
Cash may be sent through the post safely by changing it into a postal order re-encashable by its named recipient (postal orders can be crossed, like cheques, which is safest if an organisation is the named recipient).

Freepost
A means of enabling customers to return order forms, etc, in envelopes for which postage is paid by the interested mail-order company or business.

Household delivery service
For a fee, the PO will deliver leaflets, circulars, etc, to individual households.

Passports
British visitor passports can be obtained from most post offices on personal application. Full passports may also be applied for using the appropriate form from post offices.

Post boxes
Boxes may be rented from post offices to which mail may be addressed for you to collect, eg PO Box 41, Middleton, Midshire MM1 PB2.

Licences
A range of licences are applied for at post offices: television, export, vehicle, etc.

National Savings Bank
The PO operates an extensive set of savings services on behalf of the National Savings Bank.

Poste restante
Items may be addressed to a post office, on application, for subsequent collection.

Stocks and shares
Informational directories are available.

The Post Office Guide – indispensable in the office!

The Post Office publishes its *Post Office Guide* annually and also supplies numbered supplements to it on demand.

The *Guide* is an **essential** reference book for all secretaries since it contains a wealth of practical and helpful information about the full range of the Post Office's services, eg:

- posting of: letters, cards, packets, parcels, newspapers and printed matter
- express services, insurance, compensation, certification
- postal orders, savings, premium bonds, stocks
- licences, pensions, passports
- approved methods of packaging, addressing, postage to HM forces abroad, etc.

The *Post Office Guide* may be obtained from local post offices.

Top secretary tip – overseas trips

If your manager makes regular trips abroad, it is worth suggesting that he/she becomes a Girobank customer, since a Giro cheque book and card make it possible to obtain up to £100 in foreign currency from any one of 90 000 overseas post offices, which have longer opening hours than banks!

QUICK REVIEW QUIZ

1 What are the main differences between recorded and registered postal deliveries?

2 What Post Office services are available to send a letter which is urgent?

3 What services are available through the Post Office Girobank?

4 What type of postal services would be of value to a mail-order firm from the Post Office?

5 What is Intelpost?

6 Explain what services are provided by:

poste restante, Datapost, Swiftair, 'Nightrider'.

7 What services are provided by private sector letter and parcels carriers?

8 What sort of information does the *Post Office Guide* provide?

RESEARCH AND REPORT BACK ASSIGNMENT

Draw up a schedule of the major UK *or* overseas postal services and a tariff of current associated costs, which you consider would provide a useful reference source for a busy secretary. Select the best UK and overseas schedules from your group and copy them to all for reference.

6.5 Travel services

Travelling in the UK by rail; travelling in the UK by air; hotel reservations in the UK; travel services and IT; foreign travel; the travel itinerary.

Despite the world-shrinking effects of computer networks and telecommunications, managers still need to make trips out of the office, whether to UK or overseas destinations, because face-to-face communication still matters.

As a result, an essential plank in the raft of your secretarial skills must be your ability to make travel arrangements for your manager which:

are completely reliable, having been meticulously researched and checked.

are not over-busy, and do not result in your manager suffering from nervous exhaustion or heat rash from trying to keep to the Olympian itinerary you designed!

look ahead and anticipate, by checking, say, the need for your manager to have preventive vaccinations or to obtain a visa.

provide in advance all the documents needed – while fax can work wonders, not every foreign country is oversupplied with transceivers!

TRAVELLING IN THE UK BY RAIL

A favourite slogan of British Rail's in the 1980s was, 'Let the train take the strain!' and this is still good advice for the businessman with little time to waste, since a valuable opportunity is available for a final reading of papers or checking of figures from the comfort of a carriage compartment. A helpful reference here is BR's *Intercity Guide to Services*, published annually. Its information includes:

- Details of car parking and car hire at each destination, including Rail Drive Europcar
- Prestel, Ceefax and Oracle page numbers and details
- Traveline up-to-date information access details
- Credit card booking telephone numbers by region
- How to make reservations
- BR's Business Travel Service details a comprehensive service to businesses which includes hotel bookings and executive ticket service, covering all linked travel elements and 24-hour free parking, etc.
- Intercity Pullman, Sleeper and Motorail services

For travellers who are able to avoid the peak times of intercity journeys (notably Fridays), BR offers its Intercity Saver tariff of fares, through which up to a third of normal costs may be saved. Intercity Savers are always available to Scotland.

Keep in mind also BR's facilities for you to make reservations in advance (for a small extra fee) by credit card and to stipulate first-class, non-smoker, etc. On long journeys, also ensure you check that the train has at-seat dining, restaurant or buffet facilities. Remember to double-check departure and arrival times for inclusion in any **itinerary** you are asked to produce. Also, note that a useful service on some Intercity trains is BR's trainphone, which takes standard BT phone cards or credit cards.

TRAVELLING IN THE UK BY AIR

Many executives today accept the higher costs of air travel because of the saving in time. The UK enjoys a developed network of regional airports – East Midlands, Birmingham, Manchester, Leeds, Glasgow, Teeside, Belfast, etc – in addition to the Greater London airports of Heathrow, London City and Gatwick. Passengers are also able to fly to many European and more distant destinations from the major regional airports.

Tickets are available from local travel agents, airline desks (bookable by telephone and supportive credit card number in advance) or from service companies specialising in business travel. Air travellers may also take advantage of car valeting services (parking and securing a car during its owner's absence) within the airport complex. Additionally, a number of UK airports have Business Centres where executives are able to make use of sophisticated fax, telephone and secretarial services as well as private conference rooms – all for hire on a membership basis. Nor is the secretary overlooked! Some leading international airline companies run executive secretary clubs which offer expert administrative help, hotlines and updating bulletins as well as social events for secretaries whose managers are regular air travellers.

Airline tickets for the UK and overseas may be reserved in either smoking or non-smoking areas and window seats may be requested. Some planes may also carry the Skyphone telephone service. Generally in the UK, baggage is restricted to one piece, not exceeding 22kg and a single small cabin bag as 'hand luggage'.

> **Top secretary tip**
> While stand-by and similar cheap flights are a welcome saver for tourists with plenty of time, always ensure that you book UK or overseas flights as *scheduled flights*. No manager can afford to take the risk of arriving late for an important meeting. The extra costs of scheduled flights are justified by their advertised and usually maintained departure and arrival times and secure reservation facilities.

HOTEL RESERVATIONS IN THE UK

Generally, hotels will accept telephoned reservations supported by a credit card number. Otherwise, the hotel usually requires a written confirmation of booking – as evidence of intent (and for charging) if the traveller does not turn up. Alternatively, fax or telex may be used to make and confirm a booking. Today, many companies negotiate special deals with hotel chains and may have all bookings for their employees made through a single centralised account. Indeed, some national hotel chains employ staff full-time to service such accounts and business needs. Needless to say, the ever-ready 'plastic money' credit card is most widely used to secure hotel accommodation and allied facilities. Several major hotel groups operate their own credit cards with built-in attractions like: guaranteed reservations held for 24 hours, 'best room available on booking', express check-in and out, **bill forwarding** for checking, **extended late check-out** at no extra cost, cheque encashment, etc.

The facilities which hotels offer business travellers naturally vary, but larger hotels will have fax and modems available, as well as room and telephone services, early morning call and newspaper ordering, clothes and shoe valeting, secure car parking, private suites for hire, sports and leisure facilities, from sauna to surfboarding, all supported by computerised billing and reservations systems.

For the busy secretary, some national chains operate centralised booking services through which a number of hotel reservations may be made at one time to cover a manager's business route.

> **Checklist for making a hotel reservation**
>
> **1 Before you start**, make quite sure you have definite details of: estimated arrival and departure times, duration of stay, particulars of any special requirements – dietary, telecommunications, reprographic, etc.
>
> **2 Write down the major features you wish to book before telephoning** and go through them with the receptionist. This way you won't forget any.
>
> **3 Check acceptable mode of payment with receptionist** – no manager likes to be embarrassed by, say, proferring a credit card not accepted by the hotel.
>
> **4 Check car-parking arrangements** – Secure parking is essential in most localities. Imagine if your manager has to park on the highway overnight and finds the car vandalised at the start of a busy day!
>
> **5 Make written notes of your negotiated arrangements** – particularly of a guaranteed reservation and either fax, telex or confirm by letter so as to create a written record. Ensure a written note with clear details of major aspects of the reservation(s) is included in your manager's travel pack

Travel services and IT

The travel industry, like banking, makes extensive use of information technology to provide a faster, more reliable and sophisticated service, so make sure you update yourself regularly about:

- Prestel and viewdata information and booking services, from air travel to theatre tickets
- ISTEL/TRAVICOM/ABC Corporate Services databases for instant advice on facilities, itineraries ticket issue, etc.
- Branch up-to-the-minute computerised reports on items such as exchange rates, snow reports, industrial disputes, hotel availabilities.
- Computerised convergence to scan multiple airlines for next available flights, and to effect EFTPOS payments, etc.

FOREIGN TRAVEL

A wise man once observed that: 'There are two kinds of knowledge, the kind you have to carry around in your head, and the kind you need to know where to get when you need it!' Nowhere is this truer than in the field of foreign travel, which is, in itself, a demanding and complex specialism. It pays, therefore, to foster a good relationship with a local or company – approved travel agency which will provide you with the following areas of service and specialist advice:

Travel agency services

- Making reservations for air or sea travel
- Arranging for car hire at destination airport
- Making worldwide reservations in approved (good quality) hotels and advising on their telex, fax and cable addresses, leisure facilities, and price tariffs
- providing personal, valuables and baggage insurance
- Advising on public holidays, customs and procedures of foreign countries and also on vaccination and visa requirements
- Working out in advance optimum travel routes and economic costs for travellers using various airline routes between countries and continents
- Securing tickets (including rail or coach tickets) and other documentation for collection or onward posting and accepting (by arrangement) payment on account or by credit card
- Obtaining traveller's cheques and foreign currency for clients

As the above checklist indicates, travel agencies provide a range of support services which are designed to save the busy secretary's time and energy. Travel agency staff rely extensively on directories like those produced by *ABC Corporate Services Worldwide Hotel Guide*, *ABC Guide To International Travel* and *ABC Air Travel Atlas*. These are updated on a monthly basis and comprise encyclopaedic details of airline companies' current scheduled flight costs, worldwide hotel facilities and costs, airline routes and connections and a further range of advice and requirements on vaccinations needed and recommended medication to carry, etc.

Airline reservations are generally made through either ISTEL or TRAVICOM, two companies which provide a network of computers in travel agency offices operating a **'real-time' booking system**. This means that the operator can check the 'up-to-the-minute' extent of a scheduled air flight's bookings and add a further number of seat reservations there and then. This process may be conducted while operator and secretary are connected by telephone and confirmed upon supply of a credit card number or central account number.

Details of a typical airline reservation slip

The illustration indicates the information needed to secure a computerised airline booking:

Secretary's checklist for making foreign travel arrangements

Start well in advance and avoid haste; set up a file and create a list of the jobs to attend to; then prioritise them.

Essential documents (to be checked out early)

- Valid and current passport (note that regular travellers can obtain 90-page passports for visa stamps, etc).
- Valid **visa** and certificates of vaccination; remember to allow enough time for the doctor to undertake these and for the after-effects to wear off (check with the travel agency for the latest requirements).
- Current driving licence, international driving licence and **Green Card insurance**, if driving and/or taking a car abroad; consult AA/RAC handbooks for individual countries' vehicle and equipment requirements.
- Form E111 for free medical treatment in EEC countries (available from the Department of Health).
- Travel tickets and hotel reservation(s) confirmations.

Services and the secretary

Fig 6.10

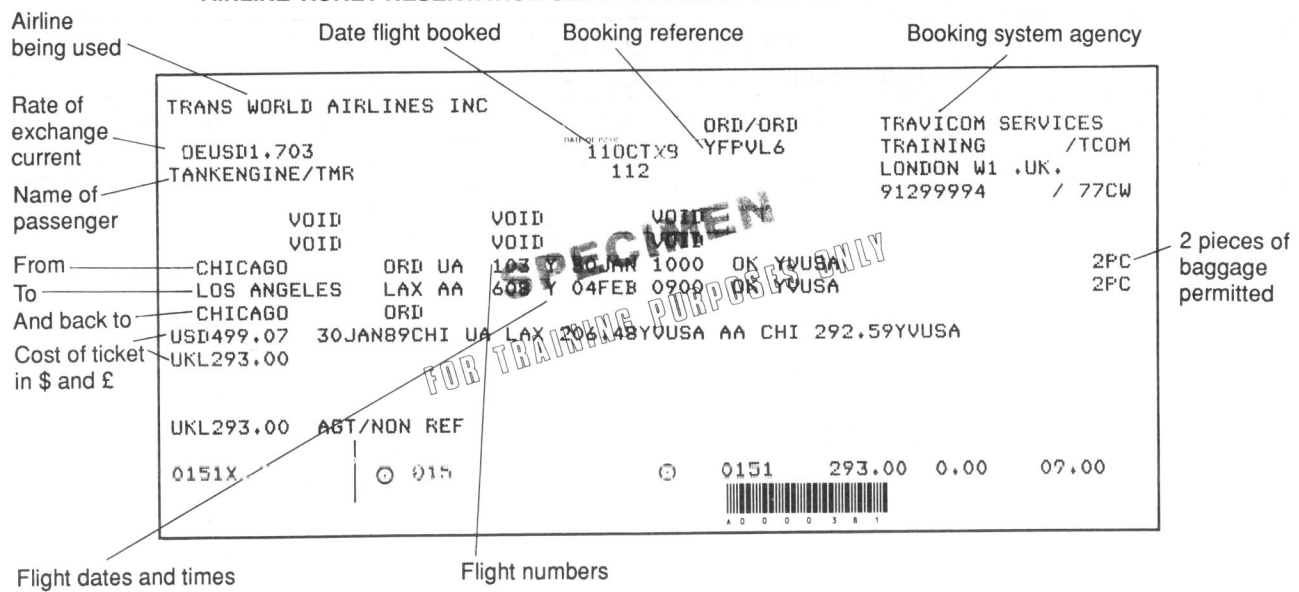

AIRLINE TICKET RESERVATION SLIP: PRODUCED ON COMPUTERISED SYSTEM

- Airline being used
- Date flight booked
- Booking reference
- Booking system agency
- Rate of exchange current
- Name of passenger
- From
- To
- And back to
- Cost of ticket in $ and £
- Flight dates and times
- Flight numbers
- 2 pieces of baggage permitted

```
TRANS WORLD AIRLINES INC          ORD/ORD        TRAVICOM SERVICES
                                                 TRAINING      /TCOM
 0EUSD1.703            11OCTX9  YFPVL6           LONDON W1 .UK.
 TANKENGINE/TMR                112               91299994    / 77CW

          VOID           VOID         VOID
          VOID           VOID         VOID
     CHICAGO      ORD UA 103 Y 30JAN 1000 OK YVUSA       2PC
     LOS ANGELES  LAX AA 605 Y 04FEB 0900 OK YVUSA       2PC
     CHICAGO      ORD
 USD499.07   30JAN89CHI UA LAX 206.48YVUSA AA CHI 292.59YVUSA
 UKL293.00

 UKL293.00   AGT/NON REF
 0151X        O 015                 O  0151   293.00  0.00   07.00
```

(Reproduced by kind permission of Hogg Robinson (Travel) Ltd)

- Business documents for the trip, including itinerary and factsheet(s) for each country to be visited, itemising the main features of political/social life, customs, religious practices, etc. Also checklist of names, job designations, addresses, fax and telephone numbers of all principal foreign contacts. Note: Don't forget to list home office fax, telex and other contact numbers!
- Travel guides and leaflets from the Department of Health.

Money and financial resources

- Foreign currency(ies), Eurocheque card and cheques,
- UK cheque book and Visa/Mastercard-based credit card and international cards (American Express, Diners Club, etc).
- Any **bankers' drafts**, or international money orders.
- Details for cabling money from UK in emergency, etc.

Personal travel resources

- Advice on appropriate clothing for season (remember heat plus humidity factor in many countries), travel iron/valeting kit, handy dictating machine and cassettes, lap-top computer, batteries and disks, calculator, foreign language dictionaries and phrase books, first-aid/medication kit, books for light reading, etc.

Make time for a time check!

Don't forget the time zone differences across the world – or British Summer Time, etc. Remember that airports, railway stations and ferry/port timetables always show *local* times which may be as much as twelve hours ahead of or behind UK times. Also, make it a habit to check your office time chart before telephoning San Francisco or Sydney, only to raise the overnight cleaner or caretaker! And of course, international times must be closely checked when producing an itinerary for an overseas visit.

Summary of free baggage allowances

1 Internal UK flights
2 pieces not exceeding 62 inches (combined length, height and width)

2 USA and Canada
2 pieces not exceeding 32kg per bag

3 Rest of world Economy Class: 1 piece
First/Club Classes: 2 pieces
Concorde/First Class: 40kg
Superclub/Club: 30kg
Economy: 23kg

All plus a single piece of hand luggage

Source: British Airways Travelwise Baggage Information

Fig 6.11 International time chart

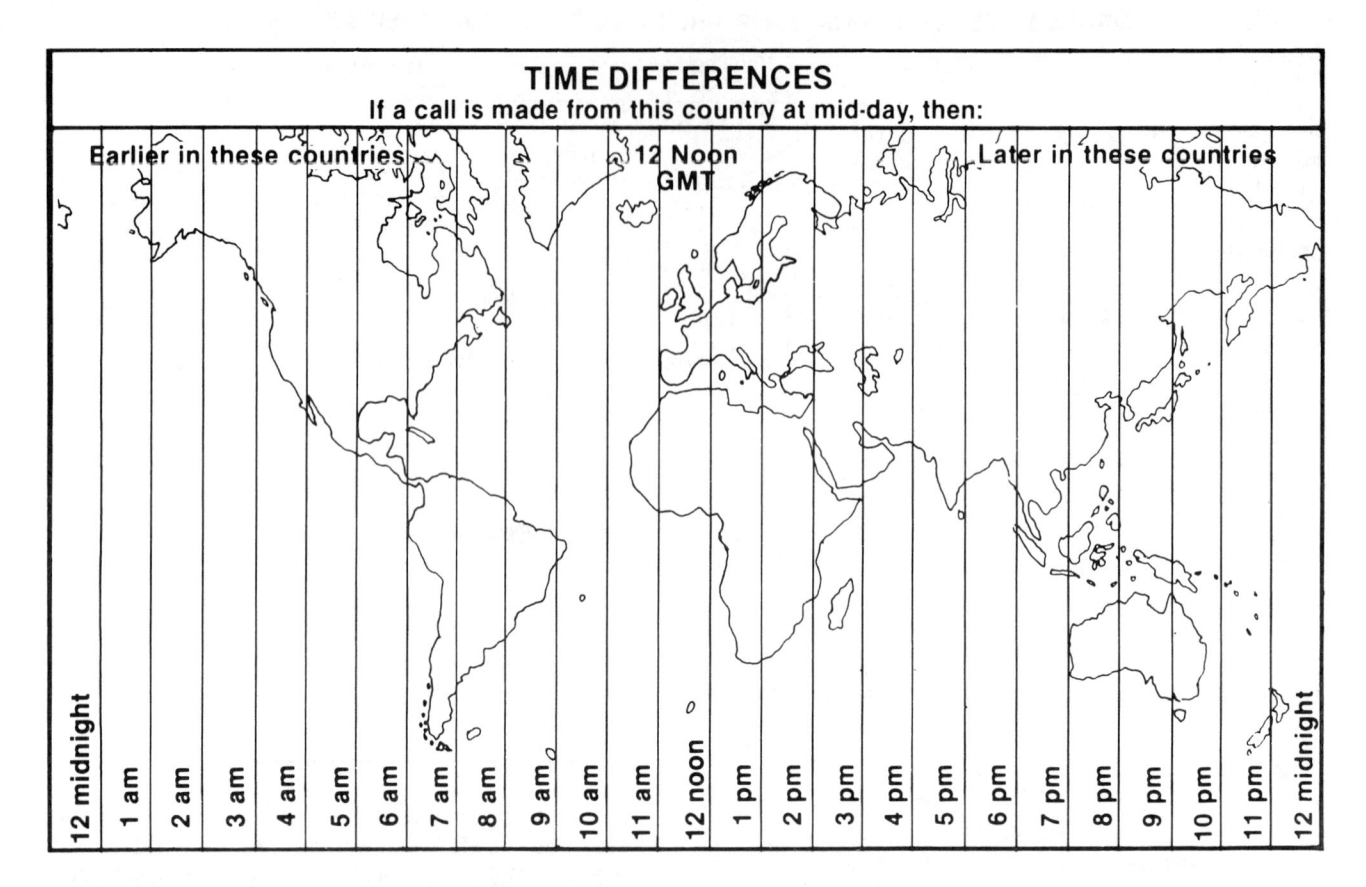

```
                    TIME DIFFERENCES
        If a call is made from this country at mid-day, then:

Earlier in these countries          12 Noon        Later in these countries
                                     GMT
```

| 12 midnight | 1 am | 2 am | 3 am | 4 am | 5 am | 6 am | 7 am | 8 am | 9 am | 10 am | 11 am | 12 noon | 1 pm | 2 pm | 3 pm | 4 pm | 5 pm | 6 pm | 7 pm | 8 pm | 9 pm | 10 pm | 11 pm | 12 midnight |

(Reproduced by kind permission of British Telecom)

THE TRAVEL ITINERARY

The word 'itinerary' derives from the Latin word for journey. Today it stands for a printed schedule which details:

The days, times and dates of a projected journey

The locations to be visited

The people who will take part in the journey, eg multinational company colleagues, overseas customers, politicians or diplomats

Brief explanatory details of what is due to happen, where and when

Illustrated is an extract of a specimen itinerary to show its structure and format; but bear in mind that these are not fixed, but rather for you to design to best effect.

DISCUSSION TOPIC

What sort of training programme would you devise for secretaries who frequently have to arrange overseas business trips for their managers?

DISCUSSION TOPIC

In Unit 1, at the start of your course, you were asked the question, 'What qualities and skills do you consider important in a secretary?' Now, near the end of your course, consider this question again, and discuss the ways in which your views have changed, and why.

ITINERARY

SIMPLEX BUSINESS SOFTWARE LIMITED

Export Sales Visit to Japan, Australia & New Zealand

Visiting Sales Team:

Susan Peters, Export Sales Manager
David Richards, Financial Consultant
John Dickinson, Far East & Australasia Sales Coordinator
Petra Zybieski, Chief Programmer and Technical Advisor

Tuesday 23 May 19--

    1630   Arrival Heathrow, Terminal 4, Check in
                at British Airways Desk & Executive Club

    1730   Scheduled departure time
                Stopover: Anchorage

Wednesday 24 May 19--

    20.15   Arrive Tokyo Haneda Airport
(local time)

                Chris Harrison, Japanese Sales Agent
                will meet Team and escort to Eastern
                Dawn Hotel

Thursday 25 May 19--

  0900 - 1200   Travel Recuperation Period
                  in Hotel Solarium/Swimming Pool/
                  Beauty Salon/Complex

  1215 - 1500   Welcoming Reception & Lunch

                  Tokyo Chamber of Commerce Delegation:
                  President Mr Ahiro Akaihito
                  (approx 25 delegates: see travel
                  pack listing of company representation)

                  Hotel Lotus Blossom Suite

  1500 - 2000   Visit to Head Office of Taniko Computer
                  Company, Tokyo to meet Directors and
                  Senior Managers

QUICK REVIEW QUIZ

1 What services are provided by British Rail's Intercity service?

2 List the major regional airports in the UK.

3 How would you make an effective hotel reservation in the UK for your manager?

4 What services does an international airline supply for its first-class and club-class business passengers?

5 What services does a good travel agency provide for international travel to businessmen?

6 Make a checklist of the items you would check and arrange to ensure a trouble-free foreign trip for your manager.

7 How does world time affect foreign travel arrangements?

8 What information is available from the ABC Corporate Services directories to aid foreign travel administration?

9 What major items of information are conveyed in a well drawn-up itinerary?

RESEARCH AND REPORT BACK ASSIGNMENTS

1 In groups of three to four, arrange to visit the offices of a local travel agency with the brief to find out what services they provide for foreign business travel, and what advice they can give to help secretaries make effective arrangements through them. Take careful notes and produce a factsheet of helpful guidelines intended for secretarial reference on your return.

2 Select *one* of the external agencies/bureaux listed in Appendix 1. In pairs, arrange a visit and find out at first hand what sort of services are provided and how staff liaise with local firms to provide them. On your return, compose a 300-word summary of your findings, to be word processed as part of a single class document for general reference and hard copy printout.

Top secretary tip
Reliability and keeping to deadlines are essential qualities in any external servicing agency you may use. So make sure you maintain details and addresses/phone numbers of those *you* know you can rely upon. Such a database will save precious time in an emergency.

UNIT 6
Summary of main points

1 **Main functions of a personnel department**: Recruitment of staff, induction, training/career development, personnel records maintenance, employee appraisal and salary review, coordination of disciplinary and grievance procedures, negotiations and relationships with trade unions, staff welfare and social activities, confidential counselling service, pensions administration, preparation for retirement services.

2 **Major personnel documents**: Personnel specification – lists the essential and useful qualities and skills needed in specific jobs; job descriptions – lists those duties and tasks which go to make up specific jobs and denotes 'responsible for/reports to' structures; personnel requisition, job application, interview assessment, disciplinary report and personnel record forms – now largely held on computer.

3 **PAYE documentation: P45** – coordinates transfer of pay details from one job to the next; **P11** – records weekly/monthly pay and NIC details for employer/IR use; **payslip** – records all sources of pay and deductions made before net pay is received; **P14** – employer's annual PAYE return; **P60** – employee's annual detail of pay and deductions for income tax and national insurance; **Tax Tables** A and B–D used to compute pay.

4 **Imprest system for recording petty cash**: System starts with a 'float' from which payments are made as needed; twinned with recording system which lists money coming in and payments made, in sets of columns; injection of cash at end of each week restores imprest to initial level; vouchers are made out to record cash given for purchases and all receipts are kept.

5 **Major accounting documentation: Ledgers** – record purchases and sales transactions and general running expenses; double-entry bookkeeping techniques record all movements of money into and out of a firm and regular **trial balances** are made to ensure the system is error free: **bank reconciliations** are made to ensure that the bank's records tally with in-house records on a monthly basis; **trading** and **profit and loss accounts** are drawn up at intervals to monitor the extent of trading profits and net profits being made; at the end of the trading year, a **balance sheet** is drawn up to record the firm's overall financial status, taking into account the value of goods and buildings held, profits made, monies owed, monies due in, and dividends due to shareholders.

6 **Principal banking services**: To manage current, deposit and currency accounts; to provide cheque clearing services, pay standing orders and direct debits, store valuables, lend money, give tax advice, service overseas trading and travel; provide credit card/cash dispenser card services, etc.

7 **Types of 'plastic money' cards**: Cheque guarantee, cash dispenser, credit, leisure, debit, Eurocheque, charge account, telephone credit and 'smart' programmable cards.

8 **Major Post Office services**: Letter service – first and second-class, special delivery, express delivery, Datapost, railway and airway, Swiftair, recorded and registered; parcels – county, national, Superservice, Nightrider, Datapost, UK and international. Other services: Girobank plc, Intelpost fax service, Freepost, Business Reply service, poste restante, motor vehicle licences, passports, postal orders, etc.

9 **Main travel services: UK** – rail/air/coach travel, hotel reservations, entertainment reservations, car rental; **international** – flight bookings, car rental, hotel reservations; **general** – personal and baggage insurance, advice on preventive innoculation/vaccination, visa/entry requirements, route-planning, foreign currency/traveller's cheques.

10 **Checks for foreign travel arrangements**: Valid passports; innoculations still current; visas needed; driving/international driving licences;

'green card' insurance certificate; form E111 for EEC free health care; personal/baggage insurance; all travel tickets – rail, air, etc; hotel reservation confirmations; foreign currency/traveller's cheques; Visa/Mastercard; cheque books and supportive cards; factsheets, itinerary and business trip documents; office fax, telex and telephone numbers; names and designations of personnel to be seen.

Sources of further information
Personnel Management Theory and Practice, G A Cole, DP Publications
Modern Business Administration – chapter on Personnel , R C Appleby, Pitman
Finance for BTEC National – PAYE and petty cash sections, J Hopkins, Pitman
Financial Accounting – An Introduction, J Blake, Hutchinson Management Series
The Elements of Banking, F E Perry, Methuen
Banking for Students, M W Downey, Pitman
Elements of Banking, D Palfreman and P Ford, Pitman
The Post Office Guide, The Post Office
ABC Corporate Services –
Worldwide Hotel Guide, Guide to International Travel, Worldwide Travel Atlas
The Times Atlas of the World, Times Newspapers Ltd
The European Year Book: A World Survey (for factsheets and factual data)
Euroguide and Travel Planner, published annually, Hallweg
Fodor's Europe, 33 countries, published annually, Hallweg
Egon Ronay's Hotels & Restaurants, published annually
The Good Food Guide, published annually 'Which?' Books
Tutor's Pack, Inland Revenue Educational Service
British Rail Passenger Timetable published annually by British Rail

---

ACTIVITIES

Have workstation, will travel!
A case study

You work as personal secretary to Richard Keys, deputy office administration manager of Industrial Pumps Limited, at their head office in Milton Keynes.

Industrial Pumps Limited is a UK company employing some five hundred staff – manufacturing, sales, marketing and administrative personnel – to make and sell a wide range of electrically powered pumps. The pumps are used in a host of different ways – to pump water into irrigation canals in third world countries, to control the movement of chemicals and fluid products in manufacturing processes, to assist in land drainage, and so on. Indeed, it is difficult to think of a pumping situation for which IPL has yet to design a suitable pump! For example, they also manufacture valves which surgeons insert into human hearts to restore their pumping capabilities.

As a result of years of ingenious design work, excellent craftsmanship and resulting reliability, IPL pumps are selling at an ever-increasing rate all over the world. The export sales department staff has doubled in size over the past five years and today there are 20 export sales executives who devote most of their time to travelling across the world to sell IPL pumps to government installations, hospitals, chemical plants and so on. Additionally, IPL employs a home sales force of some 25 sales executives to sell their products throughout the UK.

Hitherto, the home sales executives have tended to make their own travel arrangements, according to their sales itineraries and then submitted monthly expenses for petrol, hotels, meals and so on. As a result, there has been no real underlying organisation of their needs, and IPL is spending money it could save by making agreements with national hotel chains, for example, and securing a group discount. Also, claimed expenses have come to be paid 'on the nod' with little monitoring.

The export sales executives have usually made their travel arrangements with the help of two clerical assistants, Julie Halliday and Carol Parker, who have developed close links with the local branch of Global Travel Limited, a nationwide travel agency chain. The counter assistant they usually like to deal with is called Sally Owen. However, the Global local branch has become increasingly busy over the past six months, partly as a result of a sharp increase in the influx of retired businessmen and their wives, who have the money for foreign holidays and plenty of time on their hands to seek the most detailed guidance and advice from Global staff.

As a result of these developments, there has been a rash of mistakes and errors over the making of travel arrangements, both at home and overseas. Hotel bookings have not been confirmed and arriving executives have been turned away. Two export executives recently missed their flights as a result of typing errors on their itineraries, and one had to postpone an important sales visit to India because of a slip-up in vaccination arrangements.

'Start right, stay right'
This morning, Mr David Searle, office administration manager, called you into his office and briefed you as follows:

'The MD is pretty fed up with the problems he's been hearing about over faulty travel arrangements and the steeply rising cost of our UK and overseas sales teams' travel expenses. He wants us to tackle the problem and has delegated its solution to me.

'This is how I am proposing to solve it – or at least to improve matters substantially. I want to second you for three months to develop our own internal travel services unit. I've arranged to have Julie Halliday and Carol Parker transferred from export sales to work for the unit full time.

'I think that what is needed here at IPL is an integrated approach that arranges all travel, home and overseas. So, assuming you are in agreement ... (You nod!) ... I'd like you to produce your ideas on equipping a travel office. I've made room C231 available.' (It is some 5m wide and 6m long and fully 'plumbed' for LAN/modem communications and PABX phone extensions, etc.)

'Draw up a layout for me that you think would be most appropriate, and let me have your list of reference books and materials and any communication facilities you think you will need. Essentially, the MD wants us to speed up the travel arrangements process, cut out these vexing mistakes and look to running our sales teams' travel needs as cost-effectively as we can, not forgetting our image as a world leader! He says he doesn't mean us to try to take on the travel agencies at their own game, but to see how we might help them to help us do it better.

'I need you to give this one your best shot – the MD's pretty fired up! If you like what you've created, we can talk in three months' time about whether you want to stay with it, or return to being Richard's secretary. Oh, and by the way, just in case you said 'yes', I've set up a desk and phone and so on in room C321, and Richard's allowing you to start straight away! There's an old proverbial expression we engineers like to quote: 'Start right, stay right!' and I'm sure its true of this new travel servicing venture!'

CASE STUDY QUESTIONS

1 What advantages do you think are likely to stem from the setting up of the travel services unit?

2 What routine procedures would you establish to help the unit:

    (a) To make UK travel arrangements efficiently?
    (b) To make overseas travel arrangements efficiently?

    Are there any forms which might be designed which could aid these processes?

3 What management information systems (IT based) would you want installed in room C321? And what software applications packages to do what tasks?

4 What books, directories, guides and timetables, etc, would you select as part of your reference/information database in room C321?

5 In what ways would you like to liaise with Global Travel's local branch? Can you suggest any new procedures which might improve their service – bearing in mind that IPL are very good customers of Global?

6 How would Julie and Carol be most efficiently employed on the unit? What individual tasks would you allocate to them? They can both process text and data on the firm's LAN workstations and operate fax and telex equipment.

7 How would you 'sell' the new travel services unit to IPL's sales teams and their departmental office administrative staff?

CASE STUDY ASSIGNMENTS

1 Design your proposed layout for the travel services unit office in room C321.

2 Produce your initial list of reference source books and guides, etc.

3 Design a software database file (or form), for making travel arrangements for export sales executives shortly to travel abroad for periods of one to two weeks. Your form should seek to assemble the essential information needed to allow a clerical assistant to make the basic arrangements for the visit.

4 Having carried out your research, compose a memorandum to the office administration manager, outlining how the travel requirements of the UK sales force could be organised so as to save money and avoid the passing of excessive expense claims.

5 You can assume that all sales team personnel use IPL's electronic mail system. Compose an Email message to *either* the UK *or* the export sales executives which provides instructions on how they should take advantage of LAN/WAN networks to communicate their planned work schedules in advance so as to enable your unit to make any needed reservations and bookings and to confirm them back to the executive(s) concerned.

WORK SIMULATION ASSIGNMENTS

1 You work as the secretary of Mr Jim Broadbent, personnel manager of Regency Furnishing Limited, which makes high quality reproduction furniture, in a factory employing 250 people, and with some 40 administrative personnel.

Mr Broadbent said to you yesterday: 'We don't seem to be attracting the right quality of secretarial staff lately, and I think our job application form is at fault. I'd like you to design a draft job application form for me, intended for secretarial appointments, which will help us to separate the wheat from the chaff during the job selection process.'

Design a form which you think will meet Mr Broadbent's requirements.

2 As secretary to Mr Bert Franklin, managing director of Franklin Office Cleaning Services Limited, a small but growing company with registered offices at 14–16 Templeton Street, Sandowns, Westchester, Wessex, WS2 4SD, telephone: Westchester 765489, you find yourself having to tackle a wide variety of

jobs at short notice. This morning, Mr Franklin arrived in the office with these words:

'Linda, Mrs Cartwright (copy typist and filing clerk) rang me up over the week-end to say she's made her mind up to retire at the end of the month. Can't honestly say I'm sorry. She never really wanted to make a go of the WP software ... Anyway, I want you to draw up a sits vac advert for the *Westchester Clarion*. Wanted, highly intelligent WP operator, able to use Viewrite, not a clock watcher, willing to turn hand to range of office jobs, very sympathetic boss who expects hard work, etc, pay and conditions top rate – check the rate for the job in the *Clarion*, and what we offer for holidays with Freda – three paid weeks a year plus bank hols, I think. Emphasise the "lovely people to work with and high class surroundings" ... you know the sort of thing. I'll look at it this afternoon. Got to go now to see Faversham's about the new contract ...'

Draw up a display advertisement to be published in the *Clarion*, about 12 cm wide and 19 cm deep, which you think will appropriately communicate the sense of Mr Franklin's brief.

3   Having made a success of Mr Broadbent's secretarial job application form, he delivered a fresh task for you this morning:

'The MD's keen for us to transfer our personnel records onto the new database software as soon as possible. This being the case, I should like you to design a personnel record layout suitable for our office support staff records. It'll need to record the bread-and-butter items like name, age, date of birth, address, etc, but I think it should emphasise skills brought to the company and those acquired since joining, records of any training courses, and the type of equipment and software they are competent with.

'See what you can produce on the new database package and I'll go over it with you next week – say Wednesday morning.'

Form a group of three students, and, using a database package with which you are familiar, design the personnel record file which Mr Broadbent has outlined. Hint: draw up your proposed form on paper first and decide which parts you think will need to be set in sortable fields. Then divide the work between you. Compare your database file with those produced by other groups.

Alternative approach: by arrangement, work with a group of your college's or school's computer programmer/science students to produce the file, and check out how they create the fields needed and organise layout, etc.

4   Jenny Perkins has just joined your office to work as your junior. She is single and has the income tax code 260L on her P45. She started on Monday of this week, week 9 of the tax year. Her pay details are as follows: from weeks 1–8 her gross pay was £90 per week. By week 8, Jenny had paid £66.00 tax. She was and will remain 'contracted in' for Class 1 NIC payments which are levied at 7% of salary. With you her pay will increase to £100 gross per week. She has elected to pay £2.00 each week for her Social Club membership, which the firm collects and transfers. Work out her payslip details for week 9 and present them in the form of a simulated payslip.

5   Part of your job as secretary to Miss Thomas, office administration manager of Harlow & Dawson Engineering Limited, is to maintain the department's petty cash account, which is run on the imprest system. As part of the company's transfer to electronic record keeping, Miss Thomas has asked you to design a petty cash recording system, according to imprest principles, on the new spreadsheet software package recently installed on the firm's new LAN. If your design works, it will be used in each department.

The following information is available to you from your manual petty cash book records:

Your Received 'DR' columns are: Date, Folio, Amount £ p
Your last entry was: FO: 345   £36.87 fresh imprest
Your Paid 'CR' columns are:

Date, Details, Voucher No, Amount, Stationery, Fares, Postage, Beverages, Sundries, VAT.

Your original imprest was for £75.00.

Your first week's transactions to be entered onto the spreadsheet are:

Voucher	256	Milk and coffee	£3.60
	257	Stamps	£5.90
	258	Fares	£1.85
	259	Johnsons Office Supplies:	
		Envelopes	£6.40 inc VAT
	260	Dawkins DIY:	
		Cleaning fluids	£4.25 inc VAT

Using the information given above, design a petty cash imprest system on a spreadsheet package with which you are familiar, which will provide the information as recorded in a petty cash book system.

6   Your company sells a range of tyres, batteries, and motor-car accessories from a group of fitting centres in the West Midlands. Yesterday, a Mr Ken Davidson, who has been running a taxi service in Wolverton for the past six months asked your manager if he could open an account for tyres and batteries. He trades as:

Kaydee Taxi Service Limited
14A Aston Road
Wolverton
Worcs
WL3 4AV

He gave the Wolverton Branch of the Midwest Bank as a financial referee, together with Wolverton Garage Limited. Your manager has had a few nasty experiences recently over bad debts and has asked you to compose a letter to seek financial status references to both referees for an amount not exceeding £750 per month.

Produce a suitable letter for your manager to sign.

7 You work as personal secretary to Miss Hilary Wells, company secretary of Global Finance plc. Recently a new chairman was appointed, Sir Edward De Lacy. At present he has just begun a month's honeymoon with his second wife in Lima, Peru. They are staying at the Hotel Montana. Miss Wells has just received a telex to the effect that Sir Edward and his wife have been invited to attend the annual British Embassy Ball in ten days' time. Sir Edward wants a package made up of some jewellery for his wife to wear, his own gold-chased cufflinks and other personal effects to be sent as quickly as possible to him. The package is expected to weigh 3kg and be valued at £1750. His housekeeper has been charged with bringing the items he wants to your office.

Find out the quickest and most secure way of getting the package to Sir Edward, the costs involved and any other necessary action. Write out what you discover as a memorandum to Miss Wells for her to progress as soon as possible.

8 Your manager, Dr Julian Manston, is the export sales manager of Biotechnics Research Limited, a company which specialises in developing products which promote the growth and yield of a range of cereal crops. He has just finished fixing up a sales trip to a number of Far Eastern countries to promote a new product which improves the yields of rice crops. He plans to be away for a fortnight and to give sales briefing seminars in Singapore, Hong Kong and Seoul. He needs to convey a first-rate corporate image as he will be dealing with top-rank government officials and company executives. The MD has therefore authorised first-class travel and first-rank hotel accommodation.

In groups of three, carry out the following (researching as appropriate one country and destination each):

(a) Produce an itinerary giving Dr Manston a minimum of three days in each centre. He has a preference for flying with UK airlines whenever possible
(b) Find out the costs of his air travel
(c) Decide which hotels you will book him into and provide details of facilities, etc, with costs
(d) Produce a factsheet for each country and centre to brief Dr Manston, who has never before travelled to the Far East. He will be travelling in July
(e) List any helpful guidelines for Dr Manston about arrangements he will need to make before his visit, any items he should take with him, and helpful advice regarding his journey.

WORK EXPERIENCE ASSIGNMENTS

1 Find out how computers are used to keep personnel and financial records, and how, for example, the organisation's payroll and petty cash systems are operated.

2 Interview two to three sets of managers and their secretaries and find out how overseas travel arrangements are made and what aspects are considered to be important items for careful administration.

Set out your findings as a checklist for your group to share.

3 Find out how the organisation manages expense accounts and foreign travel expenses. Explain to your group the procedures followed.

4 Seek an interview with senior management and ask the following questions:

1 How do they see IT affecting what they do in the next five years?
2 How do they think secretarial work is likely to change in the next five years?
3 What advice could they give you in embarking upon a secretarial career?

5 Find out what Post Office services the organisation uses, what they cost and what support they provide. Make a checklist of your findings to share with your group.

PRACTICE QUESTIONS FROM PAST EXAMINATION PAPERS

1 Two vacancies are to appear on the Vacancy Board for the District Council, one for a shorthand typist and the other for a personal assistant to the executive director. Under the appropriate headings, give FOUR qualifications which you consider suitable for the shorthand typist and FOUR further qualifications which the personal assistant will require. (RSA Secretarial Duties Stage II)

2 You work as secretary to Mr Thomas Ruppin, head of the business studies department at Fotheringay College of Further Education. You have just prepared an itinerary for Mr Ruppin for his visit to a college of further education in Birmingham on 21 May. He asks you to define an itinerary and draw up a set of guidelines which must be considered when preparing an itinerary, so this job can be delegated in future. (RSA Secretarial Duties Stage II)

3 You have recently been on a Health and Safety course. Mrs Pritchard, your chief and personnel manager has suggested that this year you take a more active part in the forthcoming YTS Induction Course by giving a short talk to new employees on Health and Safety in the company. On today's tape she leaves you the following message:

'Jane, regarding the forthcoming YTS Induction Course – can you let me have a memo outlining the content of your talk please – which Acts you will mention and a summary of the main points of importance which relate to the employees themselves. I suggest you include some visual aids in the talk, so can you give me a list of, say, 6 examples of potentially hazardous situations and how they should be demonstrated.'

Write a suitable memo. (RSA Secretarial Studies Stage II)

4 Comlon International plc is a company designing and marketing fashion wear. Its London Sales Department is hosting a two-day Designer Dress Exhibition in Portugal. Through its local company Comlon has hired a government-owned palace 16 km from the company's offices and factory.

Draft an itinerary for the visit from arrival of the party's aeroplane (carrying 30 purchasing executives from English, Canadian and USA stores) at 1200 on the first day until their departure at 1800 on the second day.

Mr Adrian Rogers is director of sales, Mr Tom Carter is marketing manager and Mrs Sheila Abrahams is head of fashion design. (LCC/PSC)

5 Describe what action you would take in the following cases:

(a) A cheque paid into the company's bankers is returned 'RD'.
(b) You have just been informed that a cheque sent to a creditor more than a week ago has not been received.
(c) The cashier is absent unexpectedly at 15.00 and your manager brings you cash and cheques collected from the cashier's workstation. You are asked to make it up for collection by a security company's armoured cash transit service at 15.45. (LCC/PSC)

6 You are in charge of the administrative arrangements for the day-long interview of six candidates for the post of marketing assistant. Briefly outline the steps you would take to organise:

(a) the order in which the interviews will take place
(b) expenses procedures for the candidates
(c) an informal tour of the company works
(d) catering arrangements (LCC/PSC)

7 You work as secretary to Mr John Brown, director of office design division of Comlon International plc, a company which manufactures and markets office equipment and stationery.

Choose *three* of the following cards and explain how they are used. Suggest an occasion when John Brown could make use of each card.

a charge card, b cheque card, c service card,
d business card, e phone card. (LCC/PSC)

8 Mr Brown frequently goes on tour seeking potential markets. He uses a car for travelling within the country he is visiting.

(a) Which books of reference would you need to consult?
(b) List the arrangements to be made before he leaves.
(c) State the items Mr Brown should take with him in his briefcase. (LCC/PSC)

9 There are considerable time zone differences between Perth, Brisbane, Auckland, Melbourne and London. Sam Dale (director Australasia) needs continuous contact with all of these places and thus has problems in spoken communication. Describe machinery and methods to overcome these difficulties. (LCC/PSC)

10 You work for the sales manager of a small company which manufactures stereo equipment. Your employer is shortly to visit the Middle East to promote sales, and has asked you to make the necessary travel arrangements. Prepare a list of the items to be attended to. (PEI Secretarial Practice Intermediate)

11 Your employer is to make a three-day visit to a distant town. Prepare an itinerary from the following outline:

Taxi to station for early morning train to destination –
lunch with Mr Green at George and Dragon –
afternoon conference in Acorn Rooms –
Grand Hotel overnight –
dinner there with Mr Black and wife –
morning visit to new factory site –
afternoon free for report –
evening dinner with Mr & Mrs Brown, same hotel –

visit new retail store in morning –
return to office pm.

Include other relevant information as necessary (eg dates, times, etc). (PEI Secretarial Practice Intermediate)

12 Your company is advertising for a Junior Receptionist. Brief details of the position have already been given in the advertisement, but those called for interview will be given a full description of their responsibilities in order that they can clearly see what the job entails. Using a main heading of 'Post of Junior Receptionist', and sub-headings of 'General Requirements', 'Duties', and 'Terms and Conditions of Employment', write such a Job Description. (PEI Secretarial Practice Intermediate)

13 (a) In order to make a cheque as safe as possible, what items would you enter when writing it?
    (b) Why do holders of a current account receive a statement from the bank at regular intervals, and why might the balance on this statement differ from the balance shown on the bank account in their cash book? (PEI Secretarial Practice Intermediate)

14 Your travelling representatives are complaining that it is becoming increasingly difficult to carry sufficient coins in order to ring in to the office regularly. Name two Post Office telecommunications services of which use could be made to avoid this situation, and state clearly how each would be used. (PEI Secretarial Practice Intermediate)

15 It is necessary to employ a junior to help with some of your typing and other routine work as a result of your recent promotion.

Draw up a job specification to submit to your employer before advertising the post, stating clearly what the new employee will be expected to do and to whom she is to report. You work in a large department. (PEI Secretarial Practice Advanced)

16 The Office Manager has given you the names and addresses of four candidates to be interviewed by a panel for the post of Chief Accountant. He asks you to make all the necessary arrangements in connection with the interviews. Give an account of what you would do. (PEI Secretarial Practice Advanced)

17 You have recently taken up a post as assistant to the Marketing Manager. At your interview you were told that you would be a part of the management team, but so far your job has involved only typing, filing and answering the telephone. What suggestions could you put forward to your employer as to how he could make better use of your talents as his assistant? (PEI Secretarial Practice Advanced)

UNIT 6
Glossary of terms and phrases

annual audit
Usually an examination and report of an organisation's financial transactions – such as that required by the Inland Revenue; audits may be taken of stock held, time spent on given activities, etc.

bankers' drafts
In order to obtain some goods or services, such as purchasing a second-hand car, the seller may require the protection of a bankers' draft – in effect the purchaser pays the money to his bank and obtains the **bank's** cheque for the amount, which the seller will trust.

bill-forwarding
Employees of organisations who have made arrangements with hotel chains sign their bills, which are forwarded to the organisation's accounts department for payment.

clearing bank
A bank which processes payments by cheque which are credited to or debited from each customer's account; clearing banks also offer a wide range of financial services.

credit/leisure card
Plastic identity cards which enable their holder to purchase a wide range of goods and services on credit, to obtain cash (as cashpoint cards), to secure bank loans, etc.

direct debit/credit
By arrangement, payments are made electronically to organisations supplying services and deducted from a customer's bank account on a regular basis; unlike standing orders, direct debits may be increased from one month to the next without especially seeking the customer's permission.

extended late check-out
By arrangement guests are allowed to occupy their rooms after normal morning check-out times.

green card insurance
For an extra premium, car/lorry insurers will cover foreign travel use, and a 'green card' certificate is issued for the period needed.

job description
(see Unit 1 glossary of terms and phrases).

management consultancy
Some services take the form of specialist advice to company managers supplied by experts brought in to investigate a problem and often a way of solving it.

overdraft
A loan which has been extended to a bank customer in the form of a 'ceiling' amount of money his/her account is allowed to reach 'in the red' – 'overdrawn'; prudent customers seek permission before allowing their accounts to go 'into the red'!

paying-in books
A book of paying-in slip forms on which cheque totals and cash totals are recorded when paying money into a bank account; the customer retains a stamped stub as a record.

payroll software packages
Computer software which is used to complete the weekly/monthly pay and tax/national insurance contributions due for an organisation's workforce; operated by accounts department personnel.

pension
Regular allowance paid for past services, eg on retirement from work or leaving work due to a work-related injury or other infirmity.

real-time booking system
Travel agencies use computer networks to book seats on flights, rooms in hotels, etc, in a process in which the availability is continuously being updated according to firm bookings received; the customer *knows* on the spot if the requested booking has been successful.

superannuation
Term for a pension scheme to which employees contribute in addition to the basic state pension scheme.

unfair dismissal
An industrial relations term used when an employee is 'fired' in such a way that legally required procedures have been ignored or flouted, or are deemed to have been so; cases of unfair dismissal are heard by industrial tribunals.

visa
Some countries require would-be visitors to fill out visa application forms in advance of their visit; if the visitor is acceptable, then a visa or 'entry permit' is issued authorising entry (and exit).

APPENDIX 1
External agencies and bureaux

A regularly updated database of local external agencies which are able to supply services directly relevant to the work of your manager and office can often prove invaluable in times of pressure or urgency. The following checklist indicates some of the agency services you may need to call upon. You are likely to find their addresses and telephone numbers in the *Yellow Pages* and *Thomson Local Directories*:

Agency	Service
Secretarial services	Text processing, photocopying, duplicating, fax/telex messaging, mailshots, envelope addressing, colour reprography, etc.
Employment bureaux	Provision of temporary staff at short notice, prior selection/screening of job applicants, advice on current pay scales for specific posts, training, etc.
Car and van hire	Rental of cars/vans on day or hourly basis, chauffeur-driven limousine service, pick-up and drop-off of hired car at different locations, airport collection of car service in UK and overseas, etc. Note national and international networks for this service, plus full insurance feature – accident, theft, etc.
Delivery and courier services	For letters, packets, parcels, consignments – by motorcycle, van or lorry courier; hourly service guarantee across cities and next day before 10.30 am nationally; some firms offer next day guarantee for European and New York destinations.
Interpreting and conference services	Specialist companies provide mobile interpreters for visits, eg of foreign buyers, and also to service international conferences.
Exhibitions, launches and promotions	Expert companies provide a 'total service' at exhibitions – design and mounting of stands, decor, hospitality suites, etc, leaving exhibitors to concentrate on sales aspects.
Advertising, sales promotion and public relations agencies	Agency services range from planning and delivering an entire advertising/sales campaign to a new product launch and ongoing public relations liaison with media and press.
Computer and data processing bureaux	Extensive computer-based services are offered to smaller companies including payroll, tailor-made programs for specific purposes, security back-up copying and storage of data.
Chartered accountants	Annual auditing of accounts service; tax, investment and pensions advice.
Insurance brokers	Researching and arranging insurance cover; insurance advice.
Building societies	In competition with clearing banks, building societies are providing current/deposit accounts and cashpoint services, loans and commercial mortgages, etc.

APPENDIX 2
Major legislation affecting organisations

Whether working in the private or public sector, the secretary's job is widely affected by a number of laws which have been enacted by Parliament in order to regulate business and public service life and to provide protection for the citizen.

Of course, for much of the secretary's working life the extensive body of relevant law remains in the background. However, it is important for all those who earn their living within a business or public sector organisation to have gained a thorough appreciation of the principal laws which underpin their daily tasks and activities. The checklist set out here provides you with an overview of such laws and will serve as a starting point for your own further researches.

CHECKLIST OF MAJOR LAWS REGULATING BUSINESS AND PUBLIC SERVICE

The business sector

1985 Companies Act See also Memorandum and Articles of Association.

Over the past 150 years a number of Companies Acts have reached the statute book which define and control the business activities of various types of commercial company. These are consolidated and updated at intervals. The Companies Act 1985 sets out requirements to be met by new companies being set up, the duties and rights of directors and shareholders, the requirements for winding up of companies and the statutory returns of information which have to be sent to government agencies each year.

1979 Sale of Goods Act
This Act redefined the obligations of both seller and purchaser and improved the protection of the consumer by ensuring that goods were not described in an untruthful way. The Act updated the Sale of Goods Act of 1893. A product purchased has to be 'of merchantable quality' and 'reasonably fit for the buyer's purpose'.

1977 Unfair Contract Terms Act
This Act sets out the obligations and duties of all those engaged in business who in effect contract with others to buy or sell goods or services. The Act also defines the obligations of hire-purchase contracts.

1974 Consumer Credit Act
Under the terms of this Act, consumers were given increased protection when purchasing goods within a credit agreement context, including hire-purchase agreements. Consumers are protected from inertia selling through the post (see also Unsolicited Goods and Services Act 1971) and given time to consider after having filled out credit agreement forms.

1973 Fair Trading Act
This Act gave the government (The Office of Fair Trading) the right to intervene as necessary to stop unfair or misleading trading practices from going on. In particular, it prevented businesses from avoiding obligations of liability.

1968 Trade Descriptions Act
The major impact of this Act was to ensure that advertisements, sales placards, leaflets and circulars did not mislead the public. For instance, it became illegal to pretend that a good was being sold at half-price when it had never been offered for sale at the advertised undiscounted price.

Employment legislation

1978 Employment Protection (Consolidation) Act
The Act of 1975 was further extended and modified and the 1978 Act provided a great measure of justice and protection for employees; it made it

obligatory for employers to supply written contracts of employment and to detail pay arrangements. It also regularised ways in which pay agreements were drawn up in a number of industries. Employees' rights in the case of dismissal were also included.

1976 Race Relations Act
This Act provided protection for all employees, regardless of the colour of their skin or racial background in terms of employment opportunities and conditions of work, etc.

1975 Sex Discrimination Act
In particular, this Act made it illegal for employers to advertise for staff of one sex when the job could be done by either.

1970 The Equal Pay Act
Under this Act, employers are obliged not to discriminate between male and female employees in terms of pay and promotion opportunities, etc.

Safety and security

1984 Data Protection Act
The widespread practice by the early 1980s of detailing information about employees, consumers, patients, criminals etc, on computer made it necessary for Parliament to enact a law which offered citizens protection from the adverse affects of erroneous information being kept on computer or passed from one computer network to another. Under the terms of the Act, organisations have to register with the Data Protection Registrar who vets the purposes for which data about people is being put on to computer. Essentially, the Data Protection Act enables individuals to access data concerning themselves and to have it removed or corrected, as appropriate. Organisations are obliged to follow a code of practice to protect individuals' confidentiality rights and to keep information up-to-date and (with some exceptions) open to inspection according to the provisions of the Act.

1974 Health and Safety at Work Act (HASAW)
A major piece of reforming legislation, this Act redefined the duties and obligations of both employers and employees in ensuring that the workplace was maintained as a safe working environment. This Act consolidated many previously enacted safety requirements and made employees responsible for their own safety. Employers were obliged to avoid health hazards, secure the safe working of plant and equipment and implement codes of practice for safety and emergency evacuation, etc. The Act imposes financial penalties on both employers and employees found to have breached it.

1963 Offices, Shops and Railway Premises Act
Basically, this Act defined the minimum standards which employers must maintain in terms of the space, heat, light, lavatory and washing facilities and general hygiene and cleanliness in those offices, shops and other similar premises in which male and female employees work.

For example, each office worker is entitled to at least 400 cubic feet of space in which to work (eg around a desk) and the room temperature should not be less than 16 degrees C one hour after work has commenced. The Act also specifies the requirements for separate toilets when more than five mixed staff are employed. At the time, the Act did much to improve the working conditions provided by less caring employers.

The public sector

Employers and employees working in the public sector are included in those Acts outlined above concerned with employment law, health and safety at work and working conditions, etc. The Acts outlined below identify one of the major pieces of legislation underpinning the work of local government.

1972 The Local Government Act
As a result of this Act, the administrative centres – counties, county boroughs, urban and rural councils – were completely reorganised and redrawn, a process which still continues with metropolitan counties coming into and going out of existence.

Note: The work of local government has been directed by some six Local Government Acts since 1888. Over the Years, these secured the administration of schools, local health provisions, the collection of local rates, roads (except trunk roads), police and fire services, social services, council housing, planning, public transport, library provisions, etc.

1944–1988 Education Acts
These define the roles of the local authorities, parent governors of schools, governors of colleges and teaching staff in providing statutory and 16+ vocational education.

1970 Local Authority Social Services Act
This Act redefined the responsibilities of local authorities to provide community care and social services for a wide range of local inhabitants including hospital/residential care, sheltered housing, etc.

APPENDIX 3
Checklist of reference information

Key: W = Weekly, F= Fortnightly, M = Monthly.

Weekly/monthly magazines on computer equipment and software

PC User (F), *PC Week* (W), *Computing* (W), *PC Business World* (W), *Mini-Micro News* (M), *Software* (M), *Personal Computer* (M).

Weekly/monthly magazines on office equipment and materials

Business Systems and Equipment (M)
Office Magazine (M)
Office Equipment Index (M)
Business Equipment Digest (M).
Communicate (M) (Telecommunications and Data communications)
Network (M)

Magazines for secretaries and PAs

Career Secretary – IQPS Journal (M)
Office Secretary (Quarterly)
Today's PA (Quarterly)
Girl About Town
Memo (Pitman New Era Shorthand)
2000 (Pitman 2000 shorthand)

Books for secretaries

The Secretary's Desk Book, John Harrison, Pitman
The Successful Secretary, Macdonald and Little, Macdonald & Evans
Be a Successful Secretary, P Ramage, Pitman
The PA's Handbook, Moncrieff and Sharp, Papermac Business

English language and usage

Concise English Language Dictionary, OUP
The Pergamon Dictionary of Perfect Spelling, – includes phonetic listings (recommended) Pergamon
Roget's Thesaurus of English Words and Phrases, Penguin
A Dictionary of Good English, S McKasgill, Macmillan
Longman Dictionary of the English Language, Longman
Guide to English Usage, Longman

Useful sources of all kinds of information

How To Find Out, G Chandler, Pergamon International Lib.
First Clue: The A–Z of Finding Out, R Walker, Pan
Current British Directories – checklist of current publications
Dictionary of British Associations
ASLIB Directory of Information Sources
Whitaker's Almanack: annually updated
Kelly's Business Directory
UK Kompass: Directory of UK firms and what they make/do
Who's Who
Who owns Whom
Municipal Year Book and Public Services Directory (annually revised guide to local authorities)
Macmillan Directory of Business Information Sources
UK Trade Names Directory
Chambers Office Oracle – handy office-centered information and dictionary
A Dictionary of Economics and Commerce, Pan
Penguin Dictionary of Commerce
Longman Dictionary of Business English
Mozley & Whitely's Law Dictionary
Secretarial Administration (data for company secretaries)
RoSPA Health and Safety Practice, J Stranks and M Dennis, Pitman
ABC Coach and Bus, and Shipping Guides
Banker's Almanac and Year Book
A Dictionary of Banking, F Perry, Macdonald & Evans
Titles and Forms of Address, Black
British Telecom Guide, published annually
The Pitman Dictionary of English and Shorthand

Dictionary of abbreviations (various publishers, eg Pitman)
Civil Service Year Book
Debrett's Correct Form
Willing's Press Guide
Benn's Press Directory
Directory of British Associations
Educational Authorities Directory and Annual
Directory of Directors
Stock Exchange Official Year Book
AA Members' Handbook, published annually
RAC Members' Handbook, published annually

Note: The librarians in local public reference libraries are able to provide excellent advice and guidance on the contents and data of extensive reference sources, so don't forget them!

APPENDIX 4
Reference list of sizes, dimensions and extents

1 Computer storage

A bit is a single piece of information – eg 0 or 1, 8 bits make a byte. 1,000 bytes = a kilobyte, written as 'kb'.
1,000kbs of data = 1 megabyte, written as 'mb'.
1,000mbs of data = 1 gigabyte, written as 'gb'.
Floppy Disk storage capacity is normally measured in kbs.

Note: An average A4 page of printed typescript requires about 2.5kbs of computer storage capacity.

A typical 5.25 inch floppy disk is capable of holding 0.5mb of memory, or some 250 A4 pages of typed text.

A typical hard (Winchester) disk holds some 30mb of memory, or about 15 000 A4 typed sheets.

A typical 5.25 optical disk can store some 500mb of memory, or 250,000 sheets of A4 typed text.

2 Standard international paper sizes

Size	Millimetres Deep	Millimetres Wide	Application
A7	74	105	visiting/business card
A6	148	105	postcard
A5	148	210	short memo
A4	297	210	letter long memo report
A3	297	420	tables graphics accounts data
A2	594	420	notices bulletins
A1	594	841	posters
A0	1189	841	advertisements

3 Paper quantities and weight

Quire: 25 sheets, Ream 500 sheets.

Paper weight The quality and uses of stationery depend as much upon its weight as its size:

Typical bond (notepaper) weight: 80–100 grams per square metre
Typical photocopying paper: 80gm^2
Typical bank 'flimsy' copy paper: 70gm^2

4 Standardised envelope sizes

A4 sheet folded 3 times:	DL	220mm × 110mm
A4 sheet folded twice:	C5	229mm × 162mm
A4 sheet unfolded:	C4	324mm × 229mm
A5 sheet folded once:	C6	144mm × 162mm
A5 sheet unfolded:	C5	229mm × 162mm

5 Envelope types

Most envelopes are sold in boxes of 250 or 500.

Banker; flap runs lengthways along top of envelope:

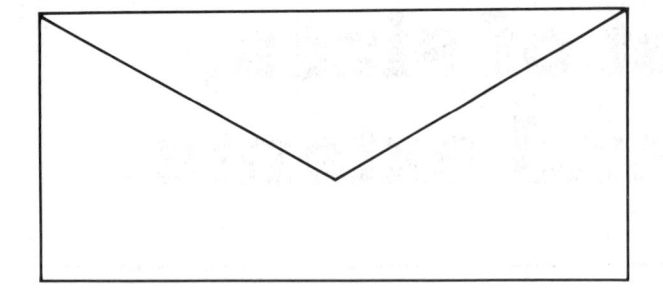

Pocket: flap runs down edgewise at one end of envelope:

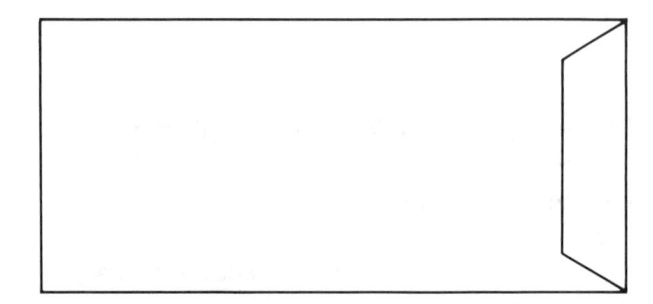

Wallet: similar to banker, running along length of envelope:

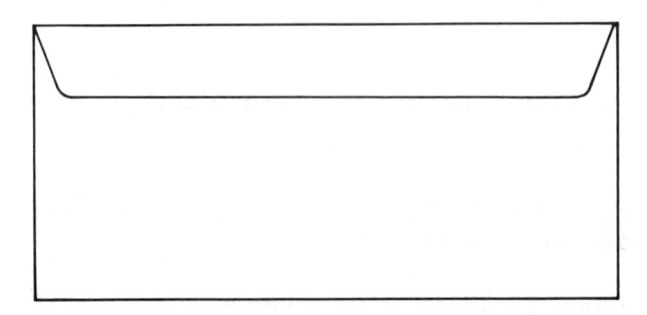

Window: 'see-through' paper constructed in part of envelope to communicate recipient's address on letter (used for mechanised mail runs)

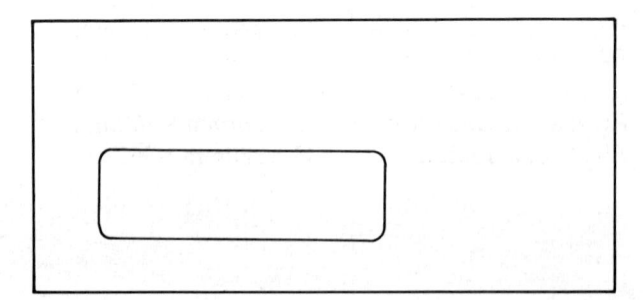

6 Envelope papers

Manilla: a cheap beige-coloured paper (for invoices, low status circulars, etc)
Watermarked woven: a high quality white/tinted paper for high-status individualised correspondence
Air cushioned envelopes: used for posting fragile items
Buttress board-backed envelopes: with a card backing for posting items like photographs which must not be creased or bent
Airmail: specially designed, lightweight envelopes for international post – weight keeps down costs – airmail lightweight notepaper should also be employed.

Note: Certain envelopes employ a 'self-seal' adhesive which eliminates unpleasant 'licking' or mechanical moistening in extensive mailshot runs.

7 Card thicknesses

Stationery suppliers offer coloured card in the sizes shown above for paper in weights ranging from 60–200gm^2.

8 Conversion factors

To convert *to* metric, multiply by the factor shown. To convert *from* metric divide by the factor

Length
miles: kilometres	1.6093
yards: metres	0.9144
feet: metres	0.3048
inches: millimetres	25.4
inches: centimetres	2.54

Area
square miles: square kilometres	2.59
square miles: hectares	258.999
acres: square metres	4046.86
acres: hectares	0.4047
square yards: square metres	0.8361
square feet: square metres	0.0929
square feet: square centimetres	929.03
square inches: square millimetres	645.16
square inches: square centimetres	6.4516

Volume
cubic yards: cubic metres	0.7646
cubic feet: cubic metres	0.0283
cubic inches: cubic centimetres	16.3871

Capacity
gallons: litres	4.546
US gallons: litres	3.785
quarts: litres	1.137
pints: litres	0.568
gills: litres	0.142

Mass

tons: kilograms	1016.05
tons: tonnes	1.0160
hundredweights: kilograms	50.8023
quarters: kilograms	12.7006
stones: kilograms	6.3503
pounds: kilograms	0.4536
ounces: grams	28.3495

Fuel consumption

gallons per mile: litres per kilometre	2.825
miles per gallon: kilometres per litre	0.354

Temperature

°C	°F	°C	°F	°C	°F
−30	−22	60	140	170	338
−20	−4	65	149	180	356
−10	14	70	158	190	374
0	32	75	167	200	392
5	41	80	176	210	410
10	50	85	185	220	428
15	59	90	194	230	446
20	68	95	203	240	464
25	77	100	212	250	482
30	86	110	230	260	500
35	95	120	248	270	518
40	104	130	266	280	536
45	113	140	284	290	554
50	122	150	302	300	572
55	131	160	320		

Freezing point of water 0°C; 32°F.

Boiling point of water 100°C; 212°F

Paper sizes

Size	mm	inches
A0	841 × 1189	33.11 × 46.81
A1	594 × 841	23.39 × 33.11
A2	420 × 594	16.54 × 23.39
A3	297 × 420	11.69 × 16.54
A4	210 × 297	8.27 × 11.69
A5	148 × 210	5.83 × 8.27
A6	105 × 148	4.13 × 5.83
A7	74 × 105	2.91 × 4.13
A8	52 × 74	2.05 × 2.91
A9	37 × 52	1.46 × 2.05
A10	26 × 37	1.02 × 1.46

Standard abbreviations

acre	acre
centilitre	cl
centimetre	cm
cubic centimetre	cm^3
cubic foot	cu ft or ft^3
cubic inch	cu in or in^3
cubic kilometre	km^3
cubic metre	m^3
cubic mile	mi^3
cubic millimetre	mm^3
cubic yard	yd^3
day	d
foot	ft
gallon	gal
gram	g
hectare	ha
hour	h
hundredweight	cwt
inch	in
kilogram	kg
kilometre	km
litre	l
metre	m
mile	mi
milligram	mg
millilitre	ml
millimetre	mm
minute	min
ounce	oz
pint	pt
pound	lb
quart	qt
second (time)	s
square centimetre	cm^2
square foot	ft^2
square inch	in^2
square kilometre	km^2
square metre	m^2
square mile	sq mile
square millimetre	mm^2
square yard	yd^2
ton	ton
tonne	tonne
yard	yd
year	a

Index

Page numbers in italics denote tables or illustrations

accounting, 237–40, 243–5
accounts department, 9
Act,
  Companies (1985), 271
  Consumer Credit (1974), 271
  Data Protection (1984), 55, 72, 272
  Education (1944–88), 272
  Employment Protection (Consolidation) (1978), 271
  Equal Pay (1970), 272
  Fair Trading (1973), 271
  Health and Safety at Work (HASAW) (1974), 82, 272
  Local Authority Social Services (1970), 272
  Local Government (1972), 272
  Offices, Shops and Railway Premises (1963), 272
  Race Relations (1976), 272
  Sale of Goods (1979), 271
  Sex Discrimination (1975), 272
  Trade Descriptions (1968), 271
  Unfair Contract Terms (1977), 271
agency services, 270
agenda, 190–2, 217
  chairman's, 192–4
  electronic, 189
alphabetical/numerical sequencing, 72
annual audit, 268
appointments, tips on making, 67
archive retention practice, 51
AVA (Audio Visual Aid), 217

back-projection, 217
balance sheet, 9, 26, *241*
bank,
  clearing, 268
  direct debits, 246
  loans, 246
  overdrafts, 246
  security services, 246
  services, *247*
  statement, 245
  terms used in, 247–8
  travel services, 246–8
bank accounts, 243–4
bankers' drafts, 268
bar-chart 173, 175, 181
  clustered, 3-D 174
bill-forwarding, 268
book-keeping, double-entry, *239*
booking system, real-time, 269
brainstorming session, 217
bring forward systems, 81
British Rail, 254
British Standards, 9
British Standards Institute, 26
British Telecom, services to business, 115
budgets, 9
business organisations, work of departments, 9–11

C/PABX (computerised or private automatic branch exchange), 111, 112–15, 138
CABX (computerised automatic branch exchange), *34*, 85, 131

CAR (computer aided retrieval), 61, 81
card,
  ATM/cash dispenser, 249
  charge account, 249
  debit, 249
  phone, 249
  Smart, 249
  telephone credit, 249
  thicknesses, 276
CCITT (International Telegraph and Telephone Consultative Committee), 138
CCTV (Closed Circuit Television), 183
chairman, in organisation, 8
chart, organisational, 5
cheque,
  crossed, 244–5
  Euro-, 247
  open, 244–5
  traveller's, 246
cheque book 244,
  components of, *244*
cheque guarantee cards, 248
CIM (computer input microform), 61, 81
circulation list, 181
Citicall, 115
COM (computer output microform), *34*, 61, 81
committee,
  roles of, 186
  type, 186
communication, *87*
company departments, *10*, 22
company secretary, 8
company support services, *12*
computer,
  decision-tree system, 81
  lap-top, 139
  mainframe, 33, 56–7
  mini, 56–7, 83
  personal, 33, 83, 105, *172*
computer files, 53
computer filing systems, advantages, 56
computer graphics, *171*, 176
  applications in the office, 171–2
  package, 94, 138
  plotter, 181
  and the secretary, 173–5
computer paper, tractor fed, 83
computer services, 11, 13
computer software, 53–5, 172–3
computer storage, 275
conference,
  administrative documents for, *208*
  booking form for, *205*
  organising, 202–8
  programme for, *207*
contract of employment, contents of, 230
convergence, 88–9, 131, 138
conversion factors, 276–7
counselling service, 224
county councillor/district councillor, 8
county councils, hierarchy in, *4*
credit cards, 248–50, 268
cross referencing, 52
currency, foreign, 246

daisy wheel printer, 122
data,
  archived, 26
  classifying,
    decimal point reference system, 50
    Dewey decimal system, 49
    hierarchical (branching) system, 49–50
  electronic, 53–7
data processing, 13
database, *55*, 94, 138
Datel *see* PSS
delegate, targeted, 217
delegation, 3, 26
department, 4–5, 22
  accounts, 9
  computer services, 11
  marketing, 10
  office administration, 11
  personnel, 10–11
  production, 9
  research and development, 9
  sales, 10
  transport, 11
desktop publishing, 26, 125–30
Dewey decimal system, 49, 72
diary,
  appointments, 43–4, 67
  electronic, 44–5, 72, 74
  management of, *44*
  routine, 72
  secretary's, 45–6
direct debit/credit, 268
director, of organisation, 8
dismissal, unfair, 269
dividends, 9, 26
document, 176
  best medium for, 143–4
  for conference, *208*
  effective presentation, 168–9, 176
  preprinted, 164–6
  sequencing, 74
  storage, 74
  well-presented, 142
DOS (disk operating system), 55, 81
dot matrix printer, 120

electronic,
  data, 53–7
  directories, 118
  file creation, 81
  notepad facility, 81
  office, 88–90
  printer, 120, 131–2
electronic office, information handling in, 88–90
EMAIL (electronic mail), 26, 32–44, 81, 89, 92, 95, 98
employees, roles and responsibilities, 3
envelope, 275, 276
  sizes, 276
ergonomics, 81–2
Executel, 112
external organisations, and private sector companies, 7

factsheet, 176

Index

Fax, (facsimile transmitted message) 32, 33, 35, 44, 131, 138
   facts on, 101–3
   and the future, 103
   how it works, 100
   receiving a message, 101
   routes for transmission of messages, *101*
   typical features checklist, *103*
file, 55
   electronic, 56–7
   non-document, 182
   saving and storage, 57
file arrangement,
   alphabetical, 51–2
   chronological, 52
   geographical, 52
   numerical, 51
   tree branching, 52
file copy, 181
file directory, 82
file server, 138
filing, 13
   and database software packages, 57–8
   disk, 72
filing system, manual and paper/card, 58–61, 73
filing techniques, and computer software, 53–5
finance terms, 237–40
floppy disk, 53, 56, 82
form,
   Post Office, *41*
   preprinted, 164–6, 176
founts, 138
franchise, 6
Freefone service, 115
frontispiece, 181

Girobank, 246, 252
government officer, local, 8
gross profit, 27

half-tone, 181
hard disk, 53
hardware, definition of, 27
HASAW (Health and Safety at work), 82, 272
hierarchical/branching database, 49, 72, 139
hierarchy, 3
   in county councils, *4*
   organisational, 4
   pyramid, 22
   stepped, *4*
histogram, 181
hotel reservations, 255–6
house style, 181

IDD (International Direct Dialling), 139
Income Tax tables, 232
industry, nationalised, 6
information management system, *54*, *55*
Inland Revenue 'P' forms, *235*
insurance, green card, 268
integrated management information package, 83, 139
intelpost, 40
international time chart, 258
ISBN (International Standard Book Number), 182
ISDN (Integrated Services Digital Network), 109, *110*, 139
IT (information technology), 27, 33, 72, 88, 105
   in organisations, 13, 22
   and secretary, 72

job description, 6, 27, *226–7*

jobs, changing in organisations, 14

keysystem telephone network, 112
Kilostream *see* PSS

LAN (local area network), 27, 33–6, 45, 82, 90–8, 105, 131, *see also* WAN
LAN,
   bus, 92
   design features of, 91–2
   and file management, 96
   and printing services, 96
   ring, *91*, 92, 140
   and the secretary, 93–4
   security, 92–3
   star, 92
LAN communications and services, 95–7
   automatic call-dialing, 95
   external communications services, 95
   internal communications services, 95
   telephone-call making, 95
LAN network Tapestry, *93*, *96*, *97*
LAN software application packages, 94–5
LAN system, 56–7
laser printer, 122
Laws, regulating business and public service, 271–2
LCD display, 87, 105
letter,
   checklist for effective creation, 151–2
   effective presentation, 143–50, *157*
   layout formats, 176
   major applications, 143
   types, 176
letter post, 42
library and technical information services, 13
limited company, 6
line graph, 174, 182
line relationship *see* scalar chain
log on, 82

mail,
   electronic, 26
   incoming, 38–40
   outgoing, 40–2, 72
mail-log, 82
mailable copy, 182
mailroom, 13, 38–40
mailshot, 182
management consultancy, 268
management system, 75
management of time, 46–7, 72
manager,
   and authority, 5
   departmental, 8
manager and secretary,
   communication, 17
   decision-making and problem-solving, 17
   delegating and monitoring, 16–17
   dissemination of information, 17
   interpersonal skills, 18
   organising the workload, 18
   roles of, 16–18
managing director, 8
map, 3-D contour, 174
market research, 10, 27
meeting,
   calling of, 188–90
   formal, 185
   informal, 186, 188
   minutes of, 194–7
   and secretary, *187*
   tele-and audioconferencing, 188–9
   terms and phrases used in, 199–200
   type, 186
memo, 176

component, 153–4
   and electronic mail, 157
   how to handle effectively, 155
menu, ikon, 139
message,
   overnight, 37–8
   taking of, 73
message confirmation report, *102*
microfiche, *53*, 60–1, 82
microfilm, 60–2
microform, 60–2, 73
micrographics, 60–2
microprocessor, 82
MIS (management information service), 139
modem (modulator-demodulator), 44, 89, 139
mouse, 83, 89, 139
MP, as chairman of public corporation, 8
multiserving, 92, 139
multitasking, 92, 139

National Insurance, 234

OCR (optical character recognition) scanner, 32, *34*
office,
   design, 69–71, 73, 82
   electronic, 32–6, 36–7
   environment, 69
   essential functions of, 31
   as information processing centre, 31–32, 72
   'less-paper', *89*
   and telephone services, 109–12
   traditional, 36–7
   visitor to, 64–6
office administration, 11, 13
office equipment, and information, 88
office filing systems, 51–2
office information,
   audio-visual communication, *87*
   aural communication, *87*
   direct communication, *87*
   media for handling, *87*
   non-verbal communication, *87*
   principal media of, 131
   visual graphic representation, *87*
   written/printed word and number, *87*
office reception, 68–9, 73
office records, 49–51
office records systems, automated, 81
office visitor, 64–7
official receivers, 217
on-line connection, 106, 139
optical disk storage, 33, *54*, 82
optical scanning equipment, 82
organisation,
   business, 3–6, 9–11
   change in, 6
   chart of, *5*
   definition, 22
   factors affecting shape and structure, 22
   hierarchy in, 27
   IT in, 22
   key people in, 8–9
   ladder in *see* hierarchy, stepped
   multinational, 6
   multiple, 6
   private sector, 7, 8
   and private sector companies, 7
   pyramid, 3, *4*, 27
   of self, 46–7
   summary of features, 7
   support services and functions, 11–13
   types, 6
   work of, 9–11
overdraft, 268

'P' forms, 231, 232, 233
PABX (Public Automatic Branch Exchange), 33-4, 84, 109-10, 112, 131
packet-switched services, 139
paper, 121
   quantities and weight, 275
   sizes, 181, 275, 277
partnership, 6, 22
PATBX (Private Automatic Telex Branch Exchange), 105
PAYE (Pay As You Earn), 231-3, 233-4
paying-in slip or book, 232, 245, 268
payroll, 233-5
   software packages, 268
PBX see PABX
PC (personal computer), 33, 83, 105, *172*
pension, 224, 268
personnel department, 10-11
   forms and schedules, 225-9
   functions of, 221-4
   record update, *228*
petty cash,
   book, *235*
   imprest system, 82, 235-6
   voucher, *236*
photocopiers, 123-5, 132, 139
   colour, 125
   costs of, 125
   departmental, 124
   desktop, 124
   the future, 125
   systems, 125
photosetting, 139
pictogram, 182
pie chart, 173, 182
pixel, 171
PLC (public limited company), 6, 22
point-of-sale material, 10, 27
Post Office, 251-3
   Guide, 253
presentation see seminar
Prestel, 91, 106-8, 139
   costs of, 108
   gateways in, *106*, 138
   and Mailbox, 107
printers, 120-23
   electronic, 120, 131-2
   ink-jet
   laser, 122
   line, 122
printing techniques, reverse, 182
private limited company, 22
private sector company,
   and external organisations, 7
   key people, 22
private sector organisation, *7*
production department, 9
profit,
   gross, 3, 27
   net, 3
profit and loss account, 9, 26, *240*
profit motive, 3
prototype, 9, 27
PSS (Packet Switchstream Service), 109, 139
PSTN (Public Switched Telephone Network), 109, 140
public corporation, 6
   chairman, 8
public enquiry inspectors, 217
public relations, 217
public sector organisation, 8
   key people, *9*, 22
pull down, 140
purchasing, centralised, 26
pyramid, organisational, 3, *4*, 27

quango, 6
quorum, 217
   radiopaging, 115, 116, *118*, 140
radiophone, mobile, 115
RAM (Random Access Memory), 53, 82
record management system, 50, 72
records and information management, 13-14
recruitment process, *222-3*
reference information, checklist, 276
reference system, decimal point, 50, 72, 181
relationship,
   functional, 22, 27
   line, 22
   staff, 22
report,
   binding and laminating, 162
   major applications of, 158-62
   referencing, typography and presentation, 162-4
   system for referencing, 164
   tip on producing, *164*
reprographics, 26, 182
research and development department, 9
retirement and pensions, 224, 268
RNL (remote network link), 92
RDM (Read Software Only Memory), 53, 82-3
Royal Mail Special Delivery, 40

sales department, 10
sales documentation, *167*
sales invoice, *168*
sales plan, 10, 27
sales revenue and cost of sales, 27
Satstream see PSS
scalar chain, 15, 27
scroll 83, see also mouse
secretary,
   and account sale cycle, 167
   appraisal, 20
   and career development, 19-20
      extending experience, 19
      forward planning, 19
      personal skills audit, 19, 20
   and computer graphics, 173-5
   experience, 20
   and IT equipment, 72
   knowledge, 20
   and LAN, 93-4
   and meetings, *187*
   and plastic money, 248-50
   qualifications, 20
   regular tasks, 36-7
   testing the market, 20
   typical day, *33*
secretary and manager,
   communication, 17
   decision-making and problem-solving, 17
   delegating and monitoring, 16-17
   interpersonal skills, 18
   organising the workload, 18
   role of, *22*, 16-18
section, 4-5
sections supervisor, 8
security clearance, 27
seminar, 209-10
shareholder, 8
shop steward, 8
SMART, 85
Smart card, 249
software,
   computer, 53-5
   definition, 27
   packages, *55*, 57-8, 83
   for processing/storing data, 72

sole trader, 6, 22
spellchecker, 182
spreadsheet, *55*, 94, 171
   package, 140
staff relationship, 15-16, 28
standing orders, 245
Star services, 115
status confirmation report, *102*
status enquiries, 246
style sheet, 140
superannuation, 269
superscript and subscript, 182
supervisor, section, 8
Swiftair, 42
symbol chart/pictogram, 174

tabled paper, 217
telecommunications, 13, 131
telecommunications systems, 83, 88
teleconferencing, 28, 140, 217
telemessages, 140
telephone, 109-19
   answering system, *38*
   cellnet, 26, 116, *117, 118*, 131, 138
   keysystem, 112
   mobile, 116-17
   services in organisations, 109-12
   ship's, 115
telephone call,
   barring, 110
   interrupting, 110
   logging and reporting, 110
   outside line access, 110
   override, 110
telephone credit cards, 249
telephone directory, 74, 117-18
telephone network, stages of, *110*
telephone services, 131
teletex, 89
telex, *38*
   features, 105
   operations, 104-5
   specimen message, *105*
temperature, 280
Thomson Local Directory, 118
trade unions, 224
trading account, *240*
transport department, 11
travel services, 254-60
   foreign, 256-8
   itinerary for, 258-9
traveller's cheques, 246
turnkey office systems, 83
typeface, elite and pica, 181

underscoring, 182
unit, 4-5
   VDU (Visual Display Unit), 83
videotex, 106-8
viewdata, 106-8, 131
viewfoil/overhead transparency, 217
visa, 269

wages and salaries, 235
WAN (wide area network) 32, *33, 34*, 36, 45, 81, 131, see also LAN
Winchester disk, *53*
word processing, 28, *55*
   packages, 94

Yellow Pages, 115, 118